BREAKING THE SEQUENCE

Breaking the Sequence

Women's Experimental Fiction

—

INTRODUCED AND
EDITED BY
ELLEN G. FRIEDMAN AND
MIRIAM FUCHS

PRINCETON UNIVERSITY PRESS
PRINCETON, NEW JERSEY

Library of Congress Cataloging-in-Publication Data

Breaking the sequence : women's experimental fiction / introduced
and edited by Ellen G. Friedman and Miriam Fuchs.
p. cm.
Includes index.
ISBN 0–691–06755–4
ISBN 0–691–01531–7 (pbk.)
1. English fiction—Women authors—History and criticism.
2. Experimental fiction—Women authors—History and criticism.
3. Women and literature. 4. American fiction—Women authors—
History and criticism. 5. English fiction—20th century—
History and criticism. 6. American fiction—20th century—
History and criticism. I. Friedman, Ellen G., 1944–.
II. Fuchs, Miriam, 1949–.
PR888.E982B73 1989
823'.91'099287—dc19   88–14001

This book has been composed in Linotron Sabon

Princeton University Press books are printed on acid-free paper, and meet
the guidelines for permanence and durability of the Committee on
Production Guidelines for Book Longevity of the Council on Library
Resources

Printed in the United States of America

7 6 5 4 3 2

For the women in our lives:
Sarah Fuchs, Lola Glazer, Rebecca Friedman, Sonia Friedman

Patriarchal she said what is it I know what it is it is I know I know
so that I know what it is I know so I know so I know so I know
what it is. Very slowly. I know what it is it is on the one side a to be
her to be his to be their to be in an and to be I know what it is it
is he who was an known not known was he was at first it was the
grandfather then it was not that in that the father not of that grandfather and then she to be to be sure to be sure to be I know to be
sure to be I know to be sure to be not as good as that. To be sure
not to be sure to be sure correctly saying to be sure to be that. It
was that. She was right. It was that.
Patriarchal Poetry.
                                            —Gertrude Stein

By obeying the improvisations born of emotions, by abandoning
myself to digressions and variations, I found an indigenous structure, a form born of organic growth, like crystal formations.
                                            —Anaïs Nin

a night of utterly other discourses that will spark out of a minicircus
of light upon a page . . . and generate endless stepping-stones into
the dark, gathering up solitude as a needed strength that will nevertheless be resented by one and all especially one.
                                            —Christine Brooke-Rose

I see myself: brown very thick skin tender low breasts with huge
violet nipples the skin below them curves downwards over man's
hips to heavy long spider's legs. . . . I'm looking down at my body
and writing.
                                            —Kathy Acker

Mary is tampering with the expected sequence. First she broke the
sentence; now she has broken the sequence.
                                            —Virginia Woolf

Contents

THE task we set for ourselves in embarking on this volume was to introduce and explore the rich tradition of women's experimental fiction in this century. This work, archaeological and compensatory, is in line with one of the important and active projects of feminist literary criticism, the recovery and foregrounding of women writers.[1]

The idea for this volume was born at a 1983 Modern Language Association Convention session on postrealism. When asked why there seem to be no women experimental writers, a panelist replied that women writers are too busy trying to enter the mainstream to be concerned with narrative innovation, suggesting that their interests are political, not aesthetic.

This panelist's assumption that literary experimentalism is dominated by men is longstanding, an element of the history of the modern novel, and reiterated in literary criticism of the last several decades. For instance, of the 27 writers listed on the tables of contents in *Literary Disruptions* (1980, 2d ed.) by Jerome Klinkowitz and *Fabulation and Metafiction* (1979) by Robert Scholes, 25 are male. The volume of *American Literary Scholarship: An Annual* published in 1986 lists 14 writers in its "Innovative Fiction" category, all male, and of the 35 writers, musicians, and artists Denis Donoghue mentions in a *New York Times Book Review* article, "The Promiscuous Cool of Postmodernism" (June 22, 1986), the only woman is Virginia Woolf, whom he quotes *about* modernism, but does not include among the modernists. Published in 1987, Brian McHale's *Postmodernist Fiction* mentions or discusses over 150 writers, about a dozen of whom are women. The bio-bibliographical guide to postmodern fiction edited by Larry McCaffery does cover an impressive number of women writers, but in the volume's essay on women, "Feminist Fiction and the Postmodern Challenge," Bonnie Zimmerman writes that feminist "experimentation usually serves the ultimate end of realism" (177).

Until recently, studies of women writers also overlooked the experimentalists. Classic works such as Ellen Moers's *Literary Women* (1976) and Patricia Meyer Spacks's *The Female Imagination* (1975) explore how social, economic, political, and psychological factors influence the way women write and the way their characters behave. Influential, pioneering studies such as Elaine Showalter's *A Literature of Their Own* (1977) and Sandra M. Gilbert's and Susan Gubar's *The Madwoman in the Attic* (1979) focus on women writers as a literary tradition separate from men writers, but for the most part, they do not concern themselves with experimentalism.

One of the early studies concentrating on women's experimentalism, *Feminine Consciousness in the Modern British Novel* (1975) by Sydney Janet Kaplan, was followed a decade later by Rachel Blau DuPlessis's *Writing Beyond the Ending: Narrative Strategies of Twentieth-Century Women Writers* (1985), an exploration of particular innovations in plot and theme as means of liberating female protagonists. Two works reexamining the formative decades of modernism are Shari Benstock's *Women of the Left Bank: Paris, 1900–1940* (1986) and Gilbert's and Gubar's *The War of the Words* (1987), the first volume of a projected three-volume study entitled *No Man's Land*. *Women of the Left Bank* situates the lives and works of American and British literary women within the sociocultural context of expatriate life in Paris, and *The War of the Words* conducts a broad, cultural discussion of the sexual battle out of which Gilbert and Gubar believe modernism was constituted. These two works focus on the social, historical, and psychological factors that impelled women to write innovatively. But as far as we know, there has been no work attempting to outline the Anglo-American tradition of twentieth-century women's experimental fiction.

The study that has made clear to us the urgency of bringing this tradition into view is Alice A. Jardine's *Gynesis: Configurations of Woman and Modernity* (1985). Jardine explores the intersection between feminism and what she calls "modernity" (the effect on traditional belief systems and structures of the new insights from physics, psychology, politics, and philosophy) as inscribed in experimental literature. She points out that although experimental literature and feminism share not only a profound quarrel with established, patriarchal forms, but also a sense of identification with what has been muted by these forms—what even male theorists of modernity call "the feminine"—practitioners and theorists of both camps are not interested in pursuing the issue of their similar concerns. Because it is largely invisible, few have speculated about the role that women's experimental literature plays in this crucial intersection. This literature may be the "missing link"—in some ways problematical and complex—in a chain of common inquiry and vision.

Our endeavor to encourage the pioneering exploration of this body of fiction and the issues it suggests has required the participation of the larger community of critics—feminist critics, as well as critics of the literature of modernity whose perspectives are not self-consciously feminist. Because we have not sought to impose our own perspective—outlined in the Introduction—the essays represent a greater range of methods and viewpoints, complementary and contrary, than is common to volumes of feminist criticism. In fact, the figures and works they treat are in some cases different from those treated in the Introduction. Other variations in the essays are due to the fact that in the case of some women experimentalists, the essays in this volume represent the first critical considerations of their works, and thus some articles are by necessity introductory. What is consistent in this volume is that all of the essays explore women's experimental fiction, emphasizing its aesthetics, within the context of modernity—many, but not all, from a variety of feminist perspectives. Moreover, because it is clearly an area in which this volume can make an original contribution, the greater portion of space is given to lesser-known writers.

In the introductory essay entitled "Contexts and Continuities: An Introduction to Women's Experimental Fiction in English," we outline three generations (pre–1930, 1930–60, and post–1960) of women's experimental fiction and view them in the perspective of feminine narrative. We pay particular attention to the formal devices by which such narrative is achieved. We have had to be selective in the writers we discuss, and we may disappoint some readers by our omissions, but we hope that they will be inspired to proceed on their own. Since an exhaustive treatment of this tradition is impossible, we have tried to suggest its continuity, as well as its variety and range. In the third generation, covering writers publishing after 1960, we concentrate on figures who may not be well known in order to give them exposure. Our decision to limit the introduction to women experimentalists who write in English was made with difficulty. Women's experimentalism is an international phenomenon, with a great many compelling writers—Nathalie Sarraute, Marguerite Duras, Monique Wittig, Clarice Lispector, Luisa Valenzuela, Isabel Allende, Christa Wolf, among them. The volume's final section, "Literature in Translation," containing essays by Germaine Brée on Nathalie Sarraute and Monique Wittig, and Maria DiBattista on Marguerite Duras, provides a kind of coda, recognizing the international scope of this literature.

As has been suggested, the 18 essays that follow the introduction take diverse approaches to the experimental fiction of women. Two broad discussions of women's experimentalism comprise the "Perspectives" section of the volume. Speaking with the authority that comes from being an experimental woman writer herself, Christine Brooke-Rose in "Illiterations" examines some of the prejudicial ideas of Western intellectual history that have marginalized the experimental woman writer to the point of invisibility. She believes that male writers should learn to identify with the feminine experience and female characters, just as women have been taught to identify with the masculine experience and male characters. The result could be what Brooke-Rose calls a "delightful bisexualism." Though recognizing that all literary experimentalism serves the feminist

purpose of "changing culture by charting alternatives to hegemonic structures of consciousness," Marianne DeKoven in "Male Signature, Female
Aesthetic: The Gender Politics of Experimental Writing," fears that a
merging of the female and the male experimental traditions may not only
elide works by women but also the link between feminist and experimentalist narratives, a link she believes is important to emphasize and
amplify.

Gillian E. Hanscombe's essay, "Dorothy Richardson Versus the
Novvle," opens the section of the volume entitled "First Generation: Before 1930." Hanscombe traces the evolution of Richardson's radical narrative, which took shape as Richardson refined her determinedly feminine
aesthetics. In "WOOLFENSTEIN," Rachel Blau DuPlessis approaches
Virginia Woolf by way of Gertrude Stein, offering an astute intertextual
study that links two writers generally regarded as polar opposites; the
essay is also a convincing demonstration of the continuities within the
women's experimental tradition.

Essays on the second generation include that of Donna Gerstenberger
who, in "The Radical Narrative of Djuna Barnes's *Nightwood*," contends
with the influential male interpretations of *Nightwood*—those of T. S.
Eliot and Joseph Frank. She argues that Eliot's conservative evaluation
and Frank's application of "spatialization" do not appreciate the degree
to which Barnes subverted "conventional readings of experience." Ellen
G. Friedman's "Breaking the Master Narrative: Jean Rhys's *Wide Sargasso Sea*" is an intertextual study of the resonances between Rhys's text
and Charlotte Brontë's *Jane Eyre*. By violating the sanctity of the
"mother-text" and rupturing its smooth patriarchal outlines, Rhys re-
casts Brontë's narrative, "edging the canonical with the subversive" and
"the patriarchal with the feminine," thus writing Brontë into modernity.
Millicent Dillon attributes Jane Bowles's inability to complete work on
her novel *Out in the World* to a failure to recognize fragmentation as a
viable narrative procedure and to a capitulation to her husband's sense of
narrative order. The essay examines Bowles's increasing paralysis as a
writer, describing her as torn between will and instinct: the conscious will
to follow traditional modes, subverted by her instinct that fragmented
forms better expressed her sense of experience. Linda W. Wagner-Martin
attributes H.D.'s elliptical and allusive style to her attempts to make prose
reveal "the idea *behind* the idea," the woman behind the writer, the "intimate moments of being" behind any specific moment in time. Sharon
Spencer shows Anaïs Nin repeatedly striving to define and practice feminine narrative. Exploring exemplary novels, Spencer proposes that Nin's
theories of lyricism, her textured imagery, and feminine subject matter
converge in a style that can be characterized as "music of the womb."

The section "Third Generation: After 1960" contains almost half of this volume's essays; this is to emphasize the least known of the three generations of women experimental writers. Richard Martin explicates the highly innovative *Amalgamemnon* by Christine Brooke-Rose in terms of "redundancy" and "generation," the generation that is paradoxically implied by redundancy. Martin characterizes this narrative strategy as a deconstruction of "male supremacy." According to Perry Nodelman, such a sense of generation or "unending" is the quality distinguishing Joyce Carol Oates's *Bellefleur* as "feminine storytelling." Opposed to phallocentric fiction, which proceeds linearly from beginning to end, *Bellefleur* is marked by the repeated interruptions and incompletions of the multitude of tales that comprise it. Indeed, the apocalyptic ending of the novel mocks the requisite climax and resolution of traditional fiction.

Miriam Fuchs presents Marguerite Young's *Miss MacIntosh, My Darling* as an exemplary feminine narrative, built on a multileveled paradox and an amorphous, but encompassing structure. Her essay "Liquescence as Form" explores ways in which Young casts her theories of creativity in terms of fecundity but not necessarily birth—emphasizing conception over procreation, potential over fulfillment. Philip Stevick's study of Ann Quin, who committed suicide in 1972, illuminates the disturbing mode in which Quin represents consciousness in the four novels that make up her life's work—a mode Stevick views as unique, evoking a consciousness that is at the same time personalized, eroticized, fragmented, transforming, and operating on "several levels of discourse simultaneously." Focusing on minimalist writers Maxine Chernoff and Lydia Davis, Marjorie Perloff investigates their attempts to mediate between what they see as a necessary return to the "real" and their acceptance of the assumptions underlying experimentalism, a mediation between the referential impulse of words and the absolute impossibility to fix the reference of words. Perloff views this attempt as a new direction in fiction, which she designates as "post experimental."

In defining the space in which Marguerite Duras unfolds her fiction, Maria DiBattista appropriates Duras's word "clandestine," the "domain (assigned or preferred?) of women's literature, the literature of an unknown and . . . unformulated language, the 'silence of women.' " Kathy Acker is more aggressive in defining female fictional space. According to Larry McCaffery, not the clandestine but the outlawed is the context for her "delirious" narratives. Against a collection of punk, feminist, and experimentalist manifestoes, McCaffery defines and measures Acker's radical texts. Kathleen Fraser explores Barbara Guest's *Seeking Air* as a fictional space comprised of elements that break the narrative surface, fragmenting it into a collage of "half-seen clues," "collapsed chapters," and "reframed genres"—methods by which the authority of traditional narrative patterns is interrogated. Germaine Brée examines Nathalie Sarraute and Monique Wittig, both of whom reshape the contours of fiction by infusing it with sensations that ordinarily lie below consciousness. Sarraute excavates what she calls the inner "magma" of the psyche through prevocal impulses and "subconversations," while Wittig finds literary strategies that uncover lesbian "truths," compelling readers to experience them as "truths," not as "stories" outside and separate from their own traditions.

The volume ends with a list—organized by generations—of primary works by writers considered in this volume and by lesser-known contemporary, "third-generation" experimentalists writing in English who are not considered in this volume. We offer the expanded third-generation list in the hope that it will open up some paths of investigation for interested readers.

We wish to acknowledge Trenton State College for its continued support of this project. The college F.I.R.S.L. Committee generously provided released time for research and writing, and the librarians at the Roscoe L. West Library, especially Patricia Beaber, Fred Chin, Robert Woodley, and Carol Miklovis, were particularly resourceful. In the English Department, Dr. Lahna Diskin, Chair, provided us with many forms of departmental support and Milton Levin gave helpful readings of the initial proposal. We are grateful to Dr. Wade Curry, Dean of Arts and Sciences, for providing extra funds for a graduate assistant and to the American Association of University Women for a Research & Project Grant. Thanks go also to Elizabeth Seton College for a sabbatical leave during the early stages of research and to Kathy Phillips of the English Department at the University of Hawaii for reading various sections of the manuscript. We also thank Linda Kuehl and John Kuehl for their helpful reading of a draft of our Introduction. Sue Sellers, who did research on this project in an undergraduate tutorial deserves our gratitude. Especially, we wish to thank Marielena Bresnen, a Trenton State College graduate assistant, for her dedication, fortitude, and thoroughness. We are particularly indebted to Robert Brown, our editor at Princeton University Press. Deeply felt gratitude goes to Max Friedman and Alan Holzman who witnessed and helped us overcome the day-to-day struggles with this project.

NOTE

1. This task is described by Nancy K. Miller as an "archaeological and rehabilitative act . . . [toward] a reconstituted record of predecession and prefiguration . . ." ("Emphasis Added: Plots and Plausibilities" 342).

Permissions Acknowledgments

For the essay, "Contexts and Continuities: An Introduction to Women's Experimental Fiction in English" by Ellen G. Friedman and Miriam Fuchs, permission to reprint "Counting" by Jayne Anne Phillips, published by Vehicle Editions, is acknowledged. Permission is granted by the author.

For the essay, "Dorothy Richardson Versus the Novvle" by Gillian E. Hanscombe, permission to reprint passages from Dorothy Richardson's unpublished letters is granted by Sheena Odle, Literary Executrix, Dorothy M. Richardson Estate. Also acknowledged are The British Library and The Beinecke Rare Book and Manuscript Library, Yale University.

In the essay, "Jane Bowles: Experiment as Character" by Millicent Dillon, permission by the Harry Ransom Humanities Research Center, The University of Texas at Austin, to reprint passages from the letters of Jane Bowles is acknowledged.

In the essay, "H.D.'s Fiction: Convolutions to Clarity" by Linda W. Wagner-Martin, the following copyrights are acknowledged:
> Reprinted, by permission of the publisher, from H.D., *Hedylus* (Redding Ridge, CT: Black Swan Books, 1980); copyright © 1928, 1980, the estate of Hilda Doolittle.
> H.D. *Collected Poems: 1912–1944.* Copyright © 1982 by the estate of Hilda Doolittle. Reprinted by permission of New Directions Publishing Corporation.

In the essay, "The Artists of Hell: Kathy Acker and 'Punk' Aesthetics" by Larry McCaffery, the following copyrights are acknowledged:
> *Babel* by Patti Smith. Reprinted by permission of The Putnam Publishing Group.
> *The Lords and the New Creatures*, copyright © 1969, 1970 by James Douglas Morrison. Reprinted by permission of Simon & Schuster, Inc. and Michell J. Hamilburg Agency.
> "Oh Bondage! Up Yours!" by Poly Styrene, © 1977 Westminster Music Ltd., 19/20 Poland St., London, WIA 3DD. International Copyright Secured. All Rights Reserved. Used by Permission.
> "The Day the World Turned Dayglo" by Poly Styrene. Reprinted by permission of Phantom Publishing Ltd.

In the essay, "One Hundred and Three Chapters of Little Times: Collapsed and Transfigured Moments in the Fiction of Barbara Guest" by Kathleen Fraser, permission to reprint passages from the poetry of Barbara Guest has been granted by the author.

INTRODUCTION

Contexts and Continuities:
An Introduction to Women's
Experimental Fiction in English

ELLEN G. FRIEDMAN AND
MIRIAM FUCHS

THE search for or theorizing of an exemplary feminine literary discourse has occupied both Continental and American critics. American critics have sought this discourse in the muted themes of women writers, particularly of the nineteenth-century.[1] They have found that women writers expressed dissatisfaction with or ambivalence toward prevailing ideas of appropriate behavior in fiction and life through covert means—subtexts, minor characters, patterns of imagery that undermine or question the values that the surface plot and major characters seem to confirm. For instance, Sandra M. Gilbert and Susan Gubar see Jane Austen's deep ambivalence toward prevailing values in the "duplicity" of the "happy endings" of her novels, "in which she brings her couples to the brink of bliss in such haste . . . or with such sarcasm that the entire message seems undercut" (*Madwoman* 169). Thus, Jane Austen and, as feminist literary criticism has revealed, other women writers provided mainly (and not always with full awareness) hidden or disguised challenges to patriarchal notions of fiction. Having turned their attention in recent studies to twentieth-century writers, American critics have searched for similar covert inscriptions. A trend in Gertrude Stein criticism, for instance, has been to suggest that her radical aesthetics were formulated to disguise her lesbianism.[2] By emphasizing the ways in which the text holds the particular writer's life or psychology, this way of viewing women's writing has advanced the cause of finding the woman in the text. At the same time, however, it overlooks other, perhaps broader achievements in producing feminine narrative. Although the woman in the text may be the particular woman writer, in the case of twentieth-century women experimental writers, the woman in the text is also an effect of the textual practice of breaking patriarchal fictional forms; the radical forms—nonlinear, nonhierarchical, and decentering—are, in themselves, a way of writing the feminine.[3] In subverting traditional modes of narrative, writers from Gertrude Stein, Dorothy Richardson, and Virginia Woolf to Christine Brooke-Rose, Eva Figes, and Kathy Acker have been undermining the patriarchal assumptions that inform these narrative modes. Plot linearity that implies a story's purposeful forward movement; a single, authoritative storyteller; well-motivated characters interacting in recognizable social patterns; the crucial conflict deterring the protagonist from the ultimate goal; the movement to closure—all are parts of dominant fictional structure. Since this fiction is metonymic, reflecting cultural values in its order and progression, its themes and ideals, this fiction represents patriarchal mastery in Western culture. In exploding dominant forms, women experimental writers not only assail the social structure, but also produce an alternate fictional space, a space in which the feminine, marginalized in traditional fiction and patriarchal culture, can be expressed. Thus, the rupturing of traditional forms becomes a political act, and the feminine narrative resulting from such rupture is allied with the feminist project.

The subject of feminine narrative occupied early women experimentalists, particularly Dorothy Richardson and Virginia Woolf, who attempted to carve out a new fictional territory, a territory of difference and otherness in which the feminine would reign. Richardson explicitly associated the modes of her fiction with what she called "feminine prose," a fluid, interior narrative reflecting a woman's mind. Woolf, criticizing the lack of a female literary tradition and dissatisfied with the conventional novel as a vehicle for women's experiences, called for sentences and narratives that were "rightly shaped for [a woman's] use" (*Room* 80). In charting a feminine aesthetic, both writers were well aware they were developing techniques for a new fiction that innovative male writers, such as Joyce and Proust, also wrote (Woolf, "Modern Fiction" 106–07). Richardson even refers to Joyce's "feminine prose" in her 1938 Foreword to *Pilgrimage* (10, 12).

French women critics such as Hélène Cixous and Luce Irigaray have taken up the issue of "feminine prose."[4] Rather than looking at specific works, these critics—for the most part—theorize. They call for a feminine literature, *écriture féminine*, that "writes the body" by imitating the rhythms and sexuality of women. Disrupting conventional narrative, this writing is nonlinear, polyphonic, open-ended, subverts hegemonic forms, and arises, in Julia Kristeva's terms, out of the "semiotic"—pre-Oedipal primary processes.[5] These theorists have rarely applied their ideas to women writers and often exemplify their theories with male models—Joyce, Proust, Lautréamont—thus leading to the improbable situation of women literary critics proposing that feminine writing has been accomplished mainly by men.[6]

American feminists regard theories of écriture féminine with interest, but Nancy K. Miller and Elaine Showalter view them largely as an "ideal"—something for the future of women's literature.[7] It seems likely that there are critics in both groups who would agree that if one locates the politics of writing in textual practice, the experimentalists, if they were women, would be the most exemplary writers.[8]

Moreover, the manifestoes of the (male) experimentalist canon, in substance, are nearly indistinguishable from Cixous's well-known manifesto, "The Laugh of the Medusa," for écriture féminine. In *Surfiction*, Raymond Federman writes, "The most striking aspect of the new fiction will be its semblance of disorder. . . . [I]t will be . . . illogical, irrational, unrealistic, non sequitur, and incoherent" (13). In more poetic language, Cixous presents a similar vision of narrative: writers "must . . . wreck partitions, classes, and rhetorics, regulations and codes . . . take pleasure in jumbling the order of space, in disorienting it, in changing around the furniture, dislocating things and values, breaking them all up, emptying structures, and turning propriety upside down" (886–87). Thus, the critics of the experimentalist canon and both American and French feminist critics define an ideal literature similarly. However, they all have overlooked the long tradition of women who have attempted to write this literature, despite the historical evidence that from the beginning the feminine and the experimentalist aesthetics were linked by common techniques, some common roots (Richardson and Woolf), and the common purpose of subverting traditional modes of discourse.

This neglect of women innovators is partially a legacy of modernism as interpreted through its male critics. Although Virginia Woolf and Gertrude Stein have been credited with helping to formulate experimental fiction, the credit inadequately expresses their achievements since they are commonly described as having been second, if not secondary, to Joyce and Proust. T. S. Eliot set the pattern for such judgments in his famous declaration that with the "immense prodigy" of *Ulysses*, Joyce had "killed the nineteenth century," leaving nothing more to accomplish (Ellmann 528). This judgment, almost universally taken up, left no doubt that modernism for fiction had a monarch and had the effect of diminishing the achievements of Joyce's contemporaries. Thereafter, Woolf and Stein appeared as after images, even imitators. In the very early study *The Novel and the Modern World* published in 1939, David Daiches proposed a minor standing for Virginia Woolf and reaffirmed this position in the "Preface" to the 1960 edition.[9] In the face of such judgments, Woolf embraced the role of "outsider," a position she rationalized as liberating (*Writer's Diary* 292). Less resigned to a marginal position, Stein met Joyce's challenge to her reputation as "arch-experimentalist" with the futile question, "But who came first, Gertrude Stein or James Joyce? Do not forget that my first great book, *Three Lives*, was published in 1908.[10] That was long before *Ulysses*" (Ellmann 528–29).

Despite their pioneering work, women were cut out or subordinated in the first assessments of early twentieth-century experimentalism, fixing the response to succeeding generations of women. However, this neglect is also partially a legacy of the last decades of feminist criticism, which has hunted subtexts and muted texts to uncover a feminine discourse while overlooking the texts by women experimentalists who may be writing that discourse in deliberate, open, and varied ways.

Alice Jardine in *Gynesis: Configurations of Woman and Modernity* probes the conjunction of modernity and feminism. Modernity (including the epistemological assumptions governing modernist and postmodernist writing) has forced a "crisis-in-narrative" by calling into question the Western paternal disciplines (or narratives) of philosophy, religion, and history. The loss of belief in, and consequent delegitimation of, these paternal narratives has provoked an exploration of "newly contoured fictional spaces" (69), spaces not dominated by discursive rationality but by multiplicity and difference. Construed by theorists such as Jacques Derrida as other-than-logocentric, these spaces have been designated as feminine. Woman, therefore, is at the core of the resulting discourse and thus "intrinsic to new and necessary modes of thinking, writing, speaking" (25). However, as Jardine points out, despite the fact that the feminine is central to the discourse of modernity, theorists of modernity and feminist literary critics resist acknowledging the similarities in their projects (61)—a resistance animated by the difference between "woman" (an abstraction) and flesh and blood "women." Theorists are interested in "woman" as an object of inquiry, but not necessarily in "women"; feminists, on the other hand, are interested in "women," but suspicious of the theorists' use of "woman." The natural convergence of "woman" and "women" would seem to take place in women's experimental narratives. Thus addressing the question posed by Jardine, "What happens when women take over this discourse [of modernity] in the name of woman?" (263) could begin with a reading of these works. The possible significance of a joint venture between modernity and feminism is articulated by Jardine: "The potentials for modernity and feminism to unite in their efforts are strong and exciting primarily because . . . the theories and practices of modernity, *when taken up by female voices*, become strangely and irresistibly subversive, promising new questions and answers unburdened . . . by the dominant ideology in the West" (258). The implications for feminism and modernity certainly seem compelling enough to warrant a persistent examination—with particular attentiveness to their radical aesthetics—of the works of modernity that women have produced. In addition to the promise of expanded horizons for feminine discourse, such investigations may eventually provide the impetus for a new alliance between male and female writing based, after so many centuries, on privileging feminine discourse with which writers of both sexes can write their lives and times. However, before such a utopia can be seriously entertained, over 80 years of women's experimental narratives need to be recovered and recognized.

In addition to Woolf, Richardson, and Stein, there has been a steady and strong tradition of women experimentalists. Subverting closure, logic, and fixed, authoritarian points of view, they undermine patriarchal forms and help fulfill the prophecy of a truly feminine discourse, one practiced by women. Their innovations stretch from the exploded syntax of Gertrude Stein to the anarchistic narrative collages of Kathy Acker; they include Dorothy Richardson's stream of consciousness, Djuna Barnes's flat, dehumanized characterization, and Anaïs Nin's blurring of genres among numerous other innovators and innovations.

Women experimentalists can be grouped into three generations, according to the publication dates of the most substantial portion of their work. Such generational grouping clarifies the evolution and continuity of this tradition and also focuses the similarities and differences among contemporaries. The reason for classifying according to publication dates is that classification according to birthdates is not particularly useful with these writers since some did not publish until late in life and some have big gaps between works. For instance, although Marguerite Young was born in 1909, only 27 years after Virginia Woolf, she did not publish her epic novel, *Miss MacIntosh, My Darling,* until 1965, 24 years after Woolf's death. Born in 1894, Jean Rhys published four novels by 1939 but did not publish her fifth until 1966, a gap of 27 years between *Good Morning, Midnight* and *Wide Sargasso Sea.*

The writers in the first generation produced a substantial body of work before 1930. This group includes Dorothy Richardson (1873–1957), Gertrude Stein (1874–1946), and Virginia Woolf (1882–1941). The writers in the second generation produced a substantial body of work between 1930 and 1960. Four major figures of this group include Djuna Barnes (1892–1982), Jean Rhys (1894–1979), Anaïs Nin (1903–77), and Jane Bowles (1917–73); H.D. (1886–1961) straddles the first two generations since she wrote experimental novels in the twenties, thirties, and forties (though some were published decades after they were composed), but seems by temperament and practice, at least in her novels, to belong here. The third-generation writers include Christine Brooke-Rose, Marguerite Young, Kathy Acker, Eva Figes, Marianne Hauser, Ursule Molinaro, Lydia Davis, Maxine Chernoff, Ann Quin—all of whom are not well known—as well as many more, some better known such as Susan Sontag, whose major work was published after 1960.

Once manifest, the tradition of experimental women writers alters received ideas of the beginnings of modernism in fiction. The singularity of the few dates and works that comprise the old timeline fades—1913, *Remembrance of Things Past*; 1916, *A Portrait of the Artist as a Young Man*; and 1922, *Ulysses*—as the dates and works of women arrive. The new timeline begins earlier with *Three Lives* in 1909. Nineteen-fourteen, the year of *Dubliners*, is also the year in which Stein published *Tender Buttons*, a virtuoso display of the possibilities of language in contrast to Joyce's collection, which still reflects nineteenth-century forms. In 1915 *Pointed Roofs*, the first volume of Richardson's *Pilgrimage*, appeared. Additionally, *Ulysses* shares 1922 with Woolf's first experimental work, *Jacob's Room*, and Stein's *Geography and Plays*. Other years and works populate the timeline: *Mrs. Dalloway* and *The Making of Americans* were published in 1925; H.D.'s *Palimpsest* in 1926; and Woolf's *To the Lighthouse* in 1927.

Presence on the timeline, accorded by publication dates, does not fully reveal the extent to which women practiced the new fiction, since women's books habitually did not see print until many years, sometimes decades, after composition. A sense of this phenomenon gives urgency to the task of recovery and revision. For instance, although H.D. finished *HERmione* in 1927, it was first published in 1981. Stein composed the first draft of *The Making of Americans* in 1903, while Joyce began *Portrait* in 1904, but a crucial and regrettable fact of literary history is that Stein's book was not published until nine years after Joyce's, and then in an abridged version, thus dulling its impact as an early experiment. Still another 40 years passed before the unabridged edition made its way into print. Yet Stein was writing years before many other experimentalists were attempting their first, tentative steps, and her early use of repetition, accretion, and nonlinearity, in addition to her grammatical dislocations, point to her pioneering role in shaping the new fictional spaces.

Even when publication was timely, women's achievements were often diminished by either the kind of attention they received or the slippage from it. Stein, for instance, experimented with narrative almost as soon as she arrived in Paris from the United States. *Tender Buttons*, complete by 1912, was in print nearly four years before *Ulysses* began to appear in *Little Review*. Both works created a furor. But the public's response to *Tender Buttons* was parody; *Life* magazine even ran a series of Stein imitations (*Autobiography* 171). She became a figure of fun. Joyce, on the other hand, was regarded as morally dangerous; his book was censored and confiscated, the subject of serious action and serious debate over serious issues. Richardson also achieved a good deal of attention during her lifetime; though regarded as an eccentric and difficult writer, she interested serious readers of fiction who watched for each volume of *Pilgrimage*. Richardson began work on *Pointed Roofs* in 1912. By the time *Ulysses* was published, six books of *Pilgrimage* had already appeared in print. Along with Joyce, she was serialized in *Little Review*. When the June 1919 issue was seized by the United States Postal Service because it contained a section of *Ulysses*, her installment of *Interim* was seized as well (Fromm 65, 118–19). The fame Richardson had 50 years ago has now dissolved, and she is generally regarded as an obscure woman writer, occasionally remembered as a practitioner of the stream-of-consciousness technique.

In studies of modernism, Virginia Woolf is the only one of the three women pioneers habitually considered with Joyce and Proust, but often not as their equal. Leon Edel expresses this view quite clearly: "I think of *Mrs. Dalloway* as a Joycean novel, diluted, and washed and done in beautiful water-color; and *To the Lighthouse* is Proustian in its time sense, but again the medium is a kind of water-color of the emotions" (128). The now critical clichés that her fiction illustrates innovative techniques that others pioneered and is flawed by its narrow scope are typified in the comments of David Daiches who found Woolf handicapped by her circumscribed subject matter, implying *female* subject matter: "delicate rendering of the different shades of experience" (*Novel* 189). *Mrs. Dalloway* and *To the Lighthouse* may focus on women and, to some extent, their private musings, but—it must be added—so does *Moby-Dick* focus on men and the male activity of whaling. Daiches's comment—if readers "have not been captured by the initial appeal of the texture . . . there is nothing more to be said. . . . [O]ne's response to her novels will depend in the last analysis on one's temperament"—reveals the kind of masculine bias contributing to the invisibility of women in the experimentalist tradition (191).

Unlike their male counterparts, early women innovators exercised distance and caution in their relations with one another, providing perhaps another partial explanation of their particular status in literary history.[11] These three women attempted to make their way independently of one another, each working to alter the course of Western fiction. In a self-addressed pep talk, Woolf writes, "I can take my way: experiment with my own imagination in my own way" (*Writer's Diary* 292). They never attempted even a loose association, let alone declaring a movement. The record of their public acknowledgments of one another is meager. Of the three, Woolf was the most generous. Reviewing *Revolving Lights* (1923), the seventh volume of *Pilgrimage*, Woolf praised Richardson's sentence "capable . . . of enveloping the vaguest shapes" ("Romance and the Heart" 124). Although she applauded Richardson's techniques, her judgment of Richardson's achievement was ambivalent, as evidenced in her 1919 review of *The Tunnel*:

> That Miss Richardson gets so far as to achieve a sense of reality far greater than that produced by the ordinary means is undoubted. But, then, which reality is it, the superficial or the profound. . . . When we are in a position to make up our minds we cannot deny a slight sense of disappointment . . . We want to be rid of realism . . . and further require that Miss Richardson shall fashion this new material into something which has the shapeliness of the old accepted forms. We are asking too much; but the extent of our asking proves that *The Tunnel* is much better in its failure than most books in their success. (121–22)[12]

The coolness of this public assessment seems more emphatic when compared with the camaraderie of Pound's salutary response to Eliot's *The Waste Land*. The relations among the women never warranted the kind of tribute that Eliot gives to Pound with *"il miglior fabbro."* Woolf did not review Richardson's fiction after 1923, and for her part, Richardson maintained a careful distance from Woolf. Without naming her, she alludes to Woolf in the 1938 Foreword to *Pilgrimage*, although she does name Proust and Henry James. Moreover, she turned down the opportunity to review Woolf's *The Years* (1937) (misspelling Woolf's name in the letter), asserting, as Gloria Fromm reports in her Richardson biography, that "none of [Woolf's] preceding books had moved her deeply, and . . . in spite of her admiration for the work . . . the book [should be] in the hands of someone to whom she meant a good deal." At the same time, she accepted an offer to review Joyce's *Finnegans Wake* despite the months of intensive study the task required (Fromm 319).

In *The Autobiography of Alice B. Toklas* (1933), which comments on and gossips about dozens of artists and writers, Stein does not refer to either Woolf or Richardson, though the Hogarth Press published Stein's *Composition As Explanation* in 1926. Stein's reputation for encouraging other women writers is not exemplary. The struggling American journalist and writer Djuna Barnes complained bitterly about Stein's insulting reception of her: "D'you know what she said of me? Said I had beautiful legs! Now what does that have to do with anything?" (Field 104).

Each of the three women was responsible for a radical reformulation of narrative. Together, they constitute a formidable force in the development of new ways of writing and thinking, a force the significance of which is clouded by their self-sustained, though relative, isolation from one another. In contrast, the largely male Imagist and Vorticist circles were supportive of their members: Pound cut and shaped *The Waste Land*, published William Carlos Williams, Richard Aldington, and H.D. in *Poetry*, and got sections of *Portrait* and *Dubliners* into *The Egoist*. In the 1930s Stein sold a work by Picasso to finance the publication of five of her books, and she did not find a major American publisher until she was fifty-nine years old (Kostelanetz xxix). Woolf knew quite well the significance of the Hogarth Press: "I'm the only woman in England free to write what I like. The others must be thinking of series & editors" (*Diary* 3: 43).

Perhaps one result of this complicated history of coolness and distance is their location in literary history as theorists who exercised their ideas in works. Richardson's reputation, for instance, is based on her Foreword to *Pilgrimage* in which she outlines her new form. However, seen together as the progenitors of a tradition, in their theories and practice, Richardson, Woolf, and Stein defined and exemplified the new fiction, providing arenas of revolution, spaces in which the West's prevailing conceptual structures were renounced with the renunciation of established narrative forms; such renunciation was also the enunciation of the feminine presence in writing and culture.

FIRST GENERATION

Although Richardson deliberately embarked on a "fresh pathway," she appears to state her goal quite modestly: to create a "feminine equivalent of the current masculine realism" (Foreword 9–10). But no one should underestimate what she meant by feminine realism—nothing less than a fiction written about women, exclusively by women, anticipating the call by some feminists for a literature in which a woman, as Claudine Herrmann writes, can "conserve some space for herself, a sort of *no man's land*, which constitutes precisely what men fail to understand of her" (169). The task of the woman writer was immense, for Richardson believed there were no models upon which to base her work. Her approach was at least twofold. First, she presented details of a woman's life—concerns with domestic chores, friends, gossip, and clothing as suitable for literature. Second, she reproduced—rather than described or summarized—those concerns without poeticizing or generalizing them. In other words, the prose had to *be* her protagonist's thoughts.[13]

In order to explore a woman's space, what she called feminine "contemplated reality," Richardson imitated the movement of the female mind as it drifts through memory and the perception of the sensible world (Foreword 9–10), thus inventing what the novelist May Sinclair, borrowing a term from William James, called the "stream of consciousness" (57–58). When she adopted this technique, Richardson changed the nature of the novel. In reproducing a character's thoughts without authorial revelation of their significance or relation to the rest of the text, the authoritarian and omniscient gave way to the tentative and impressionistic.[14]

Accommodating the flow of consciousness demanded other departures from conventional narrative. Richardson developed a fluid prose, unrestrained by unnecessary punctuation or other inhibiting "stereotyped . . . signs." As she describes it, she means her narrative to flow from "point to point without formal obstructions" (Foreword 12). Thus the thoughts and perceptions of her protagonist Miriam Henderson stream unimpeded through 13 volumes and 2,000 pages.[15]

Richardson not only challenged conventions of grammar, but also abandoned traditional plot structure. In its place, she constructed a fluid chronicle of multiple climaxes and resolutions, but no definite beginning, middle, and end.[16] To the repeated disappointment of her contemporary readers, Richardson's *Pilgrimage* has no ending. The first volume published in 1915, the novel was still in progress at the time of her death in 1957. If she had lived beyond her 84 years and if her health had been better, *Pilgrimage* might have been longer, and still incomplete. By refusing to move her narrative to closure, she took a brave and iconoclastic route, for closure in the traditional novel usually means that the heroine gets married, goes mad, or dies. Richardson's protagonist, Miriam, merely goes on. She develops, grows wiser and more complex. *Pilgrimage* confirmed that novels no longer required closure; they could be openended. In subverting the traditional plot, Richardson not only rescued her heroine from the inevitable structures of conventional fiction, but also helped carve a fictional space free enough so that the feminine could be expressed.

In *A Literature of Their Own*, Showalter writes about the necessity of demystifying "the legend of Virginia Woolf." In this view, the careful introspection and lyricism, which for many readers define Woolf's fiction, have provided a suffocating ideal for subsequent women writers. In "Professions for Women," Woolf exhorts the woman writer to kill the Angel in the House, that is, to reject the traditional idea of woman. When the Angel guides the pen of a woman writer, she cannot portray reality as she sees it, only as she "ought" to see it (236–38). Showalter astutely observes that just as Jane Austen played the Angel for George Eliot and Charlotte Brontë, Woolf has played the Angel for mid-twentieth-century writers.[17] This iconization of Woolf as quintessential *female* author, together with her reputation as a secondary experimentalist, has clouded a sense of her total achievement. It has allowed, on the one hand, attention to focus too narrowly on her introspective female protagonists, especially Mrs. Dalloway and Mrs. Ramsay, and on the other hand, allowed a dismissal of her more difficult works as interesting exercises but imperfect art.[18]

Viewed as a whole, however, her novels may be seen as having opened up narrative possibility for subsequent writers, especially innovative writers, and are in themselves forceful and progressively radical experiments in feminine narrative, which also confront the issues of her world. In each novel she foregrounds what in conventional formats would be muted and invisible. For example, in *Mrs. Dalloway* she looks between the spaces of clock time, expanding the moment, flooding it with the consciousnesses of a small number of characters. She breaks the metronome of time, making room for the ebb and flow of thought and memory, both stretching the moment and conflating the past and the present. *Mrs. Dalloway* also stretches outward to the world—to the effects of social roles, class, colonialism, and World War I. Woolf expresses her intent in her *Diary*: "I want to give life & death, sanity & insanity; I want to criticise the social system, & to show it at work, at its most intense . . ." (2: 248). Though the narrative takes place over the short course of a day, Woolf succeeds in embracing a broad, as well as deep, reality; it is a fiction that includes, not excludes.

On the surface *The Years* (1937) seems Woolf's most externally focused narrative. Bristling with numerous settings and characters, the novel is encyclopedic, yet web-like rather than linear. It follows members of the Pargiter family and their friends from Victorian times deep into the twentieth century, covering the period from 1880 to 1936, and the various characters, and their progeny and friends, become registers of the development of modern consciousness, as well as of the progress of history. But progress and development are not rendered through the cause-and-effect logic of events and their aftermath, but through reconciliations and ruptures and the confluence and clash of shifting moments and shifting attitudes. Described by Howard Spring, one of its reviewers, as "the very flesh and bones, the blood and marrow of history" (377), *The Years* moves toward no final, essential explanation.[19] Instead, Woolf offers history as meaning deferred, as multiplicity and interplay, an alternative to history as a master narrative of heroes and quests.[20]

Woolf's move toward an increasingly abstract or anti novel, which culminates in *The Waves*, begins early and radically with *Jacob's Room* (1922). Woolf builds this work around a central character Jacob, who is absent. His portrait is drawn from the echoes, imprints, and shadows left in the places he has been and in the memories of the people who knew him. After Jacob dies as a soldier in World War I, the only palpable evidence that he existed is his room, which he left as if sure he would return.

The Waves (1931), Woolf's daring attempt to do without the props of traditional narrative—particularly distinct characters and plot—is perhaps of all her works the most marked by the semiotic—the rhythmic, disruptive, and ephemeral welling up from the unconscious—in its narrative strategy. Bernard, the name Woolf gives to one of the novel's six voices, describes her narrative method by which unconscious pulsations are unleashed and engender her feminine narrative: "The crystal, the globe of life as one calls it, far from being hard and cold to the touch, has walls of thinnest air. If I press them all will burst" (354). As Woolf pressed the walls of the globe of fiction in *The Waves*, the boundary between inner and outer reality collapsed, giving way to an ensemble of disembodied voices. "What a symphony, with its concord and its discord and its tunes on top and its complicated bass beneath" (354). These voices are incantatory, more like poetic reflections than dialogue. Direct action, dramatic exchange, individual characterization are abandoned, dissolved into voices "running homogeneously in & out, in the rhythm of the waves" (*Diary* 3: 312).

Among the most undervalued of Woolf's works is *Orlando* (1928). Regarded or dismissed as a lighthearted valentine for Vita Sackville-West, the novel is as radical, deep, and imaginative a deviation from novelistic convention as *The Waves*, which it predates—though quite dissimilar. In her other novels, Woolf rejected the "ill-fitting vestments" of traditional forms because she believed neither reality nor women's life rhythms could be contained in them ("Modern Fiction" 105). Her method's purpose was a deeper verisimilitude than could be approximated with older forms.

In *Orlando*, however, she abandons verisimilitude to test the possibilities of antirealism as another means of shattering master narratives—here, the "narratives" of historical time, gender, race, and class. The novel depicts a metamorphic central protagonist who changes sex and is unhampered by the limitation of a human lifespan. After nearly 400 years, Orlando, who begins in the novel as a young man, is a woman in her thirties. This novel presaged a definite direction in the innovative novel, the picaresque and entropic impulse. It is an unusual book, even for Woolf, though experimentalists who follow her—Djuna Barnes and Kathy Acker, for example—make use of the hermaphroditic protagonist, the superficial, cartoon-like depiction of rapidly changing external events, and the violation of temporal and spatial verisimilitude, accommodating difference and otherness through an antirealistic mode.

Perhaps more than any other modernist fiction writer, Woolf was a brilliant theorist. Woolf's most prophetic and far-reaching proposal for a new fiction is in *A Room of One's Own* (1929). Here she creates Mary Carmichael, an imaginary woman writer who tampers with the expected sequence of narratives by "breaking" it. Carmichael, Woolf's alter ego, "set to work to catch those unrecorded gestures, those unsaid or half-said words, which form themselves, no more palpably than the shadows of moths on the ceiling, when women are alone, unlit by the capricious and colored light of the other sex" (88). To break the sequence is to rupture conventional structures of meaning by which the patriarchy reigns in order to give presence and voice to what was denied and repressed.

The implications of breaking the sequence extend to nearly all of experimental fiction. Djuna Barnes, for instance, breaks chronology by condensing and expanding time erratically. Time moves very rapidly in the first four chapters of *Nightwood* and then comes to a sudden halt in the monologues that follow. More recently, Kathy Acker's feminist punk narratives not only break narrative sequence, but violate all sense of fictional decorum, taking Woolf's idea to an extreme. Acker's *The Childlike Life of the Black Tarantula by the Black Tarantula* (1975) is a self-reflexive collage of plagiarized material, original fiction, pornography, and autobiography—there is no central conflict, no traditional protagonist, only a metamorphosing first-person voice. The line of development from *Orlando* and Mary Carmichael to the work of Acker seems clear. Thus, although the *legend* of Virginia Woolf may represent a suffocating ideal, the real Woolf provided instruction and strategies for feminine narrative.

Writers are still catching up to some of the innovations of Gertrude Stein, and her practices often seem anticipatory when a new literary development comes into view. Stein's focus on the "wordness" of words; her emphasis on sound, rhythm, and repetition as bearing the weight of progression and meaning; the absence in her work of linearity, conventional syntax, and climactic development; and the fusion in some works of lyric and prose are qualities that mark her prophesying aesthetics. Her writing exemplified and prefigured the ways in which the delegitimation of the paternal fictions could be expressed in literature—through necessary and radical ruptures in language and narrative. As Catharine R. Stimpson has astutely noted, her writing means the "very discovery of difference" (4). Indeed, the new writing movements (such as Language Poetry or écriture féminine) that center on language as the means of achieving revolutionary or at least new modes of discourse frequently employ Steinian techniques.[21] Some of the terms of écriture féminine were anticipated by Stein's theories of composition—that narratives be written in a prolonged or continuous present (*What Are Masterpieces* 16–17); that paragraphs and punctuation be relinquished for a sense of wholeness; and that texts should have "evenness," everything in them have the same value ("The Gradual Making" 257–58). Although, unlike Woolf and Richardson, she does not cast her theories in terms of gender, the literature she proposed—compositions countering hierarchy, countering *telos*, and freeing words of their associations—describes "writing the feminine," as well as writing that subverts patriarchal discourse.[22]

Like Woolf's *The Waves*, with which it has few surface resemblances, Stein's work is marked by the semiotic. In Kristeva's words, "The semiotic is articulated by flow and marks . . . energy transfers, the cutting up of the corporeal and social continuum as well as that of signifying material" (*Revolution* 40). *Tender Buttons* embodies such articulation by presenting (not representing) impressionistic renderings of isolated objects—a seltzer bottle, a cut of roast beef, an umbrella. Stein summons up a petticoat, for instance, with "A light white, a disgrace, an ink spot, a rosy charm" (*Selected Writings* 471), constructing a linguistic collage that does not describe as much as it creates a charged impression—like an abstract piece of sculpture. "A cool red rose and a pink cut pink, a collapse and a sold hole, a little less hot" (472) is a collection of color and texture. By force of habit, a reader could impose a storyline on these words. (Fresh cut roses are attractively displayed in a florist's shop. Someone purchases them late in the day, when the roses have begun to wilt. If the purchaser looks carefully, the rose petals are bent backwards, exposing a hole in the center of each flower.) Stein distrusted the imperiousness in the tendency to impose narratives: "The narrative in itself is not what is in your mind but what is in somebody else's" (*What Are Masterpieces* 102). She designed her syntax so that a reader would be compelled to experience the raw image evoked by her verbal composition before attempting to construct a linear narrative for it. Since the interplay of colors, temperatures, actions, and sounds in her image makes a more dynamic and concentrated linguistic structure than any possible imposed narrative, the narrative, once constructed, has no more force than an explanatory footnote, no more legitimacy than a forgery.

The recent phenomenon of Language Poetry also evokes Stein in its emphasis on composition, the privileging of words, exploded syntax, sound arrangements, and "rhythmic recurrence" (Perloff 18). For example, the style of language poet Charles Bernstein in "The Sheds of Our Webs" suggests the style of Stein in works like *Tender Buttons* and *Geography and Plays*, not least—as Marjorie Perloff suggests—in the impression of poetry being put through a "Cuisinart" (16). Compare Bernstein's "Floating on completely vested time, a lacrity / To which abandon skirts another answer / Or part of but not returned" to Stein's, "A peal is that mountain which makes a ring and is ringing. / There is no squeak, there is no touch there is no lump . . ." ("A Portrait of F.B." 176). The initial sense of linguistic incoherence in these two passages is mitigated by their tonal coherence: Bernstein's lines are elegiac; Stein's are whimsical. The reader of both, however, entertains a discourse governed by the unfamiliar and ambiguous: words are located in strange contexts; grammatical functions are open to question. (In Stein does "ring" mean a sound or a circle? And as Perloff asks of Bernstein's lines, is "skirts" a noun or a verb? [15].) For language poets, writing in this way is an act of rescue, salvaging language from the ravages of capitalist misuse. Stein's purpose was also rescue: "You had to recognize words had lost their value in the nineteenth century . . . , they had lost much of their variety and I felt that I could not go on, that I had to capture the value of the individual word, find out what it meant and act within it . . ." (*What Are Masterpieces* 100). A response to both texts must include a consideration of words in their own right. Freed from the governance of traditional syntax and grammar, words shed some of the preconceptions attached to them, an act of renewal for language that serves various ideologies, including the feminist.

As Gilbert and Gubar have noted, "Stein's books are fantastic experiments in alternative tongues. . . ." The "foreign language" that results from her writing practice is formulated, as Stein says in *Tender Buttons*, in order to "excreate, only excreate a no since." Stein dismantles ("excreates") prevailing linguistic structures to defeat their annihilating logic ("since"), which denies or subordinates what is strange to itself ("Sexual Linguistics" 529). The "alternative tongue" she devises undermines the language it interrogates, pointing the way out of silence and opening the language to new sites of enunciation.

SECOND GENERATION

For the three pioneers of women's experimentalism, the act of writing was, as Stimpson says of Stein, "the very discovery of difference." In pioneering modes to inscribe this difference, Woolf, Richardson, and Stein provided diverse and compelling examples for those who followed them. For the most part, second-generation writers such as Djuna Barnes, Jean Rhys, Jane Bowles, and H.D. were less prone to theorize than those of the first generation. Although difference no longer required discovery, it required emphatic and multiple assertion. Their works, reflecting a radical disengagement from patriarchal modes, satirize or attack traditional structures and in some cases presuppose their dissolution. In *Nightwood*, Barnes outlines a vestigial quest to delineate the oppressiveness of traditional form and expectations. In *Wide Sargasso Sea*, Rhys disrupts

Brontë's *Jane Eyre* by using her own text for the relocation of its narrative and her own characters to rearticulate its gender conflicts. Anaïs Nin's feminine narrative coalesces as genre lines are decomposed and revised, and in Bowles the feminine is revealed as traditional characters and narrative are stretched to a point just beyond the limits of realism. In several novels, H.D. breaks historical time, restructuring it and situating woman within its fractionary spaces.

Not just their fiction, but also their lives were emphatic assertions of difference—in their rejection of sexual and social norms. Although Richardson, Woolf, and Stein in many ways lived unconventionally, each found stability in a long-term relationship.[23] In contrast, the writers of the second generation led daring, unprotected lives—reflected in the sexual adventures, expatriatism, and nomadic style of living that their fiction often depicts.[24] Since their deaths, biographies, memoirs, and letters—to a greater degree than their work—have kept these writers alive in the minds of scholars. Familiarity with H.D.'s relationships with Ezra Pound and William Carlos Williams is far more common than with the larger part of her canon—written after her Imagist period.

Millicent Dillon, Jane Bowles's biographer and the editor of her letters, has managed almost single-handedly to keep Bowles's image alive while the *Collected Works* is generally disregarded. For many, Jane was the seriously troubled wife of her more famous husband, Paul Bowles, also an experimental writer. Nin's reputation rests on her erotica, diaries, and relationship with Henry Miller, and Rhys's affair with Ford Madox Ford has so far sustained a place for her in histories of modernism. Eliot's marital problems, Pound's dandyism and fascism, Hemingway's women, Faulkner's alcoholism, and Joyce's jealousy are well known, but interest in these writers' lives is inspired by interest in their works. But particularly for H.D. and other second-generation writers, their association with various men, or with a group of men, or simply with an interesting group has been the main justification for their place in literary history.

Attention to the work of Djuna Barnes has also been eclipsed by depictions of her life in Paris expatriate circles and her subsequent hermitic seclusion in a Greenwich Village apartment. Barnes's masterpiece *Nightwood* acquired a reputation as a small, obscure, overly written novel while Barnes herself became known as the ill-tempered and irascible inhabitant of Patchin Place. In *Women of the Left Bank*, Shari Benstock refers to Barnes's problematic reputation, attributing it in part to critics who have read *Nightwood* as Barnes's attempt at modernism, resulting in failure, in an "eccentric, almost inverted form of the Modernist aesthetic" (242). Unable to find a proper category for Barnes's work within the boundaries of male modernism, critics declare it "private and highly peculiar writing that addresses itself to a select audience, drawing its subject matter from Barnes's life and in form and imagery composing a pastiche of earlier literature" (242). The implications that "peculiar" means different, "private" means lesbian, and "pastiche" means derivative have added up to Barnes's work becoming a curiosity of literary history.

Nightwood's difference is its strength as well as its difficulty. As Barnes's attempt to satirize the patriarchal props of traditional fiction, it presents an antiquester pursuing a reward that is damnation and encountering characters who Barnes has denuded of character—in other words, anticharacters. If *Nightwood* seems austere, its characters unyielding, its plot in disarray, it is because Barnes employs a quest narrative that—because it is obsolete—her characters cannot sustain. Barnes fastens her protagonist, Robin Vote, to a moribund pattern from which she cannot wrench free, and through this process Barnes dislocates the form and indicts the ideology of master narrative.

Denunciation of Western patriarchy, of its sexual mores and sociocultural expectations, as well as its forms of narrative, is reflected in Barnes's dehumanization of character. Alienated, deprived of love, or sexually confused, *Nightwood*'s characters are drained of vitality except for sudden outbursts of grief or protest. Ortega y Gasset identifies dehumanization as a device of the avant garde, its aim to mitigate a reader's tendency to empathize, thus compelling objectivity and critical judgment (14). The purpose of dehumanization is to estrange rather than engage, to shock readers out of complacency and into reevaluation. Barnes uses dehumanization to condemn the quest for identity as conceived in Western culture, a quest that depends upon continued legitimation of social values upheld by a patriarchal society. Thus, flat and inscrutable, her characters move like puppets propelled by forces beyond their comprehension. As drifters, expatriates, and perennial travelers, they define themselves by their location rather than by self-knowledge. The sister in "The Grande Malade" explains: "We are *where* we are. We are Polish when we are in Poland, and when in Holland we are Dutch, and now in France we are French, and one day we will go to America and be American" (*Selected Works* 22). Drained of three dimensions, the inhabitants of *Nightwood* survive by invention, charade, and the fabrication of identities. Robin's husband, Felix Volkbein, gives himself a false aristocratic genealogy and Dr. O'Connor proclaims himself male, female, and a bearded lady. This strategy of achieving identity by proclamation, however, travesties their quest for a unified, coherent self. Rather, they achieve "roles," performing their lives much like actors perform their parts. Felix enacts what he pretends is his destiny by marrying Robin in order to have sons to continue his forged family lineage. Nora, a lesbian, imposes her own sexuality on

Robin, but finds that once they live together, love is like "the 'findings' in a tomb" (56). All her lovers, male and female, attempt to endow Robin with a sexuality that mirrors their own. But their attempts to impose on her their own life scripts fail as decidedly as these scripts fail to ensure their own identities or to put them in an authentic relation to the world.

Through Robin, Barnes undermines the traditional quester and savages the way women are expected to achieve identity in our culture. Unformed and uninformed, Robin searches for selfhood and knowledge, but her movements are random—most often directed by others. Robin offers the world the silent and docile exterior of the desirable woman, *la somnambule* as Barnes characterizes her. Behind her "desperate anonymity," however, is the unstable and volatile presence of the "woman who is beast," who must be turned into "woman" (37) by accepting the roles that others create for her, playing "other" to Felix, Nora, and Jenny Petherbridge, another lover. At the end of *Nightwood*, Robin, as woman acculturated to take the form of any strong presence, collapses on all fours in imitation of a nearby dog. Crawling after him and barking wildly, she ironically does become "the woman who is beast"—Barnes's final comment on the achievement of identity, particularly for women, within the framework of Western society. Although its tone and spirit are much darker, *Nightwood* has a number of affinities with Woolf's *Orlando*—its hermaphroditic characters, its basically picaresque movement, its deliberate effort to provide an antigenre.

In contrast to Barnes's dislocated narrative, Jane Bowles's prose seems realistic, but the realistic surface disguises an underlying and subversive surrealism. Her prose, particularly in *Two Serious Ladies* (1943), may be compared to Dali paintings in which objects have verisimilitude but are out of proportion and placed in inappropriate contexts. Edith Walton, who reviewed the novel for the *New York Times Book Review*, describes this quality, declaring the world of Bowles's novel an "almost frighteningly fantastic one—the more so because its outward lineaments are so natural and so normal. . . . Belatedly one realizes that there is hardly a character in the book who could be called really sane . . ." (14).

Bowles's two serious ladies inhabit a world that seems at first glance coherent, but at some point, one realizes that this world—as Miss Goering, one serious lady, observes of Mrs. Copperfield, the other serious lady—is "going to pieces." For Bowles and for feminine narrative, generally, this is a forward direction. It negates confirmation of the phallogocentric order and ideals, thus making way for an alternate fictional space. Bowles's fictional universe is decentered, and in it illogic reigns. She had a genius for inventing dialogue in which characters address a text other than the one they hear. Thus her prose has the feel of sense, but proceeds in non sequiturs. At a party, a man named Arnold suggests that Miss Goering spend the night at his house. "We have an extra bedroom," he says. The remark seems disingenuous, but it turns out to be sincere. Agreeing to go home with him, Miss Goering responds to what she believes is his subtext (but is not), saying "It is against my entire code, but then, I have never begun to use my code, although I judge everything by it" (19). Although her statement begins reasonably, it veers off the track and never gets back on it. This technique typifies Bowles's prose and cumulatively undermines the conventional dialogue and situations it summons.

Because they do not inhabit the predictable bourgeois world of the traditional novel, Bowles's protagonists assume they are free to follow their wills. A woman alone is at the center of much of the fiction of Rhys, Nin, and Bowles, but only in Bowles's novel are the central female protagonists both in control of their lives and independent of men. Rather than being defined in relation to men—a condition of female characters Woolf criticizes—they are defined in relation to their ideals, though these ideals are not always clear. In Richardson's *Pilgrimage*, Miriam, whose world *is* bourgeois, struggles to maintain such a relation, resisting strong social pressure to live a conventional woman's life. Unlike Richardson, Bowles does not feel compelled even to address the issue of emancipation because the world her characters populate is stripped bare of traditions and values that would demand their dependence, that would, in fact, make any demands on them. They are self-propelled and in a curious way, invulnerable.

Two Serious Ladies subtly parodies traditional novelistic structure. Bowles divides the limited omniscient point of view between Miss Goering, who aspires to sainthood, and Mrs. Copperfield, who aspires to happiness. Their separate, unrelated adventures, which take place on different continents, are juxtaposed. The two ladies meet twice, at the beginning and end of the novel. Vaguely motivated by notions of winning salvation, rich Miss Goering moves to a tiny, rented house near a glue factory on Staten Island and embarks on a series of casual affairs with unattractive and inconsequential men who happen to single her out. Meanwhile, on a vacation with her husband in Panama, Mrs. Copperfield becomes obsessed with a prostitute, Pacifica, for whom she leaves her husband. Though she has not given a thought to her since their first meeting, Miss Goering, toward the end of the novel, telephones Mrs. Copperfield, who has returned from Panama with Pacifica. At their meeting they make epiphanal-sounding, but paradoxical pronouncements about themselves and one another that are, at best, thinly substantiated by what has occurred. Epiphany is not so much forced on the fiction as it is mechanically included—Bowles's parody of the significance and closure required at the end of conventional narratives.

Unlike some of Joyce's Dubliners, Mrs. Copperfield and Miss Goering do not gain insight; rather, they sum up what they have learned in non sequiturs. Having set up the apparatus for a conventional conclusion, Bowles allows it to dissipate. Within two pages, Mrs. Copperfield describes herself as "completely satisfied and contented" and "only a step from desperation." Miss Goering reflects near the end that "certainly I am nearer to becoming a saint . . . but is it possible that a part of me hidden from my sight is piling sin upon sin . . . ?" (201). In this anticlimactic ending, nothing is resolved: the significance of experience or of attempts to achieve salvation and happiness is, as Mrs. Goering puts it in the last lines of the novel, "of considerable interest but of no great importance" (201). In patriarchal fiction salvation and happiness are commonly depicted quests that Bowles has here decentered and thus sabotaged.

These protagonists contrast sharply with the objects of male domination that are at the center of each of Jean Rhys's five novels. Indeed, Rhys perfected the heroine as other. Utterly dependent on men for survival, this heroine is nevertheless not so much forced into otherness as actively claiming it as her own territory. Julia—the protagonist of *After Leaving Mr. MacKenzie* (1931)—for instance, persists in a life of drink and tawdry hotel rooms and undermines the few and admittedly limited opportunities to escape that come her way. A reader is tempted to ask why she does not change her life, but on some level understands that Julia has, to some extent, chosen or at least allowed it. Although she hopes to find a man to keep her, she will not have a man on just any terms; she would rather be destitute. Destitution and confinement become spaces of refuge, spaces that Julia can claim as her own. Implicit in the life she leads is a rejection of normalcy and of the ordinary life course, a point made plain in the scene in which she visits her dying mother.

In *Wide Sargasso Sea* (1966) Rhys expands her narrative materials, employing two contrasting settings, the West Indies and England; a literary frame of reference, the protagonists and plot of Charlotte Brontë's *Jane Eyre*; and three first-person speakers, Antoinette (whom Rochester renames "Bertha," a "proper" English name), Rochester, and Mrs. Poole. For years the image of Bertha Mason, who like Rhys comes from the West Indies, haunted Rhys. Like Rhys's protagonists, Bertha is at the mercy of a man who does not care about her, though in Brontë's novel she is the madwoman in the attic, the obstacle to nineteenth-century happiness. Rhys was "vexed at [Brontë's] portrait of the 'paper tiger' lunatic, the all wrong creole scenes, and above all by the real cruelty of Mr. Rochester"

(*Letters* 262). One of her purposes in detailing the history of the Rochesters' courtship and marriage was to reveal what is muted in Brontë's narrative, Bertha's side of the story, and in the process question the assumptions of Brontë's text, especially those that lock away Bertha and all she evokes of the hidden and inadmissible in nineteenth-century England.[25]

Wide Sargasso Sea functions as a metatext for *Jane Eyre*. In writing it, Rhys forever qualified and altered Brontë's novel, and Rhy's novel must be seen in the light of Brontë's to achieve full significance. Rhys not only appropriates Brontë's plot, but adapts her imagery as well, particularly of birds, gardens, and trees. Rhys's narrative alters the context for the romance between Jane and Edward. The mysterious, sexually powerful male is deflated in Rhys's novel after Rhys shows him greedy and also sadistic: he marries Antoinette/Bertha clearly for her money and commits adultery shortly after his honeymoon; then he transports his new wife to an alien country and eventually locks her up in an attic.

Rhys attempts to demystify Rochester's strength by specifying its origins: control of Antoinette/Bertha's inheritance, the habit of dominance, an absolute confidence in the superiority of his moral values and culture—all backed by prevailing laws. Yet Rhys demystifies Brontë's madwoman as well, locating the sources of madness in extreme vulnerability, dependence, and a helpless passivity, depicting madness as a desperate, last-resort sanctuary. However, Rhys does not propose a simple reversal of sympathies. She portrays Antoinette's limitations as clearly as she does Rochester's, though his have a larger arena within which to unfold. With her lush and stunning novel, Rhys has established a complex relationship between the two texts and the two women writers that illuminates the difference in expectations that nineteenth- and twentieth-century women writers have of their narratives and women have of their lives.

Compared with Barnes, Bowles, and Rhys, Anaïs Nin was a prolific writer, though she worked in relative obscurity for decades. In the 1930s she tried to publish the first of her *Diaries*, but it was not until 1966, when she was sixty-three, that the first volume appeared in print. Suddenly, Nin was a celebrity. She lectured in the United States and Europe, received numerous awards, and became a cult figure to a large, adoring reading public. Nin also became a target of some feminists, who criticized her for not focusing on political issues. However, Nin's feminist impulses pulled her beyond politics of the moment toward challenging her literary heritage, which she viewed as dominated by male structures. She was determined to write in forms that were subversively feminine—deliberately searching out, with the aid of surrealism and psychoanalysis, a new discourse for women.

Somewhat like Richardson, Nin believed that women must write differently from men, and she wanted her writing to serve as an example. Harboring deep respect for the authority of dreams, Nin believed that they would lead her to shape forms that reflect feminine processes. Occurring during waking hours as well as during sleep, dream for Nin is "an idea or image which escapes the control of reasoning or logical or rational mind . . . any experience which emerges from the realm of the subconscious" (*Novel* 5).

In *House of Incest* (1936), for example, Nin summons the subconscious, synthesizing its images, blending, exploring, and recreating them in a series of fluid, transforming dream-like visions. Water imagery gives the narrative the feel of a dream. The first-person narrator says, "I am of the race of men and women who see all things through this curtain of sea, and my eyes are the color of water. . . . I cut the air with wide-slicing fins, and swim through wall-less rooms" (15). The fluid prose of *House of Incest* is reminiscent of the music of one of Nin's favorite composers, Debussy. Her narrative, like his music, flows freely, lyrically and imagistically, suggestive of moods, textures, colors, and nuances of emotion. It follows the fluctuations and permutations of Nin's narrator in a prose that Nin realized would look loose, fluid, even formless: "This accusation has been leveled at every new form. But we have to decompose in order to recompose in order to make a new synthesis . . ." (*Novel* 63).

For Nin, violating traditional genre lines was a radical act resulting from her belief that women's writing must uncover images that derive from levels of perception beyond conscious thought and recollection. Asserted as text, the writing based on these images blurs the line between fiction and autobiography, between fantasy and reality, calling into question the absolutes of history, and suggesting that history, as it is codified, is merely another form of narrative. Passages in the *Diaries* often read like a short story, her novels like autobiography, her literary criticism like personal anecdote or diary entries.[26] The altering of the shape and content of literary forms was a strategic move, an example of the woman writer who, in interrogating cultural forms, locates herself in the world.

Until recent activity pointed to a change, the legacy of H.D.'s association with Imagism promised to be immortality as a minor practitioner of a short-lived, but influential poetic style. H.D. wrote over 20 volumes divorced from this movement, and almost half of her canon consists of novels. Her first novel to be published, *Palimpsest*, was released in 1926 by Contact Publishing, a house financed by her companion Bryher and run by Robert McAlmon, Bryher's husband (Guest 160). *The Gift*, written in the forties, remained unpublished until 1982.

In *The Gift*, H.D.'s memoir of her childhood in Pennsylvania, H.D. breaks the sequence of history in which she is marginal, indeed insignificant, and makes room for an alternate arena for the exploration of her memory. In this arena fragments, shards, pieces of herself and her life have free play, effecting meaning through resonance rather than metaphor or metonym. She impels her narrative by associational flow, fusing first- and third-person points of view, and juxtaposing events from various periods of her life, instead of by chronological progression. Like Nin in her *Diaries*, H.D. recalls specific moments through heightened intensity and magnification of detail. H.D., however, provides only a single concrete date: the bombing of London for nearly the hundredth time on January 17, 1943.

Her narrative strategy is to reproduce the constellation of events that intersect in memory, though not necessarily in historical time. Faithfulness to linearity, to historical time, would require the falsification of the memoir, dependent on the erratic structures of memory and the conscious and unconscious processes that shape it. In *The Gift* exhaustion and terror shake H.D. free from historical time and catapult her into another dimension: "We have been shaken out of our ordinary dimension in time and we have crossed the chasm that divides time from time-out-of-time . . ." (141). Here, the child and the adult are contemporaneous in "the labyrinth of associated memories" (135). She recounts these memories mixing present and past tenses and uses both the first person and third person to refer to herself as a child. Her diction, too, alternates between an adult's and a child's. As a result, H.D. bridges time and "time-out-of-time" in *The Gift*, shaping a feminine narrative in which all times transverse the same narrative moment. This technique creates a space in which the "H.D." of the memoir is privileged to an extent that is not possible in the context of what is known as "history."

Palimpsest, like *The Gift*, breaks historical time, offering three versions of a woman quester, who metamorphoses through time and space and each version of whom (they are all writers) H.D. envelopes with a similar complex of images and allusions.[27] Searching through personal and ancient history, this hermaphroditic and thus more-than-human quester is torn between the world and spiritual vision as she struggles to define her quest.[28] Each of the novel's three sections depicts the quest at a more advanced stage. The first section depicts the process by which Hipparchia, in 75 B.C. Rome, decides to eschew earthly life. In the second section, as the American poet Raymonde living in postwar London, the quester has surrendered her husband to another woman in order to—in the emblematic refrain of this section—"fish the murex up," by diving "deep, deep" into the primal sea of the unconscious. In the third section, which takes place on a 1925 expedition to Egypt, Helen, echoing Raymonde, determines to "dive deep, deep, courageously . . . into some common deep sea of unrecorded knowledge," a place beyond history and ancient hieratic symbols, from which she hopes to "bring, triumphant, to the surface some treasure buried, lost, forgotten" (179). In the context of this woman-centered quest, the "buried" treasure rescued from "unrecorded" knowledge suggests not a paternal Truth as it would in a male quest narrative, but rather an image from the repressed. Through *Palimpsest*, H.D. proposes that if this treasure were brought to consciousness, it would designate what has been under erasure and prompt, by virtue of its presence, a rereading of history, a consequent reassignment of borders and boundaries, and perhaps, given the nature of the quest and the questers, a cultural transformation that would articulate the presence of women.

THIRD GENERATION

Most serious readers of fiction have at least some knowledge of Gertrude Stein and Virginia Woolf. Of the second generation, Djuna Barnes and Jean Rhys have attracted small and loyal circles of readers, and Anaïs Nin earned short-lived popular acclaim with the publication of Volume One of the *Diary* (1966) and *Delta of Venus: Erotica* (1977), though the literary establishment has largely ignored her. The writers in the third and current generation have attracted hardly any attention at all, especially compared with the attention paid in numerous studies to current innovative male writers. With only an occasional book or article on a single figure, these women writers lack the critical recognition that helps to sustain an audience and thus have difficulty staying in print. Because they are often confined to small presses and thus not widely reviewed, many writers in this category are largely unknown.

The decade of the 1960s was a turning point for both women's studies and experimental fiction. Each moved separately, however, into its current stage of activity because each field was essentially segregated by gender. Male experimental writers seemed plentiful. Along with John Barth, Thomas Pynchon, John Hawkes, and Donald Barthelme, the scene included William Gaddis, Robert Coover, Raymond Federman, Ronald Sukenick, and Gilbert Sorrentino. Their idiosyncratic forms, syntactical dislocations, and self-reflexiveness compelled critics to invent new terminology, including "surfiction," "transfiction," "fabulation," "metafiction," and "megafiction." In women's studies, Betty Friedan's *The Feminine Mystique* (1963) and Kate Millett's *Sexual Politics* (1970) offered the establishment a new feminist challenge, and many books, building on the insights of Virginia Woolf and Simone de Beauvoir's *The Second Sex* (trans. 1953), explored women's history, psychology, sociology, and literature.

By 1980 each field of activity seemed defined along gender lines. Women's literature, understood from a feminist perspective, was of interest primarily to women; experimental fiction, with its emphasis on form, seemed to be dominated by men. In this segregated atmosphere, the current generation of women experimentalists was lost between the cracks. As it produces wildly varied works, this generation stretches and redefines fictional modes, introducing the cracks and fissures through which the muted, clandestine, and thus the feminine can speak.

Its stance is, on the whole, more subversive than that taken by many male experimentalists. Despite their textual disruptions, the works of Jorge Luis Borges, John Barth, and other fabulists often display a nostalgic yearning after and grieving for the comforting authority of linear narrative—its teleology and its Newtonian certainties. In contrast, contemporary women experimentalists, for the most part, declare themselves on the side of ruptured and unreliable narrative; for in the spaces created by the ruptures and the anxiety provoked by the unreliable, they continue the project of a feminine discourse that not only can bear the meanings unbearable in the priestly and narrow chambers of master narratives, but also provides a hopeful alternative (rather than mournful alternative, as is the case in much male experimentalism) to the failed master narratives.

Writers like Susan Sontag and Ann Quin, seeking to nullify the assumption that language imparts cultural "truths," thwart the process of critical interpretation, breaking the complicity between reader and writer. Blurring distinctions between interior and exterior, between the clandestine and the overt, they uncover, but do not rationalize, the impenetrable and paradoxical. They interweave hallucination, memory, fantasy, and present action as though they were the same; the novel's "events" become a complex and shifting constellation of elements that resist coalescence, making "what happens" elusive. In her well-known essay "Against Interpretation," Sontag argues against imposing an authoritative narrative on the ambiguous text, an effort that would foreground its symbolic dimension while denying the semiotic, the dynamic interactions of the text's nonrational material. Sontag's fiction, less well known than her essays, strongly reflects her views on interpretation. When asked by an interviewer which of two contradictory interpretations of her novel *Death Kit* (1967) was accurate, she declared both of them correct, insisting on the validity of the novel's "systematically obscure elements" (Bellamy 123–24).

Obscurity is thus a deliberate mode of her fiction. In both *Death Kit* and *The Benefactor* (1963), she attempts to blur the line between dream and reality. *Death Kit*'s protagonist, Diddy, talks about his life in the third person in a matter-of-fact tone, but the reader is gradually led to suspect that the substance of the novel is a hallucination he is having moments before his death. In *The Benefactor*, dream, fantasy, and reality are confounded as well. The first-person narrator believes in the authenticity of his dreams. He believes that his waking existence—his mistress, his home, his wife—should be altered to conform to the images of them in his dreams. By selling his lover into slavery, attempting to murder her, and then becoming her benefactor, he transforms flesh-and-blood people into the phantoms that haunt his nocturnal life. But this fusion of dream and reality is, necessarily, incomplete, creating of his life a shattered text. The narrator posits various versions of his story, until the text dissolves into numerous texts and the narrator acquires multiple, conflicting histories. In *The Benefactor* the singular self is splintered and dream and reality interwoven in various permutations, none of which has a privileged validity.

Sontag offers an intransigent text, obscuring not only the line between reality and dream, but also obscuring the logic and discreteness of narrative point of view. As she undermines the difference between first- and third-person point of view, the categories objective and subjective, individual perception and omniscience fade. The first-person narrator of "Debriefing," which progresses in jolts through seven discontinuous sections, has a degree of omniscience she would not possess in traditional fiction. She describes what she saw, said, and heard. But she also describes what she could not possibly know, as well as what may have happened and may not have happened. The narrator confesses to having too much "stuff" in her head; "rockets and Venetian churches, David Bowie and Diderot, nuoc mam and Big Macs, sunglasses and orgasms" (38). Events and nonevents are presented with equal conviction, with the result that the distinction between what might have been and what actually occurred is blurred and irrelevant. Sontag forces indeterminacy upon the reader, accomplishing in her fiction what she advocates in her criticism—in other words, yielding Logos to the experience of otherness, expressed through the ambiguous, the polyphonic, and the carnivalesque (Kristeva, *Desire* 70–72).

At the center of Quin's *Berg* (1964), a similar indeterminacy prevents the text from being reduced to a single critical interpretation. Trying to discover the "truth" of his life, Aly Berg establishes a narrative that presents and rationalizes actions from his past. But even a simple report of events erupts with contradictions and inconsistencies until one must conclude that in *Berg* facts are amorphous, if not illusory, albeit tenaciously pursued. Quin's protagonist tries to fix what is real by committing murder—a clear, decisive action with verifiable repercussions. Intent on parricide, Aly pursues his father, who abandoned him and his mother years before, to his father's rented room. The murder seems simple to accomplish, but Quin denies Aly the reassurance of a corpse. Just as Sontag blurs real events and hallucination, Quin presents what happens and what Aly imagines as if there is no difference. For example, after Aly describes what seems to be his father's corpse, his father comes home drunk. Later, Aly reads a newspaper account of a corpse, fitting his father's description, which has washed up on shore. However, his death is in doubt again when his landlady says of a new tenant: "Funny thing . . . [he] reminds me a little of Mr. Berg, first thing I thought when he entered the house . . . why there's the old man himself . . ." (166). Aly hopes that murder will prove "you have done something which is having an absolute positive result" (140), but missing a murder victim, there is no result and the murderer does not exist.

Reminiscent of Barnes's, Quin's characters are dehumanized, often depicted as protean creatures, reshaped according to their environment. Like a huge "amoeba," Aly moves toward the partition separating his father's room from his own. He "smears" his face against the window and "pulls" his eye through the keyhole. These metamorphoses presage his ultimate metamorphosis in an ersatz Freudian romance in which Aly becomes his father, moving into his father's room with his father's mistress. Murder-of-the-father, which can be viewed as an attempt to subvert the very foundations of Logos, seems to be negated as Aly "becomes" the very father he has attempted to kill. Moreover, someone identical to his father rents Aly's room on the other side of the partition. In this novel, truth and reality, father and son, fantasy (murder) and action (murder) are presented as temporary imaginative or linguistic configurations momentarily privileged and then dissipating.

The wake of Stein's attack on conventionally structured discourse, as was noted, has brought other linguistically innovative narratives. Some of these narratives question the relationship between the signifier and signified in ways that Stein proposed: "Call anybody Paul," wrote Stein, "and they get to be Paul call anybody Alice and they get to be an Alice." A new name can redefine, words used in new ways can transform, or they can foreground an essence not revealed by the old name: "If you feel what is inside that thing you do not call it by the name by which it is known" because the signifying powers of that name have been diluted through use or that name has never approximated what "you" feel is that "thing's" core ("Poetry and Grammar" 210). Such ideas about words motivate the linguistic inventiveness of Christine Brooke-Rose's *Amalgamemnon* (1984), a text written almost entirely in the future tense.

Manipulating linguistic structures, Brooke-Rose stretches the signifiable. Deconstructing old words that elide a feminine presence, she builds new vocabulary to assert that presence, thus creating new possibilities for discourse. As she writes in *Thru*, "The pun is free, anarchic, a powerful instrument to explode the civilization of the sign and all its stable, reassuring definitions, to open up its static, monstrous logic of expectation into a different dialectic with the reader" (607). Brooke-Rose delights in punning, giving clichés a new twist, inventing homonyms, adding new prefixes, disconnecting existing words and assembling new ones. Her target in *Amalgamemnon* is high-tech culture. The protagonist, Sandra, who may soon be fired from her position as Professor of Humanities, imagines herself as a determined counterculture "graphomaniac," who will be imprisoned for her "graffitism" (20). Her words will take many forms, from carvings on prison walls to messages scraped in sand to the text entitled *Amalgamemnon*. Unwilling to reprogram herself "like a floppy disk," or recycle herself "like a plastic bottle" (5), Sandra decides to think about things, and the result is a dazzling display of her knowledge and thought processes, totally "redundant" in the computer culture that may do away with her job.

She puns, invents, and blends words to articulate her subordinate position with her lover Willy. Rather than always argue, Sandra "mimagrees" with his chauvinistic pronouncements. Thinking further of her role as passive partner, Sandra concludes that "mimecstasy and mimagreement will always go together, like sexcommunication" (14). When Willy "wineandines" Sandra, she resents his "sexplicit" attitude (10). Willy's "homonologue" on "sexcess" (success or sex excess) turns into a "ho-homonologue" as he explains to her why men enjoy sex more than women (18). This is a new vocabulary for courtship, one that reflects a woman's point of view in language invented by a woman. Sandra also plays with clichés, altering them for satirical effects: "Che sera sera, you shall see what you shall see and may the beast man wane," or "may the boast man whine" (30, 52). By satirically reversing or inverting stock phrases about male competitiveness, she undermines the values of the male-dominated society that has designated her as redundant.

To oppose the bureaucracy and technology that victimize her, Sandra withdraws to her imagination, an interior stage for a "minicircus" of tales spanning centuries and continents. As the space that she can claim as her own has contracted to the text itself, circumscribed but brimming with subversive intent, Sandra "amalgamates" her materials, recombining and transforming elements of history and myth. This act parallels her efforts to amalgamate and shape a vocabulary that adequately reflects her own perspective within a patriarchal system. At the end of *Amalgamemnon*, Sandra is still cooking for Willy (now Wally), but she has recast and re-formed history in her "second memory," making "weird atonal leaps through the gamut of possibilities" (21). The stories running "through the madlanes of [her] memory" will not help her to find a job, but by inscribing her presence in language, she defies the deadening and ever-growing bureaucracy around her. Through the figure of Sandra, Brooke-Rose constructs an "utterly other discourse" (5), a discourse that writes the feminine into the vocabulary of Western culture.

Brooke-Rose amalgamates words in order to inscribe a feminine pres-ence in her text, but in *The Talking Room* (1976) Marianne Hauser takes the opposite approach. By reducing characters to letters of the alphabet, she disconnects them from the patriarchal history inherent in surnames, handed down through the line of the father: "Yes, I the J and you the V. We are initials" (1). Thus, the thirteen-year-old narrator-protagonist is simply called "B," her mother "J," her mother's lesbian lover "V." J is called "J-J" when V is feeling affectionate. Visiting lesbian couples are called "GG" or "ZZ." When V believes that J has abandoned her, she finds another lover, J2. V refers to her former male lover X as her first "J." As reducing names to letters of the alphabet designates characters without giving them traditional familial contexts, it also generates an un-predictable network of associations.

Without desire for the male (most of the characters are lesbians), with-out the search for a mate, no culturally prescribed path such as the one that leads to marriage moves the text forward. Since patrilinear descent is not foregrounded, the identity of B's biological father becomes only one of many unresolved questions: was B a test tube baby, or did her mother have a heterosexual fling in order to have a child? Did B have a twin who died at birth? Why does B find information about her birth written in graffiti in a public place? Where does J go when she leaves B and V for long periods of time? Because successive pieces of information that B gains generate various possible narratives—not truth—concerning her identity, the value of language for B resides in its sounds rather than in its signifying powers. When she hears voices from the "talking room" where V and J argue and reconcile endlessly, she does not attempt to decode their dialogue; hearing their voices, she is comforted. The closest she can get to "truth" is the truth of their proximity, evidence that her mother has returned home once more and that the "family" is intact. Sounds of their living together—phonograph music and assorted noises—signify that V and J (and therefore B) are together. Since logocentric discourse deceives, Hauser's narrator settles for initials, echoes, music, and noise as sufficient reverberations of meaning.

By attending to atmosphere, mood, texture, color, rhythm, intonation, and musicality, other contemporary experimentalists like Toni Morrison, Joyce Carol Oates (in various works), Marilynne Robinson, and Eva Figes direct their texts toward lyricism and poetic language. They penetrate the world of solid objects and render them magical. Boundaries give way, surfaces become porous, and the world is charged with an otherness. As Morrison interweaves the ordinary and the extraordinary, their boundary becomes obscured by the momentum of her narrative. *Sula* (1973) begins:

> In that place where they tore the nightshade and blackberry patches from their roots to make room for the Medallion City Golf Course, there was once a neighborhood. It stood in the hills above the valley town of Medallion and spread all the way to the river. It is called the suburbs now, but when black people lived there it was called the Bottom. . . . A steel ball will knock to dust Irene's Palace of Cosmetology, where . . . Irene lathered Nu Nile into [women's] hair. (3)

The passage shifts from an unspecified time to the present, from an indeterminate "they" to the hairdresser "Irene," from the river to Nu Nile. As the mundane is described lyrically, it is liberated from its immediate context, heightened, and transformed. Although her self-declared style is "psychological realism," Oates has several experimental novels among her works (Friedman 3–17). Her lyric novel, *Childwold* (1976), for instance, is ordered by a succession of poetic and reflective interior monologues, somewhat reminiscent of Woolf's *The Waves*. The very sequence of voices, old voices succeeded by young, recalls the novel's thematic preoccupations with mutability and transience. *Childwold*'s imagery of butterflies, the river, and encroaching vegetation bears this theme more emphatically than in more traditional fiction in which imagery supports, but does not bear theme.

Noteworthy for its blending of careful, realistic description with lyrical and meditative language, *Housekeeping* (1980) by Marilynne Robinson, is characterized by a feminine perspective that evokes a realm of otherness, of nature and natural space that seems infinite. Ruthie, the narrator, moves into this realm as she reinvents the concept of family, going far beyond its patriarchal structures to discover communion and multiplicity. In her recounting of her and her sister Lucille's childhood after their mother's suicide, she evokes a world in which all that seems substantial and certain—members of her family, the house in which they live—can vanish in an instant: the sleek, elegant train carrying her grandfather slips off the bridge and is swallowed up by the dark, silent lake; their mother's car rolls off the edge of a cliff into the very same lake. The absence of Ruthie's and Lucille's father, the deaths of their grandparents, their mother's suicide, the departure of their two aunts signify the end of the familial line. The final connection snaps when Lucille abandons Ruthie to live with the local schoolteacher, who in effect adopts Lucille: "I had no sister after that night" (140).

For Ruthie, the act of redefining family, thus redefining her place within the world, begins as she relinquishes the duties of housekeeping—of occupying a single building, of trying to maintain it, of working to keep nature at a distance. Setting the house on fire, she leaves in ashes not the house, which survives the fire, but domesticity that in this novel is tied to the constraints inherent in women's roles and women's consequent loss of the natural world. In moving outward, she enacts the "process of de-evolution, of decivilizing," what Joan Kirkby calls "a gradual erosion of hierarchical social structure into a state of watery dissolution" (92, 100). Through meditation, dream, and memory, Ruthie's losses are transfigured. "Family" comes to include other families, their houses, and their disasters as well. In this way, "families will not be broken. Curse and expel them, send their children wandering, drown them in floods and fires, and old women will make songs out of all these sorrows. . . . Every sorrow suggests a thousand songs, and every song recalls a thousand sorrows, and so they are infinite in number, and all the same" (194). As the firm chronological roots of Robinson's text expand, they gradually move toward a realm whose incandescent beauty and transformative powers compel the protagonist to expand her sense of place, and thus her sense of self, far beyond the single center of her family "home." Consequently, her life acquires an indeterminacy and a poetry reflected in the lyrical dimensions of the text.

At the heart of Eva Figes's small and graceful masterpiece *Light* (1983) is the contradiction inherent in Claude Monet's dual role of great experimental painter and Victorian patriarch. Depicting a day in the life of Claude Monet, Figes moves the narrative from dawn to dusk and the imagery across the color spectrum from blue to red. She attempts to capture the quality of an Impressionist painting in words. Figes associates characters with various tones of light. Claude is depicted in all lights while his wife, who grieves for her dead daughter, is perpetually dressed in black and moves in darkness and shadow. Lily, Monet's sprightly granddaughter, is associated with bright colors and sunlight.

As the brushstrokes in Monet's paintings fragment the visible world, the narrative is broken into hours, places, and individual perceiving consciousnesses. However, the technique of following the hours in terms of the changing light and moving rapidly among the various consciousnesses of Monet's large family is halted at the novel's center. Here Figes depicts a traditional dinner party in the omniscient, authoritative manner of more conventional fiction. This yielding of the narrative's fluid, fragmentary mode is appropriate since the meal is orchestrated to cater to the reigning patriarch, Monet. His tastes and ideas dictate the culinary and conversational course of the meal. At the dinner table, there is a stifling hierarchy, established and governed by a patriarchy that denies all that is not itself. After almost 60 pages of characters rendered impressionistically and thus without hierarchical order, merely in rapid succession, Monet has a sudden privileged status. The narrative acquires an organizing center it did not possess. The other characters suddenly shift into subordinate roles as they are defined in relation to Monet: Monet's wife, Monet's son, Monet's step-daughter, Monet's servants. Monet, who tries to comprehend and capture the complexity and tenuousness of light—"a luminous cloud of changing light, a sort of envelope" (78)—is blind to these qualities in his wife and children for whom he acts the traditional authoritarian and restrictive patriarch.

In the last chapter, however, Figes distances this conflict by jumping forward in time to after World War I when all that is left is Monet's beloved (though now overgrown) lily pond, reflecting the transience of the changing light and the constancy of the eternal repetition of those changes. So distanced, the conflict dissolves, for the governing principle of life is mutability and in this context, Monet's attempt to continue a restrictive order was as doomed as nineteenth-century representational painting. Since it is set just as the new century begins, *Light* takes the hope of the new art into the life of the new century.

Marguerite Young's *Miss MacIntosh, My Darling* (1965), nearly 1,200 pages long, is a difficult, massive, and intricately patterned experiment that deserves the kind of attention paid to novels such as John Barth's *Letters* (1979) and Thomas Pynchon's *Gravity's Rainbow* (1973). Sometimes called meganovels, these works begin with length, but other criteria follow. Beneath the apparent disorder of these sprawling works are "vast, intricate systems" of coherence. Frederick Karl attributes the unity of *Gravity's Rainbow* to Pynchon's borrowing of molecular structure from chemistry; of *Letters* to its epistolary system, which absorbs systems of Barth's earlier novels to create an even larger system. There are other criteria as well—dense prose, accretion or amassing of fictional materials rather than continuous development, a narrow, sometimes skewed view of a given society, and a sense of incompletion despite enormous length (251–53, 258). Young's novel has all of these and more.

Miss MacIntosh, My Darling is built upon a complex structure, and Young uses perhaps the most complicated structure of all the meganovelists—a frame comprised of things and events that do not exist, or at least are not represented in the symbolic order. Numerous details of what is impossible or illogical flood the text—a crowd of people in an empty room, a thrilling violin recital without a single note being played. Together they constitute a discernible structure, one built on the paradox that the nonexistent and the existent are equally "real," a paradox, in fact, that dissolves when seen in the context of feminine narrative in which such distinctions have little value. Using contradiction as though it is not contradiction, and refusing to distinguish between what happens or is imagined, Young calls into question assumptions behind master narrative.

The feminine in *Miss MacIntosh, My Darling* is the writing into narrative of what is usually outside of narrative, that which would require resolution in a traditional text. Thus, Esther Longtree's never-ending pregnancy and Mr. Spitzer's belief that he is his twin brother and not himself are presented as "facts," not delusions, in Young's textual universe; and in this way the palpable world is surrendered to the invisible, the nonrational, the imagined, and the hallucinated. Catherine Cartwheel's hallucinations have concrete results. When she orders the dinner table set for a large group of imaginary guests, "there was a living servant to stand behind every chair" (223). Her servants accept her hallucinations as real, or real enough to have consequences in their world. Violating temporal, spatial, and other categorical restrictions, Catherine chooses her guest list according to the alphabet. When it is time for the Rs, servants prepare for the Egyptian pharoahs Rameses I, II, III, Roland from Roncevalles, Sirs Joshua Reynolds and Walter Raleigh, Ronsard, Rhadamanthus, Rimski-Korsakov, accompanied by "runes, roulades, rubrics, royal masts, rose windows," riddles, Roman numerals, and redcaps from Grand Central Station (187).

Practicing what Brooke-Rose calls in *Amalgamemnon* "language in random access" (21), Catherine is limited only to the extent that she chooses one letter of the alphabet at a time. Inattentive to the logic of grammar or to the differences between animate and inanimate nouns, Catherine invites both Sir Walter Raleigh and rose windows to the same dinner party. She seizes language, reassigning words to serve her ends. If "women's oppression," as Domna C. Stanton writes, "is embedded in the very foundations of the Logos, in the subtle linguistic and logical processes through which meaning itself is produced," Catherine's manipulation of language is a means to liberation (Eisenstein and Jardine 73). Similarly, the ruptures in logic, the absences and gaps that constitute *Miss MacIntosh, My Darling* liberate it from the constraints of patriarchal forms of narrative. As nonexistent details spin into circles of imaginary events that have measurable repercussions, Young's *Miss MacIntosh, My Darling* approaches alterity and moves into feminine space.

Instead of blurring, disrupting, or subverting narrative elements, writers such as Kathleen Fraser and Jayne Anne Phillips contract them. They formulate strategies for resonance and depth other than fully described settings, explicit development, deep character delineation, or detailed conflicts and resolutions. This mode of experimentation is characterized by the removal of expected elements, thus keeping the central concern of the text elusive, forcing attention on its silences, intervals, gaps, and elisions. In inverse relation to writers like Young, who fill out the spaces until they overflow, these minimalists excavate fictional space, in Jardine's words, emptying out "images, narrative, characters, and words, in order to reach their silent, but solidly significant core—an erotic core" (*Gynesis* 235). Contraction in some minimalist narratives results in ruptures in logic and dependence on tone, pacing, rhythm, repetition, and image, thus bringing these narratives into the territory of poetry. The distinction is at times a matter of authorial declaration.

According to Kathleen Fraser, only a few pieces in her book *Each Next* (1980), subtitled *Narratives*, are "connected" to prose fiction (Fraser, Letter). Though many of the other pieces are arranged in sentences and paragraphs, their lyricism, syntax, and compression, Fraser believes, mark them as poetry. One of the pieces that she names as prose fiction is entitled "Lily, Lois & Flaubert: the site of loss" (an allusion to Roland Barthes's *The Pleasure of the Text*). This two-and-a-quarter-page narrative is in three parts, each developing a concern with the way we constitute a world through language. All three of the narrative's characters use "naming" as a strategy for evoking this world. The names involved belong to dogs—Lily, Lois, and Rover, who on grey days when his owner hopes for sunshine is temporarily renamed Flaubert. The illusion created by renaming Rover is a strategy to color experience: "A guest walking in and hearing you call out 'Flaubert . . . Flaubert???' might enter a different context than he thought his steps were leading to—a configuration of narrow lanes and dark doorways opening onto courtyards. . . ." The name evokes an era—a place, a set of other names, a way of thinking and being that has passed, but persists in the imagination; thus the name, as a locus for the imagination, becomes "the site of loss." Even if the dog does not appear when he is called, "his name is enough" to suggest a "discourse that still perforates the common silence" (15–16).

In a comparison of superficial qualities, Jayne Anne Phillips's story "Counting" (1978) seems more to resemble a "story" than "Lily, Lois & Flaubert: the site of loss," although the difference is perhaps only a matter of degree. Fraser's narrative proceeds in jumps from one section to another, organized through juxtaposition, and dependent upon a gathering resonance from the intersecting silences. Connections are diffused rather than solidified. Phillips's story is more decidedly linear, relying on an orderly progression of events, but also filled with elisions and intervals. Here is Phillips's story:

> The old woman begs him to shoot it. The dog has bitten several chickens and now the young calf. They pen it up, watch the disease take hold. Spraddle-legged the hound hangs its head. Sways, rushes the mesh cage and climbs. The dog's mad eyes are marbled as a goat's, but behind the hard glass something flowers. Its rose jaws open and flare. The blooming closes and leaves him far back.
> The distance is yawning, unimaginable. It is stronger than flesh or the odor of flesh, it dwarfs all things. It ticks like a clock in the mouth. It has him at the center of his breath, he is alone.
> Rifle against his chest a hard arm. He begins to count.

Although Phillips makes use of logical ellipses, syntactic dislocations ("the blooming closes"), and sound patterns ("*h*ound *h*angs its *h*ead"), the story, fourteen sentences long, is complete with three characters, a setting, an exposition, a conflict, and a resolution: a man has been asked by an old woman to shoot a rabid dog. He recognizes something of himself in the dog's madness and finds it difficult to kill, but by "counting," thus mechanizing the killing, he makes himself do it. Fraser implies an occupation for Lois's owner (a French deconstructionist), but we know nothing more substantial about her characters or settings. Phillips's story is solidly located on a farm, though we do not know where or when. In Fraser, the narrative intensifies in the final lines. In Phillips's story, meaning wells up from character and situation, but not as in traditional fiction. The characters *have* been emptied; there is simply an old woman and a man of indeterminate age, both faceless and nameless. The situation, too, is bare, even trivial in its broad outlines. The narrative has a power derived from what is left out. Although Fraser is mainly a poet and Phillips mainly a prose fiction writer and each writer seems to maintain a sense of her individual territory, they both, in their fashion, make spaces through which the semiotic can make its presence felt. Their minimalist strategies, in fact, provoke these spaces, which are richly generative and dynamize their texts. Thus, though the surface structures are minimalist, the narratives are nevertheless expansive.

In writing fiction that observes and interrogates its own processes as those processes unfold, writers like Brooke-Rose in *Xorandor* and Kathy Acker are contributing to the development of feminine narrative. By portraying the artificial nature of imposing a particular order on a complex of events, they challenge the stance of mastery. They assert that even the conscious choices a writer makes are arbitrary, a result of having chosen from among multiple, perhaps equally valid options. In this self-reflexive fiction, the narrative voice is thus no longer authoritative; it may be one of many variables in a text. In some works, the reader is invited into the frame of the narrative to participate in its complexities. By rendering problematical the notion that fiction depicts essential truths and presents universal reality—that it tells *the* story of life—writers like Brooke-Rose and Acker perform acts of liberation. They free narrative discourse from the authoritarian postures of conventional, patriarchal fiction.

Xorandor (1986), an excursion into science fiction for Brooke-Rose, is a story about the telling and not telling of a story. The book records the efforts of Jip and Zab, computer-wiz fraternal twins, to write the story of their discovery of Xorandor, a nuclear waste-eating rock that produces offspring with a similar ability. In their endeavor, they confront the usual barriers to reproducing reality on the page. Frustrated, they soon abandon efforts at exact reproduction for artifices that convey a *sense* of reality since "all stories jumble things up" anyway (24). They debate using flashback or chronological order; they disagree over "what's really relevant and in what order" (35), what points to develop, and with what degree of detail, how to separate interpretation from real events, knowledge gained later from what they knew at the time, and what information to withhold in order to keep readers turning pages. They accuse each other of points of view skewed by their gender and also by egotism. When one of Xorandor's offspring, rather than sticking to a diet of nuclear waste, eats the nuclear material in a bomb, thereby neutralizing the bomb, politicians fear a consequent imbalance of world power. The twins are shipped off to live with a family in Germany by their well-intentioned father, thus cutting off their access to information and requiring them imaginatively to fill in the narrative gaps. The twins, like all storytellers, have privileged information, but it is so weighty that either revealing or concealing it would influence the course of history. Two of Xorandor's offspring are unknown to the adults; thus if they remain undiscovered and reproduce, there is hope yet that nuclear bombs will be neutralized. Therefore, in the end, Jip and Zab decide not to tell their story.

With *Xorandor*, Brooke-Rose has designed a puzzle of self-reflexivity: although the twins decide not to tell their story, they have told it. Since they are highly imaginative kids, after all, they may be untrustworthy narrators. Of course, on another level, the entire book is an invention—a straightforward fantasy, in fact; there are no rocks that eat nuclear material and for that matter, no Jip and Zab. This layered narrative contemplates various levels of its own fictionalizing process in the context of a science fantasy that satirizes the procedures of world politics, and in the process, *Xorandor* acts as a reminder of how the world treats its saviors, whether Christ or Xorandor.

In a penultimate passage, Brooke-Rose comments on the nature of narrative in fiction, as well as in history. In Germany, away from the action, Jip and Zab have this conversation about their predicament:

> "Poor Us! We're storytellers without a hero. . . . We're not even autobiographers since we've dropped out of our own story. Nothing is happening, Zab.
>
> "Something is happening to us, Jip, we're growing up. Even storytellers can change, during the story.
>
> "What on earth do modern historians do, Zab, when history seems to stop?
>
> "They wait.
>
> "Until something happens?
>
> "Until they discover that something has been happening all the time, away from their camera-eyes, unbeknown to them." (159)

In yet another layer of this novel's self-reflexivity, Jip expects stories to have heroes, clear plots, authoritative tellers, the kind of story that he was not able to tell, and of which he will never be the hero since he cannot publish his story. The wiser Zab understands that storytellers, whether of fiction or history, must mature in order to recognize that which has been invisible to them—that the "story" may be taking place despite the lack of heroes, clear plots, and authoritative tellers. In fact, the story may be taking place subversively, like Xorandor's offspring, growing and multiplying outside the purview or control of the patriarchal establishment.

Described by Larry McCaffery as a practitioner of "punk" aesthetics, Kathy Acker writes in a self-reflexive narrative mode as evidenced by her titles: *The Childlike Life of the Black Tarantula by the Black Tarantula* (1975), *The Adult Life of Toulouse Lautrec by Henri Toulouse Lautrec* (1975), *Kathy Goes to Haiti* (1978), *Great Expectations* (1983), and *Don Quixote* (1986). Like the youth "punkers," she obeys no rules, accepts no traditional assumptions. For instance, Acker defies the mandate for authorial originality by plagiarizing titles and stories and the mandate against prurience in serious fiction by writing almost clinical pornography. Her crude illustrations of male and female genitals in *Blood and Guts in High School* (1984) are meant to shock. Sharing qualities with punk rock, her fiction is loud, brash, violent, and disturbs the bourgeois values and complacencies her audience may possess.

Acker employs numerous strategies to underscore the contrived nature of her text. Entropic and picaresque, Acker's *The Childlike Life of the*

Black Tarantula by the Black Tarantula is, in a way, ordered by disorder, by personae and settings undergoing continual and erratic transformation. However, entropic impulses are somewhat qualified by other impulses that loosely shape the novel. The narrator, in her various permutations, is driven by the fear of becoming robot-like, a product of "parents and institutions." She is driven to her multitudinous impersonations by her fear of being frozen in an ordinary identity. Therefore, she transmutes herself into extraordinary beings—murderers, nymphomaniacs, perverts, and mystics—avoiding a solidified, pedestrian self. She says, "I'm trying to become other people. . . . I'm trying to get away from self-expression . . ." (145). Acker implies that the "self" of self-expression is packed with the culture's language and prescriptions, so that in "self-expression" it is the culture that is given voice. To reach an authentic space, the "self" must be deconstructed and emptied. The metamorphoses into society's outcasts help her to measure what remains after the acculturated self is emptied.

Like the spider that is the text's dominant metaphor, she wishes to mark and inhabit her own space. Acker's assaultive use of words, as well as the particular terms and shape of the search she depicts, strongly suggests Cixous's description of what feminine writing should express, "the forceful return of a libido that doesn't give up that easily, and also by what is strange, what is outside culture, by a language which is a savage tongue that can make itself understood quite well" ("Castration" 52).

In a pamphlet-like publication entitled *Hello, I'm Erica Jong* (1982), Acker brutalizes the self-declared radicalism of writers like Erica Jong, who seem hypocritical to Acker, offering titillation for public consumption in the name of *vérité* or feminism. Complete with crudely drawn skeletons printed in red, the pamphlet has the look of a child's storybook, as well as the tone, rhythm, and large print. Acker parodies what she perceives as the self-congratulatory mode of *Fear of Flying* with statements like "Hello, I'm Erica Jong. I'm a real novelist. I write books that talk to you about the agony of American life, how we all suffer. . . . You think booze sex coke rich food etc. are doors out? Temporary oblivion at best. We need total oblivion. What was I saying? Oh, yes, my name is Erica Jong." Acker views Jong's treatment of sex as puerile, as "googoo." To Acker, "sex" should be a path to true engagement, not an opportunity for self-dramatization. Speaking as Jong, Acker writes "I would rather be a baby than have sex."

In the last chapter of *Black Tarantula*, "The Story of My Life," the narrator asserts that in 1970 "I begin to live solely according to my desires" (133). This declaration reveals a radical defiance of the terms of adult life, especially for women, as it is defined by Western patriarchal culture. But in living differently, in living by desire, she hopes to break through to meaning and communion, "Sexual ecstasies become mystic communion. Human communion. There's nothing else I want" (103). The dominant metaphor of Acker's novel is the female tarantula, into which the persona dreams herself: "I see myself: brown very thick skin tender low breasts with huge violet nipples the skin below them curves downwards over man's hips to heavy long spider's legs" (121). Powerful and predatory, the black tarantula is able to ensure the integrity of her web, a symbol for the narrator's work. Woolf's proposal that the woman writer kill the Angel in the House of Fiction has been taken up with some finality by Acker. In the fiction of Kathy Acker, angels of any kind do not stand a chance.

THE outlining of three generations and eight decades of the tradition of women's experimental fiction is a step in the project of bringing this tradition to visibility. Viewing these writers as a separate tradition is not isolationist; rather, it is a strategy in recovering them, in making them an object of discourse. Separation is a means of offering women writers visibility that they would not otherwise possess and enabling discussions that could not otherwise proceed.[29] Not attached to a particular literary discourse, many women's experimental works slip into obscurity. Thus the tradition can give a home to many significant writers and works that are lost, neglected, or undervalued outside of this context.

The tasks concerning this tradition are manifold—foregrounding, amplifying, adjusting, and contextualizing, among them. Current practices in feminist literary criticism suggest other projects as well—for instance, the tracing of continuities and discontinuities between generations, the exploration of influence and intertextuality. Since the experimentalist and feminist aesthetics are historically and explicitly linked in the work of Woolf and Richardson, more studies substantiating the continuation of that link are in order—particularly studies that focus on second- and third-generation experimentalists. Additionally, the question of how the formal innovations characterizing experimental writing are pertinent to the whole women's tradition needs to be explored. Requiring further substantiation and documentation is the fact that the kind of prose that Cixous and other advocates of écriture féminine have been describing as an ideal, something for the future of women writers, already has a distinguished tradition and a list of eminent *women* practitioners. Also, more studies that claim or assume they are speaking about experimentalism or experimentalists in general must include women, must integrate them into their discussions.

Almost as fundamental as the recovery and situating of this tradition is the issue raised in Jardine's *Gynesis* of the intersection between modernity and feminism, an intersection that implies a role—largely unrecognized and unexamined—for women's experimental narrative in reconciling feminism and modernity. Modernity, in the name of which French male theorists are claiming the feminine for themselves, has, in essence, declared itself identified with Molly Bloom rather than Stephen Dedalus—a profound shift in identification that carries the potential for the reorganization of dominant conceptual structures of the West.[30] This shift can be illustrated through the progression in Joyce from *Portrait* to *Ulysses*. In *A Portrait of the Artist as a Young Man*, Stephen articulates his ambitious quest, "to forge in the smithy of my soul the uncreated conscience of my race." He calls on the "Old father, old artificer, [to] stand [him] now and ever in good stead" (253). In writing this novel, Joyce composed within the conceptual framework of dominant Western structures. Following the imperatives of master narratives, the (male) artist is an ersatz God who must remake the world in his own image in each work. His calling on the Father with whom he identifies is his attempt to mark his quest as sanctified, as a search for Truth that he, the blessed son, can reveal in order "to forge . . . the uncreated conscience" of his race. When we meet Stephen in *Ulysses*, he is still searching for sanctification of his quest from the Father. However, in the gap between the two books, the whole universe has been deconstructed by Einstein, Freud, and Marx—a circumstance that *Ulysses* but not *Portrait* reflects. When Stephen looks for the all-powerful Father, what he finds is Bloom, an ordinary man who as Jew is marginal and powerless. The quest so reverently formulated in *Portrait* has passed into anachronism, the ideal of the forging of "racial conscience" mysteriously withdrawn. As the quest for the unification of consciousness under the sign of the Father fades, what it has hidden emerges, what it has repressed returns. This is the "yes," the affirming feminine that does not exclude or privilege or conceive hierarchically. This feminine has been written by men, but perhaps more relevant to the reconciliation of feminism and modernity, it has also been written by women. It is time, indeed, to read Molly not only as she has been written by Joyce and his brothers, but also as she has written herself from Gertrude Stein to Kathy Acker.

NOTES

1. An early example is Ellen Moers's discussion in *Literary Women* of *Frankenstein*. Moers reads Mary Shelley's gothic tale as a reflection of Shelley's own experiences with childbirth. The novel presents a "birth myth," expressing

"the drama of guilt, dread, and flight surrounding birth and its consequences" (142). Gilbert and Gubar in *The Madwoman in the Attic* discuss
ways in which nineteenth-century women's writing is "parodic, duplicitous,
extraordinarily sophisticated . . . both revisionary and revolutionary, even
when it is produced by writers we usually think of as models of angelic resignation" (80).

2. In *Women of the Left Bank*, Shari Benstock examines critical approaches to
Stein that view her writing as either "egotistical silliness" or as a disguised
"lesbian code," a covert "confession" of her sexuality. Benstock indicates
that the relationship between Stein's lesbianism and her writing is more complex (161–63).

3. Alice Jardine examines the implications for feminism of texts that reflect a
postmodern sensibility—in her terms, the writings of "modernity." Such texts
question the ideologies of traditional Western narratives that historically
have been "narratives invented by men" (24). The attempt to challenge traditional forms necessarily involves the introduction of modes and processes
that can be characterized as "*féminine*" (25).

4. For a useful introduction to French feminist criticism, see *New French Feminisms* edited by Elaine Marks and Isabelle de Courtivron and *L'écriture féminine*. Also helpful are Carolyn Burke's and Jane Gallop's essays, which
examine the theories of Freud, Lacan, and Kristeva in a feminist context (Eisenstein and Jardine 106–21).

5. See Julia Kristeva's *Desire in Language* and *Revolution in Poetic Language*.
According to Kristeva, the semiotic in language is manifested through *chora*,
or rhythmic pulsations, disruptions, and other pressures evident in the text.
The semiotic derives from unconscious, pre-Oedipal processes. Symbolic processes, on the other hand, are manifested in the language of conscious control
and logic.

6. Kristeva notes that contemporary writer Sophie Podolski in her novel *Le pays
où tout est permis* writes écriture féminine, but she speaks of Podolski's
achievement as unusual (Marks and de Courtivron 166–67). In "The Laugh
of the Medusa," Cixous notes a few women writers such as Marguerite Duras
and Colette, but the fact that few examples of women writers of écriture
feminine have been offered has also been noted by Toril Moi in *Sexual/Tex-
tual Politics* (97, 110) and Alice Jardine in *Gynesis* (62–63).

7. Showalter in "Feminist Criticism in the Wilderness" views écriture féminine
as "a significant theoretical formulation in French feminist criticism, although it describes a Utopian possibility rather than a literary practice." In
"Emphasis Added: Plots and Plausibilities in Women's Fiction" Miller describes écriture féminine as "fundamentally a hope, if not a blueprint, for the
future." See Showalter's *The New Feminist Criticism* (249, 341).

8. Toril Moi, in "Rescuing Woolf for Feminist Politics: Some Points towards an
Alternative Reading," examines why Woolf has sometimes been considered
"insufficiently feminist." Moi believes that Woolf, "the greatest British
woman writer of this century," is also a "progressive, feminist writer of ge-

nius"—if "the politics of Woolf's writing [are located] *precisely in her textual practice*" (*Sexual/Textual Politics* 8–18). Moi's point that evidence of Woolf's feminism can be found in her formal innovations applies to other women experimentalists as well.

9. Daiches's 1942 *Virginia Woolf*, like *The Novel and the Modern World*, assessed Woolf's contribution to literature as "a very real, if in some sense a limited one." Daiches wanted the "robustness" of her criticism to appear in her fiction as well. His call for a masculine quality reveals his bias. Daiches did not alter his opinion for the 1963 edition of *Virginia Woolf*.

10. *Three Lives* was published in 1909 by Grafton Press, not as Stein says in 1908.

11. Gilbert and Gubar in "Tradition and the Female Talent" remark that early twentieth-century women writers did not have "a women's club comparable to the male society created by Eliot and his brothers." They examine the tendency of women, particularly in the nineteenth century, to feel reluctance and guilt in exercising their literary ambitions (203–04). In "Gertrude Stein, the Cone Sisters, and the Puzzle of Friendship," Carolyn Burke points to Stein's lack of enduring friendships with women: "As Natalie Barney, herself a cool observer of women's relationships, said of Gertrude's history of failed friendships, 'It is obvious that . . . her friendships ceased from the causes already detected in their beginnings' " (Burke 242).

12. In the 1923 review of *Revolving Lights*, Woolf makes similar criticisms ("Romance and the Heart").

13. See Gillian E. Hanscombe's analysis of Richardson's techniques in her essay "Dorothy Richardson Versus the Novvle" in this volume.

14. Sydney Janet Kaplan writes that the "break with tradition" for Richardson and others was more than a shift in aesthetics; it was also an assertion of "feminism," an attempt "to define a specifically feminine consciousness" (1–2). On Miriam's perceptions, Kaplan writes, "The objects [she notices] are not organized in order of their importance, an indication of the lack of hierarchical values in the feminine consciousness" (41).

15. Added to stream of consciousness, the omission of expected punctuation and capitalization alters the narrative so radically that Woolf credits Richardson with inventing the "psychological sentence of the feminine gender" ("Romance and the Heart" 124).

16. Some French feminist critics believe the pattern of multiple climaxes, which they attribute to feminist and innovative fiction, imitates female sexuality; this pattern contrasts with traditional fiction's single culminating climax, suggesting male sexuality. See Ann Rosalind Jones in Showalter's *The New Feminist Criticism* 362–66.

17. See Gilbert and Gubar in *The Madwoman in the Attic* for another discussion of this idea in Woolf (17).

18. An example of this approach may be seen in Phyllis Rose's comment, "She strove perhaps a little too hard to create beauty and so, in a work like *The Waves*, she presents too unbroken a surface" (212).

19. In *Writing Beyond the Ending*, Rachel Blau DuPlessis examines Woolf's method in *The Years*: "At first, the system of social reproduction seems forceful and intact, quite impervious to change. . . . By midbook . . . [it shows] a change not only cosmic, cyclic, and chronic (like the seasons and the day, which are, not incidentally, deconstructed by being taken out of their expected order) but evolutionary" (165).

20. "Master narrative" as used by Jardine in *Gynesis* is the discourse of Western culture that encodes its philosophy, history, central truths, and values. The "questioning or turning back" of this discourse involves a "reincorporation and reconceptualization" of what master narratives have omitted, and in France this is conceived as a " 'space' of some kind (over which the narrative has lost control), and this space has been coded as *feminine*, as *woman*" (25).

21. In her article "The Word as Such: L = A = N = G = U = A = G = E Poetry in the Eighties" for *American Poetry Review* (1984), Marjorie Perloff notes the link between Stein and Language Poetry writing about Charles Bernstein.

22. Kristeva's discussion in "Women's Time" of "cyclical and monumental" time (33–36) suggests a sense of time that is similar to Stein's notion of "a prolonged and continuous present." "The Laugh of the Medusa" (887), in which Cixous writes that "feminine" texts are governed by disruption and dislocation, brings to mind Marianne DeKoven's description of Stein: "The modes Stein disrupts are linear, orderly, closed, hierarchical, sensible, coherent, [and] referential. . . . The modes she substitutes are incoherent, open-ended, anarchic, irreducible, multiple . . ." (xiii–xiv). Catharine R. Stimpson writes, "Stein is no ideological feminist, but she does foreshadow the pulsating, lyrical polemic of much contemporary feminist theory" (10).

23. Gillian Hanscombe describes Richardson's marriage to Alan Odle as "a happy one, providing her with 'a new world' " (16). According to Rose, Woolf's marriage to Leonard "allowed her to work well, supported and loved by an intelligent man" (87). James Mellow describes Toklas as giving Stein a "sense of stability for forty years" (163).

24. Barnes lived in London, Berlin, Paris, and New York; Rhys in Vienna, Budapest, and Paris; Bowles in New York, Mexico, and Tangier; Nin spent the years between the wars mostly in Paris. Rhys was married three times; and despite H.D.'s long-term relationship with Bryher and Bowles's and Nin's marriages, sexual adventures and affairs were common to them. Barnes was hospitalized for drinking; Bowles and H.D. spent years in sanatoriums; and Rhys, Barnes, and Bowles all experienced serious financial problems. (See Field 13–18; Staley 2–19; Dillon, *A Little Original Sin* 290, 391, 419; and Guest 278, 312.)

25. In this reading, we were helped by Gilbert and Gubar who see Bertha as representing an aspect of Jane's psyche (*Madwoman* 362).

26. Sharon Spencer notes that the diary "displays the qualities . . . of fiction" (122).

27. Deborah Kelly Kloepfer, in " 'Fishing the Murex Up': Sense and Resonance in H.D.'s *Palimpsest*," describes H.D.'s method of transforming the past into

a textual palimpsest in order to "connect [the] three minds [of her protagonists into] . . . one layered consciousness" (572)

28. As pointed out by Susan Stanford Friedman in *Psyche Reborn*, H.D.'s epic
works, which she wrote after her brief Imagist period, are shaped by "myth
and mythic consciousness, by religious vision or experience, and by a new
synthesis of fragmented traditions" (5). Friedman discusses *Palimpsest* as
H.D.'s recasting of the masculine epic into a feminine form, "suited to . . . a
new woman's epic" (69).

29. Elaine Showalter in "Feminist Criticism in the Wilderness" describes wom-
en's writing as a " 'double-voiced discourse' [that is] not . . . *inside* and *outside* of the male tradition . . . [but] inside two traditions simultaneously . . ."
(263–64).

30. Jardine emphasizes that most of the theories about the "feminine" in writing
"are based almost entirely on *men's* writing and, most important, on fiction
written by men" (61).

WORKS CITED

Abel, Elizabeth, ed. *Writing and Sexual Difference.* Chicago: U of Chicago P,
1982.

Acker, Kathy. *The Adult Life of Toulouse Lautrec by Henri Toulouse Lautrec.*
New York: TVRT, 1975.

———. *Blood and Guts in High School.* New York: Grove, 1984.

———. *The Childlike Life of the Black Tarantula by the Black Tarantula.* New
York: TVRT Press, 1975.

———. *Don Quixote.* New York: Grove, 1986.

———. *Great Expectations.* New York: Grove, 1983.

———. *Hello, I'm Erica Jong.* New York: Contact II, 1982.

———. *Kathy Goes to Haiti.* Toronto: Rumor, 1978.

Barnes, Djuna. "The Grande Malade." *Selected Works* 21–28.

———. *Nightwood.* 1936. Introd. T. S. Eliot. New York: New Directions, 1961.

———. *Selected Works of Djuna Barnes: Spillway, The Antiphon, Nightwood.*
New York: Farrar, 1962.

Barth, John. *Letters: A Novel.* New York: Putnam's, 1979.

Barthes, Roland. *The Pleasure of the Text.* Trans. Richard Miller. New York:
Farrar, 1975.

Beauvoir, Simone de. *The Second Sex.* 1949. Trans. and ed. H. M. Parshly. 1953.
New York: Vintage, 1974.

Bellamy, Joe David, ed. *The New Fiction: Interviews with Innovative American
Writers.* Urbana: U of Illinois P, 1974.

Benstock, Shari. *Women of the Left Bank: Paris, 1900–1940.* Austin: U of Texas
P, 1986.

Bernstein, Charles. "The Sheds of Our Webs." Perloff 15.

Bowles, Jane. *Two Serious Ladies.* 1943. *My Sister's Hand in Mine: The Collected*

Works of Jane Bowles. Expanded ed. Introd. Truman Capote. New York: Ecco, 1978. 1–201.

Brontë, Charlotte. 1847. *Jane Eyre*. New York: Penguin, 1966.

Brooke-Rose, Christine. *Amalgamemnon*. Manchester, Gt. Brit. and New York: Carcanet, 1984.

———. *Thru*. *The Christine Brooke-Rose Omnibus: Four Novels: Out, Such, Between, Thru*. Manchester, Gt. Brit. and New York: Carcanet, 1986. 577–742.

———. *Xorandor*. Manchester, Gt. Brit. and New York: Carcanet, 1986.

Burke, Carolyn. "Gertrude Stein, the Cone Sisters, and the Puzzle of Friendship." Abel 221–42.

———. "Rethinking the Maternal." Eisenstein and Jardine 107–14.

Cixous, Hélène. "Castration or Decapitation?" Trans. Annette Kuhn. *Signs* 7 (1981): 41–55.

———. "The Laugh of the Medusa." Trans. Keith Cohen and Paula Cohen. *Signs* 1 (1976): 875–93.

Daiches, David. *The Novel and the Modern World*. 1939. 2d ed. Chicago: U of Chicago P, 1960.

———. *Virginia Woolf*. 1942. Norfolk, CT: New Directions, 1963.

DeKoven, Marianne. *A Different Language: Gertrude Stein's Experimental Writing*. Madison: U of Wisconsin P, 1983.

Dillon, Millicent. *A Little Original Sin: The Life and Work of Jane Bowles*. New York: Holt, 1981.

———, ed. *Out in the World: Selected Letters of Jane Bowles: 1935–1970*. Santa Barbara: Black Sparrow, 1985.

Donoghue, Denis. "The Promiscuous Cool of Postmodernism." *NYTBR*. June 22, 1986: 1, 36–37.

Doolittle, Hilda. *The Gift*. New York: New Directions, 1982.

———. *HERmione*. New York: New Directions, 1981.

———. *Palimpsest*. 1926. Rev. ed. Carbondale: Southern Illinois UP, 1968.

DuPlessis, Rachel Blau. *H.D.: The Career of That Struggle*. Bloomington: Indiana UP, 1986.

———. *Writing Beyond the Ending: Narrative Strategies of Twentieth-Century Women Writers*. Bloomington: Indiana UP, 1985.

L'écriture féminine. Special Issue. *Contemporary Literature* 24 (1983).

Edel, Leon. *The Psychological Novel: 1900–1950*. New York: Lippincott, 1955.

Eisenstein, Hester and Alice A. Jardine, eds. *The Future of Difference*. 1980. New Brunswick: Rutgers UP, 1985.

Ellmann, Richard. *James Joyce*. Rev. ed. New York: Oxford UP, 1982.

Federman, Raymond. "Surfiction: Four Propositions in Form of an Introduction." *Surfiction: Fiction Now . . . and Tomorrow*. Chicago: Swallow, 1975. 5–15.

Field, Andrew. *Djuna: The Life and Times of Djuna Barnes*. New York: Putnam's, 1983.

Figes, Eva. 1983. *Light*. New York: Ballantine, 1984.

Fraser, Kathleen. *Each Next: Narratives*. Berkeley: The Figures, 1980.

Fraser, Kathleen. Letter to E. Friedman. October 6, 1986.

Friedan, Betty. *The Feminine Mystique*. New York: Norton, 1963.

Friedman, Ellen G. *Joyce Carol Oates*. New York: Ungar, 1980.

Friedman, Susan Stanford. *Psyche Reborn: The Emergence of H.D.* Bloomington: Indiana UP, 1981.

Fromm, Gloria G. *Dorothy Richardson: A Biography*. Urbana: U of Illinois P, 1977.

Gallop, Jane. "Introduction"/"Psychoanalysis in France." Eisenstein and Jardine 114–21.

Gilbert, Sandra M., and Susan Gubar. " 'Forward Into the Past': The Complex Female Affiliation Complex." *Historical Studies in Literary Criticism*. Ed. Jerome McGann. Madison: U of Wisconsin P, 1985.

———. *The Madwoman in the Attic: The Woman Writer and the Nineteenth-Century Literary Imagination*. New Haven: Yale UP, 1979.

———. *No Man's Land: The Place of the Woman Writer in the Twentieth Century*. Vol. 1. *The War of the Words*. New Haven: Yale UP, 1987.

———. "Sexual Linguistics: Gender, Language, Sexuality." *New Literary History* 16 (1985): 515–43.

———. "Tradition and the Female Talent." Miller, *Poetics of Gender* 183–207.

Guest, Barbara. *Herself Defined: The Poet H.D. and Her World*. Garden City, NY: Doubleday, 1984.

Hanscombe, Gillian E. *The Art of Life: Dorothy Richardson and the Development of Feminist Consciousness*. Athens, OH: Ohio UP, 1983.

Hauser, Marianne. 1976. *The Talking Room*. New York: Fiction Collective, 1984.

Herrmann, Claudine. From "Women in Space and Time." Trans. Marilyn R. Schuster. Marks and de Courtivron 168–73.

Jardine, Alice A. *Gynesis: Configurations of Woman and Modernity*. Ithaca: Cornell UP, 1985.

Jones, Ann Rosalind. "Writing the Body: Toward an Understanding of *l'écriture féminine*." Showalter, *The New Feminist Criticism* 361–77.

Jong, Erica. *Fear of Flying*. New York: Holt, 1973.

Joyce, James. *Dubliners*. London: Richards, 1914.

———. *A Portrait of the Artist as a Young Man*. 1916. New York: Viking, 1965.

———. *Ulysses*. 1922. New York: Random, 1961.

Kaplan, Sydney Janet. *Feminine Consciousness in the Modern British Novel*. Urbana: U of Illinois P, 1975.

Karl, Frederick R. "American Fictions: The Mega-Novel." *Conjunctions* 7 (1985): 248–60.

Kirkby, Joan. "Is There Life After Art? The Metaphysics of Marilynne Robinson's *Housekeeping*." *Tulsa Studies in Women's Literature* 5 (1986): 91–109.

Klinkowitz, Jerome. *Literary Disruptions: The Making of a Post-Contemporary American Fiction*. 2d ed. Urbana: U of Illinois P, 1980.

Kloepfer, Deborah Kelly. " 'Fishing the Murex Up': Sense and Resonance in H.D.'s *Palimpsest*." *Contemporary Literature* 27 (1986): 553–73.

Kostelanetz, Richard. Introduction. *The Yale Gertrude Stein*. New Haven: Yale UP, 1980. i–xxxi.

Kristeva, Julia. *Desire in Language: A Semiotic Approach to Literature and Art*. Trans. Leon S. Roudiez, Alice A. Jardine, and Thomas Gora. New York: Columbia UP, 1980.

———. From "Oscillation Between Power and Denial." Trans. Marilyn A. August. Marks and de Courtivron 165–67.

———. *Revolution in Poetic Language*. Trans. Margaret Waller. Introd. Leon S. Roudiez. New York: Columbia UP, 1984.

———. "Women's Time." Trans. Alice A. Jardine and Harry Blake. *Feminist Theory: A Critique of Ideology*. Ed. Nannerl O. Keohane, Michelle Z. Rosaldo, and Barbara C. Gelpi. Chicago: U of Chicago P, 1982. 31–53.

McCaffery, Larry, ed. *Postmodern Fiction: A Bio-bibliographical Guide*. New York: Greenwood, 1986.

McHale, Brian. *Postmodernist Fiction*. New York: Methuen, 1987.

Marks, Elaine, and Isabelle de Courtivron, eds. *New French Feminisms: An Anthology*. Amherst: U of Massachusetts P, 1980.

Mellow, James R. *Charmed Circle: Gertrude Stein and Company*. New York: Praeger, 1974.

Miller, Nancy K. "Emphasis Added: Plots and Plausibilities in Women's Fiction." Showalter, *The New Feminist Criticism* 339–60.

———, ed. *The Poetics of Gender*. New York: Columbia UP, 1986.

Millett, Kate. *Sexual Politics*. Garden City, NY: Doubleday, 1970.

Moers, Ellen. *Literary Women: The Great Writers*. Garden City, NY: Doubleday, 1976.

Moi, Toril. *Sexual/Textual Politics: Feminist Literary Theory*. New York: Methuen, 1985.

Morrison, Toni. *Sula*. New York, Knopf, 1973.

Nin, Anaïs. *Delta of Venus: Erotica*. New York: Harcourt, 1977.

———. *The Diary of Anaïs Nin: 1931–1934*. New York: Harcourt, 1966.

———. *House of Incest*. 1936. Denver: Swallow, 1958.

———. *The Novel of the Future*. New York: Macmillan, 1968.

Oates, Joyce Carol. *Childwold*. New York: Vanguard, 1976.

Ortega y Gasset, José. *The Dehumanization of Art and Other Essays on Art, Culture, and Literature*. Princeton: Princeton UP, 1968.

Perloff, Marjorie. "The Word as Such: L=A=N=G=U=A=G=E Poetry in the Eighties." *American Poetry Review* 13 (1984): 15–22.

Phillips, Jayne Anne. *Counting*. New York: Vehicle, 1978.

"Postrealist American Fiction: The Novel Still Novel." Session No. 477. MLA Convention. New York, Dec. 29, 1983.

Pynchon, Thomas. *Gravity's Rainbow*. New York: Viking, 1973.

Quin, Ann. *Berg*. New York: Scribner's, 1964.

Rhys, Jean. *After Leaving Mr. MacKenzie*. New York: Knopf, 1931.

———. *The Letters of Jean Rhys*. Ed. Francis Wyndham and Diana Melly. New York: Viking, 1984.

Rhys, Jean. *Wide Sargasso Sea*. London: Deutsch, 1966.

Richardson, Dorothy Miller. Foreword to Volume 1 of *Pilgrimage*. Introd. Walter Allen. 4 vols. London: Dent, 1967.

——. *Pointed Roofs*. Introd. J. D. Beresford. London: Duckworth, 1915.

——. *Revolving Lights*. London: Duckworth, 1923.

——. *The Tunnel*. London: Duckworth, 1919.

Robbins, J. Albert, ed. *American Literary Scholarship: An Annual/1984*. Durham: Duke UP, 1986. 293–339.

Robinson, Marilynne. *Housekeeping*. New York: Farrar, 1980.

Rose, Phyllis. *Woman of Letters: A Life of Virginia Woolf*. New York: Oxford UP, 1978.

Scholes, Robert. *Fabulation and Metafiction*. Urbana: U of Illinois P, 1979.

Showalter, Elaine. "Feminist Criticism in the Wilderness." Showalter, *The New Feminist Criticism* 243–70.

——. *A Literature of Their Own: British Women Novelists from Brontë to Lessing*. Princeton: Princeton UP, 1977.

——, ed. *The New Feminist Criticism: Essays on Women, Literature, and Theory*. New York: Pantheon, 1985.

Sinclair, May. "The Novels of Dorothy Richardson." *The Egoist* 4 (1918): 57–59.

Sontag, Susan. *Against Interpretation and Other Essays*. New York: Farrar, 1964.

——. *The Benefactor*. New York: Farrar, 1963.

——. *Death Kit*. New York: Farrar, 1967.

——. "Debriefing." *I, etcetera*. New York: Farrar, 1978. 35–52.

Spacks, Patricia Meyer. *The Female Imagination*. New York: Knopf, 1975.

Spencer, Sharon. *Collage of Dreams: The Writings of Anaïs Nin*. Chicago: Swallow, 1977.

Spring, Howard. Review of *The Years*. *Virginia Woolf: The Critical Heritage*. Ed. Robin Majumdar and Allen McLaurin. London: Routledge, 1975. 376–78.

Stanton, Domna C. "Language and Revolution: The Franco-American Dis-Connection." Eisenstein and Jardine 73–87.

Stayley, Tom. *Jean Rhys: A Critical Study*. Austin: U of Texas P, 1979.

Stein, Gertrude. *As Fine as Melanctha*. New Haven: Yale UP, 1954.

——. *The Autobiography of Alice B. Toklas*. New York: Harcourt, 1933.

——. *Composition as Explanation*. London: Hogarth, 1926.

——. *Geography and Plays*. 1922. New York: Something Else, 1968.

——. "The Gradual Making of *The Making of Americans*." *Selected Writings* 241–58.

——. *Lectures in America*. New York: Random, 1935.

——. *The Making of Americans*. 1925. Unabridged ed. New York: Something Else, 1966.

——. "Poetry and Grammar." *Lectures* 209–46.

——. "A Portrait of F.B." *Geography and Plays* 176.

————. *Selected Writings of Gertrude Stein*. 1946. Ed. Carl Van Vechten. New York: Random, 1972.

————. *Tender Buttons*. 1914. *Selected Writings* 461–509.

————. *Three Lives*. 1909. New York: NAL, 1985.

————. *What Are Masterpieces*. 1940. New York: Pitman, 1970.

Stimpson, Catharine R. "Gertrude Stein and the Transposition of Gender." Miller, *The Poetics of Gender* 1–18.

Walton, Edith H. "Fantastic Duo." *NYTBR*. May 9, 1943: 14.

Woolf, Virginia. *Collected Essays*. Vol. 2. London: Hogarth, 1966.

————. *Contemporary Writers*. Ed. Jean Guiguet. New York: Harcourt, 1966.

————. *The Diary of Virginia Woolf: 1920–1924*. Vol. 2. Ed. Anne Olivier Bell with Andrew McNeillie. New York: Harcourt, 1978.

————. *The Diary of Virginia Woolf: 1925–1930*. Vol. 3. Ed. Anne Olivier Bell with Andrew McNeillie. New York: Harcourt, 1980.

————. *Jacob's Room*. 1922. *Jacob's Room* 7–176.

————. *Jacob's Room and The Waves: Two Complete Novels*. New York: Harcourt, 1959.

————. "Modern Fiction." *Collected Essays* 103–110.

————. *Mrs. Dalloway*. 1925. New York: Harcourt, 1964.

————. *Orlando: A Biography*. 1928. New York: Harcourt, 1973.

————. "Professions for Women." *The Death of the Moth and Other Essays*. 1942. New York: Harcourt, 1970. 235–42.

————. Review of *The Tunnel* (Feb. 13, 1919). *Contemporary Writers* 120–22.

————. "Romance and the Heart" (May 19, 1923) [Rev. of *Revolving Lights*.] *Contemporary Writers* 123–25.

————. *A Room of One's Own*. 1929. New York: Harcourt, 1957.

————. *To the Lighthouse*. 1927. New York: Harcourt, 1955.

————. *The Waves*. 1931. *Jacob's Room* 179–383.

————. "Women and Fiction." *Collected Essays* 141–48.

————. *A Writer's Dairy*. Ed. Leonard Woolf. London: Hogarth, 1953.

————. *The Years*. 1937. New York: Harcourt, 1969.

Young, Marguerite. *Miss McIntosh, My Darling*. New York: Scribner's, 1965.

Zimmerman, Bonnie. "Feminist Fiction and the Postmodern Challenge." McCaffery 175–88.

PERSPECTIVES

Illiterations

CHRISTINE BROOKE-ROSE

TO BE an "experimental" woman writer is one thing. To write about the situation of "experimental" women writers is quite another. This will not be a description of specific writers, least of all myself, and their difficulties but a general, lightly deconstructing speculation on ancient prejudices—and what are prejudices but ill iterations of untenable positions in the face of change? And what can protests against these be but themselves ill iterations?

TO BE AN "EXPERIMENTAL WOMAN WRITER"

Three words. Three difficulties. *To be a woman*: vast and vastly written up. *To be a woman writer*: narrower but proportionately ditto, and contained in the first.

Assuming that most of the problems—described by Elaine Showalter ("Women Writers") and many others since—for nineteenth-century women writers have disappeared, and that the sexes, like classes and races, have on the face of it the same chances, there are nevertheless different types and levels of critical attention, on a sliding scale that can be subsumed in the general opposition of canonical/noncanonical (or ephemeral). And as Frank Kermode has shown, only the canonical is deemed worthy of interpretation. Inside the canon interpretation multiplies wildly, while outside it a text does not even exist. Further, the pressure of the canonic is such that the self-allotted task of interpretation is to transform into qualities elements that, in a noncanonic work, would be considered as serious flaws, and this process of canonization, until recent feminist work, has been more consistently applied to male works than to the few female entries.

In theory the canonic/noncanonic opposition applies to all writers and thus cuts across sexual and any other oppositions. In practice a canon is very much a masculine notion, a priesthood (not to be polluted by women), a club, a sacred male preserve; and yet a second matrix, as Norman O. Brown would say. Or a heroic son-father struggle in Harold Bloom's terms. But a body, a corpus, something owned. And not only a male preserve but that of a privileged caste. For women are only one part, however large, of an originally much larger exclusion: that of barbarians and slaves, or, later, other races and the "lower" classes from peasants to modern workers, who were long considered incapable of any art worth the dignity of attention, indeed of an education towards it or towards anything else, even as late as Hardy's Jude.

Nevertheless, male outsiders enter the canon more easily than women do, for reasons much deeper than that of caste. At the individual level, white males of outside origin have long been able to enter the canon, chiefly because of a long (canonic) tradition of the poet as traveling minstrel, visiting rhapsode, outsider. That is how a canon is formed and slowly altered. At the collective level, the canon also absorbs. In *The Secular Scripture* Northrop Frye speaks of the central, "mythic" tradition of any one culture (in our case the Graeco-Judeo-Christian), which excludes the parallel (popular) or "secular" art forms, until in moments of exhaustion it has to turn to them for replenishment and renewed vigor (e.g., today, SF, comics, etc.).

But women's writing does not seem ever to have had that role of "tonic," or outside remedy, nor does it today. Even with the "rereading" by the feminists of a whole new area of women's literature previously relegated to oblivion (Kolodny "Some Notes"), it is still possible for Nancy K. Miller to write: "This new mapping of a parallel geography does not, of course, resolve the oxymoron of marginality: how is it that women, a statistical majority in our culture, perform as a 'literary subculture'?" (38).

Traditionally then, this notion of a canon, of a central tradition around the central myth, which is essentially male, priestly and caste-bound, underlies types and levels of critical attention, so that despite the various and increasing waves of emancipation since the nineteenth century, certain relics remain, ill iterations in the unconscious of society.

It is thus one thing for a woman to have only the usual or no difficulties in getting published today, in acquiring a fashionable success, or at least getting well known enough to continue being published, but quite another thing for a woman writer, with equivalent speed and given the usual ups and downs, to enter the canon. One need only mention names like (in order of difficulty) Barbara Pym, Jean Rhys, Christina Stead, Ivy Compton-Burnett, Isak Dinesen, Nathalie Sarraute, who all received the accolade of serious recognition very late in life. Or Kate Chopin, or Edith Wharton, both dismissed as imitators, who are being "reread" and understood long after their death.

Or Gertrude Stein, or Djuna Barnes, who are only now receiving serious critical attention. For of course, it is yet a third thing for a woman to be genuinely welcomed and attended to as an "experimental" writer. This is caught up in a second opposition, that of tradition and innovation. But let us first go back to a more deeply buried concept.

TO BE A CREATOR

Only seven years ago, Anthony Burgess wrote an article in the *London Observer* ("Grunts from a Sexist Pig"), in reaction to receiving a Pink Pig Award from the Women in Publishing Group "for outstanding contributions to sexism." The article is mildly amusing and even, occasionally, sensible and fair, until Burgess suddenly brings out—in all seriousness—the hoary old chestnut that

> Women have never been denied professional musical instruction—indeed, they used to be encouraged to have it—but they have not yet produced a Mozart or a Beethoven. I am told by feminists that all this will change some day, when women have learned how to create like *women* composers, a thing men have prevented their doing in the past.

This is nonsense, he says, and would be denied by composers like Thea Musgrave and the late Dame Ethel Smyth. He goes on: "Freud, bewildered, said 'What does a woman *want?*'" and insists that this question has not been answered, despite the writings of (here a long list, with amazing omissions, of feminist names from Kate Millett and Simone de Beauvoir all the way back to Mary Wollstonecraft "and the great Virginia herself").

That such ill iterations can still be made after some 20 years of deconstruction (of Freud among others) and other investigations, would alone justify my title. All this has been much researched and written about. It takes centuries, generations of artists being allowed and expected to practice their art and to show themselves practicing it, for a Mozart or a Michelangelo or a Shakespeare to emerge. Even today the prejudice against women painters, sculptors, and composers runs deeper than that against women writers, for precisely the reasons described by Virginia Woolf.

But where do these judgments come from if not from the canon? Jane Austen is perfect, but of course she is not Shakespeare. Nor for that matter is Thackeray or Trollope. What does it mean? Burgess himself is very careful to welcome the republication by Virago of "the masterpiece of Dorothy Richardson." Does he really mean that? Or is it really "only" a mistresspiece? His evaluation is wholly in relation to Joyce (though it is already much to recognize her as "anticipating" him), and used more to defend himself than to praise her:

> In considering . . . the masterpiece of Dorothy Richardson I did not say that here we had a great work of women's literature, but rather here

we had a great work which anticipated some of the innovations of James Joyce. I should have stressed that this was a work by a woman, and the womanly aspect of the thing didn't seem to me to be important. I believe that the sex of an author is irrelevant because any good writer contains both sexes.

Impeccable stance on the face of it, going back to Coleridge and of course to "the great Virginia herself," who however adds: "Coleridge certainly did not mean, when he said that a great mind is androgynous, that it is a mind that has any special sympathy with women; a mind that takes up their cause or devotes itself to their interpretation" (102).

The androgynous-great-mind stance is what some feminists condemn as "humanism" rather than "feminism," while for others it is the only possible option, providing it is understood properly and not used as a pigsnout mask.

Meanwhile, back to the canon: would anyone now seriously dispute the major status of writers such as Jane Austen, George Eliot, or Emily Dickinson? Probably not. For of course, they are safely dead.

One useful analogy: the nineteenth-century gentleman who would live by the classics (in dead languages), or sometimes study ancient Arabic or Persian or Hebrew, yet show no interest in contemporary equivalents (indeed there could not *be* equivalents, oral or written), and would despise any living representative of those cultures as wogs and Jews.

Another useful analogy: the performing arts, where the artists are necessarily alive, but die with their art (or did before the modern media). Thus men did not feel threatened in their real creativity, that is to say, in their desired posterity, and for this reason the performing arts (the living word) have often been considered as vaguely inferior to the creative arts. For although the *work* involved is as great and often greater for performing artists, they merely transmit, perform, interpret, what has been "created" by the "real" artists, who alone possess that mysterious quality called *genius*.[1]

The performing arts require ability, talent, hard work, but genius? No. The contradiction goes all the way back to Plato, who devalues the mere performance and interpretation of the rhapsode in the *Ion*, yet elsewhere also devalues writing as against the human voice. Writing is death, King Thammuz said to the God Thoth who offered it as a gift in the *Phaedrus*. This text is one of Derrida's earliest and most famous deconstructions ("*La pharmacie*"). Writing is a *pharmakon* (poison/potion), an external remedy, a mere technique that will kill Memory, whereas the voice is the living word, the soul in the body, the breath of life. The letter killeth the spirit. The whole tradition of Western metaphysics that Derrida has been deconstructing in complex detail for 20 years has survived on that contradiction (since it is written).

We thus have two double inversions:

(1) Writing is death, an ambiguous poison/remedy from outside that kills memory, compared to the living word; yet both the contemporary arts by descendants (the wogs) of the great classical authors and the arts of the living word and body (the performers) have traditionally been devalued in relation to the canon (wogs vs. classics) and to composing or writing (performance vs. creation); the first because *living* moderns cannot belong to a classical canon (and are wogs in addition—the same addendum applying to women but more so, for reasons we shall see); the second because performers die, and not only performers but interpretation, which limits the original and so kills infinitude, but also dies, inevitably replaced.

(2) The oral word is live, yet the body and living word of the performing arts are not creative; creation also needs hard work and "brilliance," but these are devalued compared to genius, which comes over and above.

The work/genius opposition goes back at least to Longinus, in what is basically a nature/culture opposition (*On the Sublime*, Ch. 2). The privilege is on genius (nature), with work (culture) as both a curb and a spur.

Genius is the tutelary god or demon that makes the artist. The poet may have his Muse (pre-Hellenic *montya*, from Indo-European *mon-*, *men-*, *mn-*, to remember), daughter of Zeus (supreme power), and Mnemosyne (Memory), but she merely presides or inspires, that is, jogs, or, as Beauty, she is both his inspiration and his aim. This notion goes back to an oral tradition, since writing is supposed to kill Memory, but later poets steeped in the classics never seemed to notice the contradiction and went on invoking the Muse, possibly as a Dead Letter, and in fact representing the bisexual nature of creativity.

The really mysterious creative force, however, is genius: direct contact with the gods. Plato called it divine madness, Longinus called it ecstasy, the eighteenth century Genius, the Romantics Imagination but also Genius. And whatever the name, it belongs to men.

Gender, genre, genius, genesis: all come from the same Indo-European root *gen*: to beget/to be born. Only man begets, woman bears and travails: genius vs. work.

Burgess turns this into a backhanded compliment: "I believe that artistic creativity is a male surrogate for biological creativity, and that if women do so well in literature it may be that literature is, as Virginia Woolf said, closer to gossip than to art."

Is bearing then not a biological activity? The metaphors of literary paternity are very curious indeed. On the one hand, "the text's author is a father, a progenitor, an aesthetic patriarch whose pen is an instrument of generative power like his penis" (Gilbert and Gubar 7).

On the other, genius belongs to men in a strangely passive role. He is possessed. He is pregnant. The metaphor for literary works as begotten children and their production as childbirth is older than the pen/penis begetting metaphor. As Elaine Showalter ("Feminist Criticism" 188) reminds us (quoting Gilbert and Gubar, Nina Auerbach, Tillotson, Ellmann), the eighteenth and nineteenth centuries are full of gestation metaphors, and Joyce echoes them. In fact, they go back to Plato, for whom the speeches of Phaedrus and Lysias are their sons (never, of course, their daughters). Indeed, any speech (*logos*) was a son.

But a quaint, motherless son. For what gets occulted in all this is the woman, just as the real producer, the worker or small farmer, gets occulted by the rise of capitalism.[2]

In the *Republic* it is Diotima, the only woman allowed into the dialogues (but in absentia) who has given Socrates the apparently extraordinary revelation that the purpose of love is procreation *in beauty*. For what purpose? For immortality (206e, 207a). And she rapidly moves on (in the account of Socrates) to those who have fecundity of *soul* (men, 209a), who will look for the beautiful object (a boy) and educate him, and at whose contact they will give birth to that with which they have long been pregnant (209c).

Why does Plato put this nonsense into a woman's mouth? Precisely because she is a woman and knows about "real" childbirth, the literal half of the metaphor, which gives such a solid, physical basis to her figurative sliding, that is, to the meaning Plato wants. The fecund male, though procreating through "contact" with Beauty (boy or Muse) is already long pregnant, quite independently of this contact. He has been touched with divine madness, with genius. The Muse (or boy), contrary to some feminist comments, is never a mother in this, but a memory-jogger or an "ideal." In concrete practice she is merely a titillating handmaid, a step on the Platonic ladder, at most a gorgeous midwife.

Thus in the earliest texts that echo down and influenced the European literary tradition, even to modern times (e.g., Pound), men have simply appropriated childbirth as a painless metaphor, a *bearing* over, a mater phor artistic creation. A Muse may or may not preside, but genius begets *and* travails. The woman in this does neither. Indeed, when women did start writing, the ancient metaphor was all too easily reversed: her books were produced *instead of* children, as surrogates, in the absence of the all-essential male.

For men have always had it both ways: the begetting *and* the travail (the travail which as "work" belongs to culture, but which as bearing and "labor" belongs to nature); the genius *and* the work (the genius, which is itself both passive possession and authoritative production), the penis *and* the womb. Man has in fact appropriated, to represent his relation to Truth or God, both aspects of woman's role in relation to man: the being made fecund and the travail. This in addition to begetting. It is his *supplément*: he, as God, begets a work upon himself; he, as poet, is made fecund and labors. But on a safe, metaphoric level.

How perfectly logical then, in this long tradition, that women should have no role at all in artistic creativity. The double connotation of "womb" as both birth and death has been split, men appropriating the birth process and leaving its death connotations to the woman. Just as writing is death, the outside pharmakon. Obviously then, woman cannot be included in that "tonic" aspect of "secular" culture to which the central male tradition now and again turns when exhausted. All she can be is beautiful, and hence not understand beauty.[3]

Can women, then, traditionally, never be in that "masculine" role of creativity, have they ever been supposed to have that privileged, direct contact with the gods that goes by the name of genius?

The only institutional example seems to be the ancient prophetesses, who might be supposed to be directly inspired from the gods in their oracles. Yet they were easily legended by Herodotus as twittering birds, and they uttered their "sibylline" oracles uncomprehendingly in the name of the male gods (or at most the powerful Hera, or the martial Athene, whose priestess grew a beard whenever disaster threatened). They merely transmitted blindly, they were the (hidden) spokespersonae for the gods, and rulers consulted Apollo or Zeus, not his priestess.

Women cannot have direct access to Truth, or to the divine madness of the poet, and *do* something rational with it: *her* divine madness is from the devil, she is a witch, or its modern equivalent, a hysteric (Cixous and Clément).[4]

If as in this rare case of the sibyl she *has* access to the "fecundation," she is automatically deprived of the understanding necessary for the "travail." The Church's present resistance to women priests is no different, whatever the specious (canonic) arguments given, such as lack of biblical authority. The true reason is the same time-honored, self-assigned prerogative: the divine and metaphoric power of producing one thing out of another thing through the word is deeply felt as a male power. The priest, who with the Holy Spirit produces Christ the Body (the Logos) parallels the poet, who with his genius begets and labors to produce not only metaphors (Aristotle: a sign a genius) but motherless sons. Interestingly, the resistance to woman priests corresponds exactly to the varying versions of transubstantiation from full metaphor (the bread *is* the Body) to a mere symbol: the Catholic Church says no, never; the Anglican is in agonized compromise; the Lutheran and other Protestant churches have mostly accepted.

It is thus almost normal, if any such contorted logic can be considered "normal," that beneath and despite an apparent general acceptance and praise of women in literature and the arts, there should still lie in men's unconscious, and therefore in that of society, the deep phallocratic fear of women as memory, as birth, as death, of writing as the death of memory, and hence as birth and death, leading to the total occultation of women from the writing process and the resulting but equally deep conviction that women cannot be "great" artists of "genius" or even serious "creators" with a possible posterity. As men can. As a few exceptional women have been, but they were influenced by men and they are dead, their posterity has been accommodated, it is not a new and threatening future posterity. Moreover, women writers can only write disguised autobiography, i.e., "life," but consigned to death because (a) not male life and (b) not "creative."[5]

And yet, in artistic creation, by anyone whatever and given the necessary initial conditions, life and death are shared by all, and the begetting is also the travail and vice versa.

To Be an Experimental Writer

I am aware that in this return to my main topic, the sudden juxtaposition of "experimental" writing with "genius" may seem to be equating the two. In fact, I do not even like the word "genius," and have been using it only to point up a deep-lying contradiction. I agree with Frye that the "Romantic provincialism" that looks everywhere for genius and great personality is old-fashioned, but "still around" (*Anatomy of Criticism* 62). Clearly there can be trivial as well as truly innovative experiment just as there can be trivial as well as important writing in wholly familiar forms. I shall not here define Greatness, or the Sublime, or Imagination, or Literature. But I should perhaps try to define "experiment."

I have so far put the word in quotes, because it seems to mean so many different things. What is "experimental" art, or an "experimental" novel? Is it a genre?

People often talk as if it were, although most experiment either widens the concept of a particular genre or explodes the notion of genre altogether. A writer, or a group of writers, is put into that category, as if it were equivalent to Science Fiction, Fantasy, Romance, Realism.

For Zola, the father of a certain kind of realism, "the experimental novel" meant a novel that (whatever its other qualities) had been carefully researched and backed by "experience" (of slaughterhouses, mines, peasant life, etc.), or what we now call documentary. The narrative voice had to be objective, impartial, "scientific." In other words, a new kind, or school, of realistic novel, called Naturalist, almost a new genre.

For Hardy, according to Penny Boumelha's interesting readings, it meant, on the contrary, experiment away from Naturalism, the "search for a form" revolving round the problem of the female characters, provoking "an uncertainty of genre and tone which unsettles the fictional modes in a disturbing and often provocative manner" (30). This enables Boumelha implicitly to claim Hardy as a postmodern and at times to do an elegant deconstruction job on the play of ambiguities. But the "experiments" in question turn out to be chiefly Hardy's odd but by no means novel, and to some, merely clumsy, manipulation of points of view (34, i.e., *back* from the new "objective" voice); or else his "experimental" blends of "prose romance, dramatic form, and psychological or social theory . . . an exercise in mock-heroic, replete with parodic allusions to the convention of courtly love . . . a direct descent of the ballad tradition . . . a modified pastoral" (42, 48)—in other words a mixed use of traditional forms for different purposes.

But if all this is "experimental," then every writer who develops his art is experimental, and there is indeed a sense in which every writer is. But at least Boumelha is genuinely concerned with formal experiments as they are related to the themes of the "New Woman" fiction of the nineties. Today, on the other hand, the word "experimental" is often used by feminist critics to designate new feminist *themes*, or "imaging," that come out of feminine "experience" (as opposed to "experience" of mines and slaughterhouses), whether or not these create new modes or structures.

Conversely, in the Formalist and then the Structuralist periods, the underlying opposition was often felt to be Realism *versus* Experiment, that is, a complete reversal, with the privilege of seriousness on the "experimental" side, since the presuppositions of Realism and in fact of Representation were being thoroughly requestioned. It is often forgotten for instance that the *nouveau roman*, when it burst out in the fifties, first acquired the label *nouveau réalisme*, and was linked to phenomenology, just as earlier literary "revolutions" since Wordsworth had been made in the name of a greater realism. It is only later that the nouveau roman came to be seen as, and further developed into, a much more complex poetics, linked to "postmodernism" and deriving indirectly from Nietzsche and Heidegger, challenging all our assumptions about language and truth.

So "experiment," though part of the tradition/innovation opposition, was caught up in that of realism/formalism—which itself had meant so

many different things from Hegel onward: for Hegel (and for the Marx-
ists after him), "formalist" meant superficial (Preface to *Phenomenology
of Mind*), but for the Russian Formalists (much condemned by the Soviet
regime) it meant rigorous attention to literary structures and conventions,
in other words, poetics. Thus "experiment" is often regarded as "merely"
formal, tinkering with technique (conceived quite logically as something
external in just the way Plato considered writing to be external), tinkering with the signifier irrespective of the signified, the "content," the
"truth," "the real," and other such idealist concepts, the implication
being that the real exists independently of our systems or ways of looking
at it, and even, in the case of "mere" form, that such tinkering is not
accompanied by any valid "content" at all, let alone "value." Baudelaire
was complaining of this already in 1861 in his essay on Gautier.[6]

Years ago (1956), Nathalie Sarraute reversed the realism/formalism opposition and said that the true realists were those who look so hard at
reality that they see it in a new way and so have to work equally hard to
invent new forms to capture that new reality, whereas the formalists were
the diluters, who come along afterwards and take these now more familiar forms, pouring into them the familiarized reality anyone can see. Sarraute's reversal in a way goes back to Hegel (formalism as superficial),
for it calls the imitators formalists and the innovators realists. But such a
reversal, although expressed in terms of an older dispensation (forms to
capture a preexisting reality) is basically sound, for it insists on the link
between innovation and a completely different way of looking, which is
after all another way of defining genius, for example in science. Today
one would push it much further and say, not that new ways of looking
necessitate new forms but that experiment with new forms produces new
ways of looking, produces, in fact, the very story (or "reality" or "truth")
that it is supposed to re-produce, or, to put it in deconstructive terms,
repeats an absent story (see Hillis Miller, Brooks's "Freud's Masterplot,"
Chase, Culler's "Fabula and Sjuzhet").

Both aspects of the opposition, whichever way one takes it, are as necessary to the continuity of art as they are to that of life. Both occur in all
art forms across the spectrum of genres and subgenres, both can be practiced and achieved by men and women of all origins. And the prejudice
against the unfamiliar affects all who experiment.

To Be an Experimental Woman Writer

Nevertheless, women writers, not safely dead, who at any one living
moment are trying to "look in new ways" or "reread," and therefore re-
write, their world, are rarely treated on the same level of seriousness as

their male counterparts. They can get published, they can get good reviews. But they will be more easily forgotten between books and mysteriously absent from general situation surveys or critical books about contemporary literature, even about contemporary "experimental" novels. They will not ultimately be taken up by the more attentive critics. Even "the great Virginia herself," who had the best possible position and environment in the Bloomsbury Group to be so taken up, who was called a "genius" by her husband and friends, not only became ill with agony over the reception of every book by the then predominantly male literary scene, but was not fully and widely appreciated until well after her death, and she is the "best" case, the token case. Similarly Nathalie Sarraute, another token case, was nearly sixty years old when she won recognition, at the time of the nouveau roman and thanks to the label, although her writing was and remains quite distinct from that of its main male representatives.

It does seem, in other words, not only more difficult for a woman *experimental* writer to be accepted than for a woman writer (which corresponds to the male situation of experimental writer vs. writer), but also peculiarly more difficult for a *woman* experimental writer to be accepted than for a *male* experimental writer. She may, if young, get caught up in a "movement," like Djuna Barnes, like H.D., like Laura Riding, as someone's mistress, and then be forgotten, or if old, she may be "admitted" into a group, under a label, but never be quite as seriously considered as the men in that group.

Perhaps one of the safest ways of dismissing a woman experimental writer is to stick a label on her, if possible that of a male group that is getting or (better still) used to get all the attention. Fluttering around a canon. The implication is clear: a woman writer must either use traditional forms or, if she dare experiment, she must be imitating an already old model. Indeed, the only two advantages of "movements" are (1) for the writers, to promote themselves (hence they are usually men), and (2) for the critics, to serve as useful boxes to put authors into. But women are rarely considered seriously as part of a movement when it is "in vogue"; and they are damned with the label when it no longer is, when they can safely be considered as minor elements of it.

It may well be that women artists do not like new "movements" and still shrink from declaring all over the place how revolutionary they are. Political women, and hence feminists, have had this courage. But, as well as "muted" women (Ardener), many artists, male or female (rightly or wrongly), evade the overtly political, and it seems to me that the combination of woman + artist + experimental means so much hard work and heartbreak and isolation that there must be little time or energy for crying out loud.

And here we come back to the canon, in the form of another ancient opposition within the idea of belonging: traditionally, men belong to groups, to society (the matrix, the canon). Women belong to men. And insofar as women, emancipating themselves, also behave in the same way, they are said to imitate men (and so to belong to them again). All emancipation apparently has to pass that way, just as it then apparently has to pass through a "separatist" stage to find its strength and identity. But every individual needs a mixture of withdrawal and belonging. And it seems to me that the woman artist needs more withdrawal and less belonging. She needs to withdraw, either from the man she is with who may be consciously or unconsciously punishing her for, or otherwise stifling her creativity, or from society (ditto). She will try less hard to belong, because she needs it less deeply. Thus she will tend to belong neither to a man nor to society. At best she will belong to what Ardener calls the "wild" zone, as described by Elaine Showalter in "Feminist Criticism in the Wilderness."

Showalter gives Ardener's diagram of the "muted" and the "dominant" group as one circle over another, the "muted" circle shifted slightly to the right (whereas in Victorian society the "woman's sphere" was conceived as separate and smaller).

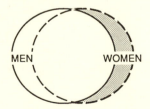

Showalter points out that spatially and experientially each group has a crescent-shaped zone inaccessible to the other, but that "metaphysically, or in terms of consciousness," the "wild" zone

> has no corresponding male space since all male consciousness is within the circle of the dominant structure and thus accessible to or structured by language. In this sense, the "wild" is always imaginary: from the male point of view, it may simply be the projection of the unconscious. In terms of cultural anthropology, women know what the male crescent is like, even if they have never seen it, because it becomes the subject of legend (like the wilderness). But men do not know what is in the wild. (200)

If this is so, there are not only very few truly experimental writers of the "wild" zone (to my knowledge only Hélène Cixous succeeds here, but my knowledge may be limited), but in theory they must also know, and accept, that they cannot enter the canon (unless of course, men were to open their minds and abolish the notion of canon). Except, perhaps, a female canon.

But then, the very notion of a female canon (the new geography) is a contradiction in terms. Feminists have not quite faced that problem, it seems to me, but I cannot deal with this huge issue here, beyond noting the danger: not only can the new boldness of feminist themes seem in itself sufficient renewal (the "wild" zone perhaps turned into a new chunk of reality to be sold), it can also help to create the stamp, the label "woman writer." As I have suggested, one *safe* way not to recognize innovative women is to shove them under a label, and one such is "woman writer." Women may feel that the dismissive aspect comes from men, but I am not so sure of this. Naturally it must be comforting to be backed and pushed and hailed by a sisterhood (a female canon), but that sisterhood is, with some notable exceptions, generally so busy on feminist "themes" and on discovering or reinterpreting women authors of the past (rather as the Deconstructionist Yale School rarely paid attention to the deconstructing "postmodern" literature all around), that it has no time to notice or to make an effort to understand, let alone to back, an unfamiliar (experimental) woman writer who does not necessarily write on, or only on, such themes, but whose discourse is, in Elaine Showalter's phrase "a double-voiced discourse, containing a 'dominant' and a 'muted' story," what Gilbert and Gubar in *The Madwoman in the Attic* call a "palimpsest." If the "wild" zone writer is inaccessible to most male readers, she is at least appreciated by feminists. The "double-voiced" writer (unless he is a man) antagonizes both, she is in the sea between two continents.

The best way, in my view, for any writer—but especially for a woman writer—is to slip through all the labels, including that of "woman writer." The price, however, is to belong nowhere. And this is, on the whole, what happens to experimental writers of all sexes and origins, but more particularly to women experimental writers, for the reasons analyzed above. On the one hand, they will not get the encouragement, or the serious criticism that a male experimental writer will get, which can help them develop. On the other hand, an indifferent experimental male writer will get more attention, qua experimenter, than any woman experimental writer—good, bad, or indifferent.

In his book *On Deconstruction*, Jonathan Culler has a chapter called "Reading as a Woman," where he quotes Shoshana Felman: "Is 'speaking as a woman' determined by some biological condition or by a strategic, theoretical position, by anatomy or by culture?" And he applies this to reading, quoting Heilbrunn and Showalter ("The Unmanning") and others, to discuss the divided structure of woman's reading: women can read, and have read, as men, and have learned to identify with a masculine experience presented as the human one. Today, women face this problem, and "try to bring a new experience of reading for both men and women, a reading that questions the literary and political assumptions on which their reading has been based."

If this is so, it would seem that the androgyny that men have claimed for *all good* writers at the *creative* end has willy-nilly been acquired by women at the receiving end, but not by men, who rarely identify with women characters as women do with male ones. Whatever the case, it would surely be a good thing if more men learned to read as women (even the "wild" zone), so that the bisexual effort, which they have metaphorically appropriated at one end, should not remain so wholly on the women's side at the other. Both should read as both, just as both write as both. And one of the ways in which this delightful bisexualism should occur is in a more open and intelligent attitude to experiment of all kinds by women.

NOTES

1. It is thus not by chance that women were admitted into the performing arts, late but much earlier than in most others (though for that reason treated as *demi-mondaines*, belonging not to *the* world but to a half-world used by men). Nor is it by chance that even today one can still hear the opinion, unwittingly echoed from the thirties, from the same type of man, of the same generation as those who say there have been no women Mozarts, that Jews are brilliant performers and interpreters but not creators.

2. See Derrida's "La pharmacie de Platon" (91–95)—though this is only incidental to my argument—who reminds us that the father is "also: a *chief*, a *capital*, and a *possession* [un *bien*]. *Pater* in Greek means all that" (my translation, his italics). Rabaté takes this up with reference to Pound: "The questions of generation and usury appear from the start as inextricably confused, for interest is the 'offspring,' the 'son' of money" (191).

3. In *Mademoiselle de Maupin*, by Théophile Gautier, the beauty-seeking d'Albert writes to his friend that women understand no more of poetry than do cabbages or roses, which is natural since they are themselves poetry: the flute cannot understand the tune played on it (206). And Mademoiselle de Maupin herself (but disguised as a man) is astonished to find herself becoming aware of beauty in women. Women (she writes to *her* friend) are usually deprived of the feeling for beauty, because they possess beauty, and since self-knowledge

is the most difficult knowledge, they naturally understand nothing of it (301–02, my rendering). See also Pound to H.D.: "You are a poem though your poem's naught" (H.D., *End to Torment* 12).

4. Hawthorne to his publisher, praising a contemporary woman "domestic" writer, Fanny Fern, author of *Ruth Hall*: "The woman writes as if the devil was in her; and that is the only condition under which a woman ever writes anything worth reading. Generally women write as emasculated men . . ." (Ticknor 1913: 141–42). (Quoted by Voloshin in "A Historical Note on Women's Fiction" not on the devil image but to correct an impression of Hawthorne's volte face, given by Kolodny in "Some Notes on Defining 'A Feminist Literary Criticism' " after his earlier condemnation of "that damned mob of scribbling women.")

5. See Kolodny in the above essay (77) even on a successful feminist author, about reviewers and TV hosts insisting that Erica Jong reveal the "autobiographical underpinnings" of her novel (*Fear of Flying*) so that, "by attributing its narrative to autobiography, the inherently sexist view might be maintained that women's productions are attributable to something less than fully conscious artistic invention." A few pages later, however, Kolodny is in danger of being misunderstood as doing this herself by insisting on feminine experience: "To cavalierly label Kate Chopin's Edna as immoral, or Joan Didion's Maria as mad . . . is to ignore the possibility that the *worlds they inhabit may in fact be real, or true*, and for them the only worlds available" (italics added). Feminists cannot have it both ways, or at least Kolodny should define "underpinnings."

6. "Among the innumerable prejudices of which France is so proud is the common notion, naturally found heading the precepts of vulgar criticism, namely that a work which is *too well* written *must* be lacking in feeling" (266, my translation, his italics).

WORKS CITED

Ardener, Edwin. "Belief and the Problem of Women." *Perceiving Women*. Ed. Shirley Ardener. New York: Malaby, 1977.

Auerbach, Nina. Review of *The Madwoman in the Attic* by Sandra M. Gilbert and Susan Gubar. *Victorian Studies* 23 (1980): 506.

Baudelaire, Charles. *L'art romantique*. 1868. Ed. Ernest Raynaud. Paris: Garnier, 1921.

Bloom, Harold. *The Anxiety of Influence*. New York: Oxford UP, 1973.

———. *Kabbalah and Criticism*. New York: Oxford UP, 1975.

———. *A Map of Misreading*. New York: Oxford UP, 1975.

Boumelha, Penny. *Thomas Hardy and Women: Sexual Ideology and Form*. Totowa: NJ: Barnes, 1982.

Brooks, Peter. "Freud's Masterplot: Questions of Narrative." *Yale French Studies* 55 (1977): 280–300.

Brooks, Peter. "Repetition, Repression, and Return: *Great Expectations* and the Study of Plot." *New Literary History* 11 (1980): 503–26.

Brown, Norman O. *Love's Body*. New York: Random/Vintage, 1966.

Burgess, Anthony. "Grunts from a Sexist Pig." *The Observer*, June 21, 1981, 37.

Chase, Cynthia. "The Deconstruction of Elephants: Double-Reading *Daniel Deronda*." PMLA 93 (1979): 215–27.

Cixous, Hélène, and Catherine Clément. *La jeune née*. Paris: Union Générale d'Editions, 1975.

Culler, Jonathan. "Fabula and Sjuzhet in the Analysis of Narrative: Some American Discussions." *Poetics Today* 1 (1980): 27–37.

———. *On Deconstruction*. London: Routledge, 1983.

Derrida, Jacques. "La pharmacie de Platon." *Tel quel* 32 & 33 (1968); *La dissémination*. Paris: Seuil, 1972. 91–95.

Doolittle, Hilda (H.D.). *End to Torment: A Memoir of Ezra Pound*. Ed. Norman Holmes Pearson and Michael King. New York: New Directions, 1979.

Dronke, Peter. *Women Writers of the Middle Ages: A Critical Study of Texts from Perpetua to Marguerite Porete*. New York: Cambridge UP, 1983.

Ellmann, Richard. *James Joyce: A Biography*. Rev. ed. New York: Oxford UP, 1982.

Felman, Shoshana. "Women and Madness: The Critical Phallacy." *Diacritics* 5 (1975): 2–10.

Frye, Northrop. *Anatomy of Criticism*. New York: Atheneum, 1957.

———. *The Secular Scripture*. Cambridge, MA: Harvard UP, 1976.

Gautier, Théophile. *Mademoiselle de Maupin*. 1835. Ed. Geneviève van den Bogaert. Paris: Garnier, 1966.

Gilbert, Sandra M. "What Do Feminist Critics Want? A Postcard from the Volcano." *ADE Bulletin* 66 (1980): 16–24.

Gilbert, Sandra M., and Susan Gubar. *The Madwoman in the Attic: The Woman Writer and the Nineteenth-Century Literary Imagination*. New Haven: Yale UP, 1979.

Gubar, Susan. " 'The Blank Page' and the Issues of Female Creativity." *Critical Inquiry* 8 (1981): 243–63.

Hegel, G. W. *The Phenomenology of Mind*. Trans. J. B. Baillie. New York: Harper, 1967.

Heilbrunn, Carolyn. "Millett's *Sexual Politics*: A Year Later." *Aphra* 2 (1971): 38–47.

Kermode, Frank. *The Genesis of Secrecy*. Cambridge, MA: Harvard UP, 1979.

Kolodny, Annette. "The Feminist as Literary Critic." *Critical Inquiry* 2 (1976): 821–32.

———. "Some Notes on Defining 'A Feminist Literary Criticism.' " *Critical Inquiry* 2 (1975): 75–92.

Kuhn, Thomas S. *The Structure of Scientific Revolutions*. Chicago: U of Chicago P, 1962.

Miller, J. Hillis. "Ariadne's Thread: Repetition and the Narrative Line." *Critical Inquiry* 3 (1976): 57–77.

Miller, Nancy K. "Emphasis Added: Plots and Plausibilities in Women's Fiction." *PMLA* 96 (1981): 36–48.

Millett, Kate. *Sexual Politics*. Garden City, NY: Doubleday, 1970.

Rabaté, Jean-Michel. *Language, Sexuality and Ideology in Ezra Pound's Cantos*. London: Macmillan, 1986.

Sarraute, Nathalie. *L'ère du soupçon: Essais sur le roman*. Paris: Gallimard, 1956. Trans. *The Age of Suspicion: Essays on the Novel*. Trans. Maria Jolas. London: Calder, 1963.

Showalter, Elaine. "Feminist Criticism in the Wilderness." *Critical Inquiry* 8 (1981): 179–205.

———. "The Unmanning of the Mayor of Casterbridge." *Critical Approaches to the Fiction of Thomas Hardy*. Ed. Dale Kramer. London: Macmillan, 1979. 99–115.

———. "Women Writers and the Double Standard." *Women in Sexist Society*. Ed. V. Gornick and B. K. Moran. New York: Basic, 1971, 323–43.

Tillotson, Kathleen. *Novels of the Eighteen-Forties*. Oxford: Clarenden, 1961.

Voloshin, Beverly. "A Historical Note on Women's Fiction: A Reply to Annette Kolodny." *Critical Inquiry* 2 (1976): 817–20.

Woolf, Virginia. *A Room of One's Own*. 1929. New York: Harcourt, 1957.

Male Signature, Female Aesthetic:
The Gender Politics of
Experimental Writing

—

Marianne DeKoven

MANIFESTOES for avant-garde (experimental, postmodern, antirealist, metafictional, surfictional, innovative) and feminine (*féminine*, feminist, female, women's) stylistic practice often sound remarkably alike without knowing that they do or taking cognizance of one another in any way.[1] A consideration of the politics of that mutual failure of recognition, my primary concern in this essay, shapes itself for me as a consideration of a few atypical successes: recognitions, all formulated by women, of the affinity of the two traditions. Julia Kristeva in fact actually conflates them. She *equates* with revolutionary avant-garde literary practice the eruption into masculine writing of the feminine pre-Oedipal, presymbolic (she also calls it "semiotic") mode of discourse, which is the language of *jouissance*, of union with the mother's body:

> For at least a century, the literary avant-garde (from Mallarmé and Lautréamont to Joyce and Artaud) has been introducing ruptures, blank spaces, and holes into language . . . in a culture where the speaking subjects are conceived of as masters of their speech, they have what is called a "phallic" position. The fragmentation of language in a text calls into question the very posture of this mastery. The writing that we have been discussing confronts this phallic position either to traverse it or to deny it. (165)

In other words, écriture féminine *is* the male avant-garde (of course, in French poststructuralist dogma, the gender of authorial signature is immaterial). Hélène Cixous, who notes "a few rare exceptions" to the rule that "there has not yet been any writing that inscribes femininity," cites Jean Genet as one of those exceptions: "Thus, under the name of Jean Genet, what is inscribed in the movement of a text which divides itself, breaks itself into bits, regroups itself, is an abundant, maternal, pederastic femininity" ("Sorties" 98). "Under the name of" is intended to signal the irrelevance of Genet's male signature.

In "For the Etruscans: Sexual Difference and Artistic Production—The Debate Over a Female Aesthetic," Rachel Blau DuPlessis and the Members of Workshop 9 address directly the question of the affiliation of the postmodernist/avant-garde tradition with the female aesthetic: "Any list of the characteristics of postmodernism would at the same time be a list of the traits of women's writing" (151). DuPlessis and Workshop 9 also say that *"women's writing is, if ambiguously . . . nonetheless profoundly revolutionary (as are, in their confusing ways, modernism and post-modernism, also written from positions of marginality to the dominant culture)"* (152). But do these traditions inhabit identical, or at least contiguous, positions of marginality? And if so, why is it only women who think so? Do the affinities in stylistic practice between a predominantly male (and often misogynist) avant-garde and écriture féminine (the female aesthetic) mask a wide divergence in cultural positioning, or are there other reasons for the failure (refusal) of the two to embrace?

Kristeva and Cixous elide the gendered signature, ostensibly in the interest of theoretical sophistication, but in political effect endorsing the privilege of the male signature, of the historical twentieth-century European male avant-garde. "For the Etruscans" approaches the dangerous intersection of feminine (female) and avant-garde (postmodern, experimental) literary practice from an entirely different direction. Where Kristeva and Cixous are concerned with inscribing the feminine in (written) culture, DuPlessis and Workshop 9 are concerned with writing by women (the female signature). They locate an affinity between the female aesthetic and modernist or postmodern stylistic practice entirely in the spirit of appropriating experimental style for women's writing:

> In women's writing, as in modernist, there is an encyclopedic impulse, in which the writer invents a new and total culture, symbolized by and announced in a long work, like the modern long poem. And women are beginning to produce just such works, often in the encyclopedic form of essay, compendia, polemic, collage (*Woman and Nature, Silences, Gyn/Ecology*). I imagine Hélène Cixous fits here, too, and her dissertation was even on Joyce! Perfect. (150–51)

In this utopian feminist literary vision, the woman writer is free to choose from among the best of what the culture has to offer, discarding the mysogynist, female-deleting tendencies within particular literary movements, notably modernism, postmodernism, the avant-garde (a number of American feminist theorists self-consciously take the same approach to psychoanalysis, semiotics, marxism, and poststructuralism). Generally, however, and most markedly in America, the anthologized, syllabized, canonized postmodernists, surfictionists, magic realists, anti-realists, metafictionists, and fabulators, virtually all of whom are male, as are the well-known critics who write about (anthologize, syllabize, and canonize) them, do not seem to need to rejoice in their similarity to Stein, Woolf, H.D., Barnes, Nin, Sontag, Wittig, Duras, Sarraute. Or Cixous. Similarly, the male heroes of Marxism, psychoanalysis, semiotics, and poststructuralism do not seem to feel the need of invoking the authority of female thinkers to legitimize their work. These are extremely well known and oft-repeated facts, which we should not use, in a spirit of bitterness, to make of "theory" or avant-garde stylistic practice a city of dead-end streets, but rather, though too simple in themselves to dictate an entire feminist poetics or politics, powerful facts of which we should not lose sight.

I do not mean to imply that the work of women writers and feminist critics can have no impact on some reified capitalist-patriarchal History "out there"; rather, it seems to me that so far, particularly in the spheres of avant-garde literature and critical theory (as opposed, for example, to film, American and Victorian studies, French), we have had very little discernible impact. But we can hope, as Teresa De Lauretis puts it in *Alice Doesn't*, that having interrogated, confronted, and submitted to Humpty Dumpty's precarious "mastery" of language, we have "move[d] on to the next square, where the echo eventually will reach us of Humpty Dumpty's great fall" (3).

De Lauretis's liberating, gleeful representation of phallogocentric discourse as a doomed and ludicrous Humpty Dumpty is at least in part, in its optimism, a product of the substantive historical link between avant-garde and feminist practice in experimental film. In her essay "Feminism, Film and the *Avant-garde*," Laura Mulvey begins by seeming to take the same position as the authors of "For the Etruscans": "feminists have recently come to see that the arguments developed by the modernist *avant-garde* are relevant to their own struggle to develop a radical aesthetic" (178). In other words, feminist filmmakers and film critics have discovered that avant-garde practice can be adapted to their purposes. That position begs the question of a historical link between the two movements.

Mulvey continues in the same vein when she says that the "questions posed by the *avant-garde*, consciously confronting traditional practice . . . arise similarly for women" (178–79), again avoiding theorizing a historical relationship between the two. But, as if her own statement raised precisely that question in her mind, she ends the paragraph by saying that "feminist film practice has come to be interested in—*almost* to have an objective alliance with—the radical *avant-garde*" (179, italics added). That very revealing "almost" speaks of Mulvey's wise reluctance to subordinate feminist film to a male-dominated avant-garde.

Toward the end of the essay, however, in discussing a 1978 meeting between the Berkeley feminist journal of film theory, *Camera Obscura*, and the London Film-makers' Co-op, Mulvey, her warm recollection of that weekend overcoming the wise reluctance of the "almost," formulates an enviable position:

> I was . . . struck by the historic conjuncture between feminist film theory, the *Camera Obscura* presentation, and the Co-op, home of *avant-gardist* film practice—a meeting, one felt, that could not until recently have taken place. It seemed to be a concrete indication, or mutual recognition, of a growing two-way traffic. (188)

Mulvey's formulation of her London experience gives us a model of the ideal relationship between the avant-garde (experimental, etc.) and feminine (women's, feminist, etc.) traditions: a "two-way traffic," an equal marriage. If this ideal can be realized, at least sporadically, among filmmakers and film critics, why is it so elusive among writers and literary critics?

To begin to answer that question, we must develop more fully the implications of avant-garde patriarchalism. The work of Sandra Gilbert and Susan Gubar has focused in part on the extreme misogyny of male modernism, arguing that the entire movement is an attempt to rescue for firm masculinity a literature made limp by Victorian-Edwardian feminization ("Tradition" 203). Susan Rubin Suleiman makes a similar argument:

> to what extent are the "high-cultural" productions of the avant-gardes of our century in a relation of complicity rather than in a relation of rupture vis-a-vis dominant ideologies? From the Surrealists to the *Tel Quel* group and to some of the so-called "postmodernists" in American writing, twentieth-century avant-gardes have proclaimed, and in a sense lived on (or off), their adversary, subversive relation to the dominant culture. But insofar as the dominant culture has been not only bourgeois but also patriarchal, the productions of the avant-garde appear anything but subversive. ("Pornography" 128–29)

In an unpublished essay on the history of her attempt to unify feminist and avant-garde literary practice in America, the poet Kathleen Fraser gives a painful account of her successive alienation first from the male-dominated avant-garde (her moment of revelation came when the prolific, accomplished, and important New York School poet Barbara Guest, along with all but one other woman avant-garde poet, were excluded from a "definitive" experimental anthology) and then from feminist literary circles hostile to avant-garde practice, committed rather to a belief in the transparency of language and its ability to represent adequately, through relatively conventional literary forms, the specificity of women's experience. Fraser's ultimate solution was to found, along with a group of feminist-experimentalist friends (including Rachel Blau DuPlessis), the journal of experimental writing by women called *HOW(ever)*. Excellent and interesting as that journal is, it avoids the question its own exclusively female authors frequently raise by citing, in their working notes, even when their closest discernible affinity is to Gertrude Stein, male avant-garde or modernist writers as primary influences. It is not enough for a female/feminine/feminist avant-garde, or écriture féminine, simply to repudiate the dominant male avant-garde: turning our backs on our father's house is a futile gesture if all we are wearing on them is the garment he has designed for us.

The Anglo-American literary feminist hostility or indifference to the avant-garde may not be merely a repudiation of a male supremacist tradition. Feminist writers and critics are also frequently suspicious precisely of the (putative) cultural marginality of the avant-garde: afraid that claiming other outsiders as allies or *semblables* will make absolutely impossible a position already quite shaky. As a class, women are so distant from hegemony, from the center(s) of power, that we should shun rather than seek allegiance with those who define themselves as the site of such distance.[2]

Even when feminists claim for women or for the feminine a privileged, transgressive marginality in relation to hegemonic culture, it seems necessary also to claim sole occupancy of that margin, exclusive rights to the territory of the Other: women must *be* difference. The oft-attacked essentialism of that position does not concern me here. It is a position dictated by the necessity of political fact. If women do not claim exclusive rights to the margin, to Otherness, then we will yet again be entirely silenced: the battle between conservative, hegemonic center and transgressive margin will yet again establish itself, over the silenced body of woman, as a battle between men. In fact, that is precisely what has happened in literature departments of the American academy, in the "battle" between what we might for convenience call the exponents of literature, or New Criticism, and the exponents of textuality, or *la nouvelle critique*. In that battle, the textualists, assuming through what Alice Jardine calls "gynesis" the privileged position of cultural margin, appropriate the subversive cultural feminine, *but not women*, as their weapon against the literarians, hovering over what is to us the birth of our new language, snatching it from our body, slapping on it their own patronymic, setting off with it down the road into the sunset on the heroic quest for theory.

Mary Jacobus identifies "textual harassment" as "the specular appropriation of woman, or even her elimination altogether." We might adapt

Jacobus's brilliant formulation to a triangle not of two male theorists, who use the annihilation of woman to enable their own confrontation, as in Jacobus's paradigm, but of male theorist and antitheorist ("textualist" and "literarian")—male (literary) center and margin: "This triangle characteristically invokes its third (female) term only in the interests of the original rivalry and works finally to get rid of the woman, leaving theorist and theorist face to face" ("Is There A Woman" 119).

Jacobus sees clearly the danger for women involved in complicity with any such triangulation. It is probably that vision of danger which prompts her to reject with little explanation an alliance of écriture féminine with the avant-garde: "Women's access to discourse involves submission to phallocentricity, to the masculine and the Symbolic: refusal, on the other hand, risks re-inscribing the feminine as a *yet more marginal* madness or nonsense" ("The Difference of View" 12, italics added). While this argument is ostensibly the one I cited earlier—that alliance with the avant-garde would place us so far from the center that we somehow would no longer even be within the orbit of a center/margin dualism—Jacobus proceeds in "The Difference of View" to describe the literary practice of écriture féminine in a way that makes it indistinguishable from experimental writing: "women's writing . . . rejects mastery and dominance. . . . The transgression of literary boundaries—moments when structures are shaken, when language refuses to lie down meekly, or the marginal is brought into sudden focus, or intelligibility itself refused . . . a refusal of mastery, an opting for openness and possibility, which can in itself make women's writing a challenge to the literary structures it must necessarily inhabit" (161). I can only conclude that her argument really points to the fear informing "Is There A Woman In This Text?": alliance with the avant-garde would not simply make us "yet more marginal," it would annihilate us altogether, making us the silenced woman out of whose mouth the male avant-garde speaks.

Therefore, like "For the Etruscans" but in a very different spirit, Jacobus suggests that we must appropriate avant-garde/experimental style, call it écriture féminine or the female aesthetic, connect it *simultaneously* to an exclusively feminine Other of discourse and to texts written under a female signature, and suppress again the question of a possible theoretical-historical convergence of the female and avant-garde traditions. Further, we should suppress altogether our knowledge of the existence of the avant-garde tradition and hypothesize écriture féminine as if it were an entirely new literary practice. If we allow écriture féminine a history, that history begins with Stein, H.D., Woolf: many analyses of those foremothers, as well as of contemporary women writers, simply relabel their work écriture féminine, as if there were no male writers who used the same stylistic practices.

The invisibility of the avant-garde tradition to most exponents of écriture féminine/female aesthetic/women's writing is superseded only by the monumental male exclusivity of the avant-garde, particularly in American postmodernism. I say "superseded" rather than "equaled" because the avant-garde is the repressed of écriture féminine, cropping up sporadically in a context of belittlement, repudiation, or flaws/holes/gaps in the critical argument. To the male avant-garde, however, écriture féminine, women's writing as a category, and, in the vast majority of cases, women writers altogether, simply do not exist. An obvious, straightforward question follows: why is experimental writing, a demonstrably antipatriarchal literary practice (DeKoven 3–27), so excessively dominated by men at a time when women writers are doing extremely well in traditional, culturally hegemonic literary forms? Why is it men who disrupt the hierarchical Sentence, in Barthes's formulation—who write écriture féminine—while women write some version of the nineteenth-century realist novel?[3]

Part of the answer is that many women *are* writing experimentally but receiving little or no recognition for it; women writers who are successful and recognized write in traditional, conservative forms. Experimental writing by women, explicitly linking the feminine subversive cultural/literary Other, the maternal repressed of discourse, with the female gendered signature, is, I would argue, simply too subversive to be supported or recognized by hegemonic institutions such as the academy or mainstream publishing.

The abyss dividing écriture féminine from the avant-garde, with which it should be at least loosely allied, is both creature and measure of the failure of subversive/transgressive literary and literary-critical attacks on hegemonic culture in the twentieth century. The question we should be asking is not how experimental writing by women, even though it looks like and describes itself similarly to experimental writing by men, is *really* profoundly different. Only the continued inefficacy of both will be served by such an emphasis. Feminist analysis of experimental stylistics, rather than pretending either that the avant-garde tradition does not exist or that it is the same thing as écriture féminine, should acknowledge the antipatriarchal potential of form in historical, male-signed avant-garde writing, but at the same time acknowledge the self-canceling countermove of that writing toward male supremacism and misogyny. We cannot claim allegiance naively, in particular, with contemporary American postmodernism, allegiance that postmodernism (with a few exceptions) would not even notice let alone bother to repudiate.

Our efforts to establish a "two-way traffic" between écriture féminine and male-dominated avant-garde, difficult but not therefore impossible, dangerous but not therefore undesirable, have as their tool the fact of commonality in experimental style. To translate that commonality into cultural-political reality is not at all to suppress the gendered signature, in what Nancy Miller calls a "postgendered poetics" (282). As Miller describes it, the "weave of indifferentiation," in eliding "gendered subjectivity" (272), appropriates women's writing to an ostensibly genderless but actually male discourse, annihilating woman just as surely as the theorists' triangulation described by Mary Jacobus. Since we (feminist critics, women experimental writers) are the ones who are in danger of being silenced, it behooves us to articulate our language clearly: to establish ourselves as an "ambiguously nonhegemonic group" *in relation to male avant-garde hegemony*, simultaneously within it and subversive of it. We (here, now) emerge in part out of the twentieth-century avant-garde, in part out of the Anglo-American feminist emphasis on writing by women. We can link those traditions consciously, making of them a new point of departure. We can write, and write about, if not a new language, then at least a new politics of language, aware of the complexities of our historical positioning, beginning here.

However, in our vigilance against the female-obliterating tendencies of the "weave of indifferentiation" in all discourse, in the margin as well as the center, we should not forget that success in bridging the abyss between écriture féminine and avant-garde—even partial, limited success—could only make more likely of realization, in a history that, so far in this century, has defeated it, the purpose of experimental style, whether in writing signed by woman or by man: to assist in changing culture by charting alternatives to hegemonic structures of consciousness.

NOTES

1. A series of disclaimers: rather than making what I consider a futile attempt to define either of these two major traditions, I assume a loose cluster of overlappingly characterized attributes for the predominant stylistic practices of each. Also, I will use "experimental," "avant-garde," "postmodernist" and, in a certain context, "modernist," as well as "feminine," "female," and "feminist" more or less interchangeably to designate those loosely overlapping or congruent subtraditions. I am not interested here in the crucial separations among them. For characteristic proclamations of both traditions, derived from various places and times, see Cixous, Irigaray, Woolf, Barthes, Federman, and Tzara.
2. Though DuPlessis and Workshop 9, and others, most notably Elaine Showalter, consider women "ambiguously nonhegemonic" because many women are

affiliated with the ruling class and otherwise partly occupy the cultural center, I would argue that the politics of antifeminist backlash, the feminization of poverty, the defeat of ERA, the antiabortion movement, etc., should make clear to us that the "ambiguity" of our nonhegemonic status does not materially alter patriarchy's essential subordination of women.

3. Margaret Homans argues "that women writers who appear confident in their positions as enfranchised speakers of the dominant discourse"—in other words, women writers who write some version of the nineteenth-century realist novel—

> share, though it is evidenced in more indirect ways, a sense of alienation from language that women writers who also have reasons of race or nationality for such a response explicitly distinguish as an alienation arising from gender. My aim in making this argument is to suggest that there is a specifically gender-based alienation from language that is characterized by the special ambiguity of women's simultaneous participation in and exclusion from a hegemonic group. . . . (205)

While it is an incontrovertible fact that the majority of the most successful, visible women writers employ conventional or traditional forms, it is also the case that their use of those forms is much less straightforward and unproblematic than it appears: as Homans demonstrates, the feminine repressed of discourse will out.

WORKS CITED

Barthes, Roland. *The Pleasure of the Text*. Trans. Richard Miller. New York: Farrar, 1975.

Cixous, Hélène. "The Laugh of the Medusa." Trans. Keith Cohen and Paula Cohen. *Signs* 1 (1976): 875–93.

———. "Sorties." Trans. Ann Liddle. Marks and de Courtivron 90–98.

DeKoven, Marianne. *A Different Language: Gertrude Stein's Experimental Writing*. Madison: U of Wisconsin P, 1983.

DuPlessis, Rachel Blau, and Members of Workshop 9. "For the Etruscans: Sexual Difference and Artistic Production—The Debate Over a Female Aesthetic." *The Future of Difference*. Ed. Hester Eisenstein and Alice A. Jardine. Boston: Hall, 1980. 128–56.

Federman, Raymond. *Surfiction*. 1975. Chicago: Swallow, 1981.

Fraser, Kathleen. "The Tradition of Marginality." The Poetry Project, St. Mark's Church. New York: June 6, 1985.

Gilbert, Sandra. "Costumes of the Mind: Transvestism as Metaphor in Modern Literature." *Critical Inquiry* 7 (1980): 391–418.

———. "Soldier's Heart: Literary Men, Literary Women, and the Great War." *Signs* 8 (1983): 422–50.

Gilbert, Sandra, and Susan Gubar. "Tradition and the Female Talent." Miller, *Poetics of Gender* 183–207.

Homans, Margaret. " 'Her Very Own Howl': The Ambiguities of Representation in Recent Women's Fiction." *Signs* 9 (1983): 186–205.

Irigaray, Luce. "This Sex Which is Not One." Trans. Claudia Reeder. Marks and de Courtivron 99–106.

Jacobus, Mary. "The Difference of View." *Women Writing and Writing About Women*. Ed. Mary Jacobus. London: Croom, 1979. 10–21.

———. "Is There A Woman In This Text?" *New Literary History* 14 (1982): 117–41.

Jardine, Alice A. *Gynesis: Configurations of Woman and Modernity*. Ithaca: Cornell UP, 1985.

Kristeva, Julia. "Oscillation Between Power and Denial." Trans. Marilyn A. August. Marks and de Courtivron 165–67.

Lauretis, Teresa de. *Alice Doesn't: Feminism, Semiotics, Cinema*. Bloomington: Indiana UP, 1984.

Marks, Elaine, and Isabelle de Courtivron, eds. *New French Feminisms: An Anthology*. Amherst: U of Massachusetts P, 1980.

Miller, Nancy K. "Arachnologies: The Woman, the Text, and the Critic." Miller, *Poetics of Gender* 270–95.

———, ed. *The Poetics of Gender*. New York: Columbia UP, 1986.

Mulvey, Laura. "Feminism, Film and the *Avant-Garde*." *Women Writing and Writing About Women*. Ed. Mary Jacobus. London: Croom, 1979. 177–95.

Showalter, Elaine. "Feminist Criticism in the Wilderness." *Critical Inquiry* 8 (1981): 179–205. Rpt. in *The New Feminist Criticism: Women, Literature, and Theory*. Ed. Elaine Showalter. New York: Pantheon, 1985. 243–70.

Suleiman, Susan Rubin. "Pornography, Transgression and the Avant-Garde: Bataille's *Story of the Eye*." Miller, *Poetics of Gender* 117–36.

———. "Reading Robbe-Grillet: Sadism and Text in *Projet pour une révolution à New York*." *Romanic Review* 68 (1977): 43–62.

Tzara, Tristan. "Dada Manifesto 1918." *Dada Painters and Poets*. Trans. Robert Motherwell. New York: Wittenborn, 1951.

Woolf, Virginia. *A Room of One's Own*. New York: Harcourt, 1929.

FIRST GENERATION: BEFORE 1930

Dorothy Richardson Versus the Novvle

GILLIAN E. HANSCOMBE

Pointed Roofs, the first volume of Dorothy Richardson's experimental novel *Pilgrimage*, was published in 1915. The writing of the succeeding twelve volumes occupied the remainder of Richardson's life, the last, *March Moonlight*, being posthumously published in 1967. She conceived *Pilgrimage* as one novel and each constituent volume as a chapter: "I told them, since they admitted they had read only one volume of mine, that each volume is a single chapter of one book & cannot therefore be treated in the manner they suggest" ("Data for Spanish Publisher").

The conception was certainly remarkable for its time. In 1915 Richardson was forty-two years old, unmarried, unknown, untrained for any particular profession and with an occupational background that seems meager when considered as a literary apprenticeship. She had spent some years as a teacher, ten years as a secretary in a Harley Street dental practice, and had embarked on some casual journalism and translation. To her advantage, however, were roughly 25 years of economic and emotional independence from her family, together with an open-minded interest in people, incidents, and places. Although *Pilgrimage* is often criticized by traditionalists for its seeming formlessness, its internal structure and its thematic cohesion present Richardson's experience, through her persona Miriam Henderson, as that of a representative woman of the period.

Fundamental to Richardson's experimentation is the conviction that women and men constitute polarities and that her own work is representative of the polarity of women. Some feminists would question the gender stereotyping implicit in this conviction; and yet Richardson's distrust of language, her dissatisfaction with a tradition that ignores women's experience, and her exasperation with male novelists and male critics make her work central to the development of a feminist literary consciousness. She is "experimental" when seen in mainstream terms. She is "pioneering" in the context of the struggle of women writers. The ironies and paradoxes uncovered in the course of examining her work arise from her basic problem of having to use a language and a tradition in which women are alien in order to produce a work in which a woman's consciousness is central. That literary critics and commentators are also trained in the mainstream tradition presents further obstacles to any accurate reading of her work.

Richardson's monodic stream-of-consciousness technique is familiar to us after more than half a century's reading of her celebrated fellow modernists, Joyce, Woolf, Proust, and others. She makes her own wry comments on being the first English prose writer to develop this technique in her Foreword to the 1938 Collected Edition of *Pilgrimage*. Yet Richardson was not only the first exponent in English; she was also unique in her exposition of a sole inner monologue. Nowhere in the long text of *Pilgrimage* is there a single paragraph extraneous to the perceiving consciousness of Miriam Henderson. Richardson saw herself, however, as a realist, setting out "to produce a feminine equivalent of the current masculine realism" and hinting that this project would be necessarily technically innovative (Foreword 1938). She loathed and repudiated May Sinclair's stream-of-consciousness tag, although its very aptness rapidly led to its widespread use in identifying the new techniques developed by the whole range of modernist writers of fiction.

Richardson commented often that a writer should write only about what she (or he) knows best; and since her own life was what she knew best, it was self-evident to her that it should provide her material and that the result would be entirely consistent with her realist aims. That she exploded the form of the English novel, recast its parameters, dissected and reassembled the syntax of its sentences, were to her all inadvertent side effects of the pursuit of her technique. The small but intense and passionate bubble of interest created by her technique among some literati seemed to her fundamentally aberrant. What she wanted, what she desired without ambivalence, was for the reader to see, feel, and think the experiences of Miriam Henderson without any comment or judgment passed upon them by the author. Richardson's pursuit of realism entailed a deliberate intention to remove the distinction between author and persona by removing the author entirely.

No ironic distance, therefore, between Richardson's voice and Miriam's is admitted. The total egocentricity of Miriam's viewpoint is sustained throughout *Pilgrimage*—in itself, no mean technical achievement. And it is this egocentricity with its corresponding absence of ironic detachment that focuses the hiatus between fiction and autobiography experienced by most readers of *Pilgrimage*. If the reader can participate without reservation in Miriam's consciousness, the conventional distinction between author and persona becomes irrelevant. Miriam's irritation with male novelists corresponds to Richardson's. They do not write about anything she—as a reader and as a woman—can recognize. It is this irritation with men's style, egoism, plot, moral stance, characterization, tradition, and language that feeds Richardson's own efforts as a writer.

In *The Tunnel*, the novelist Hypo Wilson urges Miriam to begin writing (as H. G. Wells in life had urged Richardson to do). Miriam's immediate reaction is to reject the novelist's awareness of the exercise of style, which she diagnoses to be a male characteristic:

> Rows and rows of "fine" books; nothing but men sitting in studies doing something cleverly, being very important, men of letters; and looking out for approbation. If writing meant that, it was not worth doing. . . . To write books, knowing all about style, would be to become like a man. Women who wrote books and learned these things would be absurd and would make men absurd. (130–31)

Wilson's criteria are practical: first, to have had the experience that provides the material and then to have freedom enough to devote the time. Miriam's reaction is defensive; to the degree to which authors knew what they were doing, they were contemptible, playing a "trick" on their readers. Their cleverness connotes control, together with the desire for approbation, which Miriam clearly delights in not giving. Her defense against her own ignorance, since she does not know "all about style," becomes inverted into pride that she is free from the hypocrisy of those who do. What makes this inversion possible is her contention that the contradistinction between those who know and those who do not corresponds to the difference in consciousness between men and women. Men always "know," but their knowledge makes them manipulative and therefore contemptible. Women hardly ever "know," so their reliance on instinctual life makes them more real, more alive, more authentic than men. Those women who do trouble to "know" are absurd; they are not really women, but imitation men.

Here we see Richardson's feminism as the motivating force behind her struggle to find the individual voice that characterizes any writer's sense of style. If she can identify all her distinctive differences as features particular to women, then she can avoid the crucial problems of the isolate. She is aware that her subjection to the overwhelming pressure of an alienating traditional culture cannot be lifted by a reliance on her individual ego alone; but if that ego can be made representative of a female alternative to the dominant culture, then she can become allied to half the human race, and her voice can assume a new role as the exponent of the female vision. This assertion allows her to resist conforming to a cultural model from which, by temperament and because of ignorance, she feels excluded.

But it is not just a sense of being excluded that troubles Richardson (and Miriam). The pyrotechnical display of "style" comes across as a manifestation of egoism:

> most writers have been so consciously and laboriously, literary, that in reading them . . . one is so fascinated by what they are doing, technically, by tracing exactly how they get their effects, that one is tempted to paraphrase Emerson's "What you are speaks so loudly that I cannot hear what you say" into . . . "you have really nothing to say, and are keeping back what, if anything, you want to say, in the interest of a cunning way of saying it." (to Henry Savage, August 26, 1948)

In *Dawn's Left Hand* Miriam reflects angrily on a conversation she has had with Hypo Wilson about novels:

> Hypo's emphasis suggested that the hideous, irritating word *novvle* represented the end aim of a writer's existence. . . . The torment of all novels is what is left out. The moment you are aware of it there is torment in them. Bang, bang, bang, on they go, these men's books, like an L.C.C. tram, yet unable to make you forget them, the authors, for a moment. (239)

The phonetic "novvle" here is contemptuous and yet teasing. Miriam is drawn to the form because of what she feels is "left out." She resents the measured regularity of novels—of pace and sequence—which is to her as blind and mindless as a tram, serving only to confront the reader with the personal quirks of the author; in other words, to promise to offer "life" and instead to offer the author.

As the argument proceeds, Wilson reinforces Miriam's suspicion that by "creative imagination" men mean the ability to invent and to fantasize. "Women," says Wilson, "ought to be good novelists. But they write best about their own experiences. Love-affairs and so forth. They lack creative imagination" (240). Wilson does not have the least notion what Miriam means. When she reads male egoism, he reads invention and a created universe. From his point of view, men do not write about themselves, but about "life." From her point of view, the opposite is the case.

In *Honeycomb*, Miriam expresses one of her many reactions against narrative, seeing it as not merely extraneous to the nature of the novel, but actually obstructive, due not only to servicing the cause of egoism, but also to the stance of moral authority implicit in the tone of the third-person narrator:

> People thought it silly, almost wrong to look at the end of a book. But if it spoilt a book, there was something wrong about the book. . . . It was a sort of trick, a sell. . . . Then you read books to find the author!

That was it. . . . I have just discovered that I don't read books for the story, but as a psychological study of the author. . . . In life everything was so scrappy and mixed up. In a book the author was there in every word . . . that was why the people who wrote moral stories were so awful. They were standing behind the pages preaching at you with smarmy voices. . . . An author must show himself. Anyhow, he can't help showing himself. A moral writer only sees the mote in his brother's eye. And you see him seeing it. (384–85)

For Richardson, neither plot nor moral tone should interpose between the author's representation of reality and the reader's apprehension of it. What is implicit is a rejection of the authoritative stance of the writer, either as the craftsman manipulating events, or as the seer who imbues his manipulations with moral value judgments.

Not only are plot and narrative unacceptable, so too is characterization. In *Revolving Lights*, during a visit to the Wilsons, Miriam overhears a conversation between Wilson and a novelist called Miss Prout, about proofs for her new book:

She had put people in. . . . People he knew of. They joked about it. Horrible. . . . As she gazed, revolted and fascinated, at the bundle of pages. . . . Cold clever way of making people look seen-through and foolish; to be laughed at, while the authors remained admired, special people, independent, leading easy airy sunlit lives, supposed, by readers . . . to be creators. (342)

Here again Miriam's anger is elicited by the thought of the elevated status of authors. To treat people they know as material to be manipulated seems to her a violation of their integrity, a violation they are helpless to prevent. As Miriam is a fictionalized persona of Richardson herself, and as *Pilgrimage* is peopled entirely by Miriam's friends and acquaintances, it is clear that Richardson does not object to the accurate presentation in books of living people, so long as they appear, as they do in "life," as the percepts of the observer without any attempt to give the objective facts and details that only a "godlike" creator can know. People can be perceived, but not known. What Richardson finds objectionable is the manipulation of other people's lives and qualities in order to serve the creative ends and designs of the author. For Miriam, such an activity is a kind of cannibalism.

Richardson's is not only an anti-Romantic stance; it derives from a fundamental puritanism, one characteristic of which is a dogged fidelity to literal-mindedness, a condition of mind that makes ironic detachment almost impossible. It is this puritan resistance to fantasy that provides the bulwark for Miriam's feminism against the relativism inherent in all humanist art, especially literature, which of its nature not only encourages, but endorses, imaginative engagement with the total range of experiences, however "untrue" some of them may be. Not only does Richardson reject humanist art because it is untrue to "life"; she is also unmoved by its moral stance, which seems to her to be mere preaching. When the reader can understand, if not endorse, her puritan logic, Richardson's revulsion against the portrayal of character in fiction becomes comprehensible. She was aware of the correlation between characterization and moral tone and sought to exorcise utterly a moral tone from her work, so much so, that she was shocked by the suggestion that she may not have succeeded: "You make one comment that leaves me gasping. . . . You find that Miriam has a 'high moral tone'! I feel like shrieking where is it?" (to E.B.C. Jones, May 12, 1921).

Behind Richardson's rejection of the conventions of the novel is no superficial boredom with familiar techniques, but a fundamental antipathy to any of the organizing principles of rationalism and to the traditional culture embodying them. In her view, the rationalist impulse itself and all its hierarchical classifications had to be resisted in science, in religion, in politics, and most particularly in literature. Writing with the confidence of old age to the poet Henry Savage, Richardson illuminates her hostility to tradition by revealing a hostility to all influences that could be called formative, both on the microcosmic-personal level and on the macrocosmic-cultural level. In the first instance, she denies the value to a writer of the psychological influence of other people. She sees influences necessarily resulting in the distortion and constriction of literary creativity: "Joyce remained hampered by the handcuffs firmly fixed by the Jesuits. V. Woolf, via Leslie, was a diluted male, wobbly and irrelevant" (to Henry Savage, January 5, 1950).

At the macrocosmic-cultural level, she denies any relevance to the novel of literary theory, which is

> eternally debated between the Priests who believe "the novel" to be a matter of sacred unities forever unchangeable and the Prophets who do not so believe and produce a series of formulae; labels that slip about and never quite fit. Humanists they nearly all are, both Priests and Prophets, their world a drama going forward in a resounding box, empty of all but "people." (to Henry Savage, December 19, 1946)

The weight given here to "humanists" we must take to be derogatory since humanism, contradistinguished from mysticism, is mechanistic, devoted to categorizing and systematizing experience. Late in her life, she denied any influence on her literary work from outside her own consciousness: "I was never consciously aware of any specific influence beyond the overwhelming longing to pay tribute to the marvel of existence, anywhere, of anything; to sing a song of thanksgiving to the spirit of the universe" (to Shiv Kumar, August 10, 1952).

Clearly, the social flux of the years between the 1870s and 1914 contained many of the seeds of antitraditionalism that Richardson and her contemporaries inherited. Richardson's rejection of tradition, however, was feminist rather than literary to the extent that she felt unable as a woman to identify herself within it and unable to endorse its values. Her referential framework was primarily psychological rather than ideational; unlike other novelists, she diagnoses the conventions she perceives not as cultural but as "masculine." The corresponding feminine vision, which she designates "life-as-experience," she finds lacking.

If the gestalt of narrative techniques must be rejected and transformed, so too must its unit, the discursive use of the English sentence, with its precision of tense and its ordered disposition of objects and events. The unbalanced predominance of the male modes of expression must be redressed at least in some measure. Richardson felt she had to shape a "woman's sentence," and if that attempt resulted in a restatement of the novel as a literary form, then that was accidental and unpremeditated. Her fidelity to the rhythms of her own life demanded an exactitude according to which even minutiae must be carefully selected and patiently realized; and if this meant a self-conscious manipulation of the English sentence in order to make it elastic enough to suggest the qualities of minutiae, then such a manipulation must be undertaken. It is remarkable that the force of this concern actually generated such a long novel and that the innovations were so radical.

Complaints about the language she inherits are woven through the fabric of *Pilgrimage*. They are so persistent that the reader is forced into a curious ambivalence toward the author. Since *Pilgrimage* could not exist without language, there is something aggressive in the stance of an author who so openly questions the capacity of her chosen medium to carry the burden of her vision. The problem is, of course, fictionalized to the extent that this lack of confidence is recorded as part of Miriam's developing consciousness, and the fact that the author is responsible for that record at least allows some degree of distance between author and persona. Nevertheless, because all other distancing conventions—narrative, chronology, characterization—are meticulously abandoned, that distance is small indeed. What Richardson seems to want to force from language is that it should yield reality as directly as does the perceiving consciousness itself. It is, even so, the drive to create an "antinovel," which can represent reality, that evokes from the reader an ambivalent response to Richardson, the autobiographical author, and to Miriam, the fictional persona. It follows that Miriam should dramatize that process.

But because the rejection of a calculated style entails doubt about the integrity of language itself, words become hostile rather than friendly. The highest insights seem to Miriam to be above and beyond language. Richardson writes to Henry Savage, "Language is a very partial medium of expression. Poetry indirectly more direct. Music still more so. . . . In the hierarchy of being, the mystics . . . the best of them, stand on a 'higher' or 'deeper' or further rung. Oh the helplessness surrounding the helpfulness and manifold uses of speech, the dangers within the delights of metaphor" (Gregory 11).

This distrust of the efficacy of language is one of the principal themes of *Deadlock*, the novel bridging *The Tunnel* and *Interim*, and *Revolving Lights*. The former open new horizons for Miriam, who, in the first three novels, was pursuing the life of a teacher. In *The Tunnel* and *Interim* we see her living in a boarding house and working as a dental secretary, in an attempt to shape for herself an independent existence—independent, that is, of many of the constraints imposed by society on unmarried women. In *Revolving Lights* Miriam begins seriously to try to behave in personal relationships, as well as in her social milieu and working life, as an independent individual. *Deadlock* forms a bridge between these two frontiers of the public and the personal; and the material of which the bridge is constituted is largely Miriam's ambivalence about the capacity of language to convey the development of her consciousness. Passages from *The Tunnel* refer back to *Honeycomb* where she recorded her first formulation of the problem with books, and forward to *Deadlock*, in which she begins to record her conviction that she must try to shape the language itself in a way that will allow the accommodation of her woman's view. Such passages can seem repetitious until readers accept both that the wider context is assumed to frame different nuances of emphasis and that the distortion of chronology entails an insistence on the recording of significant perceptions whenever they occur and recur in Miriam's consciousness.

And not only do we see the perceptions occurring and recurring; we see, at the same time, Miriam's efforts to interpret and rationalize them. In *Honeycomb*, she discovered for herself that what really happened when the reader read a book was that he or she "met" the author, so that the conventions of the novel were obtrusions between the two personalities. Nevertheless, it follows that she needs to explain to herself why she should see this phenomenon when others do not. In consequence, she focuses sharply on the problem of language itself. The vision of reality, which seems to Miriam both truthful and feminine, must still depend for its exposition upon the language of men, since "the very words expressing it have been made by men" (*Revolving Lights* 281).

First, Miriam surmises, men categorize facets of life and then the categorizations are built into language, so that women, for whom life is open-ended and unstructured, have to manipulate a medium whose nature is foreign to their experience. For Miriam, and by extension women, experience is reality, reality is life, life is experience. The communication of reality is thus theoretically impossible. If direct communication is impossible, so is direct contact with other people; they can only be conjoined by a mutual activity. Otherwise they become "separate disturbing personalities" (*Deadlock* 16). Richardson embodies this belief technically by introducing her characters as percepts of Miriam's consciousness, only informing the reader of distinctive personal details such as name, status, appearance, as it were accidentally. In *Deadlock*, for example, the central character involved with Miriam is Michael Shatov, an intellectual humanist, a short, shabby man with a beard. But the reader does not learn his first name until the middle of the novel (87); all his distinguishing traits emerge intermittently and randomly because they assume the status of reality only as they impinge on Miriam's awareness of him. The concentrated attention required of the reader to follow the text without becoming confused, prevents the imaginative involvement with the prose, which readers of novels are conditioned to expect. Readers of *Pilgrimage* are obliged to assess every one of its characters in Miriam's terms. Shatov's importance, for instance, consists solely in his importance to Miriam. As the text continues, we are given a more intimately observed account of Shatov and only then the information that Miriam has been about to give him an English lesson. This dislocation of the realistic sequence of relationship is a technical device designed to give psychological veracity to Miriam's perceptions of Shatov.

Clearly Miriam knows his name and nationality long before we do. Richardson was aware of this source of irritation to her readers, but her commitment to her method precluded her from modifying it. She commented about the opening of *The Tunnel*:

I attempted a compressed retrospect and achieved almost nothing at all. This business of compression, so essential, if the unity and continuity of consciousness is to be conveyed, gets of course more troublesome as the material accumulates, though at the same time it is made a little easier by Miriam's increasing articulateness. It is this last factor, I think, that must be the "explanation" of your impression of a general increase in lucidity in the books. Just as her early vagueness accounts for the sacrifice of direct information. It has been "horrible" to refrain from objective description of her family ... and surroundings. The people and surroundings that come later are clearer because you see her seeing them, for the first time, and share her impressions such as they are. (to E.B.C. Jones, May 12, 1921)

Thus, in 1921 Richardson felt the people and situations in the recent volumes of *Pilgrimage* to be clearer than they had been in the earlier volumes, precisely because Miriam's perceptions are sharper. The opposite is true, however, for the reader; simply because Miriam not only perceives more people and more things, but she does so more often and has more memories to obtrude upon her present. As a result, the texture of the volumes following *Deadlock* and *Revolving Lights* is thinner and less intense, which led Richardson to remark, again to E.B.C. Jones and this time about *Oberland*:

> I agree about "slightness"—and am fully aware. It is due partly to the need to condense that grows with each vol. and partly to M's becoming more out-turned really living, partic: for this year or so, much more on the surface than she did. ... Each episode could have filled a single volume in the old manner, but I should have been in my grave before M's fortnight was at an end and there are things calling ahead. (to E.B.C. Jones, November 1927)

In *Deadlock* Miriam's coming to terms with the novel is counterpointed against her coming to terms with people. Hypo Wilson encourages her to write; Michael Shatov challenges her to examine why she finds the novel unsympathetic. She explains that novels "only show one side of people, the outside; if they showed them alone, it was only to explain what they felt about other people" (128). It is always the author who confronts her, but not his meaning (131). The point crystallizes for her when she is correcting a lecture for a fellow boarder, during which exercise she discovers the injunction "avoid ornate alias" (133). It is the unconsciously noticed things that constitute reality and it is the remembering of them that gives shape to continuity. This is an important stage in Miriam's awareness, since it gives her access to a conceptualization of the past which need not be artificial. This in turn offers her a possible solution of her problems with language and with the novel, in the notion that the continuity of the individual consciousness has an inherent logic that rearranges perceptions into a comprehensible sequence. A language and a form of the novel which took that as a criterion would not be false to "life." Eventually Richardson realized that total fidelity to Miriam's consciousness was technically impossible to achieve and that a corresponding "slightness" of texture was inevitable.

For a writer primarily impelled to revolutionize the novel, such a real-ization may well have presented an insuperable obstacle to further effort. But that was never Richardson's central concern. What she pursued, without deviation and despite any literary anomalies her experimentation elicited, procured, or provoked, was the acting out in prose of female consciousness.

Her conviction of the essential femaleness of her perceptions she con-sistently ascribed to her work. John Cowper Powys, recollecting his meet-ing with her in 1929, remembered her saying, " 'Women plunge into life at first hand.' . . . She said that the important thing in her work was that she alone represented the feminine point of view . . ." (Gregory 99). For Richardson, the importance of the "feminine point of view" was not merely that it should negate the dominant masculine point of view, but that it should offer the alternative polarity without which a truthful ex-perience of reality would be impossible.

Unlike more orthodox critics, John Cowper Powys read Richardson in her own terms. His assessment is based upon Richardson's own philo-sophic foundation, which he wholeheartedly accepts—that is, the initial division between male and female consciousness. *Hamlet* and *Faust* he concedes to be superior in "intellectual interest" to *Pilgrimage*, but he dismisses the comparison on the grounds that the former are "essentially projections of the male quest for the essence of human experience." He dismisses other female writers, including Woolf, on the grounds that they have exploited their femininity to the limits of narcissism, together with harnessing the quality of "sheer mental power," in which men themselves excel. Not only do these women fail to use their feminine resources fully, but they also employ "the rationalistic methods of men." His argument proceeds from this premise and concludes that Richardson alone uses a unique material, the feminine vision, necessitating a different method and a different style from all previous fiction. By refusing Richardson's com-parability with all other novelists, Powys argues that an entirely new crit-ical stance is dictated by the unique literary nature of *Pilgrimage*. The critical problem from the more orthodox standpoint is to doubt whether any work of literature may justly be evaluated within its own terms of reference entirely; or, to consider the problem historically, whether any work of literature can claim absolute independence of precedent.

Richardson herself felt, however, that out of all the reviewers and com-mentators who had passed judgment on *Pilgrimage* by 1950, only one had perceived and understood the "realist" goals of her original impulse: Ford Madox Ford "saw what without-realising-its-effect-upon-the-devel-opment-of-the-novel (odious word) I was moved to do" (to Henry Sav-age, January 6, 1950). Ford considered Richardson the "most distinguished exponent" of modern English realism. The main characteristic of this style he defines as "an extreme, almost Flemish, minuteness of rendering of objects and situations perceived through the psychologies of the characters and not, as it were, motivated by the temperament of the writer" (Ford 773).

For liberal humanists, orthodox critics, and other traditional commentators, Richardson's lack of "literary" concern can occasion unfavorable comparisons with her fellow female experimentalists, Mansfield and Woolf. Unlike Richardson, Woolf enjoyed a literary background; Mansfield, like Richardson, did not. Yet Mansfield and Woolf each engaged positively with the tradition of English fiction, and this engagement, especially in Woolf's case, nourished originality and intelligence. Richardson, with her more radical and rebellious temperament, found it necessary to reject the novelistic conventions as she found them. This rejection was undoubtedly made easier by her lack of systematic acquaintance with the liberal humanist currents of thought that support the literature of the past; yet had she been given this background, either by academic training or by environment, she would almost certainly have rebelled against it.

Richardson's problem with the language of men diverges from the more orthodox, the more "artistic," dilemmas of Woolf and Joyce. Rachel Trickett points out the distinctiveness of this position: "Dorothy Richardson is an unusual case of an experimenter who was not primarily interested in time nor in formal structure for its own sake. By her own confession, her experiments had a single aim: to discover the best way of expressing one particular kind of sensibility—a woman's."

The posthumous and probably unfinished *March Moonlight* provides some insights into Richardson's resolution of her problem with these novelistic conventions. *March Moonlight* is the work of her old age, written in fitful starts, offering, at the distance of her 12 published novels, an account of the difficulty of beginning: "The first effort had aroused the almost vocal protests of the beloved shabby furnishings of this little room, as if they knew that her return to them from even a momentary absence will find her, and themselves, and the relationship between them, already a little changed" (617).

This passage shows clearly the positive side of her distrust of words. Her conviction of the power of language is so strong that it even threatens to disrupt the relationship she feels toward the inanimate objects around her. Language withdraws the attention from reality, removes the possibility of unconscious awareness. The retrospective importance of this fear and the conviction it demonstrates inform the whole of *Pilgrimage*. Later, Miriam explains that not only is her relationship with inanimate objects threatened, but also that her past life is metamorphosed: "While I write, everything vanishes, but what I contemplate. The whole of what is called 'the past' is with me, seen anew, vividly. No, Schiller, the past does not stand 'being still.' It moves, growing with one's growth" (*March Moonlight* 657).

Miriam is more sophisticated about herself than about either learning or literature. She is aware of the unstable nature of memory and of its unreliability when it comes to literal veracity. The reality of her personal past lies in its capacity for growth, its extratemporal enlightenment. Richardson provides here a subjective parallel to Eliot's theory of the cultural past, introduced formally in "Tradition and the Individual Talent" and developed poetically in *Four Quartets*. This was a discovery Richardson shared with all her fellow experimentalists—Eliot, Joyce, Woolf and, to a lesser extent, Mansfield—but with a significant difference. For Richardson, the object of writing is quite simply to demonstrate her female reality, to "materialise" it; she is not aware of any need to fashion what others call a work of art, since she dissociates herself from that literary-intellectual tradition, which for her represents only the male polarity: "Contemplation is adventure into discovery; reality. What is called 'creation' imaginative transformation, fantasy, invention, is only based upon reality. . . . If it were not, they would not recognize it. Fully to recognize, one must be alone. . . . As one can richly be, even with others, provided they have no claims" (*March Moonlight* 657).

Clearly the dissociation must not be merely cultural to be authentic; it must also be personal. Miriam's egocentricity is redeemed in her own eyes by two things: the complexities of reality, which make most things unknowable, and the generalizing power of the individual consciousness, which allows the self to be everywhere.

Women writers are necessarily experimental, since, as Richardson's work so carefully demonstrates, they work within conventions and traditions that most truly belong to others. Richardson's stature, however, reaches beyond the novelty of experimentation. It is because she is a woman that the radical examination of perception, and of the words available to frame it, is made possible. Her desire to present a female perceiving consciousness entails technical innovation; but what she discovers in the process is that by every word they utter, men and women mean different things. The relationship of men—even modern men—to language is different from that of women. For women the problem is not just one of "making it new," but one of making *the* new, of making creations that a Hypo Wilson would never recognize. It is not aggression, but insight, that leads Miriam to say "I wouldn't have a man's—*consciousness*, for anything" (*The Tunnel* 149).

WORKS CITED

Ford, Ford Madox. *The March of Literature: From Confucius to Modern Times.*
1938. London: Allen, 1947.
Gregory, Horace. *Dorothy Richardson: An Adventure in Self-Discovery.* New
York: Holt, 1967.
Powys, John Cowper. *Dorothy Richardson.* London: Joiner, 1931.
Richardson, Dorothy Miller. "Data for Spanish Publisher." Ed. Joseph Prescott.
London Magazine (June 1959): 14–19.
———. Foreword (1938). In *Pilgrimage.*
———. *Pilgrimage,* including *March Moonlight.* 4 vols. London: Dent, 1967.
New York: Knopf, 1967. (Includes *Pointed Roofs,* 1915; *Backwater,* 1916;
Honeycomb, 1917; *The Tunnel,* 1919; *Interim,* 1919; *Deadlock,* 1921; *Re-
volving Lights,* 1923; *The Trap,* 1925; *Oberland,* 1927; *Dawn's Left Hand,*
1931; *Clear Horizon,* 1935; *Dimple Hill,* 1938.)
———. Unpublished Autograph Letters: to E.B.C. Jones, May 12, 1921 and Nov.
1927 in the British Library; to Henry Savage, Dec. 19, 1946, Aug. 26, 1948,
Jan. 5, 1950, and Jan. 6, 1950 in the Beinecke Library, Yale University; to
Shiv Kumar, Aug. 10, 1952 in the Beinecke Library, Yale University.
Trickett, Rachel. "The Living Dead—v: Dorothy Richardson." *London Magazine* (June 1959): 20–25.

WOOLFENSTEIN

R ACHEL B LAU D U P LESSIS

> "What is form? What is character? What is a novel?"
> Virginia Woolf, *Letters* 3: 211, 1925.

> "What is an argument. What are forensics. What are masterpieces.
>   What are their hopes."
> Gertrude Stein, "Forensics," *How to Write*, 390, 1931.

B ETWEEN 1928 and 1931, Gertrude Stein wrote a brief essay called "Forensics," an oblique study of the role of gender asymmetry and power in the formation of discourse—the capacity to speak, the speaking, and what comes out. In 1928, Virginia Woolf wrote a book-length essay called *A Room of One's Own*, a major study of the role of gender, power, and oppression in the history of culture: unequal access to resources, intellectual harassment, recruitment and formation of artists, writing and sexual difference.

Stein wrote, "Forensics are a plan by which they will never pardon. They will call butter yellow. Which it is. He is. They will call birds attractive. Which they are. They are. They will also oblige girls to be women that is a round is a kind of hovering for instance" ("Forensics" 385). "Their" power to define, to "call," involves them in the enforcement of gender standards. Stein's essay shows her to be rather tempted by the mastery and power of this "forensic" discourse. But by the end she argues that the language practice of "she" occurs in opposition to "forensics"— the language of law courts, managers, judges. "They" have a language practice of argument, power, judgment, definition, of social replication, of a "taught paragraph" (386). In short, "Forensics is established" (394). Her critique of patriarchal values in writing and speaking illustrates and proposes another mode, called "the other" (393). The other "curves," gives pleasure, does not judge, is not backed by "union and organization" (393). And like Woolf in *Three Guineas*, Stein's arsonous proposal expresses rage at dominant modes. "What did she do with fire. She almost put fire to forensics. As useful. As usual. As vagrant. As appointed. As veiled. And as welcome" (394). "Books continue each other," said Woolf interestedly (*Room* 84). Did Stein know Woolf's feminist essay of 1928? Does "Forensics" continue *A Room of One's Own*?

To encircle and engender modernism, criticism can begin by making some monsters of the intertext, by being woolfensteins, digging up the bodies, sewing bodies into bodies, resituating women where they have been elided, erased: in the biography that precedes production, in the texts and their gender narratives, in the literary movements, in all areas of production, dissemination, evaluation. The authors are woolfensteins, too, making themselves up of dead and living bodies. And to make the monstrous intertext, all bodies of work would be intercut, depending upon critical desire and need (our historical situation) as well as on the (not neutral) tasks of historical reconstruction.

"Contemporary discussions of intertextuality can be distinguished from 'source' studies" because they treat the porous "multitude of ways a text has of not being self-contained, of being traversed by otherness" (Johnson 264).[1] Source studies involve a "linear" and "developmental" (as well as cumulative and progressive) notion of authorship and its authority, while the intertextual model makes a new cut into the material, "creating new dividing lines not *between* the two oeuvres but *within* each of them" (264).

One such intertext is the conjuncture of Woolf and Stein, both major cultural workers. Between them there is at least one documentable—and linear, one-way—conjuncture: Woolf read a little Stein; Woolf met Stein once (without pleasure). It could plausibly be argued that the Stein Woolf evidently read challenged her and became part of the multiplicity of originating influences on Woolf's *The Waves*. But more, our desire makes just as plausible that the Stein-Woolf conjuncture need not rest only, though interestingly, on an influence but on the existence of a "feminine" practice of otherness, which can be proposed through them. A practice stirring up difference and undermining closure. A practice that increases difference. The terms are from Cixous's "The Laugh of the Medusa." The complex coincidence of "feminine" writing by female cultural workers with an arguably feminist poetics has yet to be fully explored.

The "influence" of Stein on Woolf begins, for the normal fiction of criticism, in 1926, one year after Gertrude Stein delivered "Composition as Explanation" at both Oxford and Cambridge. An undergraduate who had attended the lecture wrote to Woolf about it; she responded blandly, pleasantly in June 1926 that "We had meant to suggest to [Stein] that she should write something of the kind for the Hogarth Press. . . . We have now written and asked her to let us see her paper. It sounds most interesting . . ." (*Letters* 6: 510). Gertrude Stein's *Composition as Explanation* was indeed published by the Hogarth Press in November 1926, and Woolf may then be said to have read this Stein.

But Woolf's reading was mediated through the ambivalence formed by an encounter one year earlier (1925) with an enormous manuscript and (that year) with Stein's presence.[2] The manuscript sat on the Woolf desk in August 1925 and, in a letter to Vita Sackville-West, it is called "the whole of Gertrude Stein" (*Letters* 3: 198). It is clearly *The Making of Americans*.[3] When faced with the manuscript, Woolf can do no more than "flutter [it] with the tips of my little fingers, but dont open. I think her dodge is to repeat the same word 100 times over in different connections, until at last you feel the force of it." That same manuscript figured in a letter a month later to Roger Fry: "We are lying crushed under an immense manuscript of Gertrude Stein's. I cannot brisk myself up to deal with it—whether her contortions are genuine and fruitful, or only such spasms as we might all go through in sheer impatience at having to deal with English prose" (*Letters* 3: 209). A suspicious, reluctant, and provoked Woolf, using words like "dodge" and "contortions," and "spasms." She resists the manuscript, yet appreciates, as if sidewards, the author's project. For there is no final negative in these remarks despite the daunting, taunted text. As she says to Fry, the manuscript is either "genuine" or it is at least provocative because provoked, "impatient" at what seems then to be a reasonable target: "English prose." As early and middle Woolf was challenged by Dorothy Richardson's *Pilgrimage* and its critique of narrative, one might equally attempt the notion that later Woolf (including *The Waves* and *Between the Acts*) was challenged by the formal designs, the repetitions, the grids, the critique of the center, the other otherness of the work of Gertrude Stein.

Woolf's subsequent remarks to Roger Fry show that vital and fruitful tension in her work between—baldly—the nineteenth and twentieth centuries. For Woolf sets down, in response to the literary and personal irritations of Stein, the most thoroughgoing impatience with that "movement" to which she and they, willy-nilly, both belonged, irritations that probably went a long way to animating her (arguably) most Steinian book and, at the same time, incited her to write it with a lush organicism, which helps to control the potential of the experimental mode for "irritating."

> Edith Sitwell says she's gigantic (meaning not the flesh but the spirit). For my own part I wish we could skip a generation—skip Edith and Gertrude and Tom and Joyce and Virginia and come out in the open again, when everything has been restarted, and runs full tilt, instead of trickling and teasing in this irritating way. (*Letters* 3: 209)[4]

"Composition as Explanation" Woolf read, then, in 1926. But the making of intertextual analysis (beyond influence study) need not turn on what Woolf read, but may incorporate other Stein upon which to ruminate. *Tender Buttons*, for instance, which scans "Objects," "Food," "Rooms," in a meditation, often sentence, but not statement based. Bright with tasty and spectacular signifieds, a signifying process is engaged to "suppose" varieties of statement made of just about any language manipulation that can be postulated: there are visual impressions abstractly "described," sound associations, translingual puns, writing from prior writing (nursery rhymes, for instance), slid phonemes, expanded or contracted words. Yet no tactic is patterned, nothing can be gotten used to, nothing "organically" recurs. Stein unmakes, by transgressive "change," dutiful assumptions about verbal artworks: generic associations, mimetic assumptions, lexical categories, and thematic recurrence. She rejects the creation of reading context. No surprise that "suppose" and "change" are two recurrent words. One means "project the possibility" or "assume to be true for the sake of argument" and thus all is position, relativity, a possibility as easily negated by as extended by "change," the dear companion of "suppose." Because *Tender Buttons* (tender butter, tend her butter, fresh buds, delicate buttons, tend her butt on, aider may day) is not self-consistent. This is different from *The Waves*.

But both renegotiate the question of difference. In a binary system, women are different from men; but to repeat this gesture or to reverse it offers no break with binary thinking. Stein and Woolf both attempt to make a matrix unrestricted to gender as ordinarily conceived, and thus the unmaking of gender binaries in both texts (in Stein by a decisive subplot of lesbian allusions when there is no plot; in Woolf by the enfolding of manifold characters into a male writer) is expressed as a high sense of desire and engorgement.

For *Tender Buttons* is "about" desires: plural desires, polymirthful desires. A desire for orality, therefore food; a desire for sexuality, therefore specific anatomical allusions and charms like "please butter all the beefsteak" (*Selected Writings* 496); a desire for sensuality and bliss, therefore pleasures of couture, of cooking, of expansiveness, of a presexual "chora"; a desire for visual pleasure, and therefore colors and shapes streaking through the text; a desire for writing, and therefore writing. And *The Waves* is "about" that leman of desire, sensation: the flickers of insight, the responsiveness to sight, to taste, to thought; the flashes of bliss and pain given as plot, as character, as the novel.

Stein offers precise (if participial) terms for the aesthetic goals she sought in her early writing: "a constant recurring and beginning," which is "a continuous present."[5] Second there is "beginning again and again." (Woolf: "her dodge is to repeat.") And finally there is "using everything" (*Selected Writings* 518). The portrait genre was a synthesis of these aims, compressing into "one small thing" her grammatical studies in tense ("continuous present"), in inclusive totalizing ("using everything"), and in rhythms of repetition ("beginning again"). A difficult dialectic between sameness and difference animates her work: "everything being alike it was simply different." One of the formal implications of this remark was Stein's use of "lists . . . and by lists [she says curiously] I mean a series" (*Selected Writings* 519).

The Waves may be described as portraits in narrative form, with a programmatic de-emphasis of change and development in character. "In my portraits I had tried to tell what each one is without telling stories and now . . . I tried to tell what happened without telling stories" (*Lectures* 121–22). This provocative "description of Woolf's novel" comes in fact from Stein's meditations on Stein's practice. *The Waves* is without story, without causality, suspending normal reaches of plot—courtship, sexuality, marriage, success, failure, death. Even Rhoda's choice to kill herself— its narrative presence and meaning, its causal connections—is incomparably less than Septimus Smith's suicide in *Mrs. Dalloway*. Indeed, in her desire to make portraits without telling stories, Woolf may be said to resist a different novel in each character: in Susan, Hardy; in Neville, Forster; in Bernard, some of herself; in Louis, Bennett; in Jinny, Mansfield.

The Waves is definingly organized by "beginning again"—the italicized portions that provide the incipit of each section make just one of the larger and more noticeable expressions of beginning again. Every speech by every character in turn is "beginning again," since it does not (with brief exceptions between Louis and Rhoda) occur in dialogue or in response. And like Stein, Woolf is led by this work to lists ("and by lists I mean a series") with a consequent tension between grid and sequence.

The Waves is a driven book, willed, compelled. Like Monet's studies of the cathedral or the haystack in changed light, the object of attention is diminished against the grid achieved by beginning again and again. The waves means to be the endless monotony of small varients. Woolf called *The Waves* an "experimental" work. She used that word in a context of high seriousness, about her impulse to write this work, in passages that also contrast the "serious, mystical poetical" with "innumerable little ideas and tiny stories which flash into my mind" (*Writer's Diary* 104). This is to be a text of otherness, other in relation to the generic frames of novel and story, other in relation to an idea of humanity or personality, other in regard to the humanism of such a book as *To the Lighthouse*. It was to be an almost inhuman work, almost, because it does retain its attachment to the mimesis, not of an action but of time.

Woolf's word "inhuman" along with her word "eyeless," also repeated in considerations of this text, are meant to suggest the abstract, patterned quality she sought, freed from conventions of narrative representation

(*Writer's Diary* 134). Like the "objects" and "food" in *Tender Buttons*, one might consider these characters "still lives," human material arranged in visual patterns and pulses. At one and the same time, she retains her attachment to characters (giving them highly colored names like Neville and Rhoda—even any name, like Susan) and intends no characters. Indeed, an early review baffled Woolf: "Odd, that they . . . should praise my characters when I meant to have none" (*Writer's Diary* 170). None? No distinctive characters? Critics have continued to find intricate, satisfying differentiae among the voices. Yet there are no characters in a novelistic sense—those to whom happen events typical of novels. There is no dialogue or conversation; the capacity to voice is interior and occurs in an automatic round. All the "objects" and "food" of *Tender Buttons* might be viewed like the characters of *The Waves*: as voicing their soliloquies of otherness, in the languages of "shoes" or "roast beef."

Like Stein's, Woolf's experiments led her to paradoxes of difference and sameness. *The Waves* creates a space in which the trappings of social division (class, gender, sexuality, ethnicity) are not relevant—to the text, even if formative for the characters. The brotherly and sisterly characters seem never to be divided by the text (this is one explanation for the sublime space from which they speak), despite separations and despite institutions like school, business, and family, which demand different kinds of social insertion by gender. Thus—is it a remake of *The Mill on the Floss*? Or even, the asocial utopia of the word? The characters, each speaking from a core of being, are as if beneath gender, or prior to it, in a state of desire, awe, boundless affiliation, and sensuality.

This aim—of writing an almost inhuman (meaning both abstract and asocial) book—can be traced from the beginning, in 1927, of Woolf's planning for *The Moths*, a provisional title: "the idea of some continuous stream, not solely of human thought, but of the ship, the night etc., all flowing together: intersected by the arrival of the bright moths" (*Writer's Diary* 107). The implacable confrontations with otherness about which Woolf speaks in this diary passage—ship, night, moths, and later "age of earth," "the death of humanity"—are all indications of an attempt to minimize or criticize the hegemony of the human. The criticism of the human and its orders and priorities is one version of a formal and critical complex that is proposed variously in Woolf's later work: formally to pluralize, and ideologically to decenter any hegemony; to make comic or pathetic any unitary perception, especially when such are further encumbered by desire for power; and to value the many-pointed perceptions, the checks and balances of an idiosyncratic, and, in her final book, a more-than-human community.

This note on *The Moths* offers much information about the tendencies and large projects, including the writer's attachments to character and to love plot, all of which will drop away. Even when she considers it seriously, Woolf never talks of love plot as telos but as frame for ineluctable motion: moths "keep on coming." Another pre-*Waves* plan proposes to tell the life of a woman in the time one flower falls. The highly readable organic cycle here doubly evoked—"life" and "flower"—will be Woolf's major tool in *The Waves* for naturalizing and normalizing the Steinian grid. How to reject story, yet maintain communicable shape or structure; how to make a critique of the expectations for action and resolution, which evoke complacent values while at the same time remaining relatively readable—these were Woolf's dilemmas. The organic lushness of the text allows an inhuman grid to come in sub rosa.

"A beginning again and again within a very small thing" is Stein's phrase for her recursive rhythm in which nothing goes far to anywhere, but starts repeatedly (*Selected Writings* 519). Beginnings elide with and incorporate middles: in both *Tender Buttons* and *The Making of Americans* statements are both always new and always relentless, either in the constant unsortable overload of interpretive frames or in movementless multiplicity. In Stein is a glut of "beginnings," especially in her muting of development and closure. Despite the strongly sexualized endings of the first two sections of *Tender Buttons*, Stein shows strongest disinterest in climax, closure, finality, clarification of thematic purpose. The sections of *Tender Buttons*, of "Composition as Explanation," fold over upon each other, much as Bernard's final soliloquy folds over upon the whole of *The Waves*.

Of course, if everything is perpetually beginning again and again, it is also finishing again and again, but once everything is finishing again and again, finishing is simply another version of beginning. The moral and ideological function of finishing is disregarded. This prying away of the (corrupting) vitality of closure may be a central reason for beginning again. Stein's tactic may serve some of the many subversive functions boldly graphed by Barthes: "an anti-theological activity, an activity that is truly revolutionary, since to refuse to fix meaning [at the end] is, in the end, to refuse God and his hypostases—reason, science, law" (*Image-Music-Text* 147). The notable and concerted antilogocentrism of this Stein has been clearly remarked.[6]

Woolf seems, in Steinian fashion, to experiment with "beginning again and again." In Woolf each monologue of each character begins again. Virtually every sentence begins again. But with a slight alteration, indicative of Woolf's modification of Stein's extremism: in Woolf a unit of several sentences may repeat in a psalm-like pattern. "I will walk by the river. I will pace this embankment. . . . I will pace this terrace . . ." (*The*

Waves 164). And in Woolf, structures of repetition, changing scale as they do not in Stein, form arcs across the terrain of writing: the description of the sun illuminating a still life of cups, chairs, pots will arc among the sections, each moment recalling, alluding to another in a weaving dependent upon remembering.

Woolf's desire for a Steinian repetition and allover grid of language, that is, Woolf's experiment with "beginning again," is indicated by the major shift in conception from *The Moths* to *The Waves*. The evidence is compelling that *The Moths* as narrative design was involved with closure and climax: "one must get the sense that this is the beginning; this the middle; that the climax—when she opens the window and the moth comes in" (*Writer's Diary* 140). That "beautiful single moth" so clearly climactic and symbolic is in increasing tension with monotonous otherness, totalizing and ineluctable (141). In her transition between the two conceptions, a turning point occurs when Woolf indicates a need for "some odd irrelevant noises," which disperse meaning into ground. Perhaps—and suddenly we are inside the text she wanted—"could one not get the waves to be heard all through?" (141). A pulse, a hum, that Kristeva locates in a realm of (renewed, postsymbolic) access to the "semiotic": the imagined realm of pre-Oedipal connection to, desire for, fulfillment with the maternal.[7] The "odd irrelevant noises" of this world of otherness make climax (can one now use this term?) occur everywhere, epiphany changes into bliss.

The loss of the moths, associated with dramatic climax, to the waves as a central image of intention indicates a distinctive change, in this book and, plausibly, in her two subsequent major novels, one consistent with Woolf's development, but one that may assimilate that Steinian experimentalism she had found so provoking. The waves serve as a notion of style: in which every sentence or unit is a wave, ineluctable ("one wave after another. No room") like the banal, undifferentiated language of *The Years* (*Writer's Diary* 156). The waves are a notion of structure—the dramatic soliloquies Woolf describes as "running, homogeneously in and out, in the rhythm of the waves" (156). The waves, different yet homogeneous, simply the same/simply different are an image of the antiauthoritarian and critical poetics that animate her later books, with their group protagonists, their political critique, their psychic boundlessness figuring in and as the next necessary step, of history. The waves are an allover perpetual pattern of "beginning again."

"Lists [said Stein] . . . and by lists I mean a series" (*Selected Writings* 519). "But if there are no stories, what end can there be, or what beginning?" Woolf asks, in the voice of Bernard (*The Waves* 267). Closure in *The Waves* is natural (death, the organic cycle of people's lives) and therefore assimilable. But the wave is "last," it is the final last. And that final wave makes out of sequence (series) a list or its lateral extension, a grid. The famous "fin in the waste of water," a frightening and mysterious vision that began the composition process of this work in 1926, an image Woolf (in my view) domesticates and of course commemorates in Bernard's voice, is a grid that contains one enveloped mark (*Writer's Diary* 165). Rosalind Krauss is one of the grid's most cunning theorists: "The absolute stasis of the grid, its lack of hierarchy, of center, of inflection, emphasizes not only its anti-referential character, but—more importantly—its hostility to narrative" (158). For the final wave that breaks (which is the life of each character, and which contains the life of each character, and which frames the life of each character) also washes (as death does, "O Death") over the organic seasonal cycle from youth to age, and shows the author's investment in the "eyeless" repetition of a process that is forever the same. *"The waves broke on the shore"* (*The Waves* 297). This is the sustaining contradiction of the book, that natural closures of several overlayered organic cycles—a person's life, the seasons, the progress of a day, and the endless anticlosural, grid-like movement of the ocean—confront each other throughout. So *The Waves* animates the Steinian paradox "by lists I mean a series."

Stein elides the formal tension between these terms, which Woolf takes as her ground. For a list—an item-by-item arrangement of persons (guest list) or things (shopping list) usually of a specific nature or category— need not necessarily be arranged in a particular order. Series, a group of events or objects related by order of occurrence, especially succession— with its suggestive synonyms sequence, chain, train, string, and set—provides teleological pleasures. Stein collapses the two as if lists could do the work of series, while Woolf made a strategic compromise with a very readable organic series (birth to death, sunrise to sunset, spring to winter) in order to allow the baffling, associative, and random quality of the list to billow in this work as never before; list here floods series, everything seems to be interrelated (which Woolf commented on in her diary). In Stein's terms, "everything is used."

A remark in *Tender Buttons* is often isolated as an instruction: "act so that there is no use in a centre" (*Selected Writings* 498). And the text makes a pluralized sensation of all kinds of language (bilingual puns, phonemic slides, sound or visual associations, rhythmic evocations of Mother Goose, echoes of feminine chitchat, harumphings of manly syntax, etc.) occur continually, disperse in small pressures, defer most sense almost forever. Something close to this language is Woolf's projected ideal in *The Waves*. Although stylistically she holds, almost without wavering, to the firmness of a thoroughly referential sentence (which often has an absolutist quality as each character makes certain relentless generalizations), she posits a more fragmentary and labile language: "some little language such as lovers use, broken words, inarticulate words, like the shuffling of feet on the pavement" (238) or "half-finished sentences and sights" (255). A language, centered, that speaks its yearning for dispersal is parallel to a structure, centered, that erases its high pole, and thus calls attention to the device of, the ideology of, the center.

Some character suspiciously authoritative, desirable, distant in life as later in death seems to act as the center, before we find that he is sidelined. Percival preserves the allusive possibilities of a central focus (e.g., for desire) while allowing Woolf to intensify her debate with centralizing narrative order. If Percival's fault in that quest plot from which his resonant name comes is, through the desire to hide his innocent naiveté, never to ask any obvious healing question, Woolf herself will not commit the same error. She asks of Percival, of heroism, of the quest plot, and inferentially of the novel: "why does all this need to be here? Can we act so that there is no use in a centre?" (*Selected Writings* 498).

"Percival" as a function makes statements about social, cultural, and narrative hegemony. All the characters "love" Percival, yet Woolf pointedly wonders whether the deep emotion drawn to that center can or should be called "conveniently . . . 'love of Percival' " [her inner quotation marks] or whether it should lose this "too small, too particular a name" and become that boundless diffuse love for which her bisexuality is biographically, and homosexuality is narratively, an avatar (126). By the enacted dissolution of that center, the book narrates what language, "plot," and "character" look like when "Percival" ends. ("But without Percival there is no solidity" [122].) Released by his death, although often recollecting their mourning, the characters are enabled to "use everything," for they are no longer obsessed by one thing. Each can become hero, quester; all elements and roles of narrative, which had been located, locked in one spot, now may reappear, holographically, in every spot. "No other form of fiction suggests itself except as a repetition [of what had already been done]" (*Writer's Diary* 150).

The rupture with the center and a centralizing figure of desire breaks the thrall of story, and allows for a plurality of statement and focus, which is the felt antithesis of conventional narrative. To make character the essence of character; to make action the essence of action; to debate and parry "story"—this is certainly a cluster of projects that is undertaken by *The Waves*.

It also parallels Steinian projects. Both the play and the portrait were genres to which Stein turned exactly to avoid "novels . . . which tell a story [which] are really then more of the same much more of the same"

(*Lectures* 184). For Stein, "In my portraits I had tried to tell what each one is without telling stories and now in my early plays I tried to tell what happened without telling stories . . ." (121–22). Woolf enacts that same debate not only in Bernard, the novelist, but in all the voices. Although the book begins in assurance: "Bernard says there is always a story. I [Neville] am a story. Louis is a story" (*The Waves* 37), many of the speakers offer a critical (antinarrative, experimentalist) poetics in the course of the work. "They want a plot, do they? They want a reason? It is not enough for them, this ordinary scene" (197) is just one of a number of critical remarks about "impos[ing an] arbitrary design" (188). Because "there is always more to be understood" (202), because meaning is dispersed without a center, located generic gestures are valueless; so, too, are end and beginning. "Life is not susceptible perhaps to the treatment we give it when we try to tell it" (267). If one does not "tell" as development and change, motive and reason, social function of the speakers and the pressures upon them, how does one "tell"?

One is not supposed to be convinced by the sociality and connection of the personages in *The Waves* to much outside the statement and expansion of their root images, deep images that never change decidedly, and indeed seem to be at the core of the first words each speaks. Say it Stein's way: "Soon now there will be a history of the way repeating comes out of them comes out of men and women . . ." (*Selected Writings* 263, from *The Making of Americans*). Or "Every one always is repeating the whole of them and so sometime some one who sees them will have a complete history of every one" (263). In *The Waves*, Woolf assumes what Stein assumes in *The Making of Americans*: that the essential self expresses itself again and again, and it is the novel's job to explore in characters what Stein called their "bottom nature[s]" (265). In this book, Woolf too narrates "bottom natures." Rhoda's hopeless yearning, her buffeted self, her vulnerability, Jinny's vision in which "all is rippling, all is dancing," Louis's outsider's vision—these do not change (*The Waves* 46). The social life of profession, intimacy, loss, *bildung* is ignored. We learn little about Susan's motherhood, about the bond between Louis and Rhoda, about Bernard's success as a writer. These are not their bottom natures. Being always what they were from, and even before, the text's beginning, the characters avoid social insertion. Neither the compromises nor the transfigurations of adulthood jostle them.

It is a world that tries to explore difference without touching on social (including gender) inequality, without pernicious judgments of value. In that sense, a utopian text, leading to the more overt political utopianism of *The Years* and *Between the Acts*. This ultimate exploration of difference (along with an articulation of dispersed desire) are the gender narratives in a work that otherwise might seem to ignore that question—or even, curiously, center on female voices more traditionally feminine than Woolf usually proposes, and without the spinster-artist or intellectual so important to her oeuvre as a whole. But to explore difference as pleasure, variety, texture of lives, one needs the presence of the undervalued—the feminine female (flighty and fashionable, fragile and suicidal, repressed and maternal) and the marginal ("androgynous," homosexual, Australian) male; as narrative center dies in Percival, it should surprise no one that centrist masculinity does also, and we are left with the dispersion of pleasure and sensation across the text—irrespective of the "borders" of each identity.

The opposition to plot, narrative, story (often by name), and their critique by various means from a *raisonneur* figure (like Bernard), to built-in manifesto, to thematic and developmental integrations, make a feminist project of modernist aims: an antiauthoritarian project against the tyranny of conventionalized plot and therefore a critique of certain gender relations long traditional in fictions. It is necessary to tie this formulation to general critical readings linking narrative to authority, with particular attention to Roland Barthes's theory of the pleasures afforded by conventional narrative.[8] Barthes has posited that "the pleasure of the text . . . [is] an Oedipal pleasure (to denude, to know, to learn the origin and the end), if it is true that every narrative (every unveiling of the truth) is a staging of the (absent, hidden, or hypostatized) father—which would explain the solidarity of narrative forms, of family structures, and of prohibitions of nudity . . ." (*Pleasure of the Text* 10).

Thereupon it is possible to understand something quite uncanny in Woolf's text, certainly in relation to other of her novels. *The Waves* seems to be a book about children, not adults—about children perpetually children, despite the passage of time. Yet *The Waves* is a novel entirely, almost absolutely, without family. The children begin quite young—one may put their first words in relation to Woolf's brilliant visual and emotional first memories in *Moments of Being*; yet no child has a narrated or surrogate mother. No child, except Susan, has a father, and he is in no way narrated; although her yearning for the life he represents is central to her, Woolf does not compose on that point, but simply alludes to it. There are no family houses depicted, although several characters (Bernard, Susan) are said to marry; indeed, Woolf here begins her habit of setting most narrative events in relatively public spaces—gardens, playing fields, parks, restaurants, streets. And with the lamented end of Percival, the brotherly figure who could be a stand-in for the Oedipal father or his softened substitute is swept away, so that in the filial, maternal, paternal

cluster he represents, it is arguable that Woolf jettisons the whole complex of Oedipal emotional formation and thereby its narrative meaning.

The absence of family—unique to her novels, even to *The Years* and
Between the Acts, and so intensely realized as to constitute an experiment
in such an avoidance—may be explored with recourse to Barthes. Avoiding conventional narrative structures, especially any plot of disclosure
(for nothing is revealed, all are what they are), one is in a parallel way
implicated in an avoidance of family structures: the authority of the generation above, paternal and patriarchal authority, the inequalities of gender, the enclosures of space. What is buried in each character, what impels
or prevents, the times of luminosity or self-doubt that occur in them are
stated without reference to causal or traumatic moments in the past,
which may be recalled and even healed. The negotiation of such recalling
and healing is, after all, the project of another important novel by
Woolf—*To the Lighthouse*. And without relation to any future, which
these might cause. *The Waves* is written (say it again in Stein's way) in the
"continuous present."[9]

This gives renewed importance to the fact that the only major change
The Waves records is the unfolding of Bernard's changed relation to
story. After intensities of narration, after spending a lifetime keeping
phrases in a notebook, he abandons story as a useful mode and even, in a
many-layered gesture of release, abandons his own diary, his writer's
source book, letting it fall from the table at which he lives his last moments. He lets go of identity; he lets go of remembering. Beginning by
asserting authority over, making sense of, even controlling by means of
his tales, Bernard finishes by postulating an alternative poetics of narrative. This is not of disclosure, but of enclosure or enfolding. Woolf is precise about the fusions and junctures (as opposed to the separations and
distinctions), which are thereby satisfying. If, as children, Bernard remembered, "we suffered terribly as we became separate bodies," it is fitting that the work's end proposes the end of such individuality (241). His
monologue enfolds his friends (who are him as he is them) and as the
wave enfolds him, being, even identical with him. "What I call 'my life,'
it is not one life that I look back upon; I am not one person; I am many
people; I do not altogether know who I am—Jinny, Susan, Neville,
Rhoda, or Louis; or how to distinguish my life from theirs" (276). Bernard is a perfect multiple individual. Division, individuality, novels called
Emma, Tom Jones, Moll Flanders, Mrs. Dalloway, Orlando—it is such a
root assumption of value that Woolf is working to disallow: "How describe the world seen without a self?" that is, without identity (*The Waves*
287). Disavowing the Oedipal story, Woolf's experimentalism pivots into
a non-Oedipal narrative of fusion and bonding without parental and filial

figures to fix desire, without the authority of disclosure. Disavowing the individualist story of the social (as well as psychic) borders of the self, Woolf's experimentalism pivots into a collectivity of enfolding, in which the language contains, the language nourishes, the language rocks and succors.

NOTES

1. The interest in a social intertextuality of discourses in dialogue occurs in M. Bakhtin's *The Dialogic Imagination: Four Essays*: that any discourse is "entangled, shot through with shared thoughts, points of view, alien value judgments and accents" (276). The interest in a fluid and heterodox conjuncture of readings occurs in Barthes's *Image-Music-Text*: "We know now that a text is not a line of words releasing a single 'theological' meaning (the 'message' of the Author-God) but a multi-dimensional space in which a variety of writings, none of them original, blend and clash" (146).

2. The face-to-face meeting between Stein and Woolf, at Edith Sitwell's (June 1926), was a testy flop as far as Woolf was concerned. "Jews swarmed. It was in honour of Miss Gertrude Stein who was throned on a broken settee. . . . This resolute old lady inflicted great damage on all the youth. According to Dadie, she contradicts all you say; insists that she is not only the most intelligible, but also the most popular of living writers; and in particular despises all of English birth. Leonard, being a Jew himself, got on very well with her" (*Letters* 3: 269–70). Dour and repugnant comments upon Jewishness frame this, a rival queen animates it, damage abounds (from the furniture to the intellectual impact), and Stein's smugly provocative business as an American vanguard gadfly stings Woolf, most of whose information comes at second hand, after a retreat.

3. It is symptomatic of the irregular state of literary history where female modernism is concerned that this manuscript is not adequately identified in Woolf's *Letters*; despite allusions to its crushing length, the notes propose the very short "Composition as Explanation." Further corroboration occurs in James R. Mellow's *Charmed Circle*, citing Donald Gallup's 1953 collection of letters written to Stein to observe that Edith Sitwell was quite disappointed in her failure to convince the Woolfs to bring out an English edition of *The Making of Americans*. Robert McAlmon, of the Bryher-H.D. circle, published that novel, in his Contact Editions, in 1925.

4. "She" is Stein. Tom is, of course, T. S. Eliot; Woolf's ambivalent irritations with *Ulysses* are well known (*Writer's Diary* 46, 48, 49). The use of James Joyce's last name in a list of first names seems charmingly to add one more woman writer to this tally of modernist inventors.

5. "Composition as Explanation" proceeds to a developmental and formal analysis by Stein of her own writing, with major stops at *Three Lives* (w. 1905–06, pub. 1909) and *The Making of Americans* (w. 1906–11, pub. 1925), up

to, but only implicitly including *Tender Buttons* (w. 1912, pub. 1914) and early portraits (1909, 1911–12). Stein's "portraits" ("of anybody and anything") are importantly described as a compressed and miniaturized version of tactics that were invented extensively in her long (Woolf: unreadable chronicle), *The Making of Americans* (*Selected Writings* 518). I am not interested here in Stein's own self-presentation but in the poetics Stein proposes and Woolf may be said to confirm.

6. Especially by Michael Davidson, Marianne DeKoven, and Neil Schmitz.

7. Julia Kristeva, "From One Identity to An Other."

8. In *Writing Beyond the Ending*, I emphasize Oedipalization and its rescripting as part of the project of female modernism. Recent work by Susan Friedman and Gayle Greene connect the female critique of narrative explicitly to poststructuralist theory.

9. J. W. Graham has a subtle analysis of the verb tenses in *The Waves*, whose "pure present" makes all actions seem momentary, without a before or after. And, as well, the pure present removes narrative voice from omniscience and superior knowledge, to "omnipercipience," or saturation in perceptions; in the long course of revisions, which Graham analyzes, the narrator moves from, in Kristeva's terms, symbolic to semiotic processes (106).

WORKS CITED

Bakhtin, M. M. *The Dialogic Imagination: Four Essays*. Ed. Michael Holquist. Austin: U of Texas P, 1981.

Barthes, Roland. *Image-Music-Text*. Trans. Stephen Heath. New York: Hill, 1977.

——. *The Pleasure of the Text*. Trans. Richard Miller. New York: Farrar, 1975.

Cixous, Hélène. "The Laugh of the Medusa." Trans. Keith Cohen and Paula Cohen. *Signs* 1 (1976): 875–93.

Davidson, Michael. "On Reading Stein." *The $L=A=N=G=U=A=G=E$ Book*. Ed. Bruce Andrews and Charles Bernstein. Carbondale: Southern Illinois UP, 1984. 196–98.

DeKoven, Marianne. *A Different Language: Gertrude Stein's Experimental Writing*. Madison: U of Wisconsin P, 1983.

DuPlessis, Rachel Blau. *Writing Beyond the Ending: Narrative Strategies of Twentieth-Century Women Writers*. Bloomington: Indiana UP, 1985.

Friedman, Susan Stanford. "Lyric Subversions of Narrative in Women's Writing: Virginia Woolf and the Tyranny of Plot." *Reading Narrative: Form, Ethics, Ideology*. Ed. James Phelan. Columbus: Ohio State UP, 1988.

Graham, J. W. "Point of View in *The Waves*: Some Services of the Style." *Virginia Woolf: A Collection of Criticism*. Ed. Thomas S. W. Lewis. New York: McGraw, 1975. 94–112.

Greene, Gayle. "Margaret Drabble's *The Waterfall*: New System, New Morality." *Novel* 22 (1988).

Johnson, Barbara. "*Les fleurs du mal armé*: Some Reflections on Intertextuality." *Lyric Poetry: Beyond New Criticism*. Ed. Chaviva Hosek and Patricia Parker. Ithaca: Cornell UP, 1985. 264–80.

Krauss, Rosalind E. "The Originality of the Avant-Garde." *The Originality of the Avant-Garde and Other Modernist Myths*. Cambridge, MA: MIT P, 1985. 151–70.

Kristeva, Julia. "From One Identity to An Other." *Desire in Language: A Semiotic Approach to Literature and Art*. Trans. Leon S. Roudiez, Alice A. Jardine, and Thomas Gora. New York: Columbia UP, 1980. 124–47.

Mellow, James R. *Charmed Circle: Gertrude Stein and Company*. New York: Praeger, 1974.

Schmitz, Neil. "Gertrude Stein as Post-Modernist: The Rhetoric of *Tender Buttons*." *Journal of Modern Literature* 3 (July 1974): 1203–18.

Stein, Gertrude. *The Autobiography of Alice B. Toklas*. 1933. Harmondsworth, Gt. Brit.: Penguin, 1983.

———. "Forensics." *How to Write*. 1931. New York: Dover, 1975. 385–95.

———. *Lectures in America*. 1935. Boston: Beacon, 1985.

———. *The Making of Americans*. Paris: Contact, 1925.

———. *Selected Writings of Gertrude Stein*. Ed. Carl Van Vechten. New York: Modern Library, 1962. Contains "Composition as Explanation," *Tender Buttons*, and an excerpt from *The Making of Americans*.

———. *Tender Buttons*. New York: Claire Marie, 1914.

———. *Three Lives*. New York: Grafton, 1909.

Woolf, Virginia. *Between the Acts*. New York: Harcourt, 1941.

———. *The Letters of Virginia Woolf*. Vol. 3: 1923–28. Ed. Nigel Nicolson and Joanne Trautmann. New York: Harcourt, 1977–78.

———. *The Letters of Virgina Woolf*. Vol. 6: 1936–41. Ed. Nigel Nicolson and Joanne Trautmann. New York: Harcourt, 1980.

———. *Moments of Being: Unpublished Autobiographical Writings*. Ed. Jeanne Schulkind. New York: Harcourt, 1976.

———. *Mrs. Dalloway*. London: Hogarth, 1925.

———. *A Room of One's Own*. 1929. New York: Harcourt, 1957.

———. *To the Lighthouse*. London: Hogarth, 1927.

———. *The Waves*. New York: Harcourt, 1931.

———. *A Writer's Diary*. Ed. Leonard Woolf. New York: Harcourt, 1953–54.

———. *The Years*. New York: Harcourt, 1937.

SECOND GENERATION: 1930–1960

Breaking the Master Narrative:
Jean Rhys's *Wide Sargasso Sea*

ELLEN G. FRIEDMAN

"I AM sure that it needs a demon to write it. Or a fraud." Writing to Francis Wyndham in November 1958 concerning her work-in-progress, Jean Rhys thus expressed her sense of violating Charlotte Brontë's *Jane Eyre* (1847) with her own revisionary novel, *Wide Sargasso Sea* (1966), for which she usurped Brontë's characters and plot (*Letters* 158). Brontë's material did not lead Rhys to create a wholly independent narrative. In fact, maintaining the connection with Brontë was crucial: "It might be possible to unhitch the whole thing from Charlotte Bronte's novel, but I don't want to do that" she wrote to Wyndham in March 1958 (153).

In an unprecedented and aggressive revisionary move, Rhys enters and reimagines Brontë's text—glossing and subverting, reversing and transforming it—writing it into her own time and into her own frame of reference. Rhys wished to get closer to what she called "the real story," a hidden story, suggested to Rhys by the figure of the Creole madwoman Bertha, a story probably inaccessible to Brontë, who wrote within the context of the largely amiable alliance of nineteenth-century English imperialism, Christianity, and patriarchy (*Letters* 153). When the novel was within two years of completion (she wrote it over more than a 20-year period), Rhys declared to Wyndham, "I have the right to take lost Antoinette," Rhys's name for Rochester's first wife (whose middle name in *Jane Eyre* is "Antoinetta") (318). "Charlotte" was "wrong . . . her Bertha is impossible" (*Letters* 271).

The text generated by Rhys's struggle with her precursor is not quite separate, and therefore somewhat different than a Bloomian revision or misreading.[1] Rhys's relationship to Brontë has an unusually overt and conscious element, though it bespeaks a buried struggle as well. In a letter to Selma Vaz Diaz dated November 6, 1957, Rhys wrote, "Finally I got Jane Eyre to read and reread and hook on *my* Mrs Rochester to Charlotte Bronte's. I was a bit taken aback when I discovered what a fat (and improbable) monster she was. However I think I have seen how to do it though not without pain struggle curses and lamentation." She understood the audacity of her project: "Whether I have any *right* to do it is a question which I'll face later" (*Letters* 149). She calls herself "impertinent" and voices a superstitious fear of Brontë's retribution (175). She attributes some of her struggle in writing *Wide Sargasso Sea* to the difficulty of wrestling with her precursor: "Sometimes I have wondered if Miss Bronte does not *want* her book tampered with!" (175).

In a number of subversive moves, Rhys does tamper with Brontë's book. For instance, she attaches her text to the mother-text through a sly allusion to the physical book *Jane Eyre*: in Part III of *Wide Sargasso Sea* Antoinette/Bertha, whom Rhys foregrounds and fleshes out, speaks of leaving her attic prison and entering the world of "cardboard." In this cardboard world live the forces that victimize her, that have driven her into the attic and inward into her own psychic spaces. These forces were born in Brontë's novel, the physical book "between cardboard covers" (Spivak 250–51) that Rhys's nineteenth-century precursor produced and to which Antoinette refers: "Then I open the door and walk into their world. It is, as I always knew, made of cardboard" (*Wide Sargasso Sea* 180–81).

In addition to alluding to *Jane Eyre*, Rhys directly connects the two texts near the conclusion of her novel by constructing a door leading into *Jane Eyre*. At the end of Part III, Antoinette describes a fiery dream: "I got up, took the keys and let myself out with a candle in my hand. It was easier this time than ever before and I walked as though I were flying" (187). Imitating Brontë's Bertha in this dream, she sets Rochester's house on fire. When Antoinette awakens, she realizes "Now at last I know why I was brought here and what I have to do" (190). What she must do, as readers of *Jane Eyre* know, is set Thornfield on fire. However, she does not force reality to conform to her dream until she enters *Jane Eyre* as Brontë's madwoman, Bertha. Thus, the end of *Wide Sargasso Sea* explodes into Brontë's novel. It is the madwoman in Brontë's attic who sets the house on fire with her candle and then leaps to her death, enacting what is only a dream in Rhys's novel.

The result of this unusual textual violation, this audacious grafting, is the shifting of the place from which *Jane Eyre* is enunciated. For instance, if Rhys's novel is seen as background, Bertha's act in *Jane Eyre* becomes a willed act of desperation rather than a helpless act of lunacy. The resolve of Rhys's Bertha (Rochester renames Antoinette) to make her dream come true is the resolve of the victim who, rendered helpless, dreams of punishing her oppressor and ending her pain in a suicidal conflagration. This prelude justifies Bertha's act, places it in a moral context (as well as a political context, since Bertha is West Indian and Rochester represents imperialist England). Rhys thus frees the madwoman from her bestiality

and lunacy. In contrast, Brontë's Bertha, as Jane encounters her, is a grov-
eling, bellowing beast that "stood tall on its hind-feet" (321). Since she
does not comprehend the world she negotiates, she cannot be called to
account; she is not responsible.

This shift in the site of enunciation disrupts the smooth surface of inevitability in *Jane Eyre*. A desperate, victimized first Mrs. Rochester completely changes the context in which Brontë's hero and heroine play out
their roles. Despite his emotional and physical suffering (he is blinded and
maimed in the Thornfield fire), Rochester seems no longer to deserve Jane
and happiness, and who is Jane in relation to this altered fiction? In the
light of *Wide Sargasso Sea*, even Jane, whom Gayatri Spivak has called
the "feminist individualist heroine" must be reconsidered, reevaluated
(251). Brontë's Jane bears a variety of cruelties to achieve selfhood on her
own terms. However, if she equates such achievement with marriage to
Rochester, whom Rhys portrays, at least in part, as greedy and sadistic,
Jane herself must be doubted. Confronted with contradictory or ambiguous imperatives, the reader loses sympathy for Jane Eyre's quest, loses
faith in the worth of such a quest, for the object of the quest, embodied
by Rochester, has been rendered problematical.

The devices that connect the two texts also rupture the boundary between them. Although this rupture completes Rhys's text, it results in a
breakdown of the integrity of Brontë's; the mother-text is maimed and in
essence, disarmed. Rhys's sense of the literary work in *Wide Sargasso Sea*
coincides with that of Maurice Blanchot in his 1949 essay "Littérature et
le droit à la mort" ("Literature and the Right to Death") in which he
writes that a "work exists only when it has become [a] public, alien reality, made and unmade by colliding with other realities." While the author,
who "exists only in his work" remains constant, "the work itself is dis-
appearing" (26). Although Blanchot describes a process natural to the
passage of time, Rhys manipulates that process in regard to Brontë. In the
collision betweeen *Wide Sargasso Sea* and *Jane Eyre*, Brontë's text is
muted and altered so that it does begin to "disappear" and with it the
authority (encompassing the writer and the context of the writing) that
created it. Rhys ruptures the nineteenth-century text, making holes and
blank spaces through which a reader is compelled to look with a self-
consciously twentieth-century vision that will necessarily transform what
it sees. In a cunning and spectacular extension and reversal of intertextual
relations, Rhys transverses Brontë's text with an otherness[2] that postdates
it, forcing Brontë's narrative to be measured by a set of assumptions outside those of the master quest narrative in complicity with which Brontë
wrote her novel.[3]

Fulfilling Rhys's motive in recreating her, Antoinette wishes to "see what is behind the cardboard," to penetrate the veneer of beliefs that legitimate the plot of *Jane Eyre* (180). Through her character, Rhys attempts to question the truth of Brontë's "England," a metonym in *Wide Sargasso Sea* for a large constellation of elements in Brontë's universe—including its patriarchal laws, morality, and assumptions. Antoinette states, "This cardboard house where I walk at night is not England" (181). That is, the England depicted between the covers of *Jane Eyre* is a deceptive image. The new narrative Rhys creates by attaching hers to Brontë's unveils a different, other "England," an England enunciated from the site of the (returned) repressed, the incarnation of which is the West Indies where the first two parts of *Wide Sargasso Sea* take place.

Jean Rhys was born in the West Indies in 1894. According to Thomas F. Staley, "More than anything else, her early years in the West Indies formed her imagination and shaped the restlessness of her identity" (4). In the late thirties, Rhys returned to the West Indies for a visit. In 1945, she wrote to Peggy Kirkaldy, referring to what would eventually become *Wide Sargasso Sea*, "I have a novel half finished" (*Letters* 39).

One of the moments in the process by which the West Indies came to be associated in Rhys's imagination with the repressed, as well as the oppressed, took place when she read *Jane Eyre* upon first arriving in England from the West Indies at the age of sixteen or seventeen. Rhys recalls her shock at Brontë's portrait of the "poor Creole lunatic" and her conviction "That's only one side—the English side" (*Letters* 297). Significantly, Rhys began to write almost solely about the West Indies when she herself had slipped into obscurity, perhaps identifying with these islands. Of them she writes, "never was anything more vanished and forgotten. Or lovely—" (*Letters* 133).

The West Indies (Rhys emphasizes that it was an English colony) as alternate landscape operates as a competing frame of reference, not powerful enough to supplant the dominant landscape, represented by England, but with enough force and conviction to delegitimate the dominant. Erotic and wild, the nature imagery with which Rhys describes the West Indies is emblematic of the repressed forces inimical and antithetical to Brontë's neat and orderly England. Antoinette describes her garden:

> Our garden was large and beautiful as that garden in the Bible—the tree of life grew there. But it had gone wild. The paths were overgrown and a smell of dead flowers mixed with the fresh living smell. Underneath the tree ferns, tall as forest tree ferns, the light was green. Orchids flourished out of reach or for some reason not to be touched. One was snaky looking, another like an octopus with long thin brown tentacles bare of leaves hanging from a twisted root. Twice a year the octopus

orchid flowered—then not an inch of tentacle showed. It was a bell-shaped mass of white, mauve, deep purples, wonderful to see. The scent was very sweet and strong. I never went near it. All Coulibri Estate had gone wild like the garden, gone to bush. (19)

Here, Rhys presents a different, noncanonical version of the Garden of Eden; with its blatant sexuality and danger, this is the "other" garden, which Rhys draws in opposition to the "sheltered and . . . Eden-like" (276) orchard at Thornfield with *its* tree of life, the giant horse chestnut that lightning strikes and splits when Rochester proposes to commit bigamy. One of Rhys's purposes in proposing this other Eden is to undermine the clear, rigid equations for right and wrong operative in Brontë's Eden and by implication in England.

In sharp contrast to Rhys's landscape, Brontë's is controlled and measured. Notice the metaphors of control in this passage in which Jane Eyre describes Thornfield:

I surveyed the grounds *laid out like a map*; the bright and velvet lawn closely *girdling* the gray base of the mansion; the field, wide as a park, *dotted* with its ancient timber; the wood, dun and sere, *divided* by a path visibly overgrown, greener with moss than the trees with foliage; the church at the gates, the road, the tranquil hills, all reposing in the autumn day's sun; the horizon *bounded* by a propitious sky, azure, marbled with pearly white. *No feature in the scene was extraordinary, but all was pleasing.* (Italics added; 137–38)

The two landscapes represent two frames of reference in dialectical opposition, akin to the "symbolic" and the "semiotic" in Julia Kristeva's scheme. Although all language is marked by a dialectic between the semiotic (expressed in the disruptive dimension of language) and the symbolic (expressed through logocentric discourse) according to Kristeva, the degree to which each exerts its presence determines the type of resulting discourse—"narrative, metalanguage, theory, poetry, etc." (Kristeva 24). Part of Rhys's feat, then, is to qualify the dominance of the symbolic by positing a transforming semiotic presence, introduced through the wild nature imagery, the Creole ethos, the "madness" of Antoinette, and various other narrative strategies and moves.

The operation of this dialectic is evident even within *Wide Sargasso Sea*. In a particularly telling instance, Rochester, representative of England, which colonized the West Indies, confronts a West Indian primeval forest. In the delusion that he can conquer it, he persists in following what he imagines was once a paved road. But rather than taking him through and then out of the forest, this, perhaps imaginary, road leads only into it. Without a road to follow, he is vulnerable: "I was lost and afraid among these *enemy* trees" (italics added; 105). Bereft of a road or a controlling and taming mechanism (e.g., law), Rochester, as well as the patriarchal society he represents, is helpless against the force of the unconscious. So disarmed, Rochester is paralyzed, unable to respond at first to help when it comes. One of the purposes of the scene is to reveal his insufficiency and therefore the insufficiency of England as viewed from the alternate frame of reference Rhys provides.

Following a culturally inscribed pattern, Rochester deals with his inadequacy by denying the value of what he cannot master, by calling it "madness" and locking it away. In fact, Rochester becomes his own author and creates a narrative in which he is no longer insufficient, in which he achieves mastery. He renames Antoinette "Bertha," thus transforming her into Brontë's lunatic, and he also calls her "marionette," a puppet he can control. In an extraordinary passage in which Rhys demonstrates the malevolent potential of narratives, their power to narrow reality, Rochester reports that he drew "a house surrounded by trees. A large house. I divided the third floor into rooms and in one room I drew a standing woman—a child's scribble, a dot for a head, a larger one for the body, a triangle for a skirt, slanting lines for arms and feet. *But it was an English house*" (italics added; 163). England and being English, Rhys suggests, empower Rochester both to imagine and to realize this plan, to write the narrative in which the repressed, represented by the Creole Antoinette, is in its "proper" place—under lock and key in the attic.

HAVING cast doubt on the credibility of the quest, the hero, the heroine, and the villain, Rhys succeeds in breaking the quest narrative that shapes Brontë's novel. [4] Rhys delegitimates this master narrative, and by implication master narratives in general. Jean-François Lyotard defines "modernity" as "incredulity with regard to the master narratives" based on the "obsolescence of the master narrative device of legitimation. . . . The narrative function loses its foundations, the great hero, the great perils, the great quests, and the great goal" (qtd. in Jardine 65). Fostering a sense of disbelief and even the superannuated in regard to *Jane Eyre*, Rhys's amalgamated text is, then, perhaps above all, a work of "modernity."

The value of works of modernity, according to Roland Barthes, "proceed[s] from their duplicity. By which it must be understood that they always have two edges," the subversive and the conformist or canonical (6–7). While Barthes's focus is on single works within which the canonical and subversive edge each other, Rhys attempts this uneasy alliance between two different texts.

Rhys edges Brontë's canonical imagery, plot, and characterization with a subversive revision of them. She edges the orderly, proper, and hallowed discourse of *Jane Eyre* with the discourse of *Wide Sargasso Sea* in which the chaotic, the improper, and the profane are dominant. In other words, she edges "Same" with "Other."⁵ Thus, the Christian ethic explicit in *Jane Eyre* is edged with the voodoo and obeah of *Wide Sargasso Sea*; the English Garden of Eden countered by a West Indian Eden; the romantic patriarch, Rochester, with his malevolent and afflicted double; the *deus ex machina* lunatic Bertha with her haunting twin, Antoinette. The English setting and sustained first-person point of view in Brontë is edged with a West Indian setting (for most of the novel) and shifting first-person point of view in Rhys. Indeed, although the brief Part III of *Wide Sargasso Sea* is set in England, our perception of it is colored by the hostile Antoinette through whom this section is filtered. Moreover, the shifting point of view prevents the reader from settling into any privileged or comfortable narrative site and thus aids in destabilizing master narrative and its facilitating conventions, in this case the authoritative narrator.

In the gaps between the edges, according to Barthes, the canonical and subversive make a difficult compromise, a compromise essential to modernity (7). Barthes is speaking of internal gaps in the text, but in Rhys these gaps are the products of the grafting on of alien material. The effect is a disconcerting and complex play and resonance between the two texts. For instance, the plot in *Wide Sargasso Sea* has, even for a modern narrative, an unusual internal illogic often explainable only by reference to *Jane Eyre*. When Antoinette seeks the help of her former nursemaid, the obeah woman, Christophine, to deal with Rochester's infidelity and hostility, Christophine advises her to "do battle" for herself (116). In effect, Christophine is asking her to be Jane. However, this option is closed off to Antoinette not only because of her own nature, but primarily because there already is a Jane. Antoinette's fate is to be Bertha. That is, Antoinette's helplessness is explained partially by imperatives from another novel. Through the figure of Antoinette, Rhys illustrates how her precursor has restricted her to a predetermined narrative. Yet this very illustration liberates. In order to see the confinement and predetermination, one must be outside, know otherwise. Thus, Brontë's text acts as both a limit and a point of departure.

Another passage in which *Jane Eyre* provides both the gloss and a confining presence occurs during the course of Antoinette's final dream, already referred to, depicting her setting Thornfield on fire. The passage echoes the dialogue in *Jane Eyre* as Jane is being told about Bertha's suicidal jump, "She was a big woman, and had long black hair: we could see it streaming against the flames as she stood" (453). To this image in *Jane Eyre*, Rhys in *Wide Sargasso Sea* adds a "gilt frame," an image of the novel into which Antoinette gazes to learn her destiny: Antoinette recalls, "I saw her—the ghost. The woman with streaming hair. She was surrounded by a gilt frame but I knew her" (188–89). The "ghost" is herself, the part she plays for Jane, the character into which she metamorphoses once she enters *Jane Eyre*. The image offered in the frame constitutes Antoinette's script, a picture of her inheritance and her fate. That the frame, suggesting the frame of quest plot that houses Brontë's text, is of gilt (guilt?) argues its glittering but deceptive desirability. Rhys employs her edge as a subversive commentary.

Rhys's Rochester is also limited by his role in Brontë's novel. Nearing the completion of *Wide Sargasso Sea*, Rhys expresses compassion for both of her protagonists in an April 1964 letter to Wyndham, "Poor Antoinette and poor Mr. R." (*Letters* 261). Rhys's feeling is consonant with the portraits she paints. Although Rochester comes to represent the oppressive patriarchy—indeed all that Rhys sets out to challenge and undermine—she nevertheless contemplates a different development of him. As he and Antoinette are about to leave Granbois, the estate in the Windward Islands where they honeymoon, he is recaptured by its beauty: "Only the magic and the dream are true—all the rest's a lie. Let it go. Here is the secret. Here" (168). He thinks back nostalgically to when he loved Antoinette and has a momentary change of heart, "I have made a terrible mistake. Forgive me" (169). A few lines later he makes the "sickening swing back to hate" (170). Rochester's potential for change is a possibility strangled by the necessity of his playing out an inexorable role. He is as stuck in his destiny as Antoinette is in hers. Almost everything in *Wide Sargasso Sea* is calibrated by *Jane Eyre*. But it is against *Jane Eyre* that Rhys writes. Her hint at a different potential Rochester is an element of her strategy of delegitimation.

The dream sequence occurring at the end of Part 1 of *Wide Sargasso Sea*, usually seen as a foreshadowing of Antoinette's fate, also suggests how Rhys saw her relationship to Brontë and beyond that the relationship between the subversive and the canonical, the feminine (semiotic) and the patriarchal (symbolic).[6] In the dream, Antoinette has left Coulibri, where she grew up. She recalls:

> It is still night and I am walking towards the forest. I am wearing a long dress and thin slippers, so I walk with difficulty, following the man who is with me and holding up the skirt of my dress. It is white and beautiful and I don't wish to get it soiled. I follow him, sick with fear but I make no effort to save myself; if anyone were to try to save me, I would refuse. This must happen. Now we have reached the forest. We are under the tall dark trees and there is no wind. "Here?" He turns and

looks at me, his face black with hatred, and when I see this I begin to cry. He smiles slyly. "Not here, not yet," he says, and I follow him, weeping. Now I do not try to hold up my dress, it trails in the dirt, my beautiful dress. We are no longer in the forest but in an enclosed garden surrounded by a stone wall and the trees are different trees. I do not know them. There are steps leading upwards. It is too dark to see the wall or the steps, but I know they are there and I think, "It will be when I go up these steps. At the top." I stumble over my dress and cannot get up. I touch a tree and my arms hold on to it. "Here, here." But I think I will not go any further. The tree sways and jerks as if it is trying to throw me off. Still I cling and the seconds pass and each one is a thousand years. "Here, in here," a strange voice said, and the tree stopped swaying and jerking. (59–60)

This dream has been interpreted as foreshadowing Antoinette's departure from the primeval forest of the West Indies to the imprisoning, enclosed garden that is England; the phallic tree that tries to throw Antoinette off is viewed as representing Rochester (Baer 139). Described by Antoinette as a dream of "Hell" (60), its rich symbolism (soiled dress, a tree that sways and jerks) also suggests the feared but desired sexual experience. However, the dream, on a basic level, recounts the passage from one state to another—from a "white" to a "soiled" dress—and can be read in terms of Antoinette's encounter with the symbolic as represented by Rochester and patriarchal, imperialist England. The dreamer, Antoinette, enters the forest (representing the unconscious), following fearfully, with difficulty, and a sense of inevitability ("This must happen") "the man," a dual father/lover figure, who has charge of her as he holds her dress or potential self. Once in the forest, the man turns "black with hatred," for like Rochester in the West Indian forest, this dream "man" and his phallocentric laws have no force in the forest of the unconscious. The forest then metamorphoses into an enclosed garden encircled by a stone wall. This metamorphosis signals entry into the symbolic order, the enclosed garden and stone wall representing the strict patriarchal limits it poses. Here, Antoinette, a figure associated with all that is encoded as feminine, "stumbles," finds it is "too dark to see the wall or the steps." Once she has entered the realm of the symbolic, Antoinette can no longer aspire to be constituted as a subject—her dress "trails in the dirt." However, she hears a "strange voice," which says "Here, in here." This voice is not in the enclosed garden, so it must come from the repressed, offering to guide the dreamer while "the man" could only cast her away. Having refused to "go any further" to what must lead to her destruction, she follows the imperative of the voice. As she does so, the tree that tried to throw her off has "stopped swaying and jerking."

Since the context is a foreshadowing dream, the "strange voice" that calls Antoinette invites her into madness. That the phallic tree stops its violence against her as she listens, indicates this madness as a space of sanctuary. Since Antoinette cannot become a subject in the patriarchal garden, she moves into alterity, otherness, a space that she comes to occupy in the novel as soon as Rochester enters the narrative at the beginning of Part II, shortly after this dream. Significantly, the point of view shifts from Antoinette in Part I to Rochester in Part II, and in his domain, she is quintessential "other." "Madness" is simply a rendering of her otherness.

Unlike Brontë in the depiction of her madwoman, Rhys depicts Antoinette's madness and thus her alterity as a privileged state. Her madness implies special knowledge—secret, inaccessible (at least to Rochester), subversive, and desirable. As he thinks of her, Rochester says, "Above all I hated her. For she belonged to the magic and the loveliness. She had left me thirsty and all my life would be thirst and longing for what I had lost before I found it" (172). In her reimagining of the story, Rhys privileges alterity. As embodied by the West Indies and Antoinette, it is a measure of Rochester's and England's deficiencies. Rhys portrays Rochester's revenge for his being denied access to this privileged state as his marginalizing Antoinette by calling her mad: "Very soon she'll join all the others who know the secret and will not tell it. . . . They can be recognized. White faces, dazed eyes, aimless gestures, high-pitched laughter. . . . She's one of them" (172). Madness, in this novel, is a declared rather than an inherent or inherited condition, a condition arising from the place of enunciation. In England and in relation to Rochester, Antoinette is mad, the "dis-ease" inherited from her mother. In fact, Christophine denies that Antoinette's mother is really mad. Because she was treated as if she were mad, "she give up" and accepted others' perceptions of her (157). For Rochester, the cover story of madness is a way to deny the reality of Antoinette's significance and thus his insufficiency. He hopes in time he will think of her as a "legend" or a "lie": "I too can wait—for the day when she is only a memory to be avoided . . . and like all memories a legend. Or a lie . . ." (172).

The "enclosed garden" in the dream alludes specifically to the garden at Thornfield and thus to *Jane Eyre*. The "strange voice," then, also signifies Rhys's voice leading Bertha/Antoinette into *Wide Sargasso Sea*, a sanctuary for what is suppressed by and repressed in *Jane Eyre*. Although the garden in the dream is enclosed by a stone wall, representing the definite borders of this realm, it may nevertheless be invaded and ruptured and thus transformed. On one level, Antoinette's "madness" or alterity, and on another level, Rhys's *Wide Sargasso Sea* accomplish such a transforming invasion and rupture, releasing the repressed, edging the canonical with the subversive, the symbolic with the semiotic, the patriarchal with the feminine, opening the garden to the vista of the forest.

In *Gynesis: Configurations of Woman and Modernity*, Alice Jardine asserts, "Those writing modernity as a crisis-in-narrative, and thus in legitimation, are exploring newly contoured fictional spaces, hypothetical and unmeasurable, spaces freely coded as *feminine*. Gynesis [designates] the process of internalizing these feminine spaces while accounting for those crises . . ." (69). It is evident that in wrestling with her precursor, Rhys discovered what Jardine calls "gynesis" and created *Wide Sargasso Sea* out of this discovery. Provoked by Brontë's skewed, narrow depiction of the West Indies and the Creole Bertha, Rhys determined to write Brontë into modernity where such depictions are suspect, lack plausibility. Reshaping the contours of Brontë's phallocentric quest narrative, Rhys writes her into an adoption of otherness, an embracing of the feminine. In this act of conversion, Rhys, to be sure, betrays her precursor (imagine Brontë reading *Wide Sargasso Sea*), but she also discovers a mode for coming to terms with a past that if left alone is unusable and hostile.[7]

NOTES

1. The relationship between Rhys's and Brontë's texts has generated a number of studies, including those by Elizabeth R. Baer, Charlotte H. Bruner, Joyce Carol Oates, and Dennis Porter; also see Teresa F. O'Connor's *Jean Rhys: The West Indian Novels*. The penetrating essay by Gayatri C. Spivak on *Jane Eyre, Wide Sargasso Sea*, and *Frankenstein* is particularly pertinent to my reading, though Spivak emphasizes Rhys's work as a critique of British imperialism.

2. Barbara Johnson describes intertextuality as designating the "multitude of ways a text has of not being self-contained, of being transversed by otherness" (265).

3. For a discussion of the relationship between modernity and the delegitimation of master narratives, see Jardine (65–87).

4. Sandra M. Gilbert and Susan Gubar in *Madwoman in the Attic* point out that Brontë appropriated "the mythic quest-plot" in writing *Jane Eyre* (336).

5. Jardine lists some of the dichotomies at the heart of Western patriarchal culture; she makes the point that these dichotomies are "heterosexual couples": e.g., mind/body, culture/nature, techne/physis, intellect/sentiment, "same"/"other" (72).

6. Kristeva does not equate the semiotic with the feminine, but they are both allied with the subversion of dominant structures.
7. I am grateful to Maria DiBattista and Gloria C. Erlich for their helpful readings of a draft of this paper.

WORKS CITED

Baer, Elizabeth R. "The Sisterhood of Jane Eyre and Antoinette Cosway." *The Voyage In: Fictions of Female Development*. Ed. Elizabeth Abel, Marianne Hirsch, and Elizabeth Langland. Hanover, NH: UP of New England, 1983. 131–48.

Barthes, Roland. *The Pleasure of the Text*. Trans. Richard Miller. New York: Farrar, 1975.

Blanchot, Maurice. "Literature and the Right to Death." *The Gaze of Orpheus and Other Literary Essays*. Trans. Lydia Davis. Ed. P. Adams Sitney. Barrytown, NY: Station Hill, 1981. 21–62.

Brontë, Charlotte. *Jane Eyre*. 1847. New York: Penguin, 1966.

Bruner, Charlotte H. "A Caribbean Madness: Half Slave and Half Free." *Canadian Review of Comparative Literature* 11 (1984): 236–48.

Gilbert, Sandra M., and Susan Gubar. *The Madwoman in the Attic: The Woman Writer and the Nineteenth-Century Literary Imagination*. New Haven: Yale UP, 1979.

Jardine, Alice A. *Gynesis: Configurations of Woman and Modernity*. Ithaca: Cornell UP, 1985.

Johnson, Barbara. "*Les fleurs du mal armé*: Some Reflections on Intertextuality." *Lyric Poetry: Beyond New Criticism*. Ed. Chaviva Hosek and Patricia Parker. Ithaca: Cornell UP, 1985. 264–80.

Kristeva, Julia. *Revolution in Poetic Language*. Trans. Margaret Waller. Introd. Leon S. Roudiez. New York: Columbia UP, 1984.

Oates, Joyce Carol. "Romance and Anti-Romance: From Brontë's *Jane Eyre* to Rhys's *Wide Sargasso Sea*." *The Virginia Quarterly Review* 61 (1985): 44–58.

O'Connor, Teresa F. *Jean Rhys: The West Indian Novels*. New York: New York UP, 1986.

Porter, Dennis. "Of Heroines and Victims: Jean Rhys and *Jane Eyre*." *The Massachusetts Review* 17 (1976): 540–52.

Rhys, Jean. *The Letters of Jean Rhys*. Ed. Francis Wyndham and Diana Melly. New York: Viking, 1984.

———. *Wide Sargasso Sea*. 1966. New York: Norton, 1982.

Spivak, Gayatri Chakravorty. "Three Women's Texts and a Critique of Imperialism." *Critical Inquiry* 12 (1985): 243–61.

Staley, Thomas F. *Jean Rhys: A Critical Study*. Austin: U of Texas P, 1979.

The Radical Narrative of Djuna Barnes's *Nightwood*

―――

DONNA GERSTENBERGER

"Wir setzen an dieser Stelle uber den Fluss"

THE critical reception of Djuna Barnes's *Nightwood* is marked by a history of readings that focus on everything except its radical narrative achievement. This is a fate that Barnes shared with Joyce, as critics spoke to subject matter and biographical inferences, noting only in passing that the narrative method itself seemed confused or confusing. For Joyce, however, subsequent critics came more quickly to view his narrative practice as significant in itself and there to acknowledge the radical nature of his achievement. Barnes's fate has been to wait until recent years for a recognition of her narrative achievement.[1]

Barnes's first critical reader was T. S. Eliot, and the reception of *Nightwood* was at once cursed and blessed by the high priest of modernism, whose proprietary anxiousness in his well-meaning introduction to the novel seems surprising from the man who had published 14 years earlier what was to become the most influential experimental poem of the first quarter of the century. Eliot, who had worked with Barnes's novel in its various stages of publication, had read *Nightwood* a number of times; yet he clearly misses the point of Barnes's narrative form, for in his introduction he still worries the question of a genre definition. Barnes's work is, he insists, a novel, even though he knows that his contemporaries will be primarily struck by its absence of realism. Having approached the question of genre by what *Nightwood* is not, Eliot finds that he must, as one who genuinely wishes to recommend *Nightwood* to the reader, make two caveats that ignore the issue of form: that the appeal of the book will be primarily to readers of poetry and that "the book is not a psychopathic study" (xv). We need to recall that these caveats come from the author of *The Waste Land*, who had welcomed Joyce's *Ulysses* with strong praise.

One thing that Eliot's convoluted introduction to *Nightwood* does not say is that the novel must have held for him a shock of recognition, for Barnes's novel shares aspects of content and form that the writer of *The Waste Land* cannot have missed. *Nightwood* belongs, on one level at least, to a kind of modernism exemplified by Eliot himself, for on a global level Barnes's novel stakes out the same territory as Eliot's poem, which is that of a civilization (particularly Western European) in decay, an aristocracy in disarray, a people estranged from a sense of identity. Moreover, each of these works seeks to embody the contemporary situation in its fragmentary, nonlinear form, which demands that the reader come to terms with a self-referential internal coherence. And there is the figure of Dr. Matthew-Mighty-grain-of-salt-Dante-O'Connor, a character Eliot may have seen as an impolite version of that other historically sanctified male-female figure who has "foresuffered all"—identified in Eliot's *Waste Land* notes as the place where "the two sexes meet." O'Connor, mirroring Tiresias, sheds no light for Eliot; only of his own work, does Eliot say, "What Tiresias *sees*, in fact, is the substance of the poem" (50). Not until 1963 in *The Widening Gyre* does Joseph Frank spell out the connection that Eliot could not have failed to see. Finally, Barnes's title echoes Dante's dark wood as much as Eliot's poem the world of *The Inferno*, with the important difference that only in Eliot's work does the historical voice offer any promise of normative meaning.

What Eliot does and does not say helped to seal the fate of *Nightwood* for many years. Eliot's resistance to the novel's relationship to the material of his own poem may be covertly acknowledged in his comment that readers trained to poetry are the only proper readers of Barnes's novel, but that advice helped to label Barnes's book as one of interest to writers only—a label that stuck for at least 40 years. Eliot's constricted praise may well have risen from a recognition that *Nightwood*, although working with the same cultural materials, was a more radically experimental work than *The Waste Land*—which it unquestionably is. For all of *Nightwood*'s shared signatures with the avant-garde of its own time, it had, like much of Gertrude Stein's work, to wait for a period that could provide the comprehension it deserves.

For *Nightwood* demands, in a way that *The Waste Land* does not, a reading against the dominant text of binary oppositions by which the Western world inscribes itself. It is a novel that rages against the imprisoning structures of the language and narratives of the "day," which create a history built on the oppositions of night/day, past/present, reason/madness, "normal"/"abnormal," truth/falsehood, gender, and origins (both historical and textual). It is a book that relentlessly undermines grounds for categorization. The ideal and the real, the beautiful and the ugly, subject and object become irrelevant distinctions; even the language of the novel works to slip the acculturated binary assumptions of signifier and signified, and the nature of narrative itself is destabilized as traditional categories are emptied of meaning. The difficulties of confronting the totality of the experimental work called *Nightwood* must have been severe for the man who wrote "Tradition and the Individual Talent," and to argue that to fail to accept the novel's characters is to risk the "inveterate sin of pride" is to raise one more of the false trails that has kept subsequent readers from seeing the work in its totality. Monique Wittig speculates, correctly I think, that "Djuna Barnes dreaded that the lesbians should make her *their* writer, and that by doing this they should reduce her work to one dimension" (66).

As a novel, *Nightwood* asks with total commitment, how do we live outside the comfortable-because-known prison of "enlightenment" of the "day"? What narratives do we make when we acknowledge that their making is their sole existence, that there is no historical reality to validate them by? And finally, in what form can the novel exist when it destabilizes the traditional idea of narrative? For Barnes these are questions that can only be answered by a novel that proclaims itself by its process and by its refusal to rely on the old narrative assumptions of plot and character developed in servitude to a fixed way of reading and inscribing reality. To question traditional assumptions demands the abandonment of the fictions that both create and confirm them and a total reorientation toward the nature of narrative itself. Looking squarely at the radical scope of Barnes's novel sheds some light on Eliot's evasive, resistant introduction. Although *The Waste Land* predictably became the exhibition piece for the New Critics, a conspiracy of critical silence became Barnes's fate, and it is a telling irony that postmodern critics have to labor to rescue Eliot's poem from the prisoning binary readings of the New Criticism, whereas *Nightwood* offers itself to readers in the last quarter of the century without the weight of "enlightened" history to which the text refuses to bow down.

Even recent critics like Shari Benstock, who, in *Women of the Left Bank*, offers a feminist reading that understands the difficulty of female narrative in a male-constituted world, tend to read the novel in both the cultural and obligatory countercultural terms of Barnes's lesbianism and her biographical misfortunes in love. Benstock is right when she says what is culturally self-evident, that the "perversion *Nightwood* exposes is not the depravity of homosexuality, the horrors of transsexuality, or the ugliness of woman's hidden nature, but the tragic effect of woman's estrangement from her own self" (263); yet the very terms of her discourse—perversion, depravity, horrors, ugliness, estrangement—perpetuate the notions of their culturally created opposites. What may have been true about Barnes's own life is not necessarily true of the novel, which gives the lie through its narrative form to the idea that any language claims or cultural visions, patriarchal or other, can provide a grounding for "truth" or "knowledge." The claims of *Nightwood*'s narrative are too radical to admit meaning to such a reading. For this reason it is important to pay attention to the often neglected first chapter of the novel.

Barnes "opens" her novel with a mock-creation narrative, embedded in a larger narrative about the decline of Western Europe, invoking the labor of pretentious centuries that brings forth Felix, the wandering Jew of this work, who, mocked by his own name, is forever un-Felix, since his culturally inscribed goal is to find something to bow down to, the metaphysical homeland promised him by the enslaving idea of a continuous and linear historical past. The story of his birth is, in the opening paragraph of the novel, the story of his mother's death, for she gives birth, under the bifurcated wings of the Hapsburg crest, "seven days after her physician predicted that she would be taken" (1). In the biblically allotted time for making worlds, she dies toward Felix's creation, whose inheritance from his father, the Jew who has married his Valkyrie, is a phony coat of arms and two portraits of his grandparents, which turn out to be "reproductions of two intrepid and ancient actors" (7)—a version of reality neither more nor less useful for the world of the novel than any other construction of reality.

The reader learns more in detailed objective ("historical") terms about Felix's parents—the father who dies before his birth and the Austrian woman who lives seven days toward death—than about anyone else in the novel, an anti-introduction that concludes: "At this point [the acquisition of the phony ancestral portraits] exact history stopped for Felix who, thirty years later, turned up in the world with these facts, the two portraits and nothing more" (7). At this point the "present" of *Nightwood* begins for the reader who, like Felix, the wandering Jew, is abandoned by a creation narrative that gives the lie to itself, that offers only an untrustworthy grounding to hope for narrative stability. The labor of centuries has given us an un-baron seeking his nonexistent barony, clutching at the tatters of undifferentiated nobility, pomp, and pagentry. The price of Felix's obsession is the self, and he is a man so uninhabited by self that "three or more persons would swear to having seen him the week before in three different countries simultaneously" (7). His desperate desire for historical order attaches him finally to "the pagentry of the circus and the theatre," where at last he finds "a Princess Nadja, a Baron von Tink, a Principessa Stasera y Stasero, a King Buffo and a Duchess of Broadback" (11), who pander to the need for performed order in a world of flux in the same way that traditional fiction depends on characters who are fixed and fully determined in their roles so that the reader may track the "changes" they may undergo within narrative progression. Felix is willing to settle for whatever promises him a narrative order, totally unaware that, in this unconventional novel, he is one of the "empty" characters, who foolishly waits to be made full by an idealized external content, which *Nightwood* denies.

Trust in historical progression and in narrative as a means to a serviceable end has undergone its initial destabilization by the time Felix enters the "circus" present of the novel, and it is appropriate that at this point Matthew O'Connor, the doctor who is not a doctor, is introduced at a party given by a Count Altamonte, a nobleman who is probably not a nobleman. The party promises an evening's entertainment of living statues, which the count, who suspects he has "come upon his last erection," adores. The party does not take place; it is another of the promises of Barnes's narration that is canceled out. A pattern of desire and deferral, absence not filled by presence, is, ironically, an essential ingredient of *Nightwood*'s rich narrative presence.

While the guests wait for their host, O'Connor fills up absence with endless stories: "stories that do not amount to much . . . [to man] merely because they befell him without distinction of office or title—that's what we call legend and it's the best a poor man may do with his fate; the other . . . we call history, the best the high and mighty can do with theirs" (15). Felix is deeply distressed by O'Connor's definition of religion as "story," which answers in "Gothic echoes" the confessional tale of the "knotty, tangled soul" and merely fulfills the recognizable end of all traditional narratives: "Mischief unravels and the fine high hand of Heaven proffers the skein again, combed and forgiven!" (21).

Felix has fled from O'Connor before the doctor "tells" the story of Felix himself ("damned from the waist up") by recounting the story of Mlle Basquette, "damned from the waist down, a girl without legs, built like a medieval abuse" (26). Although this is one of O'Connor's many stories in which its author (not interested in unraveling the skein of narrative) seems to respond to the subject at hand by aiming in the opposite direction, it carries for the reader echoes of Felix's ancestral home with its halls "peopled with Roman fragments, white and disassociated; a runner's leg, the chilly half-turned head of a matron stricken at the bosom" (5), for Barnes's own narrative constantly calls attention to itself as narrative, validating its own existence as "story" at the same time that it destabilizes, in almost every case, the explanatory power of narrative based on the notion of historical origins. There are, for this novel, no fragments that can be shored up against our ruin.

Joseph Frank, in *The Widening Gyre*, the first serious attempt to come to terms with *Nightwood* as a radically experimental text, calls attention to this kind of "reflexive reference" as the method for approaching the novel that will solve the "mystery" of its form, a mystery that cannot be attacked by "approaching the book, as most of its readers have done, in terms of a coherent temporal pattern of narrative" (30). Although Frank's instincts about the radical nature of Barnes's narrative are sound, he seeks to solve the mystery of her experimental prose by substituting the concept of spatial form for linear narrative, a reading he comes to through Lessing and the examples of Eliot and Pound. As Alan Singer points out in his chapter on *Nightwood* in *A Metaphorics of Fiction*, although Frank understands that *Nightwood* is difficult because it abandons "the time continuum of the nineteenth-century plot paradigm," the new esthetic Frank provides only renames the problem without sufficiently accounting for the origin of the problem (48).

The substitution of spatial form for linear narrative cannot bring Frank to useful conclusions about the nature of Barnes's text. That Frank has failed to read the real intention of the first crucial chapter, "Bow Down" (which Barnes used as the working title of the novel), is made clear as he proceeds with a reading that works to reduce the whole to the story of Robin Vote and the devastating effects that follow for those who try to inscribe their own desires on her apparently blank tablet of self. Skipping to the emergence of Robin Vote and the extrapolation of conventional narrative that can be made from the "action" that follows results in a model of reading that necessarily undermines the radical integrity of the whole. The novel that Frank reads is not *Nightwood* but something that might be entitled *The Short Unhappy Life of Robin Vote and Her Lovers*.

After explaining that in *Nightwood*, "as in the work of Braque, the Fauves or the Cubists, the naturalistic principle has lost its dominance" and that "the question of the relation of this vision to an extra-artistic 'objective' world has ceased to have any fundamental importance" (28), Frank urges a narrative coherence not unlike those critical readings of Faulkner that center on Caddy Compson or Addy Bundren as "absent" characters, forgetting that the obsessions of the other characters can make equally blind the critic who prioritizes those obsessions at the expense of the language and narrative by which *they* are created. Frank's actual discussion of *Nightwood* betrays the esthetic he espouses and trivializes rather than frees the reader's sense of Barnes's narrative. Frank's problem begins in his idea that narrative must be expressed by the old notion of a *reduction* of the whole to something like the printed line of a map, which can show the journey separate from the experience of the journey itself. *Nightwood*, Frank has told us, resists such a reduction, but because Frank's ideas about narrative have not been rethought in a sufficiently radical way, he still needs to reduce Barnes's novel and in the process to destroy its narrative locus, which resides solely in the process of its telling.

Frank's limitations are evident when he takes Matthew O'Connor to task for telling Nora " 'I have a narrative, but you will be hard put to find it' " (32). "Strictly speaking," the narrative moralist in Frank admonishes, "the doctor is wrong—he has a static situation, not a narrative . . ." (32). In spite of the courage Frank has displayed in trying to find an adequate way of reading *Nightwood*, he fails to recall that Barnes deals with stasis a number of times in the novel but never in relation to the doctor. In the first chapter there are the (absent) living statues of the lofty count whose probably assumed name means "high mountain," the poseur who puts himself above the flux. The concern with stasis runs throughout the novel, but Barnes examines the idea of stasis most consistently in writing out the relationship of Jenny Petherbridge and Robin. Jenny is "the squatter," who appropriates the objects of other people's feelings and the secondhand expressions of their lives much as Felix, also identified with statues and stasis, seizes every possible remnant of a lost tradition. On one occasion, Jenny and Robin become living statues, a double shadow to the actual statue in Nora's garden. And, again, shortly after the garden scene, in a passage that sounds a good deal like Faulkner, thinking of Keats's urn: "thus they presented the two halves of a movement that had, as in sculpture, the beauty and the absurdity of a desire that is in flower but that can have no burgeoning . . . ; they were like Greek runners, with lifted feet . . . eternally separated, in a cataleptic frozen gesture of abandon" (69). The static scene in the garden brings Nora to her first felt experience of evil, her first moment of passing judgment on the world—a moment unlike any other in the book—and Barnes makes it clear that stasis marks the absence of authentic feeling.

When Felix tells O'Connor that Robin, whom he never really knew, remains to him only as an image—"but that is not the same thing. An image is a stop the mind makes between uncertainties" (111)—he, aside from sounding for us like Robert Frost, unwittingly elucidates Barnes's persistent metaphoric elaborations in the novel, which underwrite and become a part of her general narrative practice. Alan Singer's exhaustive and insightful examination of Barnes's use of tropes makes it unnecessary to repeat those observations here except to say that Barnes's refusal to rest in images, in the "stop the mind makes between uncertainties," confirms the narrative process and coherence of the novel. An image is also what Felix has of his family, "preserved," he says, "because I have it only from the memory of one single woman, my aunt; therefore it is single, clear and unalterable" (112). Precisely because it is single and unalterable it is static and inauthentic in the way the image must be for Barnes that claims in a single and unmediated act to capture the signified by the signifier.

Stasis clearly is a legitimate part of the narrative act in a theoretical sense, and for Frank to read O'Connor as static and therefore having no narrative is to be doubly wrong. One needs to recall O'Connor's narrative in "Bow Down" of the cow trembling as the bombs drop, her hide running with the water of terror, about which he says, "there are directions and speeds that no one has calculated, for believe it or not that cow had gone somewhere very fast that we didn't know of, and yet was still standing there" (23). The reader of *Nightwood* experiences O'Connor largely *as narrative*. The novel inscribes him by story and narrative act (i.e., not to be confused with Barnes or the implied narrator of the novel but as a creator within the larger narrative), whose stories often seem to exist for their own telling, glancing blows off the side of his real subjects but nonetheless inscribed within Barnes's narrative purpose. The attentive reader is surprised that the doctor is described as a "small" man at the beginning of the second chapter, "La Somnambule," because he has seemed as large as his language, as commanding as his fictions, as fertile as his imagination when first we see him in "Bow Down."

Felix, whose needs from the beginning have seemed closest to the expectations of the traditional reader, decides that "the doctor was a great liar, but a valuable liar. His fabrications seemed to be the framework of a forgotten but imposing plan . . ." (30). That Felix is no more an adequate guide than are his traditional readerly expectations should be clear. It is precisely that there is no plan and no framework but that imposed by human history and its institutions, the constructed "truths" that begin in desire and fear of extinction, that is the deepest knowledge and heaviest burden of O'Connor and his "lying" tales, which are "lies" only in the sense that they are tied to the necessities of a language, which both confirm and create the structures the "rationality" of the day has imposed.

Language, because it inscribes and is inscribed by convention, is a trap as reductive as narrative is for Joseph Frank, and one that Barnes seeks to escape in *Nightwood*. In "Watchman, What of the Night?" Doctor-Priest-Shaman O'Connor tells Nora, "we who are full to the gorge with misery should look well around, doubting everything seen, done, spoken, precisely because we have a word for it, and not its alchemy. . . . To think of the acorn it is necessary to become the tree. And the tree of night is the hardest tree to mount . . ." (83). Nora has come to ask O'Connor to tell her everything he knows of the night, and he can only by indirection truthfully tell of the night, which the keepers of rationality destroy for the sake of the day. "The very constitution of twilight is a fabulous reconstruction of fear. . . . Every day is thought upon and calculated, but the night is not premeditated. The Bible lies the one way, but the night-gown the other" (80). Nora finally asks the painful question many readers of *Nightwood* have asked of it: "How do you live at all if this wisdom of yours is not only the truth, but also the price?" (90).

For O'Connor, a surplus of language and of stories is the only way to neutralize the lie of adequacy and possession inherent in the act of narrative, and his answer is a long time coming as he follows the glancing blows of endless stories by way of saying that all answers are equally true and lying, until finally he says, "I tuck myself in at night, well content because I am my own charlatan" (96). The cost of his contentment is great because of the unreasonable demands for absolute truth put on him as a narrator, but like O'Connor, the reader knows that in *Nightwood* the only text that does not lie is narrative conscious of its own fictionality. This text as "valuable liar" does not pretend to traditional truth even within the narrative convention. The reader who comes wholly to *Nightwood* must be willing to pay the same price O'Connor has paid for his, at best, contingent wisdom. And for many readers the price has been unthinkable.

Even those readers for whom contingency and the elaborate alchemy of uncertainty have explanatory power are brought up short by the brief, final chapter, "The Possessed," which has often been seen as a coda, for lack of a better term, to the novel. It follows the silencing of Matthew's great voice with his final acceptance that there is, in the end, *"nothing, but wrath and weeping!"* (166) for the inhabitants of *Nightwood*. Only the narrator's voice is heard in "The Possessed," and this voice is straightforward and declarative, the same voice that opens the novel with the outrageous tale of Felix's birth and heritage. It is the narrator's dispassionate voice that follows Robin's circuitous path through the fields, past the responsive animals, to Nora's family chapel, where the novel ends in a tableau—a wordless scene of Nora and Robin, the latter seemingly bereft of human consciousness. Even Nora's dog, so threatened by Robin's release of the little that had held her human, gives up and lies down beside her weeping figure. In a novel that has been dominated by voices there remain only Robin and the dog, both making sounds that exist outside of (and perhaps, beyond) language. *"Wrath and weeping"* begin when the elaborating voice of contingency is silenced.

Barnes is not, however, in this last section, giving up on her narrative or speaking to its failure to sustain the "meaning" of its form as some critics have suggested.[2] She is, it seems to me, completing the novel in a way that makes clear that the narrative transaction has been between *Nightwood* and the reader. The probable failure of its characters to survive a world whose clear message is that "Thou shalt be one thing or another" within terms of established certainties is the final alchemy of a novel whose narrative has, by the very nature of its existence, demonstrated again and again that "Life is not to be told, call it as loud as you like, it will not tell itself" (129). All the conventional readings of experience, collective and individual, called history, philosophy, religion, can only create structures that substitute for a reading of life. They can only provide at best a rendering of agreements made by a collective desire for a realm of permanence and order, to which traditional narrative has become the handmaiden and language the pretender. Barnes, by questioning the narrative enterprise in the most radical way possible, has pushed her experiment further than all readers are willing to go, but those who can, those who do, no longer need a creation narrative, for all creation narratives predispose toward a desired end, one that limits and deceives. The indeterminant ending of *Nightwood* mocks the novel's already mocking beginning to remind the reader once again that, if the desire of *The Waste Land* is survival with meaning, the desire of Barnes's novel is freedom from the prison of meaning, and to accept this fact is to understand the radical experience of narrative that is *Nightwood*.

NOTES

1. Melvin Friedman in *Stream of Consciousness* makes it clear that he understands Barnes's importance as an experimental writer, but it is Joseph Frank, in his essay on spatial form, who makes the first sustained attempt to come to terms with the form of *Nightwood*, an inquiry that is continued in Louis F. Kannenstine's *The Art of Djuna Barnes* and, most successfully, in Alan Singer's *A Metaphorics of Fiction*. In 1976, Elizabeth Pochada can still begin her article, "Style's Hoax," by saying, "Judging by its modest six or so appearances in the *MLA Bibliography*, Djuna Barnes's *Nightwood* has meant a good deal less to literary critics than it has to some contemporary novelists" (179).

2. A number of critics read the collapse of O'Connor as the collapse of the novel or of Barnes's sense of the novel. Pochada is one: "Perhaps this is why 'The Possessed,' the section that follows 'Go Down, Matthew' and concludes the novel, seems an anticlimax. The novel has already jettisoned language; O'Connor has exited . . ." (188). Charles Baxter, after having asserted that the "doctor's fine talk and Djuna Barnes's fine writing conclusively and inevitably merge" (1187), sees the book reaching a crisis from which it cannot recover.

WORKS CITED

Barnes, Djuna. *Nightwood*. 1936. Introd. T. S. Eliot. New York: New Directions, 1961.

Baxter, Charles. "A Self-Consuming Light: *Nightwood* and the Crisis of Modernism." *Journal of Modern Literature* 3 (1974): 1175–87.

Benstock, Shari. *Women of the Left Bank: Paris, 1900–1940*. Austin: U of Texas P, 1986.

Eliot, T. S. *The Waste Land and Other Poems*. New York: Harcourt, 1958.

Frank, Joseph. *The Widening Gyre: Crisis and Mastery in Modern Literature*. New Brunswick: Rutgers UP, 1963.

Friedman, Melvin. *Stream of Consciousness: A Study in Literary Method*. New Haven: Yale UP, 1955.

Kannenstine, Louis F. *The Art of Djuna Barnes: Duality and Damnation*. New York: New York UP, 1977.

Pochada, Elizabeth. "Style's Hoax: A Reading of Djuna Barnes's *Nightwood*." *Twentieth Century Literature* 22 (1976): 179–91.

Singer, Alan. *A Metaphorics of Fiction*. Tallahassee: Florida UP, 1983.

Wittig, Monique. "The Point of View: Universal or Particular?" *Feminist Issues* 3 (1983): 62–69.

Jane Bowles: Experiment as Character

MILLICENT DILLON

IN THE mid-1950s, as Jane Bowles was trying to write a novel, *Out in the World*, the work kept fragmenting. To one friend and then another she would say, "I can't write—but I must write." Her husband, Paul, who had been a composer when she married him but was now a novelist, kept urging her to go on. "What's the use of my working? You're so much more successful than I," she would tell him. Then when he pressed her further, she would add, "I know you believe in me but leave me alone. I can't write—but I must write." Then he would say to her, "Just for the first page have the character come in, see this, do that." And she would answer, "No, that's your way, that's not my way. I've got to do it my way and my way is more difficult than yours."

Notebook after notebook of uncompleted fragments testify to her trying to find her way, starting, breaking off and beginning again, sometimes with almost the same words, sometimes with a new name for a character, or a new character, or a new set of characters. Each time it was as if she had to take a flying leap to get started. It would start, it would break off, and she would start again.

When I wrote the biography of Jane Bowles, I went into great detail about her anguish at not being able to go on, an anguish that she took to be a punishment for some nameless sin. The anguish went on for years and finally became punishment through the instrumentality of a stroke that afflicted her when she was forty. In fact, she never did complete another work after she began *Out in the World*.

Since the publication of the biography in 1981, I have begun to have other thoughts about what she felt to be her "block." I have come to look at those fragments in another way, as a mode of expression that was attempting to manifest itself through her but that she could not accept. The cast of her mind and feelings was expressing its intention in this form—through fragmentation and repetition—but she took the result to be only failure. If it is true that her work was psychically blocked, it is also true that had she been able to view this fragmentation as a valid expression of her own narrative vision, the fragmentation could have led her to further development—which may say something about the nature of "blocks." So that while I in no way discount Jane Bowles's own conviction of the continual disintegration of her capacity to work, I now see the history of her later writing as a flight from the form that she was being impelled toward by her very nature.

Certainly Jane Bowles was never a traditionalist. Her first novel, *Two Serious Ladies*, completed in 1942 when she was twenty-five, fits no category. It is made up of elements that are tragic and comic, yet it is neither a tragedy nor a comedy. It is the story of two women who meet at the beginning of the novel, go on their separate journeys, and then meet at the end. The first serious lady is Christina Goering (the combination of the last name of the infamous Nazi and the first name with its sacred allusion cannot have been fortuitous). She seeks salvation by making herself go out into the world and entering into relationships with bizarre, even menacing men. The second serious lady is Frieda Copperfield, married to a "handsome demanding man." Ostensibly passive, she is the one who is capable of making sudden and radical moves out of desperation as well as desire. Her most radical move is the intimate alliance she forms with the prostitute Pacifica.

This is a novel about sex and about religion and about being in the world and falling out of the world. The tone of the novel is startlingly innovative and difficult to pin down. The point of view is continually shifting and the tone itself suddenly shifts from wry humor to tragic vision—sometimes in a paragraph, sometimes within one sentence. The authorial voice is always at a distance from the reader, and it also holds itself at a distance from the characters. Reading, one feels that the relationship between oneself and the writer is constantly shifting. Yet one soon begins to know the sound of a Jane Bowles sentence, its odd jumps, the way in which it continuously confounds expectations, the way in which secrets are withheld and as suddenly revealed.

In the narrative, too, there are sudden shifts. Plot, instead of being an enveloping form, seems to be at the mercy of the tyrannical impulses of the women. Miss Goering and Mrs. Copperfield, each of whom is the shadow of the other, are mired in feminine quandaries: the desire for one's own destiny against the need to care for others, the desire for stability against the need for change, the desire for submission against the need for assertion, the love of men as against the love of women as against the love of self.

The rhythms of the book as a whole are odd, dense, and compacted. As the power of the authorial voice is not a stable one, power itself within the novel comes to be seen in a strange light. Power is imposed, shared, abdicated, inflated then deflated. A character at one instant is menacing, at the next instant pitiable. The alternations that take place from section to section, from paragraph to paragraph and even within sentences are amusing, startling, and disturbing. These alternations were also characteristic of Jane Bowles in her life, in her speech, in her gestures, in her tone of voice. The work was aptly suited to what she was at the time, a brilliant, provocative, engaging young woman, married to Paul and in the midst of a passionate love affair with Helvetia Perkins, a woman 17 years older than she.

That the novel itself has the quality of a work on a theme and variations may, in part, be due to the fact that Paul helped Jane with the structure considerably. It is now difficult for him to remember precisely what he contributed to it, but it is clear that he convinced Jane to separate a number of inchoate sections from the main story of the two women. Parts of these sections were published independently. (The story "A Guatemalan Idyll" was published in 1944 and "A Day in the Open" in 1945. A section relating to Senorita Cordoba, who was to have been the third serious lady, was published in the Spring 1985 issue of *The Threepenny Review*.) As it now stands, the novel is a remarkable organic whole, pulsating with its contained shifts. The ending is marked by a refusal of finality. Conclusion is not arrived at so much as it is dissolved or deflated.

> Miss Goering began to descend the stone steps. The long staircase seemed short to her, like a dream that is remembered long after it has been dreamed.
>
> She stood on the street and waited to be overcome with joy and relief. But soon she was aware of a new sadness within herself. Hope, she felt, had discarded a childish form forever.
>
> "Certainly I am nearer to becoming a saint," reflected Miss Goering, "but is it possible that a part of me hidden from my sight is piling sin upon sin as fast as Mrs. Copperfield?" This latter possibility Miss Goering thought to be of considerable interest but of no great importance. (201)

This is not an ending that opens out to a future. It is an ending that makes a statement, then discounts it, and even seems to discount ending itself. One's only recourse as a reader is the replaying of what has been.

"Camp Cataract," the novella that Jane completed in 1948, continues with many of the themes of *Two Serious Ladies*, though it is a much more densely focused and darker work. This is also a story of two women, but it is the story of the love and hate between them. Now, the journey that is made by one is the journey to get away from the other. Harriet and Sadie are two middle-aged sisters who have always lived with their family. Recently Harriet has had nervous "fits"—real or pretended, it is not clear. She has decided it is time to escape from Sadie and the rest of her family and has gone to Camp Cataract, a resort built around a waterfall, as her first step in going out into the world.

Sadie, whose one obsession in life is Harriet, cannot bear the separation. She decides that she will go to Camp Cataract to try to persuade Harriet to return home. When Sadie appears at the camp unexpectedly, Harriet is enraged and appalled, fearful that she will not be able to follow out her plan of escape.

Feeling alone and isolated and rejected, Sadie meets the reluctant Harriet for dinner, pulls her into a dense grove of trees with "almost brutal force" and begs Harriet to let her go out in the world with her.

> "let's you and me go out in the world . . . just the two of us." A second before covering her face to hide her shame, Sadie glimpsed Harriet's eyes, impossibly close to her own, their pupils pointed with a hatred such as she had never seen before.
>
> It seemed to Sadie that it was taking an eternity for her sister to leave. "Go away . . . go away . . . or I'll suffocate. . . ." She could not tell, however, whether she was thinking these words or speaking them aloud.
>
> At last she heard Harriet's footstep on the dry branches, as she started out of the clearing. Sadie listened, but although one step followed another, the cracking sound of the dry branches did not grow any fainter as Harriet penetrated farther into the grove. Sadie knew then that this agony she was suffering was itself the dreaded voyage into the world—the very voyage she had always feared Harriet would make. That she herself was making it instead of Harriet did not affect her certainty that this was it. (396)

But this certainty does not hold as ending. It is encapsulated in another ending, which shows this scene to have been only an imagined one. The real ending, an ending that Paul again helped Jane to achieve, comes with the death of Sadie when she jumps into the falls of Camp Cataract.

This story, which has brilliant comic moments alternating with the darknesses, shares many themes with *Two Serious Ladies*, in particular the desire for stability against the need to change and the desire to pursue one's own destiny against the need to care for others. In "Camp Cataract," however, the contrast between the two women is more fixed than in the novel. One is cared for, the other does the caring, one feels the need to change, the other wants things to stay as they are. Plot falls into a more conventional mode than in the novel. Yet within the individual paragraphs and sentences one finds the sudden turns and twists and the confounding of expectations so characteristic of Jane Bowles. That secretiveness still remains hidden at the core of the work is apparent in the description of Sadie as she realizes that she is going to make the trip to Camp Cataract:

> She often made important decisions this way, as if some prearranged plot were being suddenly revealed to her, a plot which had immediately to be concealed from the eyes of others, because for Sadie, if there was any problem implicit in making a decision, it lay, not in the difficulty of choosing, but in the concealment of her choice. To her, secrecy was the real absolution from guilt. . . . (365)

"Camp Cataract" is, I believe, a work that cuts closer to the bone than *Two Serious Ladies*. It risks more. The authorial voice allows itself to become closer to Sadie. In surrendering distance from the characters, it also surrenders distance from the readers. Sadie's dread of going out into the world and the agony of that voyage reflect a darkening in Jane Bowles's personality at the time she was writing. Her seven-year affair with Helvetia Perkins was coming to an end. She was, as she told Paul, different from the person she had been before she had started it. She was now, she said, far more uncertain. Yet the exploration of the rupture between two women in fictional form led her to a certainty of conviction, the necessity for the rupture, which was the equivalent of going out into the world. The fictional consequences of this rupture, the death of one of the women, was to have its own reverberations in Jane Bowles's life and in her later fiction.

By the 1950s when Jane was working on her new novel, she was indeed out in the world. She was in Tangier, where she had gone to follow Paul. She had fallen in love with Cherifa, an illiterate peasant woman whom Jane herself saw as sly and deceptive and possibly threatening. Jane's new life was fragmentary. Though she lived in Tangier, she traveled frequently, to Paris, to New York, to Spain—and she hated traveling. Her surroundings, her lover, the city of Tangier, the countryside of Morocco, were all new to her, inexplicable and ultimately secret from her. Her world was characterized by multiplicity of event and effect. She was partying, drinking, trying to write. She was no longer tied to Paul through the same daily intensity—he now had other interests. She was no longer tied to a single woman as she had been to Helvetia in an intense, suffocating relationship that needed to be ruptured. She was finishing her play *In the Summer House*, another work about doubleness, a work about the tie and rupture between a mother and a daughter. It is a play that has no ending (though she gave it an ending when it was performed on Broadway and elsewhere), or rather it is a play with multiple endings.

Out of this world of multiplicity and fragmentation into which she had thrown herself she struggled to construct a novel. She called it *Out in the*

World. We know, since she told Paul, what she wanted the work to be. It would be, she said, like a nineteenth-century novel. She had in mind something of the quality of Balzac, the creation of a world of sensory and realistic detail. But in addition, she wanted each of her characters to represent an abstraction, almost in the sense of a morality play.

Out in the World starts with two main characters: Emmy Moore, who is fat and in her mid-forties, has come to the Hotel Henry in a little town in New England to be alone and to write. Andrew McLain is a soldier in his early twenties who falls in love with another soldier. But the novel does not remain rooted in the experience of the two main characters. A multiplication and a fracturing take place, page after page, notebook after notebook. Emmy Moore goes out to a bar and meets other people. Their story takes over the novel's story. Jane breaks off. She begins again with Emmy Moore and with Andrew. Other new characters enter, now they too take over. Jane begins again, retelling in slightly different words. In the notebooks you can see her turning, twisting, feinting, holding off, telling, retracting, telling again. It is clear that she has given up the detached narrator of *Two Serious Ladies*. She wants to risk more, to go in deeper. But going in deeper takes her into experience that she doubts more and more until she must wonder if she was ever certain about anything.

She tries to grasp her own intention. She makes a note to herself (one of the few she ever makes on her writing): "This is a book about travesties and about two different generations. Emmy Moore represents the one and Andrew McLain the other."[1]

She tries to define Emmy Moore's travesty, trying to write and not being able to write, through a letter that Emmy Moore writes to her husband, Paul:

> I cannot simply live out my experiment here at the Hotel Henry without trying to justify or at least explain in letters my reasons for being here, and with fair regularity. You encouraged me to write whenever I felt I needed to clarify my thought. But you did tell me that I must not feel the need to justify my actions. However, I *do* feel the need to justify my actions, and I am certain that until the prayed-for metamorphosis has occurred I shall go on feeling just this need. Oh, how well I know that you would interrupt me at this point and warn me against expecting too much. So I shall say in lieu of metamorphosis, the prayed-for improvement. But until then I must justify myself each day. On some days the need to write lodges itself in my throat like a cry that must be uttered. . . .[2]

But Emmy Moore cannot go on. She stops writing, she pours herself a drink, she mutters to herself that she has not clarified or justified enough.

Now Jane tries to explore Andrew McLain's travesty through an examination of his experience of childhood:

> Looking back on those early days he realized that he must have seemed nothing like the others; he did not allow himself any close friends or companions. He was fearful that too much proximity would reveal the difference he was concealing from them. . . . His painstaking travesty had indeed lent to his face a look of flushed headiness that rendered him suspect to his companions though he had certainly not been aware of this; his eyes too had a dangerous sparkle. Very rapidly the lie changed until it was not his family that he was concealing any longer but a private monster whose shape was not even visible to himself. Like other odd children he was in the end simply concealing an oddness.[3]

Andrew, like Emmy Moore, falls into silence, one that burns his throat like sand. Yet Jane forces herself to go on writing, circling around what she does and does not know, embarking upon multiple tellings, new stories and new retractions. What she doubts most of all is the form her experience is taking. She is unable to hold on to a belief in that form or in the substance of what is evolving. Everything is breaking into pieces, an experience terrible for anyone, but for Jane Bowles one with a particular predictive meaning.

Toward the end of *Two Serious Ladies*, Mrs. Copperfield acknowledges that this is what has happened to her: " 'True enough,' said Mrs. Copperfield, bringing her fist down on the table and looking very mean. 'I *have* gone to pieces, which is a thing I've wanted to do for years. I know I am as guilty as I can be, but I have my happiness, which I guard like a wolf . . .' " (197).

But Mrs. Copperfield's going to pieces, the disintegration within her of moral choice, is counterbalanced in the novel and thereby controlled through the character of Miss Goering and through the formal aspects of their duality. There is no such counterbalance in *Out in the World*. Contained tension has given way to fragmentation. Plot begins to go wild. The willingness to go further and further into the characters without the safety of distancing ends in disorder. At the same time, the need to justify oneself becomes more and more insistent. And the only justification Jane Bowles can find is her own oddity, a judgment she pronounces upon herself.

So *Out in the World* was never finished. All of its cries were never uttered. But enough, nevertheless, was written to tell us what was at stake. Reading, almost 40 years later, one does not have to make the judgments of oddity Jane Bowles pronounced upon herself. One can value the individual fragments and respect the form that was trying to appear. The world has, after all, changed. We have grown more able to bear our own experiments and others'. We are privileged to entertain new possibilities. We no longer have to discount their importance.

NOTES

1. From a notebook in the Humanities Research Center at the University of Texas at Austin. Quoted in *A Little Original Sin* (215).
2. From a notebook in the Humanities Research Center. Quoted in *Out in the World* (74).
3. From a notebook in the Humanities Research Center. Quoted in *A Little Original Sin* (194).

WORKS CITED

Bowles, Jane. "Camp Cataract." *My Sister's Hand in Mine*. 359–401.
———. *In the Summer House*. 1954. *My Sister's Hand in Mine*. 203–95.
———. *My Sister's Hand in Mine: The Collected Works of Jane Bowles*. 1966. Expanded ed. Introd. Truman Capote. New York: Ecco, 1978.
———. *Two Serious Ladies*. 1943. *My Sister's Hand in Mine*. 1–201.
Dillon, Millicent. *A Little Original Sin: The Life and Work of Jane Bowles*. New York: Holt, 1981.
———, ed. *Out in the World: The Selected Letters of Jane Bowles: 1935–1970*. Santa Barbara: Black Sparrow, 1985.

H.D.'s Fiction: Convolutions
to Clarity

─────

LINDA W. WAGNER-MARTIN

HILDA Doolittle's reputation as a writer was first based on her brief image-centered lyrics. Ezra Pound had named the Imagist movement in 1913 when he sent some of H.D.'s early poetry to Harriet Monroe at *Poetry*, signing the author's name "H.D., Imagiste." Monroe accepted the poems. Pound edited several "Imagist anthologies," and these were followed by several more, which Amy Lowell edited when Pound moved on to Vorticism and the Continent. Faced with what appeared to be a permanent reputation as an Imagist poet, H.D. began writing more and more prose. She explored its possibilities in fiction, film criticism, journals, and letters. Her engagement to Pound, when both lived in Pennsylvania, had introduced her to the literary fashions that were to sweep London and Paris a decade later. Typical of the spirit of modernist innovation, caught so well in Pound's maxim "Make it new," H.D.'s writing set the tone for much prose of the 1920s.

H.D., however, was never a follower of trends.[1] She was much less dependent on Pound (and, later, on John Cournos, D. H. Lawrence, and Richard Aldington, whom she married) than her biography suggests. Once she had become a writer, she was intent on finding her own voice, her own form; and she chose as friends and acquaintances the avant-garde of Europe: Ivy Compton-Burnett, Dorothy Richardson, Viola Hunt, Elizabeth Bowen, Djuna Barnes, Robert McAlmon, D. H. Lawrence, the Sitwells, May Sinclair, Gertrude Stein, Kenneth Macpherson, Virginia Woolf (and William Carlos Williams and Marianne Moore, whom she had known in Pennsylvania). She read James Joyce and Robert Graves; she explored mythic and psychoanalytical approaches to literature; and in 1933 and 1934, she studied with Freud in analysis. She was by nature an innovator, and she was willing to take the range of chances that being innovative demanded.

She became expert in writing prose that sometimes resembled automatic writing, so fully did it draw on subconscious resources as well as on conscious ones. She was one of the earliest of America's modern writers to believe in organic form, in allowing the writing to express the center of the writer's psyche. Like layers of an onion, the various selves of the writer—each with personality intact—needed to fall away, exposing the nugget of self at the core. H.D. was able to achieve that sense of self in her art early, and through it, to find both method and theme. As Carl Jung was to write, "Image and meaning are identical; and as the first takes shape, so the latter becomes clear. Actually, the pattern needs no interpretation: it portrays its own meaning" (*Collected Works* 8, 402).

Because she was so surrounded by the truly experimental, so close to people such as Pound, Woolf, Lawrence, and Edith Sitwell, whose art was radical and distinctive, writing the fiction she chose was a relatively unselfconscious process. H.D. was only writing what she thought was interesting. Like the work of her other modernist friends, her fiction centered on character instead of plot, and it developed character through interior processes. It often showed as epiphanic the seemingly inconsequential happenings of daily life. Oblique and indirect, H.D.'s characterization depends for much of its effect on wordplay. The reader knows a great deal about the character of Hermione in the 1927 novel of that name, for example, because she is early identified with trees, symbol of matriarchal power as well as religion, the Tree of Life, fruition, and the "sylvania" of her home state. Yet when H.D. introduces the symbol of the tree, its positive connotation gradually shifts to negative as Hermione remembers her failure in a college mathematics course:

> The woods parted to show a space of lawn, running level with branches that, in early summer, were white with flower. Dogwood blossom. Pennsylvania. Names are in people, people are in names. Sylvania. I was born here. People ought to think before they call a place Sylvania.
>
> Pennsylvania. I am part of Sylvania. Trees. Trees. Trees. Dogwood, liriodendron with its green-yellow tulip blossoms. Trees are in people. People are in trees. Pennsylvania.
>
> Pennsylvania had her. She would never get away from Pennsylvania. She knew, standing now frozen on the woodpath, that she would never get away from Pennsylvania. Pennsylvania whirled round her in cones of concentric colour, cones . . . concentric . . . conic sections was the final test she failed in. Conic sections would whirl forever round her for she had grappled with the biological definition, transferred to mathematics, found the whole thing untenable. . . . (*HERmione* 5–6)

Omnipresent in Hermione's memory is her failure in math. Her father and brother are both scientists; her recognition was to come from them, through her participation in their world. Now she could no longer hope to enter that world, and she saw herself as useless. She also feared insanity (what was wrong with her that she could not learn this material?) and, perhaps worse, being unmarried. What could a young woman do? At the threshold of adult life, Hermione finds her ambition stifled, her resources blocked. It was a common enough story for women early in the twentieth century, but as H.D. portrayed Hermione's anguish, it is more real than fiction.

Fascinated with the effects she could achieve in prose, H.D. explored the intimate "moments of being" in various characters' lives. Exploration by its nature must be indirect. It begins in one direction, branches toward another, changes paths, burrows under or over or around obstacles. Or, as Perdita, H.D.'s child, remembers her mother saying, "Evolving. Searching. My past, the past, the past that never was . . . it's always eluding me. I think I've found it, and I find it's wrong. But the wrong way can be illuminating too, so it often points out the right way—ultimately. The idea *behind* the idea is the one I'm really reaching for" (*Hedylus* 145). Such "narrative" becomes more lyric than tale, and the progress of such a story can be described better as penetration to layers of understanding than as movement in some forward direction. H.D. chose the image of a convoluted seashell to represent her pattern of narrative. As she wrote years later, "I do not want to become involved in the strictly historical sequence" (*Tribute* 14).

At the heart of each of H.D.'s fictions lies an image (a detail, a scene, or a refrain) used with cinematic impact. She wrote essays on film for Kenneth Macpherson's magazine *Close-Up*, and transferred some of her interest from film to fiction. In her 1926 novel *Palimpsest*, the refrain "feet—feet—feet—feet—feet" recurs often, reminding the reader of soldiers leaving for World War I. The novel, set in wartime London, recounts the death of the protagonist's marriage once her husband has gone to war, her older brother's death while fighting in France, her father's death from shock at the loss of his son, and her own daughter stillborn because of her personal anguish. These pathetic events in the protagonist's life are represented by—and recalled by—marching feet. A year later in *HERmione*, the effect of H.D.'s more varied repetitions is richer: each is used sparingly, but together they form a tapestry of related effects. The novel unfolds, with the reader's consciousness playing an integral part in the narration. Each image, symbol, and refrain becomes a new way in to the meaning at the center of narrative.

The effect of H.D.'s fiction is fragmentary as well as cyclic and image-based. In that respect, too, it is modern. Modernism as a whole resisted any sense of completeness. Most modern poems were brief and "open," their meaning resulting from patterns of separate images. Modern fictions were even less traditional, and plots with clearly marked rising and falling action belonged to history. In Hemingway's words, modern fiction was to be "suggestive" rather than didactic (*Playboy*, January 1963, 123). It was also to be elliptical, its omissions as much a part of meaning as text; and it nearly always opened with an important scene instead of with description or background. The reader was intended to have a sense of haste, of disjointedness—or at least of a logic of connection that was something other than cause-and-effect chronology.

Although H.D.'s novels were modern in their fragmented and cyclic structures, they were also cohesive. Their randomness was something more than arbitrary: it suggested the hesitancy of a mind determined to uncover important psychic events. In this, her novels fit the narrative patterns recently described by Rachel Blau DuPlessis in *Writing Beyond the Ending* as a "rescripting" of the usual novel form. Just as the conventional novel presents either heterosexual romance or death as a woman's reward or punishment, so the plot line will reinforce that pattern. When a writer emphasizes a subtext or a formerly repressed discourse, or chooses to end a fiction with an unexpected resolution, such deviation from the norm is significant. It is even subversive (Chs. 1, 2, 5). It is clear that H.D.'s seemingly "different" prose (though very like prose by Woolf, Richardson, and Stein) carries many implications about her sense of herself as both writer and woman.

As H.D. wrote in *Helen in Egypt* (1961), "She herself is the writing." This kind of bravado came late in her career, but she wrote throughout her life as if she did believe in her power to write what she felt was important, in ways that pleased her. She felt no embarrassment at returning to the events of her own life, emphasizing her relationship with Lawrence and Aldington in one text, her love for Frances Gregg in another, her longing for acceptance by both her parents throughout. The events of her narratives were repeated, but their treatment differed in each work. The extent of H.D.'s production in fiction—and its importance to her development as both writer and person—has been suggested by Susan Stanford Friedman: "her desire to develop a new 'H.D.' involved fiction to a greater extent than her critics imagined. She left in manuscript form three thinly disguised autobiographical novels about her relationships with Gregg, Pound, Aldington, Bryher, Lawrence, and others of the imagist and postwar circles. An unpublished historical novel, *Pilate's Wife*, was begun in 1924, completed in 1934, and served in her mind as an answer to Lawrence's *The Man Who Died* [the novella in which the character the priestess of Isis is supposedly based on H.D.]" (*Psyche Reborn* 6).

Another of DuPlessis's points relevant to H.D.'s work is that women writers often choose themes and subjects that are as subversive as their narrative structures: they tend to dwell on brother-sister bonding, same-sex relationships, and reparenting, instead of on heterosexual romance.

H.D.'s themes follow DuPlessis's pattern. *HERmione* might appear to be the story of H.D.'s engagement to Ezra Pound, but it is also the story of her breaking that engagement in order to love a woman friend. Perhaps more important, *HERmione* is the poignant story of the protagonist's desperate aloneness within her immediate family.

Rather than "romance," the theme of the novel is Hermione's angry isolation from her mother, who preferred husband and son to her daughter—her brilliant scientist father, and her brother Bertrand. Even though the work begins as a quest novel, it is that because Hermione is forced to question her identity because of unexpected changes in family relationships. "Her"[2] planned to go to college and join the scientific community shared by her father and brother. Instead she failed a mathematics course. She had thought she would go on being Bertrand's favorite, sharing Jane Austen with him. Instead he married the vapid Minnie, who usurped not only her brother but her parents as well. Her had thought she would eventually come into her mother's favor; instead she must contend with Minnie. When she becomes engaged to the unacceptable George Lowndes, she creates even more distance between her mother and herself; and once she breaks the engagement to George to have an affair with Fayne Rabb, that situation is even more reprehensible in society's view. The final plot event of *HERmione* is doubly ironic, however, because Rabb and Lowndes have formed their own alliance and Her is twice betrayed.

Not surprisingly, Her becomes ill. As H.D. wrote later in *Tribute to Freud* about the use of the breakdown (in her own life and in her fiction), "There are various ways of trying to escape the inevitable. You can go round and round in circles like the ants. . . . Or your psyche, your soul, can curl up and sleep like those white slugs" (31). In the fiction, the marvelous breakdown section begins: "It might have been February. It might have been August. Heat pulsed and burnt but the flowers were wrong. There were great king-carnations, maroon, the colour of paper on chocolate—that thick colour. . . . It might have been May with flowers drooping from a branch. Someone had sent white lilac. 'What month is it?' Someone said 'Sh-ssh' and she turned over on a pillow" (195). The 30-page monologue that follows the description of Her's mysterious illness rivals the better-known sections of Joyce's *Ulysses* or Faulkner's *The Sound and the Fury*. "Events" are shown to be the catalysts they are in the protagonist's consciousness, shown in their pristine and unexpected impact as well as in their shrouding of social convention. Lowndes is imaged as a literal wolf; Rabb is shown repeatedly in scenes of such passion that the two women slide off davenports in their physical transport. The effect of Her's sexual initiation, coupled with her various emotional bereavements, is shown to be plausible. The text convinces. Disjuncture, stream-of-consciousness narrative, associative transition: all work for powerful impact in *HERmione*.

Yet the novel does not end with Hermione's illness, but instead with her recovery. The conclusion of the novel is a coda-like layer of seemingly unconnected material, as Her walks alone across wintry fields, has tea with a neighbor whom she knows only slightly, and plans to go abroad with his family, using her trousseau money to escape from the Pennsylvania environs—complete with loving family and lovers—that have brought her only illness and grief. Although she returns from her walk to find Rabb waiting for her, the impression of the ending is that Hermione has decided to go to Europe alone, and that she is once more in control of her life.

Narrative shape also suggests an optimistic ending. The book begins with a fragmented litany of loss, expressed in childlike syntax:

> Her Gart went round in circles. "I am Her," she said to herself; she repeated, "Her, Her, Her." Her Gart tried to hold on to something; drowning she grasped, she caught at a smooth surface, her fingers slipped, she cried in her dementia, "I am Her, Her, Her." Her Gart had no word for her dementia, it was predictable by star, by star-sign, by year. . . . She could not see the way out of marsh and bog. She said, "I am Hermione Gart precisely." She said, "I am Hermione Gart," but Her Gart was not that. She was nebulous. . . . (3)

The repeated statement of identity does little to convince the reader; indeed, later in the text, Her cries to Lowndes, after their abortive sexual encounter,

> "It's funny with me. I'm so strong. I feel strong, so right. Nothing can ever hurt me. Then—" Humiliation choked Her. Tears choked and humiliated Her. And George had turned the lamp down a little as the flick and flare of the light had burnt against Her. Now she said "I'm too strong and I'm nothing and I'm frightened." She achieved a very ugly voice that blubbered unbecomingly from somewhere, saying it over and over like a prayer wheel. "I am frightened. I am the word Aum, I am Her. I am Her." Her blubbered in a child voice against the somewhat London shoulders of a George Lowndes, "I am—so—very—frightened." (175–76)

By the end of the text, however, the distorted and shortened sentences have lengthened and assumed a more comprehensive narrative direction:

> Thought drove Her forward like the avid pulse and beat of some motor in a bleached yacht. . . . Feet pulsed forward, drove Her homeward, her

feet were winged with the winged god's sandal. Everything will be right. I'll get the money they said they'd give me for my trousseau. I was really going to keep it for the nursing. The money *is* mine. Gran left it for my marriage . . . this will be my marriage. The thought sustained Her. (234)

Avoiding a digression that should be made here—to connect this important fiction with the patterns of breakdown and madness discussed so ably by Elaine Showalter, Smith-Rosenberg, and Gilbert and Gubar—I suggest that in this narrative, structure and theme reinforce each other, conveying dramatically to the reader the subversion of each segment of the text. Because H.D.'s subject matter was so controversial (a defense of bisexuality, of woman's independence and psychic disruption from family as a way to health), the form of the fiction needed that same resilience of choice. *HERmione* includes comedy (the image of Fayne Rabb's mother in her practical rubber overshoes appearing at Lowndes's apartment in the early morning, looking for her wayward daughter; Lowndes jumping dramatically to announce to Her that she is a great poet); sexuality; ambivalence about love and friendship and family; pathos; dialogue that carries the weight of both character and plot; and sheer suspense in that the reader truly cares about the outcome of the protagonist.

H.D.'s narrative is successful partly because everything in the novel is reified through Hermione's mind (a tactic somewhat different from the self-consciousness of internal monologue). In *HERmione*, the reader believes in the mind of a character named Her. By writing a text that is so completely subjective, so located in Her's consciousness, H.D. convinces the reader that her character's impressions are the only validating "facts." In the vocabulary of DuPlessis's study, this approach leads to the valorization of what might have been—in another telling of the tale—only a "muted story."[3] Because Her's feeling of being trapped in Pennsylvania in a static and preplanned life is central to her psychic breakdown and recovery, H.D. emphasizes that emotion from the beginning. The text, accordingly, ends with at least some suggestion that she does manage an escape, ironically through the use of dowry money, which—had it been spent in its intended way—would have trapped her even more completely. DuPlessis links the muted story with what she calls "subtle memories" and concludes:

What appears in these memoirs, as sometimes in the poetry, to be an infinite retardation of narrative telos is instead another kind of story, with the definition of what has finally "happened" never completed, always capable of modification, always doubling and questioning itself. These narrative tactics bring this muted female area into focus, as it slowly emerges into speech. (121)

DuPlessis also describes a characteristic shift in women's writing that illustrates the pervasiveness of the use of muted story. If many narrative patterns depend on Oedipal drama, suggesting the dominance of male-female relationships, the woman writer's emphasis on same-sex bonds is radical. In the case of the quest plot, for example, the emphasis in a woman's fiction may be on mother-child attachments, rather than on the child's relationship with the father (37). Throughout H.D.'s fiction—and extending to her last major poem, *Helen in Egypt*—her primary narrative focus is on the character of the protagonist's beautiful, alluring, and decidedly withdrawn mother. The protagonist's psychic health is intimately connected with the character of the mother. Susan Gubar sees this emphasis of H.D.'s as her defiant and intentional reversal of the male-encoded myths—both of theme and form—so prevalent in literature of her time. Because H.D. saw herself as "a woman writing about female confinement," she was forced to use disguising tactics in much of her fiction ("Echoing Spell" 201–02).

H.D.'s disguising tactics are less in evidence in *HERmione* than in any other of her fictions, and perhaps that explains why this novel was published only recently. In 1926, H.D.'s three-part *Palimpsest* appeared from Robert McAlmon's Contact Editions in Paris; in 1928 *Hedylus* was published by Basil Blackwell in London and Houghton Mifflin in Boston. Yet in 1927 she had written *HERmione*, a text that remained known only in manuscript until New Directions published it in 1981. The incisive clarity of the Her story must have jarred with H.D.'s concepts of literature, because in both *Palimpsest* and *Hedylus* the autobiographical elements are subordinated to the classic. Both novels are set in Rome, at least partly; both speak to the issue of disguise. In *Palimpsest*, the title names the revisionary process of narrative ("a parchment from which one writing has been erased to make room for another"), just as a key passage in the text explains its necessity:

> Behind the Botticelli, there was another Botticelli, behind London there was another London, behind Raymonde Ransome there was (odd and slightly crude but somehow "taking" nom-de-guerre) Ray Bart. There was Ray Bart always waiting as there was behind the autumn drift and dream-anodyne of mist, another London. A London of terror and unpremeditated beauty. A London of peril and of famine and of intolerable loveliness. (104)

Just as there are several Londons, so there are several women: Raymonde/Ray echoing Hermione/Her and Hilda Doolittle/H.D. Identity, like story, remains mysterious, fluid, evanescent. In *Hedylus*, the image of veiled or transformed reality shifts to become a question about that more literal "meaning" as the mother character muses about the birth of her name-sake son, Hedylus.

> "Climax and anticlimax. That is what life is. Things slide over things. I mean, it was like the Acropolis that day you left me. It seemed as if a perfect image of the Acropolis had been slipped across the old one, as if a thing of transparent ice, crystal, had been slipped over the old stone." (138)

The self-knowledge of the observer changes even fact, as Hedyle continues:

> "There comes a moment when life seems overlaid with immortality as a flower with pure dew; like a flower-bud sustained beneath water, held and nourished. So this super-life seems to descend sometimes, to lie across one's whole vision. It was so with Hedylus . . . she had come back to the beginning, a serpent biting its own tail." (138)

In H.D.'s 1928 text, the intentional confusion between the name of mother and son, Hedyle and Hedylus, mirrors the confusion in their relationship. Even to the mother, that relationship is unclear, vacillating as it does between negative and positive. What is more unclear is her role toward the child, and yet her sense of her own self-identity is not shaken. Few writers have made fiction from so puzzling an ambiguity as woman's identity as child, self, and mother. Like the circled serpent, the physical and psychological unity of these three roles creates—for a woman who is at once all three people—an ever-changing identity. And as H.D. admitted later, she did not pretend to give answers: "I could not get rid of the experience by writing about it. I had tried that" (*Tribute* 40).

If H.D.'s fiction seems difficult to comprehend, it may be partly because the themes she chooses to work with are inherently difficult. Society would prefer pat answers: of course, women love their children, remain true to original loves, deny feelings of homosexuality, never question their relationships with parents or siblings. The woman writer knows how fallacious most of those givens are, but to add the complexity of theme to the complexity of being a woman writer is almost overwhelming. Whether or not H.D. was immune to what Gilbert and Gubar call women's "anxiety of authorship," and it seems doubtful that any woman writer could be so immune, her early fiction shows clearly that she was attempting to be a modernist writer by using the mythic method. H.D. knew all too well the success of Joyce's *Ulysses* and T. S. Eliot's *The Waste Land*. But she had been so interested in myth herself for so long that finding tales from the classic world that would parallel her own circumstances was not difficult. In becoming a mythic writer, H.D. was following her own interests and inclinations, as well as following a major current in modernist literature.

In *Palimpsest*, the story of a woman friend's betrayal (the woman also a possible lover) appears in all three narratives that comprise the novel. The first, "Hipparchia," is set in Rome in 75 B.C.; the second in London in 1916. With a mastery that foreshadowed her control in *HERmione*, H.D. created the persona of the beguiling, betraying Mavis Landour in the second story, "Murex: War and Postwar London." Told from the perspective of Ray Bart, the betrayed lover, the tale coalesces with the "Hipparchia" love story as Bart convinces herself that she is, perhaps, not made for earthly love:

> Let it all go . . . to live in the real past, antiquity a blue flame appre-
> hended thought interlayers of confusing semi-transparent sensations of
> modern life that were only the shadows Plato saw from a cave and
> called life. Modern life Plato said (circa 500 B.C.) was like that. All
> Athens in its dying splendour had nothing to offer that was not simply
> a shadow seen from a dark cave. All Athens in its brilliant decadence.
> How much less had life now to offer? (168–69)

Ray Bart's concerns about herself and her place in life echo those of the historically distant Hedyle in the 1928 *Hedylus*.

Going beyond any predictable literary use of myth, H.D. posited the classic existence as a choice. Withdrawal from a contemporary world (and its many and sometimes contradictory expectations for women) is less negative than it might seem, so long as the withdrawal is also progress toward a life more fulfilling than the present one. For this reason, in the meshing of art and life that H.D. as writer was capable of, Norman Holland speaks of the all-too-obvious connections between H.D. and her use of myth as a process of trying to "respect the myth implicit in every human life" (*Poems* 57–58).

At its best, H.D.'s synthesis of myth and the immediate does not obscure but rather illuminates. In *HERmione*, for example, although the setting is the present time and place, many textual implications depend upon the reader's knowledge of the Itylus myth and of two Shakespeare plays, *The Winter's Tale* and *As You Like It*. Refrains from the Philomela story, the two sisters united against the betraying Tereus even to the murder of his child, Itylus, mark the narrative so long as Her believes in the great love possible between women. Once she finds herself betrayed by Rabb, the refrain is ironic, but still not without the image of the possible love women can know for each other. In the Philomela myth, woman's role as sister supersedes that of wife or mother. (H.D. quotes from Swinburne's "Atalanta in Calydon," which emphasizes the pain the sisters shared, and uses as refrain the line, "the world will end . . . when I forget.") In Greek mythology, Hermione is the daughter of Helen and later the wife of Orestes. In a life marked by anguish, she later appears as the wife of King Leontes in *The Winter's Tale* (sad tales for winter). Falsely accused of adultery by her husband, Hermione is banished from the kingdom for 16 years; her love and virtue, however, permeate the character of her child Perdita, and the climax of the play is the reunion of mother and daughter. The real-life parallels are clear in that H.D. named her only child Perdita. As her daughter wrote in the preface to *HERmione*, "The protagonist is a divided personality, Her and Hermione. Hermione of Greek mythology. . . . Also, most significantly to me, Shakespeare's misunderstood heroine of *The Winter's Tale*, mother of Perdita" (*HERmione* xi). Even *As You Like It*, with its gender confusion and mock marriages, shows the positive relationship between female cousins, and the warring relationship among brothers. All things are possible in the magical Forest of Arden, but H.D.'s ironic use of the refrain as Her and Lowndes trek to the forest for the purposes of lovemaking intensifies the sense of Her's dissatisfaction with him. His not being able to recognize trees becomes even more ominous in the context of Shakespeare's playful forest scenes.

The fabric of allusion and reference that H.D.'s narrative sets up and, tonally, comes to rely on is an important part of her formal narrative. Once again in the words of DuPlessis, H.D.'s intention becomes clear in her "everlasting exchange between tone and judgment" (8). In what she attempts with irony and myth, juxtaposed with ostensible story line, H.D. writes the complete narrative.

The novella *Nights*, written in the early 1930s under the pseudonym "John Helforth," is perhaps the best example of H.D.'s employing all narrative techniques for a subversive effect. Here, the observer-narrator of the "Prologue," which is the first part of the text, "tells" the story of the vibrant, questing Natalia Saunderson, who has taken her own life. As Helforth attempts to tell not only Natalia's story but that of various love triangles based on her passions, the irony of H.D.'s mode becomes clear. The remote and proper, uninvolved observer cannot come to terms with the story at all. He can never understand Saunderson's final act, skating purposefully out into the unfrozen center of the magical lake: "She drove two straight lines to infinity and she got her answer. . . . The finish was, as if it were, cut by diamond, on glass. The two lines ran straight out, two parallel lines—they met in a dark gash of the luminous ice-surface." As another failed woman, misunderstood by family and lovers alike, Saunderson moves bisexually through a veritable forest of relationships, and finally clears everything before her way with one defiant and successful act. Robbed of even the capacity to tell her own story (which is the second part of the novella, a sequence of separate "nights"), she becomes one more enigma, another woman who never succeeded, at least in the eyes of the supposedly omniscient narrator.

They are all too clear, H.D.'s stories of women reared to hope for heterosexual romance, and little else. Disappointed by even the most promising of men, her protagonists turn to women lovers; those, too, fail. What answer can a brilliant yet "failed" woman write to the social myths and traditional conflicts of the modern world? Only what H.D. did create: her own story, captured in her own myth, telling a tale neither sad nor comic but rather searching, wistful and yet forceful as she tried repeatedly to find ways to supplement the gnomic but extant body of women's knowledge.

It was never easy, being this kind of writer, but it was exciting. As she wrote in *Trilogy* (67), toward the end of her life:

> I know, I feel,
> the meaning that words hide;
>
> they are anagrams, cryptograms,
> little boxes, conditioned
>
> to hatch butterflies . . .

NOTES

1. See, for example, Shari Benstock's *Women of the Left Bank*; special issues of *Contemporary Literature* and *Iowa Review*; and *H.D.: Woman and Poet* edited by Michael King.
2. The distancing H.D. achieved by choosing a nickname that is objective and remote—not to mention difficult to read grammatically—ties in thematically. Her is accused of coldness by several people, and we wonder as well at the use to which the narrator/protagonist puts the nickname throughout the text.
3. Some sections of narrative seem less important than others. When an author reverses the expected emphasis, stressing the usually trivial parts "then the narrative is dominated by the muted line. . . . access to that 'trivial' part causes the transformation of the story by major readjustments of its effect and weight" (121).

WORKS CITED

Benstock, Shari. *Women of the Left Bank: Paris, 1900–1940.* Austin: U of Texas P, 1986.

Contemporary Literature (Special H.D. issue) 27 (Winter 1986).

H.D. (Hilda Doolittle). *Hedylus*. Redding Ridge, CT: Black Swan, 1980.

———. *Helen in Egypt*. New York: Grove, 1961.

———. *HERmione*. New York: New Directions, 1981.

———. *Nights*. 1935. New York: New Directions, 1986.

———. *Palimpsest*. 1926. Carbondale, IL: Southern Illinois UP, 1968.

———. *Tribute to Freud*. 1956. Boston: Godine, 1974.

———. *Trilogy*. New York: New Directions, 1973.

DuPlessis, Rachel Blau. *H.D.: The Career of That Struggle*. Bloomington: Indiana UP, 1986.

———. *Writing Beyond the Ending: Narrative Strategies of Twentieth-Century Women Writers*. Bloomington: Indiana UP, 1985.

DuPlessis, Rachel Blau, and Susan Stanford Friedman. " 'I Had Two Loves Separate': The Sexualities of H.D.'s *Her*." *Montemora* 8 (1981): 7–30.

Friedman, Susan Stanford. "Gender and Genre Anxiety: Elizabeth Barrett Browning and H.D. as Epic Poets." *Tulsa Studies* 5 (1986): 203–28.

———. *Psyche Reborn: The Emergence of H.D.* Bloomington: Indiana UP, 1981.

Gilbert, Sandra M., and Susan Gubar. *The Madwoman in the Attic: The Woman Writer and the Nineteenth-Century Literary Imagination*. New Haven: Yale UP, 1979.

Gubar, Susan. "The Echoing Spell of H.D.'s *Trilogy*." *Contemporary Literature* 19 (1978): 196–218.

Holland, Norman N. *Poems in Person: An Introduction to the Psychoanalysis of Literature*. New York: Norton, 1973.

Iowa Review (Special H.D. issue) 16 (1986).

Jung, C. G. *The Collected Works*. Trans. R.F.C. Hull. Princeton: Princeton UP, 1953–78, 8, para. 402.

King, Michael, ed. *H.D.: Woman and Poet*. Orono, ME: National Poetry Foundation, 1986.

Robinson, Janice S. *H.D.: The Life and Work of an American Poet*. Boston: Houghton, 1982.

Showalter, Elaine. *The Female Malady: Women, Madness, and English Culture 1830–1980*. New York: Pantheon, 1985.

Smith-Rosenberg, Carroll. *Disorderly Conduct*. New York: Knopf, 1985.

The Music of the Womb: Anaïs Nin's "Feminine" Writing

——

SHARON SPENCER

> The woman artist has to fuse creation and life in her own way, or in her own womb if you prefer. She has to create something different from man. Man created a world cut off from nature. Woman has to create within the mystery, storms, terrors, the infernos of sex, the battle against abstractions and art. She has to sever herself from the myth man creates, from being created by him, she has to struggle with her own cycles, storms, terrors which man does not understand. Woman wants to destroy aloneness, recover the original paradise. The art of woman must be born in the womb-cells of the mind. She must be the link between the synthetic products of man's mind and the elements.
>
> (*Diary, 1934–1939* 234)

THIS passage was written by Nin in 1937 when she was deeply involved in the process of articulating a philosophy of writing that would serve her specific needs as a woman writer. She described her unique approach to writing fiction in various ways: as "symphonic writing," as "the language of emotions," and as "the language of the womb." The phrase "music of the womb" unites the two most original—and most basic—characteristics of Anaïs Nin's body of fiction. Her writing is "musical" because it achieves its experiential impact through carefully constructed lyrical passages built up of textured, interrelated images; it is a "music of the womb" because it became (in the late 1930s) a consciously articulated expression of woman's experience, aspirations, and values. Nin wanted to endow words with flesh and blood, so to speak, to instill an inner dynamism, or *élan vital*, to demonstrate the value of sensitivity, empathy, compassion, eroticism, sensual pleasure and love of all kinds, as well as an appreciation of the arts. She believed that these qualities had been killed by many male writers' "cerebral" approach to fiction, their tendency to dissect and analyze (to "kill" their materials), and their puritanical judgmental attitudes, defensive postures arising—she believed—from a fear of yielding to feeling. When Nin set out to create an authentically "feminine" fiction, she conceived and initiated an ambitious project, the "continuous novel" *Cities of the Interior*. The five individual titles are *Ladders to Fire* (1946), *Children of the Albatross* (1947), *The Four-Chambered Heart* (1950), *A Spy in the House of Love* (1954), and *Seduction of the Minotaur* (1959).[1]

The "music of the womb" is radical in three distinct ways. First and most obvious, in the 1930s, 1940s, and 1950s Nin was unveiling and exploring themes that few women writers except Colette had taken on, tabooed subjects: love affairs between older women and younger men; single women's entanglements with married men; women's friendships with homosexual men; white women's attraction to black men; a woman's attempt to attain erotic self-expression in the absence of love or emotional attachment; father-daughter and brother-sister incest; motivations causing lesbianism. Technically as well, Nin's earliest published works were boldly experimental. Both *House of Incest* and *Winter of Artifice* were written while Nin was working out her ideas for the "music of the womb." For a time, beginning in 1933, she was working on both manuscripts simultaneously, but *Winter of Artifice* was not completed until 1939. In both books she abandoned realistic conventions of style, structure, plot, and characterization, choosing instead to create free, autonomous, and organic forms. Each book is unique; each has a distinctive conception and form. What unites these works, making them cohere as a unified *oeuvre* is the "music of the womb": their musicality (the lyrical and rhythmical organization of all literary units, ranging from the phrase to the chapter or episode) and their devoted excavation and articulation of woman's experience.[2] Although Nin has often been labeled a Surrealist, she is closer to the fundamental impulse of Expressionism; she did not want to portray appearances but *essences*, and her literary forms were dictated not by tradition, but by the special individuality of each work, by "inner necessity" (to borrow a phrase from Vassily Kandinsky).

Inspired by Rimbaud's *Une saison en enfer*, Nin wrote *House of Incest* to express woman's psychic suffering: "I felt obsessions and anxieties were just as cruel and painful, only no one had described them vividly, as vividly as physical tortures. I wanted to do in *House of Incest*, the counterpart to physical torture in the psychic world, in the psychological realm" (*Diary, 1931–1934* 265). A confession, *House of Incest* has an organic structure of seven parts that are set off from one another by calligraphs that resemble ancient runes; this design effectively enhances the overall air of torment and mystery. Throughout 72 pages densely filled with images, a nameless woman narrator broods obsessively on her state of dissociation, alienation, and emotional and sexual paralysis. She is attracted, on the one hand, to the irresponsible sensuality of a figure named

Sabina and, on the other, to a pathetic and sinister aristocrat called Jeanne, who is in love with her brother.

In this book the idea of incest is a controlling metaphor for all doomed, impossible loves, or for narcissistic self-love. The isolated and emotionally paralyzed narrator is split into parts, body separated from spirit, feeling from intelligence, love from desire. Jeanne is the narrator's guide on the perilous journey into the house of incest, a ghastly place of infertility and death. Powerful images piled on one another betray the energy of the frantic plunge: "The rooms were chained together by steps. . . . The windows gave out on a static sea, where immobile fishes had been glued to painted backgrounds. Everything had been made to stand still in the house of incest, because they all had such a fear of movement and warmth, such a fear that all love and all life should flow out of reach and be lost" (51–52). Typical of the many images of infertility is a white plaster forest, a "forest of decapitated trees, women carved out of bamboo, flesh slatted like that of slaves in joyless slavery, faces cut in two by the sculptor's knife, showing two sides forever separate, eternally two-faced . . ." (55). The book has a nightmarish intensity and a quality of suffocation. It is a nocturne: dark, foreboding, and also cruel.

Winter of Artifice is among Nin's finest novellas, both because of its unique mode of lyrical exposition—its technical distinction—and its sensitive, profound treatment of a perilous subject: incest between adults. Published in 1939, *Winter of Artifice* may well be the first work by a woman to probe deeply the nature of this attraction and its emotionally crippling bondage. After 20 years of separation, an adult daughter is reunited with her still youthful father. Naturally she experiences an almost irresistible pressure to hurl herself emotionally into the past to recapture the period of intimacy with him that she was denied at the appropriate age. (Like Nin's own father, the woman's father abandoned his family when she was a young girl.) Gradually, by accumulating intelligent insights into his character, the young woman withstands the threat to her adult autonomy that is contained in her desire to merge or to fuse with her seductive father. Her womanly way of "conquering" her vain father is to offer a form of mothering that this narcissistic man cannot bring himself to refuse. His strategy for continuing to withhold love from his daughter is to typecast her as an "Amazon," a woman who does not need men. As long as the daughter collaborates in this distorted perception of herself as self-sufficient, she tacitly permits her father to refuse any responsibility to love her. The only solution is to accept her father's inability to love anyone but himself and to relinquish the fantasy of obtaining anything from him except deceptive flattery. This accomplishment is, inevitably, the result of a long struggle during which the daughter strips away her father's masks, one after another, revealing a frightened, lonely, aging man.

An extremely sophisticated piece, *Winter of Artifice* resembles a musical composition more closely than Nin's other works. Its 64 pages are woven into 13 movements of unequal length whose theme is "Musique Ancienne," one woman's experience with the Electra complex. In the sixth—central—section, the novella rises to an emotional climax and crisis. The daughter allows herself to imagine total union with her father:

> Inside both their heads, as they sat there, he leaning against a pillow and she against the foot of the bed, there was a concert going on. . . . Two long spools of flutethreads interweaving between his past and hers, the strings of the violin constantly trembling like the strings inside their bodies, the nerves never still, the heavy poundings on the drum like the heavy pounding of sex, the throb of blood, the beat of desire which drowned all the vibrations, louder than any instrument. . . . (84–85)

This rhapsody is extended and buoyantly sustained, subsiding into a slower rhythm and more muted tone. The dangerous dance of father and daughter now becomes a solo performance for the daughter, who begins to glide away. In the seventh section she recalls having given a dance performance when she was sixteen during which she imagined that she saw her father in the audience, approving her performance. When she asks him to verify this, "He answered that not only was he not there but that if he had had the power he would have prevented her from dancing because he did not want his daughter on the stage" (99). Assured that her father wants to bind her with limitations, she tastes the foreknowledge of freedom. Regarding his "feminine-looking" foot, she fantasizes that it is really *her* foot, which he has stolen. This enables her to glimpse the truth that he wants to steal her mobility and freedom for himself. Literally, "tired of his ballet dancing" (113) (a traditional, formally patterned dance contrasted to her more modern, freer way of moving), she demands the return of her own foot, and with it she reclaims the capacity to run from him.

While working simultaneously on *House of Incest* and *Winter of Artifice*, Nin wrote:

> *It is the woman who has to speak.* And it is not only the Woman Anaïs who has to speak, but I who have to speak for many women. As I discover myself, I feel I am merely one of many, a symbol. I begin to understand June, Jeanne, and many others. George Sand, Georgette Leblanc, Eleonora Duse, women of yesterday and today. The mute

ones of the past, the inarticulate, who took refuge behind wordless intuitions . . . (*Diary, 1931–1934* 289)

In 1937 she articulated the characteristics of "womb oriented writing," thereby becoming the third woman writing in English (as far as I am aware) to have committed to paper the need for a feminine theory and practice of literature. Dorothy Richardson, of course, was the first, and Virginia Woolf the second.

In August 1937, a conversation with Henry Miller, Lawrence Durrell, and his wife, Nancy, provoked Nin to defend her subjective, lyrical, flowing fiction. Later, she reflected:

> Henry and Larry tried to lure me out of the womb. They call it objectivity.
> But what neither Larry nor Henry understands is that woman's creation, far from being like man's, must be exactly like her creation of children, that is it must come out of her own blood, englobed by her womb, nourished by her own milk. It must be a human creation, of flesh, it must be different from man's abstractions. (*Diary, 1934–1939* 235)

The writing of the womb must be alive: that is, natural, spontaneous, flowing (to use one of Nin's favorite words). It must have warmth, color, vibrancy, and it must convey a sense of movement (often Nin's characters are stuck, immobile, or paralyzed), the momentum of growth. Woman's literature (a literature of flesh and blood) must create syntheses; it must reconnect what has been fragmented by excessive intellectual analysis. Woman's creative works must be deep; they must trace expeditions into dangerous terrain. They must explore tabooed topics and forbidden relationships. Woman's art must be honest, even if the search for truth causes pain:

> Woman's role in creation should be parallel to her role in life. I don't mean the good earth. I mean the bad earth too, the demon, the instincts, the storms of nature. . . . Woman must not fabricate. She must descend into the real womb and expose its secrets and its labyrinths.
> . . . My work must be the closest to the life flow. I must install myself inside of the seed, growth, mysteries. I must prove the possibility of instantaneous, immediate, spontaneous art. My art must be like a miracle. Before it goes through the conduits of the brain and becomes an abstraction, a fiction, a lie. It must be for woman, more like a personified ancient ritual, where every spiritual thought was made visible, enacted, represented. (235)

Nin now conceived the multivolume "continuous novel," *Cities of the Interior*, a project that involved transforming the diary, or parts of it, into fiction. Characterized by a richly inventive feminine imagery (drawn from women's preoccupations and occupations like work, cooking, decorating a home, feelings about pregnancy, clothing and makeup)[3] and an organic spontaneous (thus unpredictable) structure, *Cities* takes as its theme the psychology of woman: "Theme of the development of woman in her own terms, not as an imitation of man. This will become in the end the predominant theme of the novel: the effort of woman to find her own psychology, and her own significance, in contradiction to man-made psychology and interpretation. Woman, finding her own language, and articulating her own feelings, discovering her own perceptions. Woman's role in the reconstruction of the world" (*Diary, 1944–1947* 25).

The originality of *Cities of the Interior* lies partly in its use of lyricism to convey character, situation, and action but even more definitively, in its radical concept of structure. It is a group of distinctly discreet but related volumes with individual titles, in Nin's words, "a continuous novel." The various women artist protagonists appear and reappear, now one and now another occupying the central position as "main character." The individual volumes can stand alone wholly without reference to the others, or they can be read as parts of an unfinished whole. The order of the component parts of the continuous novel does not affect the reader's comprehension of the whole. The volumes can be considered interchangeable. Nin achieved this by avoiding specific chronological references, which would have established a sequence, and by writing fluid open endings that provide links moving simultaneously forward and backward in time.

This relativistic concept of structure underscores Nin's fluid concept of personality. In her books, being is always dynamic, the focus always on the process of becoming. Therefore, the ever-developing and self-modifying structure of the "continuous novel" is the ideal enclosure, because it destroys the very possibility of closure. New "cities" can always be prefixed, inserted in the middle or added at the end. The shape of *Cities of the Interior* need not be imagined as final, because the characters possess never-ending transformational possibilities. The organic structure of *Cities of the Interior* makes it at once abstract and yet intensely personal. Because it explores the psyche of woman with unprecedented depth, the work can be considered theoretical, and because it creates memorable characters, demonstrating what Nin meant by stressing subjectivity as the means of attaining the more general, or universal level of experience. "Because I could identify with characters unlike myself, [I could] enter their vision of the universe and in essence achieve the truest objectivity of all,

which is to be able to see what the other sees, to feel what the other feels"
(*Novel* 68).

Of the five novels, *Seduction of the Minotaur* (1959) is the most fully
developed, the deepest in emotional range as well as the most technically
accomplished. This novel derives its leisurely organic structure from the
archetype of the journey; the several parts of the novel are journeys
within the larger journey. *Seduction* begins with Lillian's arrival in Golconda where the people, whose "religion was timelessness" (92) "exuded
a more ardent life" (14), and it ends with her "journey homeward" (95).
Golconda is Lillian's "territory of pleasure" (9). Escaping from her "in-
completely drowned marriage" with Larry (96), she is "maintained in a
net of music, suspended in a realm of festivities" (12). Between her arrival
and her "journey homeward," she reluctantly undertakes a perilous inner
journey. (Now we are in the "labyrinth" Nin mentioned when she expressed the need for women to confront dangers.)

Once a classical pianist, the Lillian of *Seduction of the Minotaur* has
exchanged traditional art for a more spontaneous one—jazz: "Classical
music could not contain her improvisations, her tempo, her vehemence"
(115). But "jazz was the music of the body . . . . It was the body's vibrations which rippled from the fingers. And the mystery of the withheld
theme known to the musicians alone was like the mystery of our secret
life" (18–19). Some of the novel's most brilliant passages approximate
the technique of improvisation. Perhaps the most striking is the initial
description of Golconda (a Mexican resort probably based on Acapulco):
"She had landed in the city of Golconda, where the sun painted everything with gold, the lining of her thoughts, the worn valises, the plain
beetles, Golconda of the golden age, the golden aster, the golden eagle,
the golden goose, the golden fleece, the golden robin, the goldenrod, the
goldenseal, the golden warbler, the golden wattles, the golden wedding,
and the gold fish, and the gold of pleasure, the goldstone, the gold thread,
the fool's gold" (6).[4]

The novel's major discovery (the goal of the dangerous journey) is the
minotaur in Lillian's own personal labyrinth (unconscious), and this
monster is none other than herself: "a reflection upon a mirror, a masked
woman, Lillian herself, the hidden masked part of herself unknown to
her, who had ruled her acts. She extended her hand toward this tyrant
who could no longer harm her" (111). (In contrast, Theseus murdered
the minotaur, and exploited and abandoned Ariadne.) Lillian discovers
that her belief in her own freedom is an illusion; still bound, she must
rediscover vital aspects of the "primitive." She must learn to dance to "the
music of the body" before summoning the emotional and spiritual power
to reignite her love of Larry through enlightened understanding. Before

she can be reconciled with Larry, she must seek and submit to the rite, to a *participation mystique.*

Lillian loves to walk around Golconda barefooted. But when she is dancing with Fred, he clumsily steps on her foot. Another man, Michael Lomax, tries to prevent her from dancing with the natives, but Lillian defies him. In one of several scenes depicting dancing, Lillian also defies Dr. Hernandez. Determined to touch the earth's "fiery core" (106), Lillian seeks fusion, not with any of the male characters but with Golconda itself. This is the essence of her betrayal of Larry, but it is an impersonal betrayal and its ultimate effect makes healing possible:

> A singer was chanting the Mexican plainsong, a lamentation on the woes of passion. Tequila ran freely, sharpened by lemon and salt on the tongue. The voices grew husky and the figures blurred. The naked feet trampled the dirt, and the bodies lost their identities and flowered into a single dance, moved by one beat. . . .
>
> Dr. Hernandez frowned and said: "Lillian, put your sandals on!" His tone was protective; she knew he could justify this as a grave medical counsel. But she felt fiercely rebellious at anyone who might put an end to this magnetic connection with others, with the earth, and with the dance, and with the messages of sensuality passing between them. (105–06)

Lillian has become strong enough to resist attempts to inhibit her, even in the guise of protectiveness. She exults: "The time was past when her body could be ravished . . . by visitations from the world of guilt" (107).

At its most exalted, music was for Nin, as for many European writers, a way of entering the transcendent, even the sublime realm of experience. While "music of the body" may represent a parallel to the élan vital described by Henri Bergson (the basic dynamism of life), more sophisticated musical expressions represent parallels to more complex and intricate modes of experience: The "rhythm of life" (breathing, walking, the heart beat, dancing) has its counterpoint, or counterpart, in a more spiritual music. This more intricate, more subtle music provides "the continuity . . . which prevents thoughts from arresting the flow of life" (24) as well as "a higher organization of experience" (84).

This "higher organization of experience" (transcendence, the forgiveness, the revitalized and renewed love Lillian feels for Larry at the novel's end) becomes accessible to her only after the ritual *participation mystique* has been consummated. Only then is it possible for her to leave the labyrinth, not by retracing Ariadne's thread, but by simply rising above the maze. Several transformations occur, enabling Lillian to soar at last. One such transformation (and it is crucial) is her temporary change of relationship to Larry. Becoming his mother instead of his wife, she re-*imagines* Larry, thus giving birth to him in a new, more complex form.

Finally, then, the most richly embroidered theme of "music of the womb" is the need for love, not only the power of maternal love, with its transformative powers, but also agape, the love of friends, which is the essence of Nin's fraternal vision of marriage, viewed more as lifelong friendship than as erotic coupling. All the themes that appear and reappear in Nin's writings are related to the principle of Eros, or relatedness, as well as to the need for human beings to nurture and, when necessary, to heal one another.

Having departed from the labyrinth by air (in a plane), Lillian becomes absorbed in a sustained meditation on her relationship with Larry; this occupies the duration of her "journey homeward," the novel's concluding section. Admitting that she has not listened carefully to Larry because "he did not employ the most obvious means of communication" (99), Lillian traces their relationship back to its origins and their personalities back to their respective childhoods. Earlier imagery of earth, water, and fire is replaced by celestial figurations. Painful childhood incidents caused Larry to "be flung into outer space" (134). Lillian knows that she must find a way to bring him back into human orbit. To do this, she envisions Larry as the moon, a symbol of feminine receptivity: "How slender was the form he offered to the world's vision, how slender a slice of his self, a thin sliver of an eighth of moon on certain nights. She was not deceived as to the dangers of another eclipse" (136).

Even though she is elated by her newly created vision of Larry, Lillian acknowledges the difficulty of maintaining this vision with consistency and fidelity. The novel presents marriage as a process in which the struggle to fuse or to create a union of two must be balanced by the need to maintain individual integrity or selfhood. For this, periods of separation are required (like Lillian's three-month stay in Golconda). Nin's concept involves an important duality; one always lives, she believes, in two cities at the same time (the conscious and the unconscious realms of being). Lillian recognizes that "the farther she traveled into unknown places, unfamiliar places, the more precisely she could find within herself a map showing only the cities of the interior" (80).

Seduction of the Minotaur concludes with one of Nin's most tender passages, reminding us that however exciting the daring act of exploration, the greatest challenge of all is to explore the most familiar territories, those that lie closest to home, the cities of the interior. It is only by descending in an attempt to learn the truth that we can rise again, to embrace those we have loved perhaps but have never loved well enough: "Such obsession with reaching the moon, because they had failed to reach

each other, each a solitary planet! In silence, in mystery, a human being was formed, was exploded, was struck by other passing bodies, was burned, was deserted. And then it was born in the molten love of the one who cared" (136).

The tenderness, solicitude, and acceptance of the human need to nurture and to be nurtured characterize Nin's last "novel" as strongly as *Seduction of the Minotaur*. If *Seduction* is the most mature, the most fully developed and richly detailed example of the "music of the womb," *Collages* (1964) may be her most original book. Less musical than visual, as its title indicates, *Collages* is a composition of 19 juxtaposed vignettes. There are no narrative passages, no transitions between vignettes, no plot. Unity and overall coherence are provided by the dominant presence of Renate, a painter, and by the recurrence of related themes in the vignettes. There are many settings and many "characters"; all are swiftly sketched in Nin's vibrant imagistic prose. Among them are Leontine, a buoyant black singer; Henri, a master chef; the deliriously mad actress Nina Gitana de la Primavera; Nobuko, who every day selected her kimono to harmonize with the weather; Varda, creator of exquisite airy collages of women; the betrayed wife of a French consul, who invents a new love for herself. Although all have been wounded in some way (Renate by her selfish lover Bruce), all are resourceful and imaginative; they have woven self-sustaining worlds of fantasy around themselves.

The situations depicted in the 19 vignettes are varied, but each demonstrates transformation achieved through imagination. All celebrate the vital role of creativity, whether it is the charm of playing "make-believe," the power of fantasy to invent new personalities and lives for oneself when reality becomes unbearable, or specific artistic creativity such as that represented by the book's artists: Renate, Leontine, Varda, and a writer named Judith Sands.

In a typical nurturing act, Renate rescues the neglected and bitter Judith Sands (easily recognizable as a portrait of Djuna Barnes) from her lonely garret-like hideout. In the book's witty final vignette, the name of Judith Sands is saved from the jaws of a self-destructing apparatus that "eats" the names of artists and writers before exploding and burning. Symbolically, Nin alludes to the continuity of a tradition of women writers and restores Djuna Barnes to her place in that tradition.

To look back at *House of Incest*—an expression of entrapment, isolation, fragmentation, and suffering—and then to look at *Collages*—with its light, airy, confident tone and frequent examples of mobility—is to see the trajectory of Nin's growth as woman and artist. Renate is assured and confident, entirely comfortable with her role as woman artist and with her many friendships; she is not at all dependent on her lover for her sense of value. When someone suggests that Varda make a portrait of Renate, he declines, explaining that she is *"femme toute faite."* He adds: "A woman artist makes her own patterns." Indeed, a definitively female narrative was Nin's ideal. It preceded by 40 years the theories of contemporary French writers, such as Annie Leclerc and Hélène Cixous, who argue the need for "writing the body," as Nin argued the need for writing the womb.[5]

NOTES

1. The first book-length study of Nin's writings appeared in 1968: Oliver Evans's *Anaïs Nin*. Since then, there have been a number of studies and collections, including those by Hinz, Zaller, Knapp, Scholar, and Spencer. Also see Benstock (which contains a discussion of *House of Incest*) and *Anaïs: An International Journal* (Los Angeles), an annual begun in 1983.

2. Thoroughly Latin, Nin had a personal perspective on the "Calvinist" approach to language: "Elaborate language, said the action novelist, was not necessary for our daily relationships. It was a luxury and an affectation we could dispense with. Simplifying it to basic English would lead to better communication. What it led to was an almost total atrophy of verbal expression. The Calvinist puritanism of speech weighed heavily also on color, rhythm, musicality of language which were equated with romanticism, baroque architecture and aristocracy" (*Novel* 94).

   Music was important to Nin: her mother was a singer, her father a pianist and composer, and her brother Joaquin Nin-Culmell is a composer. Nin herself experimented with a career as a dancer. Moreover, she was particularly sensitive to the musical qualities of the English language. For instance, she felt a strong affinity with jazz: "Poetic prose might be compared to jazz. Jazz does not work unless it swings. The beat must be constantly tugged and pushed across the familiar line of the four-four balance until the real rhythmic message is *felt more than heard*" (*Novel* 171).

3. Almost any page of Nin's fiction offers examples of her "feminine" imagery. When Lillian cooks, "the fruit was stabbed, assassinated, the lettuce was murdered with a machete. The flavoring was poured like hot lava and one expected the salad to wither, to shrivel instantly" (*Cities*, "Ladders" 4). Lillian's mode of dressing created "tumult in orange, red and yellow and green quarreling with each other. The rose devoured the orange, the green and blue devoured the purple. The sport jacket was irritated to be in company with the silk dress, the tailored coat at war with the embroidery" (5).

4. Gold is associated with the highest plane of existence in the symbolism of medieval alchemy, a process that became for Nin a convenient analogy for creative transformation in both art and life. Most of the images of Golconda are drawn from nature, from the world of birds, insects, flowers, and herbs. One striking exception is "golden wedding"; continuity in relationship, especially

marriage, is one of the novel's several interconnected problems. Another exception is "the gold thread," which suggests the thread that Ariadne gives Theseus to help him find his way out of the labyrinth. It is the sun that makes everything gold (the vibrancy of the light is a recurrent reference in *Seduction*). And Golconda itself suggests "gondola," which is a specific type of boat, a variation on the landlocked ship in the book's directive dream, described in the opening passage, expressing Lillian's psychological difficulty in terms of the dream of a landlocked boat. Consequently, the seemingly random associations of the passage are actually connected in ways that sustain and strengthen the novel's major themes.

5. Readers may wish to consult *New French Feminisms* edited by Marks and de Courtivron and *The Newly Born Woman* by Cixous and Clément. Also see Margret Andersen who connects the work of Nin and Annie Leclerc.

WORKS CITED

Andersen, Margret. "Critical Approaches to Anaïs Nin." *The Canadian Review of American Studies* 10 (1979): 255–65.

Benstock, Shari. *Women of the Left Bank: Paris, 1900–1940*. Austin: U of Texas P, 1986.

Cixous, Hélène, and Catherine Clément. *The Newly Born Woman (La jeune née)*. Trans. Betsy Wing. Minneapolis: U of Minnesota P, 1986.

Evans, Oliver. *Anaïs Nin*. Carbondale: Southern Illinois UP, 1968.

Hinz, Evelyn J. *The Mirror and the Garden: Realism and Reality in the Writings of Anaïs Nin*. Publications Comm. of Ohio U Libraries, 1971.

———, ed. *The World of Anaïs Nin: Critical and Cultural Perspectives*. Mosaic 11 (Oct. 1977).

Knapp, Bettina. *Anaïs Nin*. New York: Ungar, 1978.

Marks, Elaine, and Isabelle de Courtivron, eds. *New French Feminisms: An Anthology*. Amherst: U of Massachusetts P, 1980.

Nin, Anaïs. *Cities of the Interior (Ladders to Fire; Children of the Albatross; The Four-Chambered Heart; A Spy in the House of Love; Seduction of the Minotaur)*. 1959. Introd. Sharon Spencer. Chicago: Swallow, 1974.

———. *Collages*. Denver: Swallow, 1964.

———. *The Diary of Anaïs Nin, 1931–1934*. Ed. Gunther Stuhlmann. New York: Harcourt, 1966.

———. *The Diary of Anaïs Nin, 1934–1939*. Ed. Gunther Stuhlmann. New York: Harcourt, 1967.

———. *The Diary of Anaïs Nin, 1944–1947*. Ed. Gunther Stuhlmann. New York: Harcourt, 1971.

———. *House of Incest*. 1936. Denver: Swallow, 1958.

———. *The Novel of the Future*. 1968. Athens, OH: Ohio UP, 1985.

———. *Seduction of the Minotaur*. 1959. Chicago: Swallow, 1969.

———. *Winter of Artifice*. 1939. Denver: Swallow, 1948.

Scholar, Nancy. *Anaïs Nin*. Boston: Twayne, 1984.

Spencer, Sharon, ed. *Anaïs, Art and Artists*. Greenwood, FL: Penkevill, 1986.

————. *Collage of Dreams: The Writings of Anaïs Nin*. 1977. Expanded ed. New York: Harcourt, 1981.

Stuhlmann, Gunther, ed. *Anaïs: An International Journal*. Los Angeles.

Woolf, Virginia. *A Room of One's Own*. 1929. New York: Harcourt, 1963.

Zaller, Robert, ed. *A Casebook on Anaïs Nin*. New York: NAL, 1974.

THIRD GENERATION: AFTER 1960

"Stepping-Stones Into the Dark": Redundancy and Generation in Christine Brooke-Rose's *Amalgamemnon*

RICHARD MARTIN

EARLY in the 1970s, Joanna Russ suggested that for the woman author who decided to eschew the established male conventions of the novel, two options remained: lyricism and life. She defined the lyric mode as "the organization of discrete elements . . . around an unspoken thematic or emotional center . . . ; its principle of connection is associative" ("What Can a Heroine Do?" 12). Russ realized that such writing was destined to meet with denigration in terms such as "these novels lack important events; they are hermetically sealed" (13). In one sense, Christine Brooke-Rose goes a stage further when in "Illiterations" she combines the notion of the isolation of any experimental writer and the misunderstanding awaiting the woman writer: "it seems to me that the combination of woman + artist + experimental means so much hard work and heartbreak and isolation that there must be little time or energy for crying out loud." Furthermore, her own position as a writer who has found widespread acceptance neither from conventional male reviewers nor from feminist critics, exacerbates the isolation: "she is in the sea between two continents" (*Breaking the Sequence*, 65–66, 67).

Joanna Russ saw the lyric structure as able to deal with the unspeakable, that which has been set apart, which is "unlabeled, disallowed, disavowed" (16). That there is an unspeakable to be transformed into discourse is the result of a deliberate move, which is both a social and an aesthetic strategy: it implies the woman writer's need to find that mode of expression that, by being divergent, will both emphasize and validate the otherness of women artists. In the case of Brooke-Rose, the experimentation supersedes an immediate concern with feminism while not in any way canceling it from her awareness; she is, in the first instance, an experimental writer and secondly, a woman experimental writer and as such, she is concerned with "the fusion of different discourses" ("An Interview" 3).

Nevertheless, such arbitrary classification of an author is insidious; the experimenter and the woman cannot be so neatly disjoined. In what follows I shall continually be presupposing Christine Brooke-Rose the experimentalist and (perhaps) less insistently inferring her persona as a woman—it would be more sensible, maybe, simply to take her on her own terms as someone who eschews labels and thus pays the price of, as she herself points out, belonging nowhere. Consideration of her as an experimenter implies the acceptance of the opinion that such a view includes the dilemma of recognizing that experimentalism "is at once a stepping stone to something else and is gratuitous" (Poggioli 135). It is, in fact, the "something else" beyond the stepping stones that I hope to be able to clarify. For any investigation of the nature of Brooke-Rose's experimentation will inevitably reveal her particular contribution to feminist literary discourse.

CHRISTINE Brooke-Rose's 1984 novel *Amalgamemnon* is "a polygonal story" (102), essentially many-angled, a story illuminated from many different directions, many stories brought together within a multisided frame of polynarration. There are contemporary narratives of, for example, a university teacher of the humanities made redundant by the proliferation of technology, of fleeting surface relationships with would-be "helpful" men of conventional ideas and prejudices, a venture into pig farming, dialogues with students and friends, an encounter with a band of terrorists. Then again, each individual narrative gives birth to further narratives, which in turn intermingle with classical myths, legends, history, and fairy tale in a maze of paratactical juxtapositioning in which each segment of fragmented narrative is as important as the next. The novel is held together by a pattern of structural repetitions and planned echoes: "the rhetoric of repetition will protect me" (17). Moreover, this strategy of recurrence is essential to the concept of redundancy in my title. Not only does the repetition of structures, and thus of information, make for clearer reception (*A Rhetoric of the Unreal* 44), but words by engendering further discourses (Miller passim) themselves become redundant, in both a social and a narrative sense, having served their purpose.

Nearly all the underlying compositional structures of *Amalgamemnon* are established within the limits of the first page of the book. For this reason I shall use a close examination of that page as a point of departure into the novel. The opening situation is also the constant background element: a woman exploiting her insomnia by reading and listening to the all-night radio program.

I shall soon be quite redundant at last despite of all, as redundant as you after queue and as totally predictable, information-content zero.

The programme-cuts will one by one proceed apace, which will entail laying off paying off with luck all the teachers of dead languages like literature philosophy history, for who will want to know about ancient passions divine royal middleclass or working in words and phrases and structures that will continue to spark out inside the techne that will soon be silenced by the high technology? Who will still want to read at night some utterly other discourse that will shimmer out of a minicircus of light upon a page of say Agamemnon returning to his murderous wife the glory-gobbler with his new slave Cassandra princess of fallen Troy who will exclaim alas, o earth, Apollo apocalyptic and so forth, or else Herodotus, the Phoenicians kidnapping Io and the Greeks plagiarizing the king of Tyre's daughter Europe, but then, shall we ever make Europe? Sport. Rugger. The Cardiff team will leave this afternoon for Montpellier where they will play Béziers in the first round of the European championship, listen to their captain, Joe Tenterten: we're gonna win.

I could anticipate and queue before the National Education Computer for a different teaching job, reprogramming myself like a floppy disk, or at the Labour Exchange for a different job altogether, recycling myself like a plastic bottle, and either way I'd be a worker in a queue of millions with skills too obsolete for the lean fitness of the enterprise. (5–6)

In this passage, paradigmatic for the novel as a whole, the narrating voice moves from a subjective situation (the redundancy of a teacher of the humanities, lines 1–5) to the discourse generated both by that thought and by texts drawn from the cradle of literary learning, the classics (lines 6–14), to the overheard words of the radio (lines 15–18) and so back to further reflections on the subjective dilemma (lines 19–23). The insistent use of future and conditional tenses in the opening passage is one of the most obtrusive linguistic features of *Amalgamemnon*; together with the subjunctive and imperative, they are the only verb forms employed throughout the text and thus, in their expression of unrealized moods, look forward to events but preclude their realization. Everything is talked about but nothing *can* happen; actions, persons, even ideas, belong to the realm of the possible but indeterminate. Quite apart from the overall structural pattern, the passage, again characteristic of the whole, is replete with clues and signals concerning its own significance and its mode of composition.

Regardless of the intrusive and obvious subject matter, the text swings between the poles of redundancy and generation.

The opening sentence (deliberately echoing Beckett's "I shall soon be quite dead at last in spite of all," *Malone Dies*), commences with an "I" that can equally well apply both to the text and to the narrator, both are faced with the fact of their own uselessness; to what, then, does "despite of all" refer? For the text, this can suggest that in spite of all efforts, both on the part of the reader and the author, the text will become redundant once read, or even once it has been written. The narrator is threatened by the possibility that the very process of narration bears within itself the seeds of its own redundancy, and thus the narrator is fated to outlive her usefulness. These implications are then amplified by the sort of telling pun that Brooke-Rose uses to perfection: "as redundant as you [*u*] after queue [*q*] and as totally predictable." In what sense is *u* after *q* redundant? As a subservient phoneme and in its function as a bound morpheme, it has no independent existence; *as itself* it is virtually nonexistent. Further, the very fact of redundancy is predictable—an immutable law as in the *qu* combination; no sooner has a text begun, has a narrator taken up the narration, an author begun to write and a reader to read, than they are all faced with their inevitable existential inutility. Redundancy is a predicate of textuality—of narrative—and, on another level, of existence.

It is, however, characteristic of Christine Brooke-Rose's narrative that the potentially redundant text generates further discourse.

Within the limits of the opening passage of the novel, we can discern continual variations on the redundancy motif: "information-content zero," "programme-cuts," "dead languages," "princess of fallen Troy," "skills too obsolete." These variations on redundancy are matched by words and images that are part of the generation motif: "continue to spark," "shimmer out," "reprogramming," and "recycling." It is this awareness of redundancy and of the concept's capacity to give rise to variations of the motif of generation that grants the book its basic pattern. It would, however, be more accurate to suggest that it is not so much concepts, or ideas, that perform such functions as the words themselves. Discourse is binary in *Amalgamemnon*, it is both redundant and generative, everything proceeds from language.

The narrating "I" is threatened with redundancy, the loss of her job because she is a teacher of "dead languages like literature philosophy history." The redundant aspect of those disciplines lies in the fact that the past, represented in the humanities, is kept alive "in words and phrases and structures" though the future is seen as a time in which history (and by implication literature and philosophy) will have lost its significance. As Hans, one of the student terrorists, exclaims: "In the next civilization there won't be any history, let alone any philosophy of it. . . . Events will be our instant history, but history as events not history as discourse" (109). A few pages later the rhetorical question is asked, "What will prophecy be but instant history" (113). The concept of "instant history" contains the notion of history as ersatz, as a substitute, but for what?—presumably for the "real thing," for action, events, the concrete. Among the contrasts with which we are faced throughout the novel are language as opposed to events, art as opposed to technology—the concreticized metaphor for the "real"—individual psyche as opposed to collectivized conformity, thought as opposed to jargon and cliché.

It is within such a context that the question is posed, "Who will still want to read." The particular image of reading that is presented in *Amalgamemnon* is that of the "utterly other discourse," which appears "out of a minicircus of light upon a page." Quite apart from the literal level of the page of the sleepless reader's book, which appears in the cone of light of the bedside reading lamp, there is the obvious reference to the microcosmic world of the book. Nor is this the stereotypical conception that it might have been; in its opposition to the "silencing force of high technology," art ("techne") possesses the ability to transcend the moment and within the limited physical space of the reader's immediate situation is able to generate new images of past worlds and existences. It is this that technology is forced to make redundant, and at the same time, it is this that endows the written word with generative properties to overcome redundancy, or at least to transform it.

In the opening pages of *Amalgamemnon*, the necessity to create opportunities for the reader to participate in the discourse results in many a statement with signalizing function; later Brooke-Rose elaborates complex images for the central concerns of the novel. In order to clarify the notion of the text's redundancy, triggering its own regeneration, the author has recourse to two reiterated images: toads and pigs at the narrator's pig farm. "My friend the toad" is presented as a creature with whom the narrating voice can experience a (fallacious) relationship, "one day I might crush him with the mower, then miss him dreadfully and feel a murderer for ever more" (51). At a later stage in the text, the narrating voice intrudes into the terrorist theme with: "Down at the crumbling farm, I shall be surprised to tread almost on the dead toad's baby son. . . . Forgive me little one I'll look out for you till you grow big and prehistoric like your father, but you look out too" (79). Amid reminders of redundancy ("crumbling farm," "dead toad") new life has been generated, which will inevitably proceed to maturity and further redundancy. Complementary to this, a fear is iterated that in any litter of pigs there will always be one who will fail to find nourishment. The narrator, dogged by the question, "will that little one survive," encourages the runt, "fight your way to the tits, way up that vast pink wall, see? There, don't let yourself be ousted by your brothers of milk and tummy" (73). At the same time, there is the realization that ultimately the pigs will "merely be ready for the butcher," an observation that is generalized to, "Let us recognize one another before annihilating each other" (74). The very establishment of the paradigm of redundancy-generation-redundancy does not invalidate the essential appeals inherent in a humanist-literary culture. Nor is redundancy to be taken as a negative concept (although the "misquotation" of Beckett in the opening sentence generates associations of death). Admittedly on one level—that of potential plot—Brooke-Rose does employ the word "redundancy" in its negative social sense, yet within the redundancy-generation paradigm, it must be understood in its linguistic function as essential to communication (Chomsky 166–70; Lyons 88). Furthermore, syntax, by way of repetition, deliberately creates the redundancy of linguistic items.

THE main narrating voice offers a choice of source books for her reflective oppositions to the posed world of the technologically real: the *Agamemnon* of Aeschylus and the *Histories* of Herodotus. Although never used again in the novel, on the first page *Agamemnon* serves in a double function: it supplies us with the entry to the title of the novel and introduces a key figure, Cassandra, "who will exclaim alas, o earth, Apollo apocalyptic and so forth." Not only does this echo, even plagiarize, Cassandra's opening lines in Aeschylus's play ("O Apollo! oh, oh! . . . Oh, oh! O horror! O earth! O Apollo!"), but also it reminds us of the particular fate of the princess of Troy: that she was loved by Apollo, but since she resisted him, was punished by having her gift of prophecy rendered useless, causing her prophecies to go unbelieved; she thus becomes the redundant prophetess. Prophecy, moreover, is closely associated with storytelling in Brooke-Rose's novel, and the narrating voice associates herself with Cassandra: "As if for instance I were someone else, Cassandra perhaps" (7) and becomes in her manifestation as the female companion of a stereotypical male (Willy or Wally), Sandra, a diminutive of the prophetess's name (15, 23, 45, 46, 136).

The significance of Cassandra in the novel lies in her redundancy, in her femininity, and in her devotion to the word. On a later page, after a passage in which a character refers to himself as a "graphomaniac," we read: "to be imprisoned for graffitism as poor Cassandra will be enslaved by all Amalgamemnons and die with them not out of love but of amalgamation to silence her for ever" (20). Cassandra is a metaphor for the twofold victim: the victim as woman, enslaved by male domination (Cassandra, the slave booty of Agamemnon) and the victim as artist (Cassandra, the redundant prophetess caught in her own discourse). Further, she becomes a means of decoding the title figure, who is an extension of the enslaving king, extended by the coupling with "amalgam," a mixture of different elements depending for its stability on the quantity of mercury in the compound, and extended further by the connotations of "amalgamate," to merge into a single body, used both of people and of corporations. Amalgamemnon becomes, thus, the threatening overforce, the consumer and enslaver both of artist and of woman.

In a later reference, Cassandra is associated both with concealment and castration, with uncertainty and generation:

> Never let anyone see you foresee them, keep quiet Cassandra, forecaster of your own pollux [Castor and Pollux], keep your castrations in perpetual cassation [Fr. quashing, setting aside] for nothing will ever be exactly as you shall one day see it in retrospect, otherwise you would grow big with expectation and sexplode, the expected generating the expectoration or vice versa perhaps. (30)

Apart from the characteristic wordplay, in itself generative, Cassandra is once again the epitome of redundancy, unable to utter prophecy, the author condemned to silence, the potential generator of generations, condemned to suppress her own fertility. It is not surprising that later in the book a male figure is warned to be less pessimistic in the words, "The role of Cassandra will hardly suit you" (77).

It is, however, Herodotus and not Aeschylus who provides the central literary-historical focus of the novel. The *Histories* are used as a device whereby the contrast between the classical past of literature, philosophy, and history is juxtaposed with the daily events of an imaginary present reality as propagated by the radio program, and with the typical incidents of late twentieth-century civilization: diplomatic small talk, media culture, terrorism, and the daily round. Not only are references made to events in Herodotus, as here from the opening pages—the Phoenicians capturing Io, and the Greeks stealing away Europa, daughter of Agenor, King of Tyre—but at times quotations (though verbs are transposed into the future tense) appear from Aubrey de Selincourt's translation of the *Histories* as an almost ironic comment both on the degeneration of language and on the parochial localization of events in the modern world as compared with the universality of the ancients. For example, the rape of Europa, beloved of Zeus, becomes the first round of the European rugby football championship. There is also a plaintive echo of the cry "shall we ever make Europe," expressive of British nonrelations with the European Common Market and containing at the same time the colloquial punning use of the verb "make," thereby relating the phrase back to the original myth.

Amalgamemnon proceeds upon the principles already evidenced in the opening page: discourse announces its own redundancy even as it generates new discourse. In detail this involves the reproduction and multiplication of words and associations grouped around a number of fixed points; mythology, Herodotus, and astronomy provide some of these. In addition, the very mention of names implies people who in turn imply relationships, but the relations are expressed more in terms of generative grammar than in terms of human (or family) reproduction. Thus a set of names leads inevitably to the elaboration of a family tree ("I shall go in . . . and invent myself an alternative family" 37), which is more a set of related structures than a human hierarchy as in history or the conventional family-saga novel. In an extension of the generative principle, not only is this family tree later revised (100-01) but the narrator grafts herself on to it.

On the second page of the text the narrating voice gains a name and a visitor: the visitor is Ethel Thuban and the narrator has the surname Enketei. If the clues on the first page were comparatively obvious, now it becomes evident that a reader of a certain type is implied by the text, a reader with the willingness to search and with access to the means of verification. "Enketei" can be broken down to "in ceto" or "within the whale," a reference to the constellation Cetus, which contains the star Mira Ceti, the first recognized variable star. Given Brooke-Rose's method of composition, one would expect Thuban to have similar associations; it was, in fact, in 3000 B.C. regarded as the polestar and is part of the constellation Draco (the dragon). In the case of Mira Ceti, or Mira Enketei, as she appears in the text, the addition of variability to her role as narrator is important. The unreliable narrator, the narrator who shifts position and whose "brilliance" is variable is a familiar figure. In the case of Ethel Thuban the procedure is more idiosyncratic; she features as a powerful foil to the narrator, a potential threat, and at a later stage plays the role of a dragon in a brilliantly conceived appropriation of the traditional fairy tale (86–93).

In the course of the narration, other constellations appear, notably Andromeda, Cassiopeia, Cepheus, Cygnus, and Orion. Although it is outside the scope of this article to follow the multiple significances of each, it is worth pointing out that Cepheus was Andromeda's father as Cassiopeia was her mother, and as king of the Ethiopians, he generates an African theme in the novel; Cygnus is used as a pun on "signus" ("sign") and thus is related to the language motif; finally, Orion, the hunter, is the victim of Artemis, the virgin huntress, his female counterpart. As Agamemnon and Cassandra represent the enslavement of the female by the male, so Artemis and Orion signify the threat to masculinity posed by the female. It thus becomes clear that the exploitation of myth and history is by no means haphazard, or simply a game, but a deliberate manipulation within the context of the woman/artist theme of the novel. One may add to this the use made of Andromeda who appears in several guises in the novel: at first she is "Anne de Rommede," one of Mira Enketei's students with a penchant for politics, physics, and metaphysics, as well as an interest in Greek philosophy. Other variations are "Anne de Rommeda" (suggesting a change of nationality), Anna Crusis (anacrusis: not a part of the metrical pattern), Anna Coluthon (anacoluthon: a shift in construction), and Anna Biosis (anabiosis: suspended animation). All variations suggest the outsider, in itself a metaphor for the artist and, in Brooke-Rose's terms, the experimental woman writer. Also worth remembering is that Andromeda offended the Nereids, the sea maidens, was punished by Poseidon, and rescued by Perseus—thus a woman with ambivalent relations toward both sexes, the double-voiced writer.

Similarly, if we again return to the opening of the novel, we are confronted by Io, beloved of Zeus and victim of Hera; Io finally wandered to Egypt where she was worshiped as the goddess Isis, "prototype of motherhood and of the faithful wife" (Shorter 133). Europa was also beloved of Zeus and, in fact, raped by him. Thus again these mythical figures reveal themselves as having significant contemporary connotations within the context of male-female attitudes and relations.

At this point it is necessary to return to the quotation contained in my title to suggest its relevance to a discussion of *Amalgamemnon*. The phrase first occurs in the context of another repetition that refers to the opening page of the novel: A "night of utterly other discourses that will crackle out of disturbances in the ionosphere into a minicircus of light upon a page of say Herodotus and generate endless stepping-stones into the dark . . ." (15). The contrast between the radio waves from the ionosphere and the microcosmic histories of Herodotus in itself generates the passage into the unknown. The narrating voice supplies all the necessary clues, which may be summarized as follows:

1. This text is comprised of variant discourses, and thus words, utterances, grammar, and syntax count.
2. The range of narration will be contained in the tension between the abstract and the peculiarly concrete, between the indefinite and definite, between space and confinement.
3. The text within the text serving as an anchor to microcosmic reality will be Herodotus—both father of history and father of lies ("Father of fibstory" 113). The *Histories* epitomize both historiography and

fiction, both the discourses of the past and the deconstruction of the present.

4. The discourse of the text together with meta- and extratextual discourses generates further texts.

5. The text functions as a guideline, an Ariadne's thread, into the unknown; it generates not only nonknowledge but also knowledge, the puzzle and the solution.

6. The mode of composition parallels the opening sentence's insistence on redundancy; text will be created in order to be deconstructed and the deconstruction will be implicit in the creation.

After a brief and parenthetical repetition of the opening events of the *Histories,* referring to collective rape—the capture of Io and the Greeks' carrying off Medea, daughter of the king of Colchis—the narrative quoted earlier ("stepping-stones into the dark") continues,

> creating in advance as yet another distance which I'll have carefully to deconstruct tomorrow by letting him abolish all those other discourses into an acceptance of his, although sooner or later the future will explode into the present despite the double standard at breaking points. (15–16)

In this passage, "him" is ambiguous, referring ostensibly to Herodotus but actually to the narrator's current Amalgamemnon or dominant lover. Brooke-Rose invents the strategy whereby the discourses that matter will be granted gratuitous redundance in apparent recognition of male supremacy, which in its turn comes to be known as redundant. The future, that is, holds the promise of redundancy and generation or better, of deconstruction and regeneration, and that is the confidence toward which the novel is directed.

WITHIN the context of *Amalgamemnon,* the dominant female strategy is contained in a set of puns culminating in the verb "to mimagree"—to mime agreement. Redundancy is both an accepted aspect of the text, implying generation, and of female-experienced reality, so that as the novel closes, it is possible to state:

> The characters . . . will perhaps indulge in the secret vice of reading redundant textual sources of redundant psychic sources in redundant humanistic animals. . . . Secret cabinet sources will refuse to comment on these shadow-figures and I shall mimagree, how should I not? (144)

This statement puts the critic in his or her place. Having commented on the shadow-figures of Brooke-Rose's novel, one is all too aware of the redundancy of one's own remarks. Should one have refused to comment?[1]

NOTE

1. I would like to thank Christine Brooke-Rose for her generous and patient cooperation and to thank my colleagues Wolf-Dietrich Bald and Heike Schwarzbauer for their helpful suggestions.

WORKS CITED

Aeschylus. *The Oresteian Trilogy*. Trans. Philip Vellacott. Harmondsworth, Gt. Brit.: Penguin, 1956.

Beckett, Samuel. *Malone Dies*. 1951. Harmondsworth, Gt. Brit.: Penguin, 1968.

Brooke-Rose, Christine. *Amalgamemnon*. Manchester, Gt. Brit., and New York: Carcanet, 1984.

———. "Illiterations." *Breaking the Sequence: Women's Experimental Fiction*. Ed. Ellen G. Friedman and Miriam Fuchs. Princeton: Princeton UP, 1989. 55–71.

———. "An Interview with Christine Brooke-Rose." By David Hayman and Keith Cohen. *Contemporary Literature* 17 (1976): 1–23.

———. *A Rhetoric of the Unreal: Studies in Narrative and Structure, Especially of the Fantastic*. Cambridge and New York: Cambridge UP, 1981.

Chomsky, Noam. *Aspects of the Theory of Syntax*. Cambridge, MA: MIT Press, 1965.

Herodotus. *The Histories*. 1954. Trans. Aubrey de Selincourt. Rev. A. R. Burn. Harmondsworth, Gt. Brit.: Penguin, 1984.

Lyons, John. *Introduction to Theoretical Linguistics*. Cambridge: Cambridge UP, 1968.

Miller, J. Hillis. *Fiction and Repetition*. Cambridge, MA: Harvard UP, 1982.

Poggioli, Renato. *The Theory of the Avant-Garde*. Cambridge, MA: Harvard UP, 1968.

Russ, Joanna. "What Can a Heroine Do? Or Why Women Can't Write." *Images of Women in Fiction*. Ed. Susan K. Cornillon. Bowling Green: Bowling Green UP, 1972.

Shorter, Alan W. *The Egyptian Gods: A Handbook*. 1937. London: Routledge, 1981.

Marguerite Young's
Miss MacIntosh, My Darling:
Liquescence as Form

———

MIRIAM FUCHS

"She was very much confused by clarities."

MARGUERITE Young's prodigious experiment in prose fiction took 18 years to write and, according to Bernard Bergonzi who reviewed *Miss MacIntosh, My Darling* in 1965, it came to 3,449 pages in typescript and weighed 3¼ pounds in book form.[1] By Bergonzi's method of viewing *Miss MacIntosh* in equivalent forms, the book weighs somewhat less than half a gallon of water and a little less than somewhat less than half a gallon of oil—identical volumes of different liquids of varying weights.

The conversion of text to page numbers, page numbers to pounds, pounds to gallons, and gallons to corresponding volumes of water and oil is an appropriate start for examining the structure and stylistics of *Miss MacIntosh*, a novel in which things appear in equivalent or corresponding forms. Oil mixed in water will diffuse, divide into smaller parts, and the particles will suspend in the liquid before they rise to the surface. Vera Cartwheel narrates *Miss MacIntosh* by mixing the quirky, reclusive figures she recalls from her childhood in a New England mansion with the eccentrics she meets at a tavern during her bus trip through the Midwest; but the disparate time frames coalesce as Vera recalls various people, swirling them about unpredictably, dividing them into small, peculiar "particles" for close examination—Miss MacIntosh's bald head and missing breast, Esther Longtree's swollen womb, Mr. Spitzer's double vision, her mother Catherine's opium dreams, nearly one dozen outdoor sporting events that take place across the surface of Madge's blouse—and when the mixture starts to thicken, Vera restirs and the particles appear again.

The characters also experience peculiar transformations. Extending her hand to Joachim Spitzer, her lawyer and faithful visitor, Catherine insists that he is an umbrella stand. Joachim, in love with Catherine for many years, suspects that he is Peron, his dead twin brother, with whom Catherine was in love for many years. (Joachim uses Peron's passport photo for his own identification; Joachim buried Peron in his own suit of clothing; since Peron's friends did not know about Joachim until Peron's funeral, they assume Peron never really died and Joachim never really lived.) Catherine, too, equates the dead twin with Joachim because in her drugged mind the dead continue to live in altered and variable forms. Joachim, the visible equivalent of the other twin, makes Peron a tangible presence, as "real" to Catherine as the living brother Joachim, who visits her each evening.

Fragile and insubstantial, borders and partitions do not separate; each is "the thinnest line . . . a line thinner than the thinnest thread of starlight or moth spittle hanging in a cloud . . ." (401). They collapse instead, and the substances they once contained spill over, as Young liquefies the palpable world, transforming its landscape into new configurations, creating indeterminate identities for its inhabitants, transforming objects into other objects. A basket of grapes becomes a chair, a swan becomes a wash basin, a pear becomes a glove, which, when touched, becomes a basket of peaches (290). Nothing in this novel is inviolate; everything is diffused, mixed, merged, sometimes confounded, and sometimes miraculously transfigured. Everything is viewed in analogous or related forms; and it is this aspect of *Miss MacIntosh* that makes relevant my opening comparisons.

Despite Vera's declaration that she has embarked on a traditional quest—implying movement through time, herself as heroine, numerous obstacles, and a climax in which the journey will be completed—one of the most striking features of *Miss MacIntosh* is the absence of clearly delineated, objective action that occurs in a world beyond Vera's, or her mother's, or another character's memories or dreams, events whose occurrences need not be called into question. Vera Cartwheel, born of a wealthy, but utterly daft mother addicted to opium, attributes her journey to the desire to find her childhood companion and tutor, the stalwart, practical-minded Miss MacIntosh. Now an adult, Vera travels across the Midwest (Miss MacIntosh grew up in What Cheer, Iowa) in search of her "darling." But the old-fashioned quest belies the obvious illogic of Vera's journey, for Miss MacIntosh is almost assuredly dead, having deliberately walked into the cold New England ocean many years before, leaving "her corset draped over a rock in a salt pool, . . . the red wig . . . lain over the horse-shoe crab crawling in the wind . . ." (941). Since her body is never found, Miss MacIntosh seems to dissolve into ocean or to fragment into objects and creatures left on shore. The illogic of Vera's "quest," the gap between its purpose and its method—"seeking for [Miss MacIntosh] in all those places where she was not" (7)—is never resolved. The absence of logic here—and elsewhere—signals Young's insistence that her text not be reduced to what can be understood, defined, and thus controlled, but that it be enlarged by including what Alice Jardine in *Gynesis* describes as the "categorically unrepresentable . . . at the limits of the known," what "can no longer be reduced to what Man *sees* or is presented with . . ." (122, 124).

A crossing without a port of call, Vera's trip functions synoptically before it is absorbed into her memories. It solidifies toward the end of the novel when, disturbed by the ravings of mad Dr. O'Leary whose room in the tavern is nearby, Vera changes her room, only to be awakened by another uproar in another nearby room. The resurfacing of plot, after hundreds of pages, is not intended to restore traditional novelistic balance by providing closure. The return to the tavern is a humorous, poignant reminder by Young of the old-fashioned form that she eschews for most of her book—constructed on fluidity and ever-changing forms. Young gleefully works it out, ensuring that the return of plot does not signify closure, but rather skews the narrative structure even further. With only one-sixth of the text remaining, the narrative should begin to settle, the lid slowly closing on the container. But instead, the narrative begins all over again with a new character, pregnant Esther Longtree, a waitress at the tavern. Esther tells her story to Vera, who wonders if she has "come too early or too late" (1010). And Esther is no small digression, occupying 165 pages of text, on any page of which she believes she may give birth and thus start another story within the story. Young crazily tilts her structure once more, this time only eight pages from the end; Vera's extraordinary understatement that "my love was late in coming" (1190) announces the emergence of one more new character, the stone-deaf man, whom Vera hears screaming in front of her door. Six pages from the end Vera declares abruptly that she loves him (1193), and two pages from the end announces that they will marry (1197). An indispensable character, this stone-deaf man joins the cast of eccentrics when the capacious story nearly runs out of pages. Coming so late—and so swiftly—the climax to this novel of amorphous shapes and "disrelation" (5) exacerbates its disproportion and lopsidedness. When Young uses plot, she does so in order to negate its legitimacy.

Young's work is distinctly avant-garde—its structure amorphous, its density almost defying penetration, its length straining patience, the parts negating the coherence of the whole. Everything about Young's novel eludes fixed definition or explication. In fact, the very qualities that establish this novel as avant-garde are the qualities that mitigate some of its subversive impact—its insistent repetitions, its establishing "relationships where none exist" (992), then negating those relationships, its thwarting of expectations even as they are altered. The mainstay of any avant-garde work is shock, but its effect can dissipate quickly, as Peter Burger explains in his study, *Theory of the Avant-Garde*: "Nothing loses its effectiveness more quickly than shock. . . . As a result of repetition, it changes fundamentally: there is such a thing as expected shock" (81). To illustrate his point, Burger cites public reaction to Dadaist experiments in the 1920s. Once viewers knew they would be shocked by Duchamp's ready-made urinals, in effect, they could no longer be shocked; their response was diluted to amusement or annoyance. Burger could also have used *Miss MacIntosh* to make his point. Disorienting and unorthodox, it is also relentless. Twelve hundred pages of diffusion and accretion present a formidable challenge for even the most determined of readers. The work requires a reconceptualization of hermeneutic approach, but its newness is "consumed" through its repetition and length.

It is hardly surprising, then, that despite some laudatory reviews, including one by John Gardner in *The Southern Review*,[2] *Miss MacIntosh* has been overlooked by both feminist and postmodern critics. In the quarter century since publication, Young's work has earned only two citations in the *MLA Bibliographies*.[3] Interviews with Young in Roy Newquist's *Conversations* (1967) and Charles Ruas's *Conversations with American Writers* (1985) provide little more than basic information. Born in Indiana, Young has lived for many years in New York City. She published her first collection of verse, *Prismatic Ground,* in 1937, her second collection, *Moderate Fable*, in 1944, and *Angel in the Forest*, an account of nineteenth-century utopian communities in 1945 (Ruas 91). Catherine Cartwheel and the stone-deaf man in *Miss MacIntosh* were modeled on people Young once knew, and *Miss MacIntosh* was conceived as a "novel as poem." Had Young suspected the book would take so long to write, she "would have dropped in holy horror. Who could conceive spending eighteen years obsessed by one book and working from nine to five?" (Ruas 102). The interviews provide additional facts, but little to prepare us for the striking design of *Miss MacIntosh*. "Every Form is also a Value," says Barthes in *Writing Degree Zero*: "writing is . . . the morality of form, the choice of that social area within which the writer elects to situate the Nature of his [or her] language" (13, 15). The relationship between its form and its ideological underpinnings places *Miss MacIntosh* in a seminal position, one that conjoins twentieth-century avant-garde fiction (considered by many to be largely male) to twentieth-century women's fiction (considered by many to be largely traditional). It is an impassioned and innovative expression of a female sensibility and a female aesthetic.

Miss MacIntosh is an example of "feminine" writing that feminists such as Hélène Cixous have theorized will oppose traditional patriarchal writing. It will "wreck partitions, classes, and rhetorics, regulations and codes . . . submerge, cut through . . . keep going, without ever inscribing or discerning contours" ("Laugh of the Medusa" 886). Recognizing that the number of female-inscribed texts to accomplish this is very small, Cixous cites Duras and Colette and optimistically looks to the future (878–79). Other feminist critics do the same, acknowledging qualities of "feminine" writing in the works of Genet, Joyce, Lautréamont, and Proust, which break conventional sequence, tend to be multicentered and nonlinear, rupturing traditional literary forms. Rachel Blau DuPlessis also looks to the future, emphasizing in "For the Etruscans" the inevitability of a body of literature that is nonhierarchical, nontraditional and thus nonpatriarchal, which "incorporate[s] contradiction and nonlinear movement into the heart of the text," but *has a female signature as well* (278, italics added). The continuous lyrical prose that spills into poetry, the contradictory form, circular design, multiplicity and fluidity of *Miss MacIntosh* make it a vivid and significant example of feminine writing that has been written by a woman.

Cixous characterizes feminine writing in her essay "Castration or Decapitation?" as literature that opposes hierarchical oppositions, between man/woman and activity/passivity, for example.[4] For Cixous, this writing has

> no closure, it doesn't stop, and it's this that very often makes the feminine text difficult to read . . . a feminine text goes on and on and at a certain moment the volume comes to an end but the writing continues. . . . The question "Where do children come from?" is basically a masculine, much more than a feminine, question. The quest for origins, illustrated by Oedipus, doesn't haunt a feminine unconscious. Rather it's the beginning, or beginnings . . . not promptly with the phallus in order to close with the phallus, but starting on all sides at once. . . . A feminine text starts on all sides at once, starts twenty times, thirty times, over. (53)

I have quoted this passage at length to emphasize its application to Young's work. In addition to sentences that spiral down a full page before coming to an end, and to paragraphs that expand for pages at a time, encyclopedic lists about butterflies, archaic languages, shipwrecks, exotic battles, ancient rulers, the dead, the living, and the lost flow over the text, evoking a marvelous plenitude in which all things coexist. If we attempt to cut through these lists, to go directly to "significant" items, we are thwarted, finding no sequence, linear logic, or hierarchical arrangement of parts. Without fixed boundaries, there is no margin, no inside, no outside; everything is other. Abundance, fluidity, and fusion are the reigning principles, and readers who stop "midway" in these lists will need to start again; interruption of the text disrupts its coherent reception. In effect, Young's text compels us to read and to play at the same time. To remain in the world of *Miss MacIntosh* is to yield to its laws of baffling equivalences.

Young's narrative "ends" on page 1198, but projecting an open-ended textuality, it does not "finish." Always in motion, it ends neither with Miss MacIntosh, nor with the handful of characters that have occupied hundreds of pages. It ends instead with the slow-moving, uneducated Esther Longtree, who surfaces when the book is nearly complete. The novel's two-line final paragraph (its very brevity suggesting incompletion) describes Esther's shutting the restaurant to take a lunch break, a closure that promises reopening. Vera explains: "She would hang a sign in the restaurant window—Owt to luntsch. Bee bak in a whale . . ." (1198). Vera avoids the precision of the past tense (she hung a sign) and the confidence implied by the future tense (she will hang a sign) for the indeterminacy of the conditional tense (she "would hang"). Thus, the novel "ends" with an action that has yet to happen and may not happen, capturing the indefinite space between action and inaction. Exploring what a traditional novel would omit, in this instance, a space characterized by uncertainty but also by its potential, Vera's narrative takes place between possibility and fulfillment, between idea and action.

Esther's endless pregnancy reflects the novel's refusal to move toward denouement. Like Joachim Spitzer, "mindful always that he was two persons" (669), Esther is another contradiction, understandable only in the context of Young's world, which allows everything to be something else. Esther looks pregnant and feels pregnant, but there is no end—nor any certain beginning—to her condition; about to have a child, she does not have it. Pregnancy, for Esther, is like weight: "Always. Off and on. If I lose it, I gain it again" (1017). Her swollen condition has no logical explanation. She seems neither literally nor figuratively pregnant, but declares that it is "this waiting" that has made her so loving, endowed her with "sympathy" and with her "maternal heart" (1016). For Esther, pregnancy is "breathing and hoping" (1018), the equivalent of life itself. And her "maternity" extends to her other "children" as well, Vera among them: "she loved us all . . . and we were all so much like her little children . . ." (1198). Like the women's writing that Cixous envisions, *Miss MacIntosh* does not finish and Esther does not give birth. "At a certain moment the volume comes to an end," and the end—Esther's lunch break—anticipates a new beginning.

Like the particles of linear plot, patriarchy in *Miss MacIntosh* is dispersed and diluted—Young's response to the patriarchal question that

Cixous discusses in her essay: "Where do [the] children come from?" *Miss MacIntosh* is replete with mothers, mother-surrogates, would-be-mothers, about-to-be-mothers, a female cousin, and children, particularly daughters, evoking a matriarchal world that is governed by a female ethos. Esther Longtree introduces herself as "the passive policeman's only daughter" (1011), alluding to her father's impotence and the unlikelihood that she was conceived at all. Vera's mother, Catherine, barely recalls ever having had a husband who, while scaling the Swiss Alps, "disappear[ed] under a bank of snow" (13), and the Christian hangman, epitomizing patriarchal law and retribution, is taunted by the children of his first wife. They mock his role in the judicial hierarchy as they play, hanging themselves from the same tree on which their mother hanged—and killed herself.

The masculine obsession with origins presupposes a definite beginning—biologically, the moment of climax. Exercise of the phallus is tantamount to a declaration of property rights. But unable to recall any one moment of conception, Esther cannot identify the fathers, be they traveling salesmen or strangers: "The men, the men, all like moths in a storm" (1022). Only a few, usually on their deathbed, write to inquire about offspring: "at the last moment, he would want to claim it, the little one who had been forgotten . . ." (1037). If individual fathers cannot be remembered, the children cannot be claimed. In the feminine space of *Miss MacIntosh*, the foundation for paternity is the desire to nurture and protect, a spiritual gift from one adult male to a child, exemplified by Mr. Spitzer's devotion to Vera.

Young examines the concept of maternity as well, by implication expanding its meaning to include males. Catherine Cartwheel, who prefers the company of her hallucinated personages and "Mr. Chandelier," her light fixture, forgets that she ever had a daughter. It is Mr. Spitzer who watches over Vera, who hires Miss MacIntosh to teach her the basic principles of common sense. Mad Dr. O'Leary, while waiting for Esther's pregnancy to come to term, thinks that his room overflows with pregnant patients—one of them male, "and this, people specified, was a real, pregnant man—for this, they wanted to make it very clear, was not one of [O'Leary's] dream patients but rather a real, pregnant man who suffered from a dream . . ." (1004). As she does throughout the narrative, Young tilts her text in one direction—here, toward the miracle of a pregnant man—and then tilts it the opposite way—just enough to cast doubt. In the midst of clarifying the miracle, she obscures it. Without patriarchal structures dependent upon logic and reason, all things may be possible, but they are uncertain or irreconcilable as well.

In contrast to Dr. O'Leary, Mr. Spitzer is sane, methodically trying to comprehend the collapse of the old hierarchies, feeling always that he has lost something, which he has—authority, knowledge, understanding of his own (uncertain) self. Mr. Spitzer links Catherine, Cousin Hannah, Vera, and Miss MacIntosh by serving as their lawyer, managing their legal affairs. He reluctantly learns the subtleties of female sentience and the richness of female processes, which flood his powers of ratiocination. Loving Catherine—hopelessly and irrationally—he is faithful to the illusion that one day she may return his love—or shower him with her love of Peron, his dead brother. In the midst of all these women, Mr. Spitzer is unsettled by the lack of causality, predictability, and chronology. Adjusting to what Cixous calls the "chaosmos" ("Laugh of the Medusa" 888) of feminine space and feminine literature—in Young's novel disproportion, repetition, nonsequential progression, delayed entrances and surprise exits (Miss MacIntosh dies too early, Cousin Hannah too late)—Mr. Spitzer tries to maintain composure. Barely able to "see" the palpable world without its diffusing into vague, amorphous shapes, he worries as things go out of focus, disappear from sight, happen twice instead of once, occur in the wrong order, or do not happen at all.

The ruler, the yardstick, the clock, all have lost powers of signification. Mr. Spitzer arrives on time for appointments, but finds that "on time" is the wrong time. He misses the person he should have met but finds someone else instead. He notices traffic signals a moment after they change, hears the echo of notes before the music begins. Seeing multiple images everywhere, he learns that accurate vision depends upon his ability to add and subtract. Single images are destabilized further in very peculiar ways; distant objects appear huge while objects up close are tiny. When Catherine needs exercise, she takes a trip down the canal of her inner ear. The millimeters of this path explode into an expansive landscape of extraordinary beauty. Losing a sense of beginning and ending, the reader, like Catherine, is "lost" inside her ear:

> out of this vast continent where there were so many doors and porticoes and fallen columns, secret arcades and weird deserts of stone, so many vast, trembling lakes and mirrors and reflections of clouds, so many mirroring ballrooms and trembling chords and grand pianos played upon by waves of haunted sound . . . she was lost, walking up and down stairways inside her ear. There were so many winding paths and great stone walls like the walls of China, so many towers she could not count. There were many overhanging rocks and wild, fantastic faces, stalagmites and stalactites. . . . (447–48)

Catherine's "adventure," which occurs inside of the "feminine" space that is her ear, finally "ends" but it does not conclude. Like Esther's pregnancy, it has potential for infinite regeneration, and like Esther who lives in perpetual pregnancy, Catherine, Vera reminds us, has lived for years inside this space, a "great continent no one had ever ... completely explored" (447).

Because Young confounds the boundaries between interior thought and deliberate action, she is free to narrate a "nonevent" in voluminous detail. For instance, a stranger offers Mr. Spitzer a jewel from a maharajah's crown for the price of an imitation. Recognizing, but not valuing the "real" gem over the bauble, he declines. The next day he reads in the paper that a jewel from a maharajah's crown has been stolen, and the description of the thief fits Mr. Spitzer. Detectives pursue the "international jewel thief," seen as near as Boston, as far as a foreign casbah. Page after page describes the elusive movements of the thief, positively identified by those who could not have seen Mr. Spitzer in cities he never visited. Almost convinced by the "haunting description" of himself in the papers, he considers going to the police, but worried always that he is Peron, Mr. Spitzer fears "his own credentials would then be examined, and it would seem that he was not himself, that he was dead" (723). In glorious paradox, the episode rushes on, building in momentum through events that never happened, which trigger other events that never happened—which paradoxically lead to "real" results. The conflict builds, then dissipates without climax, "other events crowding this out of the headlines just as if it had never happened" (724). The nonepisode of the missing jewel "ends" but has no closure. Mr. Spitzer forgets about it, attending instead to his dead brother's business. Resilient as he regains his composure, Mr. Spitzer realizes he has lost something of the old patriarchy, but his sense of loss is just one of a multitude of impressions that whirl about. "He knew not what his frayed edges were or where he was" (575), and so he adapts.

This novel is story within story, dream within dream. Vera pours out her own "story," which is not a traditional quest, but the particles of a rich, liquid narrative. Always contradictory, *Miss MacIntosh* jolts and disrupts, but encircles as well, pouring out its secrets of life and birth and love. In her testament to the infinite potential for creation, Young casts this power in feminine terms of conception and fecundity. Feminine qualities rise to the surface and are stirred back in the text, surfacing again in male characters such as Mr. Spitzer, Young's way of emphasizing that feminine qualities—sympathy, nurturing, patience—are qualities that cross gender lines. Sixteen pages from the end, Mr. Spitzer confesses to Catherine that he is really Peron, who has learned slowly through the years to love her and to be faithful. His timing, as always, is off; Catherine has just died in his arms. One page before the end, Vera declares that she has conceived a child. And Esther Longtree is about to break for lunch.

NOTES

1. Although Bergonzi indicates that the book took 17 years to write, Young has said that it required 18 years. See Ruas 103.
2. Gardner had been Young's pupil at the University of Iowa and wrote his first two novels in her class. As Young describes it (Ruas 113–14), she was instrumental in helping him discover a distinctive narrative style. Gardner calls Young's novel "extraordinary for breadth of mind and verbal genius" (459).
3. See Duncan and Durand in Works Cited.
4. Cixous explains that "a woman's name doesn't necessarily make a piece of writing feminine. It could quite well be masculine writing, and conversely, the fact that a piece of writing is signed with a man's name does not in itself exclude femininity. It's rare, but you can sometimes find femininity in writings signed by men . . ." (52).

WORKS CITED

Barthes, Roland. *Writing Degree Zero.* Trans. Annette Lavers and Colin Smith. New York: Hill, 1968.

Bergonzi, Bernard. "Queen for a Day." *New York Review of Books,* 25 (Nov. 1965): 34–35.

Burger, Peter. *Theory of the Avant-Garde.* Trans. Michael Shaw. Minneapolis: U of Minnesota P, 1984.

Cixous, Hélène. "Castration or Decapitation?" Trans. Annette Kuhn. *Signs* 7 (1981): 41–55.

———. "The Laugh of the Medusa." Trans. Keith Cohen and Paula Cohen. *Signs* 1 (1976): 875–93.

Duncan, Erika. "A Reminiscence with Marguerite Young." *Book Forum* 3 (1975): 426–35.

DuPlessis, Rachel Blau. "For the Etruscans." *The New Feminist Criticism: Essays on Women, Literature, and Theory.* Ed. Elaine Showalter. New York: Pantheon, 1985. 271–91.

Durand, Régis. "*La fabrique de la fiction: Lectures du roman de* Marguerite Young, *Miss MacIntosh, My Darling.*" *Caliban* 12 (1975): 45–60.

Gardner, John. Rev. of *Miss MacIntosh, My Darling. The Southern Review* 3 (1967): 459–62.

Jardine, Alice A. *Gynesis: Configurations of Woman and Modernity.* Ithaca: Cornell UP, 1985.

Newquist, Roy. *Conversations.* New York: Rand, 1967.

Ruas, Charles. *Conversations with American Writers.* New York: Knopf, 1985.

Young, Marguerite. *Angel in the Forest: A Fairy Tale of Two Utopias.* New York: Reynal, 1945.
———. *Miss MacIntosh, My Darling.* New York: Scribner's, 1965.
———. *Moderate Fable.* New York: Reynal, 1944.
———. *Prismatic Ground.* New York: Macmillan, 1937.

Fiction as Language Game:
The Hermeneutic Parables of
Lydia Davis and Maxine Chernoff

MARJORIE PERLOFF

> I went to a palm reader and the odd thing about the reading was that everything she told me was totally wrong. She said I loved airplanes, that I had been born in Seattle, that my mother's name was Hilary. But she seemed so sure of her information that I began to feel like I'd been walking around with these false documents permanently tattooed to my hands. It was very noisy in the parlor and members of her family kept running in and out. They were speaking a high, clicking kind of language that sounded a lot like Arabic. Books and magazines in Arabic were strewn all over the floor. It suddenly occurred to me that maybe there was a translation problem—that maybe she was reading my hand from right to left instead of left to right.
>
> Thinking of mirrors, I gave her my other hand. Then she put her other hand out and we sat there for several minutes in what I assumed was some kind of participatory ritual. Finally I realized that her hand was out because she was waiting for money.
>
> (Laurie Anderson, "False Documents")

> When philosophers use a word—"knowledge," "being," "object," "I," "proposition," "name,"—and try to grasp the *essence* of the thing, one must always ask oneself: is the word ever actually used in this way in the language-game which is its original home? What *we* do is to bring words back from their metaphysical to their everyday use.
>
> (Ludwig Wittgenstein, *Philosophical Investigations* 72)[1]

LAURIE Anderson's "From *Americans on the Move*," from which "False Documents" is drawn,[2] is remarkable for its exclusions. Anderson's are stories singularly devoid of plotting, characterization, description, and figurative language. Even the autobiographical convention (the narrator is almost always the writer herself) is undercut in that we learn little about the "I" who tells these stories. Family history, cultural identity, psychological makeup—all these are subordinated to what we might call

Anderson's hermeneutic stance, her role as would-be decoder of a system of signs whose ability to communicate has been short-circuited. As Michel Serres has put it: "[if] at the source anything (or almost) can be emitted, everything will be scrambled at reception. Language, fragmented, defeats." In the world, that is to say, of communications technology, no message is guaranteed ever to reach its destination intact; indeed, communication is increasingly replaced by circulation within a closed system. In Serres's words, "the interchanges distribute meaning like a dictionary. Everything rolls on, speaks, goes round and round" (Owens 53). So, in "False Documents," A reads B's palm and B tries to interpret A's reading even as A is using the occasion to play a different language game. The trick, as Wittgenstein says, is to find that language game's "original home," to determine how the words are actually put to use.

Like Anderson, Lydia Davis and Maxine Chernoff, whose short fiction is my subject here, are close to forty. Their age (Davis was born in 1947, Chernoff in 1952) is significant, for both are writers for whom the first wave of postwar experimentalism—the "self-reflexive" fiction of post-modernism with its elaborate distortions of narrative time (analepses, prolepses) and its complex modalities of voice and metafictional device—has been replaced by what looks at first like the return to a normative realism, to the recounting of ordinary incidents that stand synecdochically for the larger fabric of life. A woman comes home from work and tries to figure out why the man she loves has not called her, another woman has a fortieth birthday and wonders whether it is too late to have children, a third recounts the stages of her psychotherapy.

But the realistic convention, as used in this new fiction, has a parodic dimension. For whether the mood is sardonic, as in most of Davis's stories, or exuberant and comic, as in Chernoff's, the focus is less on "character" or on moral and psychological value, than on language itself. "I am not commenting," says Chernoff in a symposium on narrative, "about the nature of one character's reaction to experience. Rather, I am suggesting that a linguistic event has been observed by a witness. . . . Thus, 'character' in many of my prose poems exists so that language can occur. . . . The linguistic event 'happens' in the sense that anything happens" ("Fence of Character" 88). And the "linguistic event" takes the form of a verbal exchange in which one witness tries to interpret the words and actions of others. Such interpretation is partly subjective, partly determined by the cultural nexus in which it takes place. For Chernoff, as for Davis, the discourses of advertising, television dialogue, newspaper caption, and literary cliché have been so thoroughly internalized that we no longer perceive them as other.

Neither writer, however, came to the mode I am describing without some false starts. In her first book, *A Vegetable Emergency*, published in 1977 when she was only twenty-five, Chernoff renders what she calls the "linguistic moment" in parables that draw heavily—and not always successfully—on the Surrealist tradition. A man holds his breath for so long that a newspaper reporter is sent to determine how he does it and is promptly blown away by the man's "polite" exhalation (13). A lion sees a woman in a leopard coat and "greets her like a favorite aunt or a college roommate," even as she "falls to the ground, her lips a panicky smear" (6). A broom decides that the only way to remove a stubbornly resistant brown shoe from under a bed is to practice standing up straight at night rather than resting in its corner (22).

Witty and inventive as these parables are,[3] it is only when Chernoff discovers a way of grounding her language games in a particular social context that her stories begin to acquire their particular stringency. The fanciful, the marvelous, the coincidental—these retain their force, but they are now woven into the fabric of ordinary life. Thus, whereas the prose poem "On My Birthday" begins with the sentence, "Words line up like racehorses at a starting gate" (*Vegetable Emergency* 8), the title story of *Bop* replaces the fanciful metaphor of words as racehorses with a scene at the xerox machine:

> The machine would not cooperate. It photographed his original, but when Oleg looked into the metal pan, the duplicate was zebra-striped and wordless. Three more times he inserted the grocery ad. He got back stripes leaning toward each other and crossing in the middle like insane skate blades. (13)

Oleg Lum, Chernoff's Russian émigré-hero, spends his days at the public library duplicating everything he reads to get a handle on America. But the more he reads and duplicates, the more facts he knows (e.g., Question: "what city has the highest ratio of pets to people?" Answer: Los Angeles), the less he understands. Alone in his small apartment (his days are free since he works as a night watchman), he "pour[s] lukewarm tea into a *Star Wars* glass" (14) and drafts Letters to the Editor. Why, for example, do Americans have so many opinions?

In the public library Oleg Lum meets an eleven-year-old girl named Carrie Remm and, having offered her a cigarette ("he kept an extra pack at all times for his generosity training"), which she refuses ("No thanks. Kids don't smoke here" [17]), he takes her to the Thirty-One Flavors for an ice cream. Carrie tells him that her mother is divorced and has had an operation that prevents her from having any more children. This sad fact—the loss of Mrs. Remm's "reproductive abilities"—now sets the comic plot in motion. Oleg Lum (misnamed Glum by Carrie) is invited to dinner at the Remms. He brings Mrs. Remm roses with a card that reads "With *extreme* sympathy." In the meantime, Claire Remm thinks her daughter has invited a boy her own age to partake of pizza. The actual "dinner party" is a series of absurd misunderstandings where every word and gesture on the part of Claire and Carrie is slightly misinterpreted by the trusting Oleg. But the evening ends happily enough with an invitation: " 'Better yet,' Oleg said, 'a trick is up the sleeve. I have procured tickets for an event of pantomime to begin in twenty minutes. We should begin our arrival now' " (22). It is Oleg's moment of triumph, the "procured tickets" being in fact the nightly gift of his upstairs neighbors who happen to work as mimes.

The "success" of this evening goes to Oleg's head. Another Letter to the Editor is written, this one questioning the meaning of size in America. Next, we find Oleg Lum at the beach on Sunday, addressing a little boy who wears "a seersucker sunsuit and a bulging diaper" (24). And the conversation between Lum and "Bop" (the child's only word, so Lum assumes it is his name) now gives way to another scene in which Lum brings little Bop to Claire's house and offers him to her as a gift. His flawless logic (Major premises: children need parents and parents need children. Minor premises: Bop has no visible parents, Claire can have no more children. Therefore: Claire and Bop must be united as mother and child) leads to an elaborate fantasy in which he and Claire, holding hands, are the parents of an adorable little son. But of course Claire common-sensically calls the police and Bop's real parents are found, leaving Lum to write a particularly sad letter to "Dear Personal View":

> Everything in America gets lost, sometimes stolen. I lose my umbrella on el train. It is never returned. Meanwhile baby is left on beach to weather, danger, criminals, drug takers, God knows. Parents come to police. Say they are sorry, so baby is returned. Why in America is easier to find lost baby than umbrella costing nine dollars? But I worry most for sandy American baby who is found on beach like walking rubbish heap called Bop. He is dirty, hungry little immigrant. I give him new life visa, which police revoke. (28)

And in a moment of despair, Lum, on the job, ignores the burglar alarm and lets the car thieves at Cusper's Ford have their way.

Like Laurie Anderson's story about the fortune teller, Chernoff's "Bop" is a comic parable about language and its failure to communicate. Although Lum's perplexity is touching, its function is not to establish au-thorial judgments about the difficulties of immigration or the social mores of TV-watching, pizza-eating households run by single mothers.

Rather, Lum's particular perspective presents us with a heightened image of the gap (a gap always present) between the emission and reception of verbal messages in our society. Any text can be duplicated and memorized (Lum knows the price of every grocery item, the name of every food product), but what does it mean? The words are everywhere but their import is nowhere. "Claire," Oleg Lum thinks, "was a lovely name. It reminded him of water"; but when he meets the real Claire, he notes, "Her eyes looked dried up, like African drinking holes" (19).

Chernoff's seemingly straightforward, literal story (a narrative quite devoid of the trappings of self-reflexive fiction with its complexity of temporal and spatial displacements, ambiguity of point of view, and so on) can thus be read as a sly parody of the mysterious-foreigner-meets-American-woman love story. Like the items in the grocery ads that Lum xeroxes, the near-rhyming names Lum (Glum) and Remm, Claire and Care (Carrie) are counters in a language game, alternately coming together and drawing apart, their fate determined by a syllable at once ubiquitous in our culture and yet wholly equivocal semantically—"Bop."

Most of Chernoff's short stories have even less overt plotting than this one. What is to my mind the most interesting story in the book, "Don't Send Poems, Send Money," is written in the first-person, present tense, and begins:

> I am talking to my friend Lori. We go back to high school, though our relations have sometimes been strained by small acts. When she changed the spelling of her name at fifteen to the then fashionable *i* ending, when I decided not to be a scientist, when my child Sari was born (Oh, how time changes one's attitude toward spelling!), there was a wedge between us. "Do you think we'll ever get along?" I once asked her. "Why should we?" she replied, and I am sure she wasn't teasing. Lori hadn't understood the problem suggested by the question. That's the way she is. (65)

From the vantage point of the reader, "the problem suggested by the question" is how these two old friends can ever communicate. Lori is thirty-four, unmarried, a nurse; she is "on speed that an old doctor friend 'lent' her." Her object in life is to find a husband. Elaine, the narrator, married very young and gave up a potential career as a chemist when she became pregnant; she and Peter have a twelve-year-old daughter who is "growing breasts." The plot revolves around Elaine's attempt to fix up Lori with a lawyer colleague of Peter's. The resulting dinner party turns out to be a disaster. Shortly before the dinner, Elaine, who is a free-lance writer, interviews a "battered husband" for a magazine article, a man who turns out to have known her husband in law school and commiserates with

Peter's unfortunate decision to have married a dropout who saddled him with a child. Her ego somewhat battered, Elaine decides to make her best Sunday roast for the party. The guests having arrived, Peter, who has driven Sari to a friend's house for an overnight, phones from the emergency room: he has had a slight car accident and his lip needs stitches. By the time he comes home, Lori and Mike Larson have exchanged enough bland conversation to convince themselves and Elaine that they have nothing in common, and to top it off, Larson turns out to be a vegetarian. Since, as is now evident, neither man can eat roast, the women announce they are not hungry, and the four decide to forget dinner and go to a movie.

These variations on what might be called the "Let me tell you what a bad day I've had" motif are interwoven with the "I"-narrator's deadpan observations on contemporary urban life. Returning from the market, where she has bought rolled rib roasts, "Idaho potatoes to bake and chives for the sour cream and fresh wax beans and ingredients for a lemon meringue pie" for her dinner party, Elaine finds her daughter "manipulating her Rubik's cube without even looking." And we read:

> She is watching one of those reassuring kids are likewise human Saturday morning shows. They're interviewing the youthful editor of a magazine that prints writing "of children, by children, and for children." "And how should kids in our TV audience send to your magazine?" the cheeky emcee asks. "Don't send poems, send money," the twelve-year-old with the Frankenstein's forehead and shiny glasses says. "We need to establish a broader base." Do children have to be shaken down so young, I wonder. (75)

This hilarious account of media manipulation provides Chernoff with the paradigm that governs the behavior of her characters. Elaine's generous gesture toward Lori is a case of "sending poems," whereas what Lori really needs is, so to speak, money in the bank. For Lori's own language orientation does not allow for the conventions of pleasant dinner-party discourse.

> Lori is sure that the man intended for her died somewhere in Little League. 'He probably played second base, and one day a stinging liner got him in the Adam's apple." That's something else about Lori. She likes using baseball as a metaphor for life. When she had an abortion, it was "like sliding home without kneepads." When my father died, she kept repeating, "How can a Cubs fan die?" (65)

Lori's baseball lingo is emblematic of her larger need to literalize language. In her radius of discourse, nuances of meaning (Elaine points out that she cannot call herself a "widow" since she has never been married) are of no consequence in the face of hard facts: "You're married. Your mom was married. My mother is married. I'm thirty-four. Your daughter is growing breasts, and I'm not married" (66). Peter has a similarly practical nature: his suggestion is that Lori advertise for a husband. "She can say SWFRNRS desires A for marriage." "What are all those initials, Dad?" Sari asks. " 'Single white female registered nurse roller skater,' Peter smiles." As for "A," it designates "Anyone." And Sari agrees that it's "numb" "to be as old as Lori and not be married" (68).

The narrator's own language game is different. She knows that Mike Larson, the prospective date for Lori, is said to be a "creep," that many marriages are like those of the "battered husband" she interviews, that Sari's little friend Julia has a mother whose new live-in boyfriend is a drug pusher. More important, she knows that Lori has nothing to say for herself:

> "Lori and I met in high school," I say. "She was always a good athlete."
>
> She nods politely. "And Elaine was always a brain. She was going to be an astronomer."
>
> "Chemist," I correct.
>
> Larson smiles. "I once wanted to be a pilot."
>
> "Me too," says Lori, "only I wanted to be a stewardess."
>
> I look at the two, Ken and Barbie, only Barbie is a little jowly and Ken is subject to fits of choking. (78–79)

Despite such healthy cynicism, Elaine is bent on applying her own marriage paradigm to Lori's case. Like Lori herself, she "hasn't understood the problem suggested by the question." To "broaden the base," as "the twelve-year-old with the Frankenstein forehead and shiny glasses" puts it, is to send money, not poems. What Lori wants and needs is a specific material change in her life. Elaine, on the other hand, operates on the principle of what her husband calls "all surmise and misinterpretation" (73). As such, their two closed language systems can never make contact.

"ORDINARY LANGUAGE," says Maurice Blanchot in a famous essay that Lydia Davis has translated,[4] "is not necessarily clear, it does not always say what it says; misunderstanding is also one of its paths. This is inevitable. Every time we speak we make words into monsters with two faces, one being reality, physical presence, and the other meaning, ideal absence" (Blanchot 59). The "misunderstanding" inherent in ordinary language is the subject that animates Davis's own remarkable fiction. The word as physical presence: in Davis's work, vocabulary is stripped down to a bare minimum, words—frequently function words and pronouns—being put to the test through a series of permutations that yield, not knowledge of the signifieds to which they refer, but precisely the absence that Blanchot talks about.

If Chernoff's first book is written under the sign of the French Surrealists, Davis's first collection, *The Thirteenth Woman and Other Stories* (1976) draws upon the tradition of Eastern European folk tale and Kafkaesque parable. "The Mother," reprinted in *Break It Down*,⁵ is typical of this early mode:

> The girl wrote a story. "But how much better it would be if you wrote a novel," said her mother. The girl built a doll's house. "But how much better if it were a real house," her mother said. The girl made a small pillow for her father. "But wouldn't a quilt be more practical," said her mother. The girl dug a small hole in the garden. "But how much better if you dug a large hole," said her mother. The girl dug a large hole and went to sleep in it. "But how much better if you slept forever," said her mother. (119)

This fable captures perfectly—perhaps too perfectly—the despair that accompanies a young girl's fear of maternal rejection, but here, and elsewhere in these early stories, the schematic treatment of "girl," "mother," "woman," or "universal lady" keeps the reader at bay. Davis's precocious cleverness is circumscribed by an equal dose of caution. "It was not possible," begins a story called "The Transformation," "and yet it happened; and not suddenly, but very slowly, not a miracle, but a very natural thing, though it was impossible," and the detached and distanced fabulist tells the ironic tale of "A girl in our town [who] turned into a stone" (*Thirteenth Woman* 10). Again, the story is clever rather than memorable.

The solution—and here again we find a similar development in Chernoff's fiction—is to place girl, mother, daughter, lover, son, or husband in specific situations that elicit both the narrator's and the reader's interpretations and emotional responses. "I get home from work," begins the first story (simply called "Story") in *Break It Down*, "and there is a message from him: that he is not coming, that he is busy. He will call again" (3). How the "I" responds to this equivocal "message" from the nameless "him," whom she evidently loves to the point of obsession, is now relayed in three chilling pages that contain neither exposition about the past nor characterization of the principals, nor, for that matter, a rendition of the narrator's stream of consciousness. The focus of "Story" is entirely on the network of action and reaction, event and interpretation.

In a sequence of mounting tension, the "I" phones "him," receives no answer, goes to his house where she finds his car but not him, writes him a note, goes home, receives his call, argues with him about his account of his evening, hangs up, calls back but receives no answer, goes back to his house, finally confronts him in a short scene whose import remains unclear, and goes back home for the last time. Davis's short staccato "I do this, I do that" sentences foreground temporal and causal conjunctions: "then," "finally," "but," "since," "so," "even so," "either," "or." "I can't see him very well," says the narrator, "*because* it is dark in the narrow lane beside his door and he is wearing dark clothes. . . . I think he is not speaking *not because* he is feeling so much *but because* he is preparing what he will say" (5). Logical reasoning, it is implied, can lead us to the truth. Especially when logic is accompanied by precision of temporal and spatial reference: "at nine o'clock," "at ten-forty-five," "I call him back five minutes later," "I am in my nightgown, it is after twelve and I have to leave the next morning at five. Even so, I get dressed and drive the mile or so to his place." Again, the other woman in this tale of obsessive love is known only as "his old girlfriend," as if the temporal designation might satisfy the narrator's need to consign "her" to a past that is no longer a threat.

But is "old" equivalent to "former"? Or to what has been and still is? The greater the precision, the more exact the detailing of the evening's successive incidents, the less the narrator's ability to draw inferences. Indeed, evidence is inevitably contradictory:

> I try to figure it out.
> So they went to the movies and then came back to his place and then I called and then she left and he called back and we argued and then I called back twice but he had gone out to get a beer (he says) and then I drove over and in the meantime he had returned from buying beer and she had also come back and she was in his room so we talked by the garage doors. But what is the truth? Could he and she both really have come back in that short interval between my last phone call and my arrival at his place? Or is the truth really that during his call to me she waited outside or in his garage or in her car and that he then brought her in again, and that when the phone rang with my second and third calls he let it ring without answering, because he was fed up with me and with arguing? Or is the truth that she did leave and did come back later but that he remained and let the phone ring without answering? Or did he perhaps bring her in and then go out for the beer while she waited there and listened to the phone ring? The last is the least likely. I don't believe anyway that there was any trip out for beer. (6–7)

Here the narrator's re-recounting of what she has already told us, this time adopting what she takes to be the man's point of view, gradually blocks all possibility of interpreting the signs. Statement leads to question, one alternative leads to another, until finally, in the last sentence, the one premise that seemed to be a fact ("he had gone out for a beer") is rejected. In the final paragraph of "Story," the word "truth" appears six times, each repetition casting further doubt as to its nature. As "Story" ends, the narrator is trying to "come to such conclusions as: whether he is angry at me or not; if he is, then how angry; whether he still loves her or not; if he does, then how much; whether he loves me or not; how much; how capable he is of deceiving me in the act and after the act in the telling" (7).

Evidence and inference, quantification ("how much") and simple op-position ("either . . . or")—these categories, so Davis implies, can never bring us closer to "the truth." The "story" can never approach closure; just the same, it is only human to "try to figure it out." And ultimately the "events" that have generated the hermeneutic puzzle all but fade into the background, for it is the puzzle itself that has become the narrator's obsession.

Davis's minimalism recalls the Beckett of *Texts for Nothing* or *Fizzles*. Like Beckett, Davis presents us with a series of images and word clusters at once highly concrete and yet indeterminate.[6] But the repetitions and permutations that structure her stories are charged with greater personal feeling than Beckett would allow or desire. As readers, it is all but impos-sible for us not to sympathize with the woman of "Story," who wants so desperately to know where she stands with her lover; as readers, we in-evitably engage in her particular language game, trying to establish a se-miotic code that might account for the nameless lover's behavior. But—and here is the irony—in another sense, our aim, like the narrator's, is to be unable to account for it. For isn't it clear that if this man really cared about the woman, he wouldn't engage in (or invent?) such complicated maneuvers?

An even more powerful version of these motifs appears in "The Letter." Again, plot and character are at a minimum. The narrator, this time "she" rather than "I," is obsessed by the memory of her former lover or hus-band. Although there is a new man in her life, she goes over and over in her mind what "he" said at their last meeting, what he might be doing now, and so on. The mere glimpse of "an old Volvo" is taken as a sign: after all, "he" owns a white one. In this context, the sight of "his hand-writing on an envelope in her mailbox" sends her into a tailspin. And Davis's story now poses the question: how can the woman understand what the import of this letter is?

Again, the question of interpretation is Davis's real subject. The first step is supposition, generated by the envelope of the as yet unopened let-ter: "she decides that this envelope will have a check in it for some of the money he owes her. He owes her over $300. If he has been embarrassed about the debt, this would explain the year of silence, and if he now has some money to send her, this would explain the fact that now he is breaking the silence." But "this would explain" leads nowhere for "There is no check in it, and it is not a letter but a poem in French, carefully copied out in his handwriting. The poem ends *compagnon de silence*. Then his name" (52).

So enigmatic are these contents that the narrator, who is on her way to meet "some people she doesn't know very well," begins to "feel dizzy and sick. She drives slowly in the right-hand lane and pinches the skin of her neck until the faintness goes away" (53). Only later that night, when she goes to bed, does her detective work begin. The letter, taken to bed, is, of course, a supplement or substitute for the absent lover: thus the textual and the sexual become inextricable. Every mark on the page becomes erotically charged.

But the "evidence" is as contradictory and misleading as that of "Story":

> She examines first the postmark. The date and the time of day and the city name are very clear. Then she examines her name above the address. He might have hesitated writing her last name, because there is a small ink blot in a curve of one letter. He has addressed it a little wrong and this is not her zip code. She looks at his name, or rather his first initial, the G. very well formed, and his last name next to it. Then his address, and she wonders why he put a return address on the letter. Does he want an answer to this? It is more likely that he is not sure she is still here and if she is not still here he wants his letter to come back to him so that he will know. His zip code is different from the zip code of the postmark. He must have mailed this somewhere out of his neighborhood. Did he also write it away from home? Where? (53–54)

The only "clear" datum is the postmark and even this "fact" gives way under the realization that the zip code of his return address and of the postmark do not match. The attempt to read into his handwriting (the "small ink blot in a curve of one letter") leads absolutely nowhere, but the very sight of the writing makes the absent lover oddly present to the narrator. Absurdly, she wonders where he was when he wrote it.

The letter itself is a French poem. The date, May 10, in the upper-right-hand corner may have been inserted before or after the copying of the poem. As for the poem itself, Davis refers to the standard Romantic paradigm about lost love and regeneration, a paradigm familiar to anyone who has studied French in high school, even as the actual text poses peculiar difficulties. Some words are illegible and can be "deciphered" only by finding their rhyming partners: thus *pures* (pure thoughts) / *obscures* (dark, referring to dark flowers). Again, the narrator infers that the capital *L* at the beginning of the last line of the octet must lead to "*La lune*, the moon, the moon that is generous or kind *aux insensés*—to crazed people" (55).

By this time, the reader is completely caught up in the narrator's act of interpretation. The references to green meadows, the moon, and dying on the moss now take on a possibly sublime meaning: although the poem's lovers had to die, *nous nous retrouvions*, "we found each other again, up above, in something *immense*, somewhere, which must be heaven. They have found each other crying. And so the poem ends, more or less, we found each other crying, dear companion of silence." The single word "retrouvions" holds the key to the narrator's fate: "If there can be no doubt about *retrouvions*, and there seems to be no doubt, then she can believe that he is still thinking, eight hundred miles from here, that it will be possible ten years from now [his original suggestion for their next meeting], or five years [her countersuggestion], or, since a year has already passed, nine years or four years from now" (55–56).

Thus, the decoding process has transformed the mere reproduction of someone else's poem into a startling personal confession. Or has it? Is no other reading possible?

> she worries about the dying part of it: it could mean he does not really expect to see her again, since they are dead, after all; or that the time will be so long it will be a lifetime. Or it could be that this poem was the closest thing he could find to a poem that said something about what he was thinking about companions, silence, crying, and the end of things, and is not exactly what he was thinking; or he happened on the poem as he was reading through a book of French poems, was reminded of her for a moment, was moved to send it, and sent it quickly with no clear intention. (56)

Once the chain of possible inferences is set into motion, there is no end to the desire for knowledge. Given the fragmentary state of the text, as Davis's narrator presents it, we can invent any number of possible contexts for the word "retrouvions." The very absence of graphic emblems, the limitation on the corpus of signifiers, brings imagination into play.

And this is finally what the letter is worth to its recipient. "She folds up the letter and puts it back in the envelope, lays it on her chest with her hand on top of it, closes her eyes, and after a while, with the light still on, begins to fall asleep." The letter that took the place of a lover: what the words say no longer matters for the sheet of paper has become an emblem, the source of a subtle perfume that may be the lost lover's smell.

What Davis achieves in "The Letter," and in such related stories as "Five Signs of Disturbance," "A Few Things Wrong With Me," "Therapy," "Once a Very Stupid Man," and "The Sock," is to create a language field at once totally familiar and yet rigidly defamiliarized. I doubt if there is a woman alive who has not, at one time, received a letter charged with the emotions defined in Davis's story, and who has not tried to decode it as does the nameless "she" of the tale. But the telling of the incident might easily have been banal. Had Davis included references to the couple's former life together, to the factors that drove them apart, the reactions of their families and friends, the relation of their love to their work, and so on, she would have diffused the intensity of the hermeneutic process that is presented for our contemplation. More austere than Chernoff, Davis does not place her characters in the social frames that characterize a story like "Don't Send Poems, Send Money." She rarely, for that matter, reproduces dialogue, preferring the distance and undecidability achieved by the use of indirect speech. Thus, the surface of a Davis narrative is so smooth and seamless that its gaps are all the more startling.

In "Once a Very Stupid Man," a confused young woman, who can never find her clothes or even her glasses in the morning and relies on her lover to help her get dressed, wants to share with him a Hasidic tale she has come across in her subway reading, a tale that begins "There was once a man who was very stupid" (the copyright page gives as its source Martin Buber's *The Way of Man*), and tells of a man who, having with great mental effort remembered where he has put his various articles of clothing so that he can get dressed in the morning, moralizes: "This is all very well, I have found my clothes and I am dressed, but where am I myself?" (139). Banal as this statement of lost identity may be, the narrator concludes that it applies neatly to her own situation.

But in the process, the import of the Hasidic tale is subtly transformed, its hero's question about identity giving way, as so often in Davis's fiction, to the paramount question of logic:

> She was sitting in a café and a bearded man was writing two tables away from her and two loud women came in to have lunch and disturbed the bearded man and she wrote down in her notebook that they had disturbed the bearded man writing at the next table and then saw that since she herself, as she wrote this, was writing at the next table, she was probably calling herself a bearded man. It was not that she had changed in any way, but that the words *bearded man* could now apply to her. Or perhaps she had changed. (140)

Proposition 1: the person at the next table is a bearded man; proposition 2: vis-à-vis the "two loud women" having lunch, the woman narrator is at the next table. Therefore: she is a bearded man. Weighing the logic of this conclusion, the nervous heroine begins to probe the *post hoc, propter hoc* theorem. Did she want to read the tale because it reminded her of her trouble in finding her clothes, or did she have trouble finding them because the story suggested the motif to her? Does the rain cause tears or do her tears make her aware of the rain? And finally, in response to the noise of a "great clashing of metal" in the street outside, "Has the noise really come into me, or has something in me gone out into the street to make such a great noise?" (141).

Here the "scramble system" within which we try to communicate is electrically charged. Text folds over text. The Hasidic parable seems to apply to the woman's own situation so neatly. Or does it? By the end of the story, we sense that nothing is in fact farther apart than the rabbi's sententious fable about the man's recognition that clothes do not make him, that "identity" is spiritual, and the woman's quite contrary perception that we cannot, so to speak, tell where the "clothes" end and the inner person begins. Hence Davis's title "Once a Very Stupid Man" is a sentence that cannot be completed; the noun phrase, embedded in a temporal clause, hangs in midair.

IN a review of Clark Coolidge's *Mine: The One that Enters the Stories*, Lydia Davis praises the poet's subtly evocative imagery, his distinctive syntax, his "almost perfect ear"—"he rarely writes anything less than a perfectly beautiful sentence" (94)—but she wonders whether *Mine* does not go too far in the direction of nonrepresentation:

> No doubt [Coolidge's] intention is to write an uneasy work, he wants to upset language and upset the way we read language, he wants us never to forget the barrier of words. . . . But because the text is tied to nothing, or because its referent is so elusive, confused, shadowy, the text floats in isolation. . . . And after all, Coolidge is not the first writer to fragment his text by questioning the act of writing. This articulate doubt, this articulate trouble, has by now been exhausted. (95)

In thus criticizing what she calls Coolidge's "refuge in experiment," in arguing that fiction must transcend "the inherent negation involved in writing" and renew, however elliptically, the contact words make with their referents, Davis suggests that her own poetics of fiction marks a return to "the real," to what she refers, with reference to Beckett, as "the attempt to see and to say" (96). It is a distinction Maxine Chernoff would surely endorse. In what we might call the "postexperimental" fiction of these young writers, the *mise en question* of the language event, a mise en question that many of us first associate with the name of Wittgenstein, is centrally important, but it must be construed pragmatically. In the "scramble system" that is ours, their stories imply, the word can never approximate the world. And yet—each and every language event continues to yearn for such approximation.

NOTES

1. Numerical references are to Propositions not pages.

2. "False Documents" first appeared in a slightly different version as "A Duet for Paper and Hand" in From *Americans on the Move* (46). These texts and lyrics are drawn from the early stages of a performance first presented at The Kitchen Center for Video, Music, and Dance in April 1979. The version of "False Documents" cited here appears in *United States*.

3. Chernoff's second book, *New Faces of 1952*, which alternates free verse lyrics with prose poems, carries on the Surrealist mode of *A Vegetable Emergency*. Thus a poem named "Breasts" begins: "If I were French, I'd write / about breasts, structuralist treatments / of breasts, deconstructionist breasts, / Gertrude Stein's breasts in Pere Lachaise / under stately marble" (10). *Bop*, published only a year after *New Faces of 1952*, marks a real departure from this fantasy strain.

4. "Littérature et le droit à la mort" (1949), translated by Davis as "Literature and the Right to Death" in *The Gaze of Orpheus* (59). Davis is also the translator of Blanchot's *L'arrêt de mort* (*Death Sentence*), *La folie du jour* (*The Madness of the Day*), and a number of other Blanchot works. She has translated Sartre, Foucault, Leon-Paul Fargue, and Michel Leiris, and is regarded as one of the leading translators of avant-garde French literature. The influence of Blanchot and Leiris on Davis's own writing deserves to be studied.

5. Of the 35 stories in *Break It Down*, 6 first appeared in *The Thirteenth Woman* and another 16 in *Story and Other Stories*. The stories in *Break It Down* are not, however, arranged chronologically nor are they dated, so that the book gives no clear sense of Davis's development.

6. See, on this point, my discussion of Beckett in *The Poetics of Indeterminacy*.

WORKS CITED

Anderson, Laurie. "From *Americans on the Move*." *October* 8 (Spring 1979): 45–58.

——. *United States*. New York: Harper, 1984.

Blanchot, Maurice. *Death Sentence*. Trans. Lydia Davis. Barrytown, NY: Station Hill, 1978.

——. "Literature and the Right to Death." *The Gaze of Orpheus and Other Literary Essays*. Trans. Lydia Davis. Ed. P. Adams Sitney. Barrytown, NY: Station Hill, 1981.

Blanchot, Maurice. *The Madness of the Day*. Trans. Lydia Davis. Barrytown, NY: Station Hill, 1981.

Chernoff, Maxine. *Bop*. Minneapolis: Coffee House, 1986.

———. "The Fence of Character." "Symposium on Narrative: 'What is the Status of Narrative in Your Work?' " *Poetics Journal* 5: Special Issue, *Non/Narrative* (May 1985): 69–121.

———. *New Faces of 1952*. Ithaca, NY: Ithaca House, 1985.

———. *A Vegetable Emergency*. Venice, CA: Beyond Baroque, 1977.

Davis, Lydia. *Break It Down*. New York: Farrar, 1986.

———. "Coolidge's 'Mine.' " *Poetics Journal* 3: Special Issue, *Poetry and Philosophy* (May 1983): 91–96.

———. *Story and Other Stories*. Great Barrington, MA: The Figures, 1983.

———. *The Thirteenth Woman and Other Stories*. New York: Living Hand, 1976.

Owens, Craig. "Sex and Language: In Between." *Laurie Anderson: Works from 1969 to 1983*. Ed. Janet Kardon. Philadelphia: Institute of Contemporary Art, 1983. 48–55.

Perloff, Marjorie. *The Poetics of Indeterminacy: Rimbaud to Cage*. Princeton: Princeton UP, 1981.

Wittgenstein, Ludwig. *Philosophical Investigations*. 3d ed. Trans. G.E.M. Anscombe. New York: Macmillan, 1958.

The Artists of Hell: Kathy Acker and "Punk" Aesthetics

LARRY MCCAFFERY

I. IF YOU'RE LOOKING FOR TROUBLE, YOU'VE COME TO THE RIGHT PLACE
(Elvis Presley)

The artists of Hell
set up easels in parks
the terrible landscape,
where citizens find anxious pleasure
preyed upon by savage bands of youths.
(Jim Morrison, *The New Creatures Poems*)

And when we tell ourselves we have reached the paroxysm of horror, blood, and flouted laws, of poetry which consecrates revolt, we are obliged to advance still further into an endless vertigo.
(Antonin Artaud, "The Theater and the Plague")

Disasters, revolutions, and volcanoes do not make love with the stars. The erotic revolutionary and volcanic deflagrations antagonize the heavens. As in the case of violent love, they take place beyond the constraints of fecundity. In opposition to celestial fertility there are terrestrial disasters, the image of terrestrial love without condition, erection without escape and without rule, scandal, and terror.
(Georges Bataille, "The Solar Anus")

we aroused pity by cultivating the most repulsive of wounds. We became a reproach to your happiness.
(Jean Genet, *The Thief's Journal*)

Unfasten chains, remove masks.
(K.A., *Great Expectations*)

Someday there'll have to be a new world. A new kind of woman. Or a new world for women because the world we perceive, what we perceive, causes our characteristics. In that future time a woman will be a strong warrior: free, stern, proud, able to control her own destiny, able to kick anyone in the guts . . . .
(K.A., *Kathy Goes to Haiti*)

Money gives power to make change stop, to make the universe die; so everything in the materialistic society is the opposite of what it really is. Good is bad. Crime is the only possible behavior.
(K.A., *Blood and Guts in High School*)

I feel I feel I feel
(K.A., *Great Expectations*)

I'm me: I'm lonely I'm miserable I'm crazy I'm hard and tough I

Nothing was holy to us. Our movement was neither mystical, communistic nor anarchistic. All of these movements had some sort of programme, but ours was completely nihilistic. We spat on everything, including ourselves. Our symbol was nothingness, a vacuum, a void.
(George Grosz, "on Dada" [Hebdige])

work so much I'm determined to see reality I don't compromise I use people especially men to get money to keep surviving I juggle reality (thoughts of reality) I feel sorry for myself I love to hurt myself . . . .
(K.A., *Kathy Goes to Haiti*)

within the context of neo rock we must open our eyes and seize and rend the veil of smoke which man calls order.
(Patti Smith, "the salvation of rock")

As long as the freedom whatever my lust wishes to say. poetry! poetry!
(K.A., *Blood and Guts*)

"Actually we're not into music. Wot then? We're into chaos."
(A Sex Pistol [Chambers])

Fuck art.
(K.A., *The Adult Life of Toulouse Lautrec*)

II. IF EVERYTHING IS MOVING-ALL-OVER-THE-PLACE-NO-TIME, ANYTHING IS EVERYTHING. IF THIS IS SO, HOW CAN I DIFFERENTIATE? HOW CAN THERE BE STORIES?
(K.A., *Great Expectations*)

In 1973 Erica Jong published *Fear of Flying*, a novel greeted warmly by some critics (mostly male) and denounced by others (including many feminist critics); certainly the novel was controversial and popular enough to make "the zipless fuck" the best known literary catch-phrase since "Catch-22." In 1973 Kathy Acker also published her first novel, *The Childlike Life of the Black Tarantula*, although this book—appearing as it did without fanfare from a small press—caused scarcely a ripple of critical or popular reaction. These two first novels shared a number of things: both presented lusty (perhaps semiautobiographically based) narrators willing to talk about their sexual longings and histories in ways certain to shock an American public whose notions of female sexuality often went no deeper than those provided by media images of Cher, Patti Hearst, and air-brushed

HELLO, I'M ERICA JONG. ALL OF YOU LIKED MY NOVEL *FEAR OF FLYING* BECAUSE IN IT YOU MET REAL PEOPLE. PEOPLE WHO LOVED AND SUFFERED AND LIVED. THAT'S WHY YOU LIKED IT. MY NEW NOVEL *HOW TO DIE SUCCESSFULLY* CONTAINS THOSE SAME CHARACTERS. AND IT CONTAINS TWO NEW CHARACTERS. YOU AND ME. ALL OF US ARE REAL. GOODBYE. . . .
WHAT WAS I SAYING? OH YES, MY NAME IS ERICA JONG I WOULD RATHER BE A BABY THAN HAVE SEX. I WOULD RATHER GO GOOGOO. I WOULD RATHER WRITE GOOGOO. I WOULD RATHER WRITE: FUCK YOU UP YOUR CUNTS THAT'S WHO I AM THE FUCK WITH YOUR MONEY I'M NOT CATERING TO YOU ANY MORE I'M GET-

Playboy Bunnies; both also dealt specifically with male oppression, social hypocrisy, female role-playing, repression. But these are really very superficial similarities; of much greater significance is what their fundamental differences suggest about the value, even the necessity, of women developing experimental strategies in order to portray the reality of their experience.

It can be argued that *Fear of Flying*, like a number of other, similarly popular, controversial female initiation and victimization novels from that same period (Lisa Alther's *Kinflicks*, Judith Rossner's *Looking for Mr. Goodbar*, Alix Kates Shulman's *Memoirs of an Ex-Prom Queen*, Marilyn French's *The Women's Room*) served an important social function by helping to eliminate various clichéd notions about women's sexuality and by presenting a sympathetic, more realistic depiction of women's lives and the sources of their oppression. For all the controversy these books generated, however, these novels were ultimately limited mass-market fare whose "radicalism" was of a decidedly nonthreatening (but readily marketable) variety. To my mind, the limitations and inadequacies of these novels are crucially related to their reliance on traditional novelistic features. These features—the presentation of characters whose personalities can be analyzed (usually via psychology), the construction of a coherent plot involving a carefully orchestrated sequence of events leading to a kind of resolution, and so forth—not only perhaps fail to provide a means to examine the nature of the female self but they imply that women's desires and the sources of their victimization can be "contained" and made sense of by the same procedures (logic, rational analysis) and by the same public discourse that have served our male-dominated, exploitative systems so effectively. My point, then, is that women who

TING OUT I'M GETTING OUT I'M RIPPING UP MY SKIN I HURT PAIN OH HURT ME PAIN AT THIS POINT IS GOOD. ME ERICA JONG WHE WOO WOO I AM ERICA JONG I AM ERICA JONG.
(K.A., *Hello, I'm Erica Jong*; also included in *Blood and Guts*)

Capitalism leaves the subject the right to revolt, preserving for itself the right to suppress that revolt.
(Julia Kristeva, *Revolution in Poetic Language*)

As far as literature is concerned, heroines are still restricted to one vice, one virtue, and one occupation. In the novels of Doris Lessing, an authoress concerned with a great many other things besides love, the heroines still spend most of their energy and time maintaining relations with their lovers (or marrying, or divorcing, or failing to achieve orgasm, or achieving it, or worrying about their sexuality, their men, their loves, and their love lives).
(Joanna Russ, "What Can a Heroine Do?")

Unable to use the myths of male culture (and apparently unwilling to spend her life writing love stories) Woolf uses a structure that is basically non-narrative. Hence the lack of "plot," the repetitiousness, the gathering-up of the novels into moments of epiphany, the denseness of the writing, the indirection. There is nothing the female character can *do*—except exist, except think, except feel.
(Joanna Russ, "What Can a Herativeoine Do?")

rely on the conventions, myths, and language of traditional fiction are complicitly aligning themselves with the authority of language and meaning-structures that have oppressed them. Thus women need to become literary "criminals," break the literary laws and reinvent their own, because the established laws prevent women from presenting the reality of their lives—a reality that generally lies outside the laws of the text.

Kathy Acker is exactly such a literary criminal. Even in her early works, she succeeds in developing a literary aesthetic capable of rendering a radical, brutally honest exploration of female identity, role-playing, and sexuality—and of the ways these relate to wider social, political, and linguistic structures. Her aesthetic, which is intimately related to the "punk" aesthetic that evolved in music during the mid 1970s, has led Acker to produce a series of novels that are deliberately crude, violent, obscene, disjointed, surreal. Her methods are designed to force a confrontation between readers and *all* conventions (literary and otherwise), to shock them out of complacent acceptance of hierarchies, received traditions, meanings, stable identities. My sense is that Acker's approach serves her much better than Jong's in finding a suitable means to construct and deconstruct female existence. If Acker's works fail to supply a satisfying sense of "resolution" and coherency to this existence, this is because she feels such concepts distort the reality of women's lives. The only "resolution" in her works is like that produced in the aftermath of an explosion; with all familiar structures destroyed, one must begin reassembling the elements of existence into newer (and hopefully more liberating) patterns.

It is perhaps a new source of anguish for the black man to realize that if he writes a masterpiece, it is his enemy's language, his enemy's treasury which is enriched by the additional jewel he has so furiously and lovingly carved.
(Jean Genet, "Introduction" to *Soledad Brother: The Prison Letters of George Jackson*)

C'est un demon, vous savez ce n'est pas un homme.
(Arthur Rimbaud, "Delires I")

The task of art—we know—is to give form to life, i.e., the very form that women writers cannot use.
(Joanna Russ, "What Can a Heroine Do?")

one cannot simply write a book. utter speech. one must discover something. i have no patience yet require to organize. rooms, windows, i keep building. i can never rest and repetition makes me nauseous. to build monsters. to hit the plunger and spray neo graffiti in the mouth of a river. to remember a word too sacred to remember.
(Patti Smith, "babel")

The Lords appease us with images. They give us books, concerts, galleries, shows, cinemas .... Through art they confuse us and blind us to our enslavement. Art adorns our prison walls, keeps us silent and diverted and indifferent.
(Jim Morrison, "The Lords")

III. FORMULATED, SPRAWLING ON A PIN

foul mouthed . . . street tough . . . visionary experimentalist . . . French Symbolist dream of . . . Marxist underpinning which . . . the gold front tooth and spiked hair immediately signal a . . . dada . . . *jouissance* . . . motif of the demon or criminal so familiar to . . . presence indicated by a perpetual displacement . . . nihilism . . . pornographic clichés actually reveal a central feature of the reality of . . . cut-up methods . . . shocking but doubly so due to her role . . . punk stance as coded gestures of defiance . . . fundamental distrust of language's ability to express . . . *differance* . . . surrealism . . . recuperation of marginalized forms, topics, identities . . . crime, it appears, *does* pay, at least . . . frontal assault on the meaning system . . . decontextualization . . . imagination as plagiarism . . . primacy of sensation at the expense of rationality . . . madness and delirium . . . the mundane forms and objects transformed into . . . "adolescence" here seen as . . .

IV. IN THESE PLACES

IN WHICH ALL REALITY TURNS INTO
A HOWL AND MAKES ITSELF GO AWAY
SOMETHING HAPPENS
(K.A., *Blood and Guts*)

In linking Acker's novels to the punk rock movement, I do not mean to damn her with faint praise. Although ridiculed by the media and critical establishment for its adolescence and offensiveness, the punk movement was arguably the most significant artistic movement of the 1970s. The vitality and energy of the punk phenomenon is evident in various ways, but its chief importance was its creation of a style perfectly suited to undermine the complacency of the dominant power groups that had marginalized its members' lives. Emerging in part as an angry reaction against the elation of so much 1960s art (with its intoxicated dreams of social change, peace, aesthetic renewals, new possibilities), punk projected a parodic and deeply disturbing image of victimization, alienation, and hopelessness.

Rimbaud's early tendency to lewdness, sullenness, and debauchery was a perverted form of asceticism, as it is in most adolescents, a means of purification and protection.
(Wallace Fowlie, *Rimbaud*)

Blondie
The Clash
The Damned
The Dead Kennedys
Fear
Gang of Four
The Germs
Richard Hell & the Voidoids
The Ramones
Siouxsie and the Banshees
The Sex Pistols
The Slits
Patti Smith
Television
X
X-Ray Spex

V. PERTURBATION AND DEFORMATION ARE IN DEMAND HERE FOR THEIR OWN SAKES.
(Andre Breton, "The Crisis of the Object" [Hebdige])

Punk aesthetics are rooted in the notion of style as a form of refusal developed by the

Antonin Artaud
Georges Bataille

Dadaists and other precursors of punk. Punk art explores the status and meaning of revolution, the elevation of crime and perversity into art, the reworking of familiar public archetypes and icons into unsettling new forms, the undermining of all accepted forms of discourse, the recuperation of the trivial and ugly elements of our daily existence into forms that would baffle and anger the systems producing this existence. At the heart of punk aesthetics is a challenge to the conventions governing traditional artistic forms—conventions that, by analogy, apply to other areas of life. In particular, punk art emphasizes power, obscenity, passion, incoherence, delirium, pure sensation at the expense of refinement, order, logic, beauty. Convinced that the traditions and language of Great Art had derived from the same elitist, authoritative sensibility that had elevated profit and reason at the expense of human needs and feelings, punk art uses primitivism, noise, cut-up methods, perceptual alterations, and a celebration of the perverse and forbidden—all this designed to subvert the usual ways meaning could be transferred.

Charles Bukowski

William Burroughs

Dada

Jean Genet

Arthur Rimbaud

Marquis de Sade

Surrealism

Velvet Underground

Andy Warhol

Walt Whitman

Despite the restrictions of school, we did exactly what we wanted, and it was good. We got drunk. We used drugs. We fucked. We hurt each other sexually as much as we could. The speed, emotional overload, and pain every now and then dulled our brains. Demented our perceptual apparatus. We knew we couldn't change the shit we were living in so we were trying to change ourselves.
(K.A., *Blood and Guts*)

VI. AN OASIS OF HORROR IN A DESERT OF BOREDOM

The view of a world of banality, insensitivity, and oppression was vividly drawn by Baudelaire 100 years ago, and his call for artistic productions that would produce *some* powerful emotive response—even horror or revulsion—has been taken up by punks and punk's precursors ever since. Feeling themselves existing in a state of perpetual bondage where there was "no future" (as the Sex Pistols put it), punks dressed themselves in an outrageous collage of coded emblems (chains, leather, belts, and other sadomasochistic imagery, symbolically defiled public uniforms, clothes in tatters held together by safety pins or

Ordinary life is so dull that I get out of it as much as possible.
(Steve Jones, a Sex Pistol, quoted in *Melody Maker* [Hebdige])

We don't hate, understand, we want to get back. Fight the dullness of shit society. Alienated robotized images. . . . No to anything but madness.
(K.A., *Blood and Guts*)

tape)—a sartorial breakdown that bespoke larger disorders and victimizations. Even the names of the groups—The Damned, The Slits, The Voidoids, X, The Sex Pistols—reflected their status as willfully alienated and anonymous, doomed.

And yet in their actions, dress, and extreme physical and emotional responses to the world around them, there remains barely concealed within the punk aesthetic a perverse optimism: a hope in the potentially liberating effect of the perverse or shocking gesture. Often this is achieved by crossing images together unexpectedly (the shaved head of a woman, a safety pin emerging from a cheek) or by profaning, mocking, and otherwise decontextualizing sacred texts (Johnny Rotten blaring out "God Save the Queen," the Dead Kennedys opening their song "Moral Majority" with the Mickey Mouse theme song) into blasphemous metatexts; punks also reveled in physical repulsiveness: spitting, vomiting, the shaved head or mohawk, the obscene or stupid tattoo, giving the finger, exposing needle marks on the arms, chewing broken glass and then spitting bloody remarks at the audience. It is at such moments where the artist and audience achieve a brief moment of transcendence, where we are transported to a sacred place beyond dull rationality and blind adherence. In a sense, Kathy Acker's fiction can be seen most simply as an extended effort to produce such moments of liberation.

I manufacture a notion of escape. I rush off in any wrong direction my blood takes. I close the eyes of my intelligence and open my mouth to the speech of the unspoken; I give myself the illusion of a system whose vocabulary escapes me. But from this minute of error there remains the feeling that I have snatched something real from the unknown.
(Antonin Artaud, "Fragments of a Journal in Hell")

Any action no matter how off-the-wall—this explains punk—breaks through deadness.
(K.A., *Great Expectations*)

inherent within us is the dream and task of the alchemist . . . to re-create from the excretions of man pure and soft then solid gold.
(Patti Smith, "the salvation of rock")

VII. THE FEMALE ARTIST CAN NOW LOVE
(K.A., *Great Expectations*)

For obvious social, historical, and cultural reasons, an aesthetic based in part on images of violence, drugs, obscenity, vulgarity, and sexual perversity would forbid women from participation as surely as one of those placards on the clubhouse wall: "No girls allowed." And yet it was the punk movement that first permitted women in

Bind me tie me chain me to the wall / I wanna be a slave to you all / Oh Bondage! Up yours! / Oh Bondage! No More! / Oh Bondage! / Up Yours! / Oh Bondage! No more! / Chain store chain smoke I consume you all / Chain gang chain mail I don't think at

rock to present themselves as something more than picturesque objects and targets of songs; and not only did punk attract a number of gifted writers and performers—Excene Cervenka (of X), Blondie, Poly Styrene (of X-Ray Spex)—but it was a woman (Patti Smith) who was most responsible for demonstrating that punk *art* was not a contradiction in terms.

In fact, punk was a natural area for certain women artists to investigate. For one thing, punk's emphasis on breaking with rigid traditions and defying authority and public discourses was an obvious attraction. Then, too, precisely because women artists had been excluded from earlier versions of punk movements (if it was difficult for de Sade or Jarry or William Burroughs to find a niche for their extremist creative expressions, it was virtually unthinkable for a woman to do so), there were any number of intriguing new possibilities that had been left unexplored. Reacting to and playing with societal expectations about the "proper" nature of women artists and their work, punkers like Patti Smith, Acker, and Poly Styrene created a space where alternate, often androgynous identities could be discovered and expressed and where women could openly explore passions (even ugly, violent, sexually perverse passions). It was one thing for Jim Morrison to make obscene gestures and call for libidinal release and a merging of the self with the primal ("lizard") energies within us; but when women began to examine the sources of their separation from love and fulfillment by dramatizing violence, sexual oppression, and hidden desires, they were making an assertive, defiant break with restrictive cultural and aesthetic assumptions.

Acker's fictional strategies, like those underlying punk music, are designed to liberate herself and her audience from a number of linguistic, psychic, sexual, and social networks. Most centrally, of course, her fiction shares with punk a certain wild, anarchic

all / Trash me crash me beat me till I fall / I wanna be a victim for you all / Oh Bondage! Up Yours! / Oh Bondage! No more . . . .
(Poly Styrene, "Oh Bondage! Up Yours!" [Burchill])

At this point . . . in my life politics don't disappear but take place inside my body.
(K.A., *Blood and Guts*)

lets birdland lets stroll / lets rock lets roll / lets whalebone lets go / lets deodorize the night.
(Patti Smith, "rape")

I clambered up the miles and miles of Polystyrene foam / Then fell into a swimming pool filled with Fairy Snow / I wrenched the nylon curtains back as far as they would go / Then peered through perspex windows at the acrid orange glow / I drove my Polyproperty car so far on wheels of rubber sponge / Then pulled into a Wimpy bar to have a rubber bun / The Day The World Turned Day-Glo / The Day The World Turned Day-Glo / . . . Oh-oh!
(Poly Styrene, "The Day The World Turned Day-Glo" [Burchill])

i am reckless. i never do anything according to the rules . . . . i have been deprived of communicating in english. i am the eye of the eagle circling the arena of life. i am the eye, liquid and sour, poked and

spirit, a reveling in vulgarity and sexual passion, an impulse to explore one's feelings wherever they lead, a flaunting of all the familiar conventions governing her art form.

Part literary parody, part autobiography, part plagiarized snippets of other works, part visionary flights into a realm of pure madness, Acker's books refuse to cohere, control, organize themselves into an illusion of continuity and meaning. Thus she refuses to distinguish between fantasy and reality, her own words or those of others; she creates voices, characters, and scenes that emerge momentarily and then dissolve, characters who exchange identities and names, episodes that repeat themselves verbatim. Always, however, this is a concentration on the "now" of the text, on its coming-into-being, on creating a lexical space of free play where she can discover new possibilities, affirm her existence while yet dramatizing the impossibility of anyone ever being able to explicate the "meaning" of this existence. The persona who emerges from Acker's fiction is always a figure perpetually isolated from her basic drives for love, sensual gratification, self-understanding; one's "identity," Acker implies, is a discontinuous shard of fragments, an "absence" obsessively driven to speak itself into being without the pretense that such articulations can unify or explain identity. And while it may be true that this view of identity is as true for men as for women, it might also be argued that women traditionally have been forced (by men, by social and biological restrictions) to limit their choices of roles, to "be" what men want them to be, to express themselves through certain conventions. For all its disturbing emphasis on violence and delirium, there is a liberating feel to Acker's fiction because she is affirming a freedom to say and be anything her imagination can invent or plagiarize; thus while the "real" Kathy Acker's identity is perpetually displaced in her works, its refusal to be constrained by the inertia of lan-

sucked from the curious bird. trembling to express the inexpressible. filled with the objective lust of the archeologist. i crave discipline, self contradiction. i am incapable of plot. skin graphs perhaps but not plot. we pray to break our fear of submission to sensation. to strap within the movement of the roller coaster. to give in. exhale. to scream. to offer up oneself to the sacred bull charging and tearing into the skirts of repression.
(Patti Smith, "a fleet of deer")

When objective conditions [in nineteenth-century Europe] were not such that this state of tension could be resolved through revolution, rejection became symbolized in the avant-garde texts where the repressed truth of a shattered subject was then confirmed.
(Julia Kristeva, *Revolution in Poetic Language*)

Truth and falsehood, memory, perception, and fantasy: all are toys in this swirling that is him-her.
(K.A., *Blood and Guts*)

To say that the text is a signifying practice implies that it has a subject, a meaning, and a logic, but the logic is one from which the subject is absent and it is through this very absence that the subject reveals himself. One could say that, as a signifying practice, the text is the active form of madness, or rather, an active, which is to say socialized madness.
(Julia Kristeva, *Revolution in Poetic Language*)

guage habits encourages the reader to concentrate on the process of *becoming* (of the text, of "identity"). Rather than "resolving" the dualities and irrational desires within her surrogate protagonists, Acker allows them to emerge, mediated through her consciousness and a variety of discourses, and confront one another: Acker's "I" is therefore utterly vulnerable and a street-tough guttersnipe, a perennial victim and a successful criminal, a seeker of love and sexual fulfillment and an inflictor of pain and abuse, a woman who feels trapped and abandoned and yet whose wildness and alienation place her outside the bounds of societal (and linguistic) entrapment.

A narrative is an emotional moving.
(K.A., *Great Expectations*)

Significance is a *process* in the course of which the "subject" of the text, escaping (conventional logic) and engaging in other logics (of the signifier, of contradiction) struggles with meaning and is deconstructed ("lost"); significance —and this is what immediately distinguishes it from signification—is thus precisely a work; not the work by which the (intact and exterior) subject might try to master language . . . but that radical work (leaving nothing intact) through which the subject explores—entering not observing— how the language works and undoes him or her.
(Roland Barthes, *Image-Music-Text*)

It [the avant-garde text] is a *practice* calling into question (symbolic and social) *finitudes* by proposing *new signifying devices*. In calling the text a practice we must not forget that it is a new practice, radically different from the mechanist practice of a null and void, atomistic subject who refuses to acknowledge that he is a subject of language.
(Julia Kristeva, *Revolution in Poetic Language*)

VIII. THE IMAGINATION AS PLAYGARISM
(Essay title by Raymond Federman)

The words that appear on the cover of Acker's first available novel—*The Childlike Life of the Black Tarantula by the Black Tarantula*—together with the passage that

One text must subvert the meaning of another text until there's only background music like reggae: the inextricability of relation-

opens the novel—"I become a murderess by repeating in words the lives of other murderesses"—immediately display the motif of the writer-as-role-player-or-plagiarist evident in all her works. Although her early works usually contain the equivalent of footnotes or credits at the end of sections, Acker (like Burroughs and Federman) later discards all acknowledgments and allows her voice to intermingle freely with those of other authors. Just as various punk musicians played with the desire for an equation of name and identity by adopting obvious aliases—Richard Hell, Darby Crash, Johnny Rotten, John Doe, Sid Vicious, Jello Biafra—so, too does Acker deconstruct the concept of "author" (and related concepts as authorial "originality" and self-expression) not only by using the words of other writers but by adopting a shifting series of names and roles: in *The Black Tarantula* the narrator becomes the main person in the pornography books she copies; in *The Adult Life of Toulouse Lautrec* the narrator plays the role of Lautrec as a woman, while other "characters" become "real" actors or artists who are also playing roles; in *Blood and Guts in High School* and *Great Expectations*, the narrator fluidly moves in and out of different verbal masks and discourses (Janey Smith, Jean Genet, Clifford Still, Jackson Pollock, Jimmy Carter, as well as numerous purely invented personae); and in two of her books, even the author wears a pseudonym—"The Black Tarantula" being listed as the author of *The Black Tarantula* and "Toulouse Lautrec" for *The Adult Life of Toulouse Lautrec*.

Part of the point behind such strategies is to foreground textual jouissance, to insure that readers perceive that the "unity" found here is not produced by the questionable concept of an authorial ego or character "identity," but results from a confrontation with a consciousness presenting moments in its experience-in-practice. We are also re-

textures the organic (not meaning) recovered.
(K.A., *Great Expectations*)

Everything has been said. These are not my writing.
(K.A., *Great Expectations*)

One thing that I wanted to bring back to rock 'n roll was the knowledge that you invent yourself. That's why I changed my name.
(Richard Hell, in *New Musical Express* [Hebdige])

Indeed, the transition from Lautréamont to Ducasse, from narrative to law, from the domination by the semiotic to that of the symbolic, designates the scission in the process of the subject, which is the precondition of the signifying practice.
(Julia Kristeva, *Revolution in Poetic Language*)

Scott's, the young artist's, real name is James Dean. Marcia's real name is Janis Joplin.
(K.A., *The Adult Life of Toulouse Lautrec*)

Genet doesn't know how to be a woman. He thinks all he has to do to be a woman is slobber. He has to do more. He has to get down on his knees and crawl mentally every minute of the day. If he wants a lover, if he doesn't want to be alone every single goddam minute of the day and horny so bad he feels the tip of his clit stuck in a porcupine's quill, he has to perfectly read his lover's mind, silently, unobtrusively, like a

minded that men and (perhaps especially) women are perpetually doomed to live out the roles and speak the words that others have devised for them. When characters such as Jean Genet, James Dean, and Clifford Still appear in scenes with Agatha Christie's Hercule Poirot or Acker's own literary inventions, she demonstrates how questionable the distinctions are between "identity" and "role-playing"—and how intermingled with cliché, story, and fantasy *all realities are.*

corpse, and figure out at every changing second what his lover wants. He can't be a slave. Women aren't just slaves. They are whatever their men want them to be. They are made, created by men. They are nothing without men.
(K.A., *Blood and Guts*)

In REBEL WITHOUT A CAUSE Jimmy Dean plays himself. He's a victim and hero: the kid who learns to be bad cause he can't be good in a society whose goodness stinks. The kid who keeps his innocence and vulnerability while he learns. The corrupted society. Jimmy not only played in this film, he also helped director Nicholas Ray create the film.
(K.A., *The Adult Life of Toulouse Lautrec*)

IX. TEACH ME A NEW LANGUAGE, DIMWIT. A LANGUAGE THAT MEANS SOMETHING TO ME.
(K.A., *Blood and Guts*)

From the nineteenth century onward, avant-garde artists have consistently defined their role as creators of contexts that question the power and sanctity of the language and syntax that control their medium of expression (be it the language and syntax of music, painting, poetry, fiction, whatever). Such a process of inquisition has important implications for broader issues, and it is not surprising that many of the most important women writers of the past 100 years have focused their attention on developing language structures capable of liberating themselves from exterior sources of control and definition. The writings of Emily Dickinson, Gertrude Stein, Anaïs Nin, Djuna Barnes, Virginia Woolf, to cite just a few prominent examples, are united by a conviction that experimental strategies are required to disrupt the validated way words

[Language is] of all social institutions, the least amenable to initiative. It blends with the life of society, and the latter, inert by nature, is a prime conservative force.
(Ferdinand de Saussure, *Course in General Linguistics* [Hebdige])

It is by revolt against the ego and the self that I disemburden myself from all the evil incarnations of the Word, which have never been anything more for man than a compromise between cowardice and illusion.
(Antonin Artaud, "Revolt Against Poetry")

Culture has been chattering and chattering but to no purpose.

ordinarily function—and that only by devising such strategies can the nature of
womanly experience be accommodated in
language. This challenge to the normative
world and to the normative operations of
language unites avant-garde writing of both
sexes, and links Kathy Acker's punk fiction
to the innovative works of earlier women
authors.

Acker shares with her her punk precursors an evident contempt and impatience
with words that designate and describe
rather than create, words that generate the
illusion of clarity in a world of perceptual
ambiguity, words that illuminate only ab-
stractions rather than perception and sensations. Punk artists of the seventies shared
with Rimbaud, Artaud, Burroughs, and the
Dadaists a confidence that the creation of
"noise"—i.e., any disruption in the usual
orderly sequence that leads from "real
events" and phenomena to their representation—has a genuinely revolutionary potential to disorient (and hence disturb) the
consensual social order. Punk art is a response to the awareness that the orderly exchange of goods, the legal and political systems that produce this exchange, the
academic institutions inculcating the values
and meanings of society all tightly control
what is and is not the "proper" or accept-
able nature of linguistic expression (just as
language, via legal definitions of what constitutes a "drug" or "sexual abnormality,"
controls what is "proper" to do with our
perceptions and our bodies). Not interested
in merely creating metaphors for potential
anarchy and chaos, Acker and punk musicians directly *dramatize and express* disorder by producing a kind of antidiscourse of
madness and sensual delirium.

Punk musicians found the equivalent of
Dada's mockery of "civilized" artistic conventions: while cultivating an appearance
that rejected rock's usual romanticism and
turned performers instead into objects of
abuse and neglect, punkers forced an en-

When a sentence becomes distinct,
it makes no more sense or connection. Wherefore the watcher says
again "Unintelligible," nods his
head, and smiles gloomily.
(K.A., *Great Expectations*)

All writing is pigshit.
People who leave the obscure
and try to define whatever it is that
goes on in their heads, are pigs
.... Those for whom certain
words have a meaning, and certain manners of being; those who
are fussy; those for whom emotions are classifiable, and who
quibble over some degree or other
of their hilarious classifications;
those who still believe in "terms";
those who brandish whatever ideologies belong to the hierarchy of
the times; those about whom
women talk so well, and also those
women who talk so well, who talk
of the contemporary currents of
thought; those who still believe in
some orientation of the spirit;
those who follow paths, who drop
names, who fill books with
screaming headlines are the worst
kind of pigs.
(Antonin Artaud, "All Writing is
Pigshit")

Mr. Fuckface: You see, we own
the language. Language must be
used clearly and precisely to reveal
our universe.
Mr. Blowjob: Those rebels are
never clear. What they say doesn't
make sense.
Mr. Fuckface: It even goes against
all religions to tamper with the sacred languages. Without language
the only people rebels can kill are
themselves.
(K.A., *Blood and Guts*)

counter with musical forms by an abrasive, chaotic mixture of vocals, instrumentation, and gestures. The characteristic sound of punk music—the screeching feedback, ear-splitting, discordant wall of noise that drowned out most of the lyrics—turned "music" into a cacophony of primal sound sensations, babble, with all sources of rational "meaning" and "structure" further undercut by the drugs, alcohol, and violent behavior of the performers and audience. This is not to say that punk music failed to "communicate" anything—it powerfully expressed pent-up anger, frustration, confusion, sexuality—but that it did so by openly defying the traditional notions of musical structure and beauty. Likewise, Kathy Acker's fiction produces a kind of literary "noise" that fiercely communicates her alienation, victimization, and longings for a means to transcend a world of accumulation, images, repression. Acker's "noise" is often shrill, insistent in its desires, troubling in its vision, but it is also a noise that makes one want to move and feel. It is fiction to slam dance by.

all our gestures and rhythms fit the pattern of social rule like the bits of glass shaping the harmony within the kaleidoscope. but what if one rebelled? one jagged edge pulling itself from the mire of melody up into the tube and choosing to scrape and puncture the open end of a predictable merger. what if one refused and another still another until we all came to grips with this wonder of true love? of rock and roll?
(Patti Smith, "a fleet of deer")

Other Rock Deconstructionists:
rap
scratch
dub
industrial noise
and: Laurie Anderson

It is conventional to call "monster" any blending of dissonant elements . . . . I call "monster" every original, inexhaustible beauty.
(Alfred Jarry, *Selected Works* [Hebdige])

One night I wandered into a rock-n-roll club named CBGB's. The light went boomp boomp boomp the drum went boomp bomp boomp the floor went boomp boomp boomp. . . . Boomp boomp boomp entered my head. My body split into two bodies. I was in a new world. I was pounding. BOOM BOOM was reality . . . . I couldn't hear any of that poetical music shit I just wanted to kiss the guy again and again. The music made it so you couldn't hear the words and the music was so

loud music couldn't be heard
you weren't hearing
this is beyond hearing
you is just vibrations so there's no
difference between self and music.
(K.A., *Blood and Guts*)

X. BY WAY OF CONCLUSION:

Kathy Acker: I'm too ugly to go out into the world. I'm a hideous monster.
                    (*The Adult Life of Toulouse Lautrec*)
Patti Smith: i step up to the microphone
                    i have no fear.
                    ("babel field")

WORKS CITED

Note: I am especially indebted to Dick Hebdige's fine analysis of punk "style"—in *Subculture: The Meaning of Style*—for supplying some of the methods used here to "decode" punk musical elements.

Acker, Kathy. *The Adult Life of Toulouse Lautrec by Henri Toulouse Lautrec.* New York: TVRT, 1975.

——. *Blood and Guts in High School.* New York: Grove, 1984.

——. *The Childlike Life Of The Black Tarantula By the Black Tarantula.* New York: TVRT, 1975.

——. *Great Expectations.* New York: Grove, 1983.

——. *Hello, I'm Erica Jong.* New York: Contact II, 1982.

——. *Kathy Goes to Haiti.* Toronto: Rumor, 1978.

Alther, Lisa. *Kinflicks.* New York: NAL, 1977.

Artaud, Antonin. *Anthology.* Ed. Jack Hirschman. San Francisco: City Lights, 1965.

——. *The Theater and Its Double.* New York: Grove, 1958.

Bataille, Georges. *Visions of Excess: Selected Writings, 1927–1939.* Ed. Allan Stoekl. Minneapolis: U of Minnesota P, 1985.

Burchill, Julie and Tony Parsons. *"The Boy Looked At Johnny": The Obituary of Rock and Roll.* London: Pluto, 1978.

Chambers, Iain. *Urban Rhythms: Pop Music and Popular Culture.* New York: St. Martin's, 1985.

Federman, Raymond. *Take It or Leave It.* New York: Fiction Collective, 1975.

Fowlie, Wallace. *Rimbaud.* Chicago: U of Chicago P, 1965.

French, Marilyn. *The Women's Room.* New York: Harcourt, 1978.

Genet, Jean. "Introduction" to *Soledad Brother: The Prison Letters of George Jackson*. London: Penguin, 1971.

————. *The Thief's Journal*. New York: Grove, 1967.

Hebdige, Dick. *Subculture: The Meaning of Style*. New York: Methuen, 1979.

Jarry, Alfred. *Selected Works*. New York: Grove, 1965.

Jong, Erica. *Fear of Flying*. New York: Holt, 1973.

Kristeva, Julia. *Revolution in Poetic Language. New York: Columbia UP, 1984.*

Morrison, Jim. *The Lords and The New Creatures Poems*. New York: Simon, 1970.

Rimbaud, Arthur. *Complete Works, Selected Letters*. Ed. Wallace Fowlie. Chicago: U of Chicago P, 1966.

Rossner Judith. *Looking for Mr. Goodbar*. New York: Simon, 1975.

Russ, Joanna. "What Can a Heroine Do? Or Why Women Can't Write." *Images of Women in Fiction*. Ed. Susan K. Cornillon. Bowling Green: Bowling Green UP, 1972.

Shulman, Alix Kates. *Memoirs of an Ex-Prom Queen*. New York: Knopf, 1972.

Smith, Patti. *Babel*. New York: Putnam's, 1978.

Voices in the Head: Style and Consciousness in the Fiction of Ann Quin

PHILIP STEVICK

THE conventions for imagining and rendering character are, of course, infinite in their permutations, and it surprises no one to read any number of recent novels and find that the human figures in them look, talk, and move through their worlds in ways unlike characters in Dickens or Flaubert or Dostoevski or Conrad or anyone else. The conventions for rendering the inner life more or less directly, on the other hand, are rather remarkably limited, remarkable given the obvious fact that we are all at least as different from each other on the inside of our heads as we are on the outside. The narrowness of those conventions is a product of literary history. In the mere 41 years from Dujardin's *Les lauriers sont coupés* to Faulkner's *The Sound and the Fury*, the major modes for the presentation of consciousness were discovered, the great models written. And during the decisive last half of those 41 years, the dominant system underlying those fictions, virtually the only system, was that of Freud. Those great models lie there, seeming to have defined the limits if not exactly of mind then mind caught and fixed in words on a page. If it surprises no one to discover an original character in last week's novel, it also surprises no one to find modes of consciousness, in last week's novel, that are heavily derivative, that still, after all these years, seem Joycean or Woolfian or Faulknerian.

In 1964 Ann Quin published her first novel, *Berg*. It was very well received for a first novel, especially in view of the usual British distrust of unconventional fiction. What those first reviewers could not have known about that strange and haunting novel is that it was written remarkably close to the bone. *Berg* takes place, for example, in a seedy seaside resort town: Quin, it turned out, was born and raised in Brighton. The novel dramatizes a complicated hostility toward Berg's father: Quin's own father deserted her and her mother at birth. What some of the early reviewers guessed was that *Berg* bore a relationship to Nathalie Sarraute and some of the modes of the new French novel. What they could not have known is that Quin had not read the French novelists whom she was seen to resemble and, in fact, had little interest in the conventions for rendering mind, either early modernist or recent French.[1] What they could not have known but now seems obvious in retrospect is that, from the start, she began to invent ways of representing the inner life by drawing on her own troubled mind, by introspection and a set of conventions largely of her own devising, and that is why the representation of consciousness in her fiction seems so different from that of anyone else, classic or contemporary, akin, if anything, to slightly later writers whom she could not have known such as Peter Handke. Her talent was restless, original, and her four novels are all quite different from each other. But each of them extends the possibilities of *Berg*, rendering the inner life in ways that "feel" to the reader unlike every classic model from which Quin might have been expected to derive.

The opening of *Berg* establishes some of the features of her unique mode. "A body rolls upon a creaking bed," writes the narrator, as if watching from above, naming the figure as "Alastair Berg, hair restorer," yet describing him as if he were amphibian: "White-scaled," "curled webbed toes." There are fragments of his situation, serving as exposition. But almost immediately there is talk, not dialogue, since Berg is alone, but talk in the head. It is not the inner monologue of a character in Virginia Woolf, let us say, registering sensation, conflating past and present, musing on other people, all in a kind of watercolor voice. It is not the inner talk of Joyce, as Bloom or Stephen observe the phenomenal world and interrogate themselves. Berg's talk scarcely seems "inner" at all, seems rather actual speech, acted out in the theater of the mind, and one imagines Berg talking aloud to himself, at least shaping his words with his lips. "Shall I go there again, select another one?" he asks himself of the dance hall girls across the street from his room. "WANTED one downy, light-hearted singing bird to lay," he speaks to himself, as if dictating a classified ad. And finally, by the bottom of the first page, an imagined confrontation with his father establishes the mode: "Oh yes I have seen you with her—she who shares your life now, fondles you, laughs or cries because of you." It is not remembered conversation. No such conversation has taken place, or will. It is mind as a theater both of remembered wound and of desire, possibility, projection, rationalization, aggression, in which the subject is the leading character with the best lines, often the only lines.

A page later, Berg finds, under the mattress, a newspaper photograph of his father. The photograph evokes a fragment of conversation by his mother. "Oh it's him Aly, no mistaking your poor father. How my heart turned, fancy after all this time, and not a word. . . ." Berg's mother's conversation is indented, a block quote, remembered whole, as a unit, seemingly with not only the words but the rhythms and intonations intact. A little later, an encounter with a dance hall girl in which Berg was embarrassed by his impotence is recalled, as talk. "Well I must say you're a fine one, bringing me all the way up here, what do you want then, here are you blubbering, oh go back to Mum. Lor' wait until I tell them all what I got tonight, laugh, they'll die" (4). Or later, in no particular context, Berg recalls his schoolboy humiliations as speech. "Hasn't got a dad, his mum pawns herself to pay the fees; silly cissy Berg, he's so cold he can't even crap" (10).

There are, to be sure, a multitude of ways in which the identity of Berg is imagined and presented. But it is that highly rhetorical inner speech, those scenarios of recollected hurt, projected confrontation, and imagined triumph that, at first and to a large extent at last, characterize Quin's method. There are immediately obvious reasons for her choosing such a method, given the nature of her central character. No one, in experience, uses such patterns of inner speech by way of imagining pleasant encounters, curious phenomena, and nonproblematic tasks. It is a mental strategy that results from unresolved anger, resentment, the badly damaged ego, so that the mind is endlessly obliged, first, to remember those social moments that have made one feel so awful, second, to imagine those small victories that experience denies. In all of the pages of Joyce and Woolf and Dorothy Richardson and Proust (Faulkner may be a special case), no character brings so heavy a charge as Berg of aggression, defeat, and imagined triumph as the principal part of his psychic baggage. Indeed, reading backwards from Quin, one is struck by the incredible sweetness of temper in most of those classic characters in the modernist literature of the inner life. Once Quin has touched that particular area of the self, however, it seems altogether compelling and inevitable that she should have done so. And, quite far from seeming a gratuitous experimentalism, Quin's fictional technique comes to seem a perfectly natural way of rendering a mode of mind that is, in its way, at least as central to the general experience of the last two decades as the benignly assimilative mind of Joyce's Bloom.

IT IS easy to respond to *Berg* in a double way, with admiration for its craft but with a rather distanced and disengaged feeling for its central figure. I have suggested that Berg's mode of sullen introspection, in which he finds old wounds, like a tongue looking for a lost tooth, constructs scenarios of revenge and vindication—I have suggested that such a richly resentful mode of consciousness is representative of vast areas of mind in our century. It is a hard contention to prove, of course, especially since nothing in the presentation of *Berg* suggests that he is meant to seem an emblematic figure. Rather he is made to seem a special case—neurotic, obsessive, and unstable. In any case, Quin, in effect, answers the objection that Berg's mind is anomalous and marginal, therefore of only limited interest as an arena of consciousness. Following *Berg*, she published three more novels in which the characters lack much of the grotesque or hallucinatory quality of Berg. They are, to be sure, in their rather more muted ways, quite as mad as he. But they are made to seem far more "normal" than Berg. Berg commits a ritual murder upon a ventriloquist's dummy. None of the characters in the other three novels is portrayed, or can be imagined, as doing anything so overtly and explicitly unbalanced. Yet those characters display and extend the patterns of mind and style Quin had established in *Berg*.

First, in all four of the novels, the characters are never at home. Even if they occupy a place where they have been for some time past, it is not perceived as home. Physical surroundings tend to be perceived in the way in which one sees them on a trip. Features of the landscape are seen as being strange and unaccustomed, their shapes and textures foregrounded. If objects seem intended to appear beautiful or tasteful, their aesthetic status is ambiguous. It is not that the phenomenal world is neutralized, in the manner of the French *choisistes*, merely registered, verbally photographed. On the contrary, surroundings in Quin tend to be sensuous and personalized. Yet, as if at some polar extremity from Joyce's Dublin, there is no ritualized, routinized base. The merest detail seems unfamiliar. Places look like this in Quin: "The hotel. A room. Three beds. Cupboards that never close. Turn about. Green wallpaper. An old man bears hot chocolate on a silver tray" (*Three* 22). And people look like this: "Leonard leaned forward, legs apart, body suspended in an enclosed area" (*Three* 40).

Second, the whole of experience in Quin's fiction tends to be eroticized. There are, to be sure, scenes of explicit sex, "real" and imagined. And characters, even when they are in situations far removed from the sexual, seem preoccupied, implicitly, with the erotic. But, far more than that, the phenomenal world tends to appear as if charged with sexual energy. There are those images in which the conventions of Freudian symbolism are reimagined. "In the empty swimming pool a balloon floated. Oblong. Yellow. That bumped. But did not burst. Against the sides" (*Three* 103). Or,

We climbed the spiral staircase to the top of the house, and found a large vacant room. The woman opened a pill box with many compartments, and round, oblong coloured pills. She handed me one. I asked

her what it was, what it might do. She smiled, nodded, her arms like
large wings came out at me, over me. I took the pill. (*Passages* 58)

But, more pervasive, there are those ordinary images in which, by some
turn of diction, some nuance, the erotic is potently suggested. No one
makes water more sexual than Quin: the sea, the river, the wash basin,
the hot-spring pool, the hotel shower, the swimming pool. Sun, moon,
vegetation, the wind, potentially erotic, are almost inevitably sexually
charged in her work.

L arrived back a day earlier than expected. He brought some white
robes for our mime plays. He tried on over his clothes. R declared hers
was too small. As the heatwave continues I wear mine, and nothing
else, giving a freedom of movement around the flat, that strangely
enough also gives me a sense of power. You look like a priestess—a sort
of goddess. He said. You might wear something underneath you know
it's rather transparent. R said. (*Three* 142)

Clothes, in Quin, are always erotic.

Third, extending through the four novels, wholes, perhaps more properly gestalts, tend to be fragmented. The tree, the rock, the shoreline tend
to pull away from the whole of the landscape. The relationship of chair
to room, room to house, house to neighborhood, neighborhood to town
is never clear; these are all discrete details and they do not connect. The
mirror gives back a flat and unrecognizable image of the thing reflected.
The relationship between a phrase or a sentence to a larger intentional
discursive pattern is obscure. It is with people, physically, that such a trait
is most evident. Nearly any writer, of course, will permit one character to
fixate on a portion of another—the tilt of an eyebrow, the curve of a
mouth, a wrist, a breast. But in Quin such fragmentation is ubiquitous
and pervasive. It serves not so much to highlight the observation of a
conspicuous feature of another. Rather such fragmentation is the norm,
other people being *ordinarily* perceived as fractions of the whole. "In the
mirror, he had propped up at the end of the bed, she saw angles of her
own body that surprised. Parts he and others had delighted in. He
watched his movements, and her face as she watched her own. Shifting
around she saw her legs. His back" (*Passages* 74–75).

In a way related but roughly opposite, the whole of anything threatens
always to erode, split, merge into another thing. At the point at which
events in the fictive present seem about to come together as a significant
action, they break apart and become mixed with events of the fictive past.
People blend into the scenery, threaten to metamorphose into animals. It
is the outer limits of the person that are most critical. In *Three*, for ex-

ample, Ruth and Leonard bathe together, try on each other's clothes. They listen to music on the radio, aware of how the other's response affects one's own, aware of how the live studio audience's response affects one's own response, the other's response. They make love, sometimes tenderly and artfully, sometimes coldly and coarsely, but always aware of the fact that in sex at its best and sometimes at its worst, it is impossible to tell where one's self ends and the other begins. In *Berg*, it is all a bit cruder and certainly more pathological: Berg's mother, father, and father's lover invade Berg; he impersonates, later seduces, his father's lover. At one virtuoso moment in *Passages*, the experiencing self merges with a street procession.

> She thought a woman held her hand. Wrists, fingers, whiteness of skin between the paint. A glimpse of his shoes, made her look for the mouth. But he had gone. Her arms pinned, unable to move backwards or forwards. Sideways she bent a little, head raised for air. The procession passed out of the town. She moved with those in front, behind her. (72)

In *Tripticks* a local image suggests the same principle extended. "A fluid dance, and all our limbs flowing into, out, through, until I had no idea whose hands, breast, leg I touched, or was touched by" (64). More generally, in *Tripticks*, the outer limits of the self give way to the American world of billboards and self-help, tabloids and soaps, mom, pop, and the kids.

Finally, it is the nature of Quin's fiction that it takes place at several levels of discourse simultaneously, alternately, contrapuntally. Recollection merges with experience and observation. A conversation with one figure coexists with a remembered conversation with another. Pronouns move about so that a passage referring to "him" comes to refer, only a little later, to "I." The media interpenetrate the fiction so that while the television rambles on, characters ignore it, or watch it, half aware, their consciousness on display, as other characters watch them watching. It is *Three* that assembles its levels most audaciously, splicing the playing of the spoken tapes and the reading of the journals of the dead S. into the experience of Ruth and Leonard, as they attempt to understand the triangular relationship of which she was a part and which her tapes and journals in part record. But the other three novels present an image of multileveled experience that is just as pervasive, if less explicit.

Such structures as these serve the thematics of Quin's fiction, which always involves the dialectics of a highly narcissistic self and another or others, each threatening and impinging upon the other, each making unignorable claims upon the other, insight alternating with opacity, desire alternating with defensiveness. They serve as well the spatial sense of

Quin's world, a claustrophobic, hothouse world, largely cut off from history and larger patterns of social action, in which the slow dance of a very small group of egos is as important as it is because it is all there is. And they serve also that sense of the texture and density of mind, which is where I began.

THE texture of mind. Classically, of course, fiction, even densely interior fiction, operates on the assumption that the mind tells stories. Even when the story cannot be found, the mind remains in pursuit of story, as if the Aristotelian beginning, middle, and end were not properties of artifice and art but irreducible properties of mind. Such an implicit conviction has, to be sure, undergone a substantial erosion in the hands of a few novelists in recent years. But Quin, it seems clear, comes to her version of mind not from the example of someone else but from a private conviction that the mind not only does not ordinarily tell stories—it doesn't even try to. Berg comes closest to being a storyteller. His novel abounds with anecdotes, most of them abortive and inconclusive. And it does, after all, have its own telos. Berg hopes to humiliate and kill his father. After that, in the remaining three novels, story virtually ceases to exist. Although quest motifs abound, they remain just that—motifs—unsustained and unrealized. Linearity is abandoned, not, apparently, in pursuit of some "poetic" effect, not because of critical convictions about the role of the novel in the modern world, but rather because Quin, quite simply, does not see the mind as narrator.

Classically, fiction operates on the assumption that the mind seeks to understand. Deriving one's sense of mind from the fictional canon, one would assume that minds, inside and outside of novels, are restlessly in pursuit of cause, the significant whole that embraces the part, in a word, "meaning." What Quin's novels suggest, again, is that the analytical is not merely a property that a novelist can dare to jettison. Rather, it is not *there*. The abstracting, intellectualizing function of mind is thin, extremely specialized and intermittent, all but ignorable as one projects a version of the inner dimensions of self onto the page.

What mind, in its intimate texture and its local detail, actually consists of in Quin will always, to some extent, elude any accounting, since it is clear that she wished to allow for the fluid, the random, and the quotidian. In trying to describe those successions of images and sensations, words like "surreal" do not help at all, since they suggest kinship with a movement. It is not a movement that interests her but the odd and inscrutable recesses of the mind. Nevertheless, mind, in Quin, tends to organize itself as a reflection of *sensory* experience, rendering the visual, the tactile, and the auditory, creating a movement among them (again, one shrinks

from established words like "synaesthesia") in which the visual is perceived by the eye, the ear, and the skin. Likewise, speech, natural sounds,
the world of the ear, become, in some uncanny way, "seen" and
"touched."

Fire, for example, draws Berg. It is rendered as seen, a bonfire, gathering a crowd. His father may be a part of the crowd. Berg looks at the fire,
looks for his father, feels the heat. It is Guy Fawkes Day. The effigy burns.
Berg wishes his father dead. Burning would be just fine. Meanwhile, he
feels the press of the crowd, wishing to withdraw, yet happy to join (72).
It is an image characteristic of Quin, visual, highly charged, yet tactile at
the same time.

In *Three*, Leonard plays the tapes of S. The switch clicks, the spools
turn, and the machine speaks. Yet the machine speaks of desire and distance, the weather, the morning, the sky and the garden, Leonard and
Ruth—aural, visual, and tactile. So it is in Quin. The world is seen, as in
a visual composition, often simultaneously heard. And as it is seen and
heard, it presses against the musculature of the body, against the nerve
ends, and is felt on the skin.

After *Berg*, the play of voices in the consciousness is never again so
explicit, although *Tripticks* comes close. "You, there, a rotten, no good
stinking, cowardly snickering, stupid squirming yellow bastard with your
stupid creakng ugly voice I am still so disgusted with you that I don't ever
want to hear your answer. I have only this to tell you: WATCH OUT!"
(113–14). But the fiction never ceases to be the fiction of voice and those
small units that make up the continuity of mind never cease being inner
speech. Consider the transition in this passage.

> Hands above his head, marking the design of some unfamiliar birds.
> Slant of wings to the slant of their bodies under, caught the light falling.
> They turned from a straight course into a curved one, remained at the
> same height, wings on the convex side of their curving movements,
> moved in line. Lines under his eyes, mouth. His mouth betrayed the
> eyes' attention on the play we saw that night. (*Passages* 18)

There is no visual connection between a line of birds and a line on a face.
What happens is that the mind hears the word "line," making the transition from birds to face on the basis of a word. The whole of the image is
visual. Yet the transition reminds the reader that it is silently spoken and
is experienced aurally, the voice in the head. "He came in, said they must
leave at once. He flung clothes in cases. A cab was called. The negative
would have to wait. She had waited long enough. Wanted to go on waiting. Await developments. He said he would go on ahead, she could follow
soon after" (*Passages* 82). A small contrapuntal invention, turning not so

much on the idea of waiting, going on, developing, turning rather on the experience of those words as inner speech.

IN MARCH of 1970, 2½ years before Quin's apparent suicide, at the height of one of her several breakdowns, the attending therapist wrote to Miriam Boyars, her publisher, requesting copies of her novels. It is clear, in the letter, that the novels were to be read and used as diagnostic tools in helping Quin reorganize her badly damaged life. There is a sense in which the letter is naive, shocking even, as if an attending therapist at St. Elizabeth's had sent for the Cantos in hope that it would help in treating Pound, or as if a clinician had read the *Dream Songs*, hoping it would tell him how to keep Berryman from the bottle and the bridge. Yet there is another sense in which Quin's therapist was both perceptive and compassionate. Her novels do give a record of a mind that is, at once, artful, distanced, dispassionate and raw, immediate, its tensions unresolved. And that is what makes those four novels so powerful and so unusual. They take the self and others, one's voice, the voice of the nonself into areas not quite occupied before. "I opened my mouth, but no words," reads the end of Quin's last novel, *Tripticks*, with an accent so unusual that, even now, it startles. "Only the words of others I saw, like ads, texts, psalms, from those who had attempted to persuade me into their systems. A power I did not want to possess. The Inquisition" (192).

NOTE

1. There is only one piece of sustained, substantive criticism of Ann Quin. It is the brilliant essay by Judith Mackrell in *Dictionary of Literary Biography*, vol. 14, *British Novelists Since 1960*, pt. 2. Detroit: Gale, 1983.

WORKS CITED

Quin, Ann. *Berg*. New York: Scribner's, 1964.
———. *Passages*. London: Calder, 1969.
———. *Three*. New York: Scribner's, 1966.
———. *Tripticks*. London: Calder, 1972.

One Hundred and Three Chapters
of Little Times: Collapsed and
Transfigured Moments in the Fiction
of Barbara Guest

——

KATHLEEN FRASER

> And there are nervous
> people who cannot manufacture
> enough air and must seek
> for it when they don't have plants,
> in pictures. There is the mysterious
> traveling that one does outside
> the cube and this takes place
> in air.
> (Barbara Guest, "Roses," *Moscow Mansions* 58–59)

IN HER antinarrative novel, *Seeking Air*, Barbara Guest has chronicled a remarkable struggle between her protagonist—a fantasy-prone and well-barricaded urban American—Morgan Flew and a world that refuses his control (essentially his lover, Miriam, and a doppelgänger figure called Dark). Guest's subject is that which cannot be directly or simply told. We live in her characters' imaginations of each other (in the displaced subjunctive of what they *might* be more than in the certain and determined world of traditional narrative where one is given fully reasoned explanations and familiar conversations).

To enter into Morgan Flew's mind is to collapse or fly apart with him, to hide inside the intricacies of his hedged bets, to understand from the beginning that we are not to be granted the fictional coherence of knowing "everything" of his origins and reasons for being. Instead, Guest has brought to her novelistic experiment the practiced hand of the collagist, the eye of a film editor and a word-on-word attention to *constructed* reality that marks the modernist poetic sensibility.

Drawing on her years of association with the New York School—as poet, collagist, and art critic—Guest has appropriated visual solutions proposed by European and American artists who prefigured (and influenced) abstract expressionism. Her intention is to create a disrupted narrative text and through this, to underscore the fragility and ambivalence of her characters' personas in the world. Within this context she has forged a strikingly innovative fictional model based on discrete units and intervals, strengthened by peculiar juxtapositions that resemble certain Cubist paintings or experimental films in their overlapping planes and abrupt shifts.

Guest consciously situates her book in the spirited tradition of Virginia Woolf's later novels and, to some degree, Dorothy Richardson's prose (wherein the abstinence from conventional plot and the avoidance of verifiable climax mark an escape route from determined consequence). But instead of Woolf's expanding perceptions or Richardson's circuitous full-blown revelations, Guest opts for the half-seen clue, the private notation, the broken surface, and the fleeting thought as they collide, impinge upon, and elucidate one another.

Her genius lies in the poetic compression she brings to the text. While her structuralist/Cubist perspective provides the innovative frame for *Seeking Air*, her prose diction proposes a contrast of almost nineteenth-century formality and limpidity. Her sentences are classic; her experiment is, rather, *how* she puts them together. Like the Cubists, she has not given up the elegant brushwork, the good painting. Her book aims an affectionate salute at the history of English prose, while at the same time making a conscious critique of its literary formalisms and extending our idea of how narrative "truth" can be delivered.

An introduction to Guest's working method throughout the novel can be made by considering the character and scale of her "chapters," usually from one paragraph to five pages in length. Each chapter in *Seeking Air* provides a new cut in the crystal, a clue or a book of clues. There are passages whose energies are sustained by the sheer speed of metaphor, the humor derived from surprised couplings:

> Berg changes to Shostakovitch. The Cyrillic alphabet just out, crosses in front of, enters the space the bus vacated. The poem laughs back and forth and comes the caw-like repetition. Strength comes to blows with Joy. The violins fly from steppe to steppe and in the Caucasus valleys stones skim and fall. A stocky tremolo with light flashing on the flung scabbards. Numbers work for you. Desire trudging beyond the golden mean. (119)

The shortest chapter is composed of a fragment, a half-sentence with ellipses—"This diary of a place . . ." (W. S. Graham)—and is meant as a notation on her esthetic intentionality. It echoes the epigraph of *Seeking*

Air, in which Jonathan Swift amuses himself by proposing, in a letter to his friend, Vanessa, a plan for a new sort of novel:

> It ought to be an exact chronicle of twelve years from the time of spilling the coffee to drinking of coffee. From Dunstable to Dublin with every single passage since . . . two hundred chapters of madness, the chapter of long walks, the Berkshire surprise, fifty chapters of little times. (*Vanessa and Her Correspondence With Jonathan Swift*)

One feels an enormous empathy and attraction between Swift's sensibility—the scale and location of his passions—and Guest's as she hunts down not only the spilled coffee, the chapters of madness, and the "little times" but also the elusive language in which to snare them. Her "long walks" are discovered on city terraces, not in the Irish countryside; her "madness" chapters locate themselves in the narcissism of Morgan's inbred fantasies—for example, his imagined seduction by a woman in a blue dress, painted by Ingres, staring down at him from a wall in the Frick Museum; her "Berkshire surprise" is an unexpected indoor picnic of tinned white asparagus and other gourmet items squirreled away by city-dwelling Morgan.

Guest quotes Swift in order to set the stage for her own compositional scale, in which certain moments will be foregrounded and heightened, others abstracted or reduced, refusing the more conventional novelistic balance and proportion. She wants to remind us that the investigation of human nature has resulted in a variety of narrative solutions. From this perspective—this sense of scale—she will build the lives of her characters, leaving ample room for mystery and abstraction.

Guest's fictional surfaces are further complicated by her whimsical homage to other literary genres, a device that reinforces the reader's awareness of multiple and skewed time frames. Tiny metafictions appear inside the ongoing story of Morgan and Miriam: after a difficult course of love and a prolonged separation, they are suddenly featured in a little Shakespearan comedy scene called "Act the First," in which they say their healing lines, but in voices thrice removed from the late twentieth-century language one might expect following a lover's quarrel:

> M[iriam]: *'Tis odd. Though I long for homeland yet loathe am I to leave this land. An enchantment lieth here that graspeth still my girdle.*
> M[organ]: *A like feeling steals o'er me. 'Tis as if we live half awake and half in dream. The dream is here and there awakeness tarries. Yet must I shake this dream and hasten to the harbour.*

M[iriam]: *Sweet was our rest, though troubled by Eustace's sorrow. That lent a shadow to our ends.* (174)

Critical distance is created between reader and romantic plot through dislocation of the present moment, and one's perception of surface unity dissolves.

In another "genre" scene, Morgan and Miriam reestablish their intimacy through the staged ritual of cooking a meal together, discovering and replaying their own private style of amusement while consulting instructions from a 1930s cookbook in which each recipe, each gesture in the kitchen, is thoroughly laced with appropriate attitudes, clichéd lines, and reassurances once widespread in the institutions of American domesticity. The reader is not told how or why this happens but is, instead, given chunks of the literal cookbook text verbatim:

> *Creamed tuna on toast strips*
> *Canned peas with butter sauce*
> *rolls   butter*
> *Strawberry preserves*
> *Hot chocolate with marshmallows* (144)

The recasting of Morgan's and Miriam's reconciliation deflects what could be a predictable exchange and colors it with historic precedent, treating the reader to apposed perceptions, socialized and historically changing love-scripts. Guest's layering of what we think of as time-bound experience tilts our expectations, much as the shifting Cubist planes of a Juan Gris interior can alert the eye to multiple perspectives of the material world, challenging traditional assumptions.

Guest's affinity for the clue, the allusive fragment, contributes to the modeling and revelation of her characters. She names her female character Miriam, after Dorothy Richardson's Miriam in *Pilgrimage*. In a kind of homage to Richardson, which is also a revision, Guest rigorously edits what might be a very long and programmatically detailed narrative script into a more poetic structure of swift cuts and enigmatic dialogues, which are never meant to be fully explained. Duplicating the blow-by-blow nature of "real" time is not her goal. However, the homage may not be immediately apparent partly because the luxuriant winds and turns of Richardson's sentences in *Pilgrimage* are located in the female monologue. The voice of Richardson's Miriam is urgent in its attempt to understand and break with the confining social expectations that flood and diminish her. In Guest, this question is displaced by the fact that Morgan, the male protagonist, is the seer. Guest's Miriam, while sharing a similar passion to resist category and interpretation, is seen from a cooler, spliced perspective because the point of view is predominantly Morgan's and Morgan is never of a single mind, but awash with disintegrating memories and shifting discriminations. He is an obsessive man, out of step with his time, and locked into a self-absorption so delicious that it threatens to reduce his days to collapsed past events at the expense of his tenuous hold on the present "real" world—particularly as regards Miriam, whom he tends to see at a slight and somewhat literary remove. He must assure himself that he has the upper hand in their relationship; his perspective cannot admit to her strength nor her separate life outside his imagination.

We are made to feel the paradox of his situation since we come to know Miriam as a "successful" contemporary woman, yet find this fact slipping away from us given Guest's narrative design. Miriam is not often allowed a direct comment in *Seeking Air*. Her attachment to Morgan sustains the unresolved mystery of the book. But this is part of Guest's strategy. She has turned Richardson's telescope around; we are not given the certain advantage of Miriam's longing for presence and authenticity through continuous access to *her* interiority. Instead, we are looking at a contemporary Miriam through the multiple projections of her male lover. Rather than locating us chiefly inside *her* sensibility, we are primarily privileged to a view of her from the book's narrator who appears to claim objectivity, even as he exposes the fragility of his psyche. Morgan's questionable authority is presented and then dismantled. The sacred tablet of objective narrative is shattered.

Although they handle it differently, Guest and Richardson share a love of the elaborate interior monologue. Guest shifts perspectives as one might shift camera angles to render missing information. In the middle of Morgan's self-serving observation, we are quite suddenly allowed to enter Miriam's mind. One feels she is outwitting the ever-watchful Morgan in this brief reflection that *must* be hers, though its tone would appear to be impersonal:

> If idly she were to go out onto the terrace and from the snow take a snowball. A snowball and hurtle it through the air. Could it truly be said that for a few seconds that snowball had been hers, the choice had been made freely by her, Miriam, to throw it into the air? Or would Morgan when she told him what she had done, would he create another action out of hers, would he call it a performance, would he make of the terrace a stage, would he deprive her even of the scenery by causing a scene to take place between the woman alone on the terrace and the snow held in her hand? (84)

Morgan's need to appropriate Miriam's experience—to edit it along the lines of his Pygmalion script for her—is at odds with other views we have

of her. A quick gloss of Miriam shows her as self-directed and self-sufficient. Yet she is still lonely for Morgan when away from him. Again, we
are refused the ease of narrative in favor of multiple readings.

The other effect of this is to cast Miriam in the dilemma that is classic
to modern woman. She craves autonomy, self-determination, yet feels
partial without the constancy of a primary love. Miriam's fragmented
and unstable perception of herself is aligned with ours, because her character structure is parallel to and supported by the overall narrative plan
of the book. Miriam is seeking the air of her own spontaneous choices,
the adventure of discovering who she might become, independent of a
primary relationship. But she is also compelled and moved by Morgan's
passion, his imagination, his apparent confidence as he navigates the
world. At the same time, she often feels engulfed by his admiration and
devoted smothering of her tentative self-rule. Morgan seeks reprieve, escape from a rule-bound and competitive regime only hinted at. Miriam's
substantiality, her grace in negotiating daily life, holds for Morgan the
promise of pleasurable relief and allows him to avoid his own struggle
with the dark forces threatening him.

Clearly, our understanding of Miriam's dilemma—her tenuous hold on
her own identity and autonomy—is being shaped by the voice of experience. Guest enters Morgan's power base, lays bare his willfulness and his
dogged recasting of the motives and intentions of his love object (Miriam)
to suit his own ego-serving impulses. In this way Guest explores the baffled and ambivalent position Miriam finds herself in vis-à-vis Morgan and
their restless embarkation upon a shared life and its insidious under-
minings.

It is here that Guest's collapsed chapters, displaced viewpoints, reframed genres, and collaged quotations both erode and question a more
traditional narrative ordering; furthermore, they enunciate her perception of time as elastic, subjective, circular, and multidimensional. Morgan
is implicated, drawn into her less deterministic time frame; Guest's ease
with and insistence on this perspective succeed in making of Morgan a
man who struggles toward the appropriation of a woman's soul. His attempt to take over and mold Miriam's life is really an attempt to save
himself.

In his journal, Morgan concedes to his intrusive desires (his self-aware-
ness would be admirable, if only he could align it with a different attitude
toward Miriam). His desire is congruent with his need to subjugate and
objectify her. He confides: "It has been noted of Karenin that: 'not until
the storm is about to break does he actually concede that Anna might
have her own destiny, thoughts, desire . . .' "; and then he continues:

My attitude toward Miriam was interwoven with my preoccupation with her as a person whom first I had discovered and then one who I believed I might recreate in the image I desired. It can be said to my distress that I never let her alone. I persistently meddled with her character. I left her only to solitude. When with her, that is in the same room with her, my imagination infused itself into desire.

Osip Mandelstam's wife explains this state quite clearly when she tells us that Mandelstam's endearment for her was "my you." (72)

Morgan's very literary and dissembling mind is here revealed in three swift moves. His journal entries, their collaged sources and shifts, display his character without need of belabored analysis: in the first paragraph, he somewhat painlessly allows himself to view *his* refusal to accept Miriam's separate destiny, by noting another man's blindness under similar circumstances—this man appears in a Tolstoy novel—thus Morgan's lack borrows some sympathy and weight (in his mind), while linking him to a male dilemma that is obviously historical. In the second, he confesses his guilt (within the privacy of his secret pages), admitting—but in the *past tense*—that he has allowed his own egoistic needs constantly to tamper with and attempt the reshaping of Miriam's separateness. Morgan's instinct to remove himself, even as he reveals himself, is most clearly evident in the third section where he remembers a little story told by "Osip Mandelstam's wife" in which her husband's term of endearment for her was "my you." In one sentence, Morgan reduces Mandelstam's wife to both possession and object in failing to call her by her own name. Yet *she* is the conduit for Morgan's point. The reader, by now, has been several times removed from Morgan's original observation, in the same fashion that he distances himself from troubling insight. He desires to know and not to know.

Perhaps Guest's most extreme use of dislocation is in the construction of Morgan's character. She takes us beyond the monologue and into his mental graffiti. Throughout *Seeking Air*, Guest constructs her portrait of Morgan from the inside. She reveals pages intact from his journal, looks into his pocket and finds a little double-columned list and presents it as a "chapter," prefaced by this note: "I found these . . . in my pocket, in the jacket I had worn on that last trip to Washington. Placed there when I picked up my nephew, Neil. The second column was my own addenda":

In case of illness or absence for any other cause, please notify the school as soon as possible. In an emergency in the morning, please call your driver between 7:15 and 7:30. . . .

expectancy, forgiveness, betrayal, detective stories, paintings, lights (electric) buying paper, pens, post-office, heels of shoes fixed, the river, the sun. . . . (76)

The reader is asked to make sense of, to participate in Morgan's private order, bits of detritus from the street and from his mind's foraging. We begin to build up an actively shifting picture of our protagonist, a less static view of him than if we were directed smoothly through the difficult channels of his life by a single observing voice. Guest's collaged perspective gives us a visual way of participating in Morgan's multiple and often warring sides. In this instance, she places the left-hand column—"Transportation Regulations for the Sheridan School, Grades I, II, III" (evidence of his chosen obligation to some distant family life and institutional order)—next to a random list of words and thought fragments from his day, perhaps scrawled in a single minute or during an extended bus ride. One is invited to imagine how these bits of paper have arrived in his pocket, by the fact of their presence as material evidence. Neither the episode of picking up his nephew, Neil, nor the contents of the list requires further elaboration.

It is within Morgan's continuously observing, reasoning, chattering, and obsessive mind that we are introduced to the third and in some ways major "character" of this unusual book—the presence called Dark. Morgan's story unfolds, often, through the moods and levels of his psychic journey. He talks to himself; he confides to us; he both lures and banishes his doppelgänger, this insatiable haunt, Dark. While Morgan and Miriam are seeking each other and their inventions of each other, the character of Dark is always hovering in the shadows of Morgan's mind, a kind of vampire of the present moment who divides and often conquers Morgan's attention. Dark is "not the thing, but its effect" (Mallarmé), a ghostly projection, carbon paper's smudge, Morgan's comforting pillow, *and* his resistance to a world he finds too demanding and often not as interesting as his own daydreaming. He prefers his fantasies, his lineage among the gazelles, his continuously revised histories (he likes to think of himself as the war hero, the gentleman planter).

Dark encourages Morgan in this activity and is his caustic but reliable phantom companion. Morgan works at Dark like a text, almost a biography. He gathers research notes, goes into retreat, pursues his subject shamelessly. We are never really sure whether Dark is a literal manuscript he is working on or a perpetual (ongoing) narrative in his head. Where his "writing" takes place is always in question. Miriam and close friends shift between tolerantly assuming a place for Dark at every table or being frustrated and appalled by Morgan's obsessive pursuit.

Morgan claims that his colleagues take the easier path of "grey" or "beige" and believes his investment is in something much deeper:

And I returned to "Dark's" exegesis. Which if ever finished I shall deliver No. 3 in the series of "Evenings Of and About Literature." Transforming the wild evenings of Alaska into something less raw, translating the kayak noise into black clefs, white floes into Dark. Don't tremble Miriam when I put the bandage over your eyes; we shall only slide into the underground. And we can read standing up the gold emblems of Dark. A nest of swallows clinging to the sooty bridge. (25)

Morgan's thralldom to Dark assumes mythic proportions and is, at the same time, annoying. Guest's accomplishment is that, amid her filmic fades and close-ups, she provokes our concern for her protagonist's embattled psyche while, at the same time, accusing him of infantile Wertherian excesses completely unsuitable to the man *we* want for Miriam. Morgan anguishes: "Why must I be so constant to Dark, tracing its outline everywhere like a prisoner his shadow?"(40), and we wince at his romantic self-indulgence. Soon after, Guest interposes a little answering chapter, a kind of tonic to Morgan's angst, a scene in which Miriam discovers Morgan's unawareness of a piece of disturbing news in the morning paper: "Yet you did hear about it—didn't you?" (121). A dialogue follows, in which his numbness to an exterior world of people and events becomes evident. Miriam finally comments in exasperation: "You must be living in a private world entirely" and he counters: "Doesn't everyone" (122).

She refuses his simple equation: "Oh of course if you put it that way, but most people try at one point or other to get outside themselves, they even want to become involved with others" (122). Nothing is settled, but the question is on the table. A brief moment of exchange serves beyond simple character development: to implicate the reader in the dialogue and to discourage dependency on authorial finality and closure. One can draw a conclusion, shift allegiances, feel the priority of either attitude.

Guest imagines her reader as curious and avid for the pleasure of active intellection; she asks us to approach her juxtaposed lists, events, quotes, and bits of interior monologue in the same way we stand before a Cubist painting of a [tablewindowpipeguitar] by Braque or a Joseph Cornell three-dimensional box, in which a blue-and-white map of the Northern Celestial Hemisphere is placed as a background for six wine glasses, an opaque glass "shooter" marble, and two bluish-white Italian marble spheres to suggest (among other things) the earth twice seen from a great distance.

In *Seeking Air*, we must put together a "meaning" via the subject's angles, materials, functions, and planes; we must read the gaps, the overlapping clues.

Miriam's life force and the spirit of poetry finally triumph, albeit tentatively, in this complicated dance. Miriam provides Morgan with materiality, an engaged world of both playfulness and fury in which to receive the present moment. Conversely, Morgan gives Miriam access to the inaccessible, the claims of mythic time. She becomes his white page, he her dark script. Guest has personified two orientations toward life, finally hinting at a difficult shift for Morgan from perpetual brooding to a somewhat lighter and dynamic possibility. Dark is jilted and "White" begins to appear as a presence and a tonality of experience. White is absence of shadow. White is Miriam dozing on the couch, her perfume.

Morgan struggles to *get* it. He characteristically stays up all night in an insomniac battle to incorporate this new element, so long beyond his grasp. He mumbles, and it is poetry:

> Dark being edged out by White.
>   Impossible!
> I had thought if I could insert a fleecy thing Dark might find more comfort. Instead I kept finding white threads, and worse white soft lumps like cotton. Comfortable, undoubtedly, but *white*. And the white multiplied so fast. Dark the tyrant, Dark the fastidious, kept turning his back, refusing to face that at all. (180)

And he continues:

> Yet wait. White had appeared very late in the game. There had been intimations. The quarrels. The disputes. The bad timing. It had not been until he had sensed, vaguely sensed a need for, or a lack of, the Whiteness. . . . Until he had recognized the wholeness of White. It had taken some catching up and a degree of modesty unusual for him. Also a humility to accept Dark's real even urgent need for White. (183)

Mere mortals these, Morgan and Miriam, in whose modern yet timeless souls Guest has waged the battle of the century: loving versus selfhood, partnership without ownership. What has resisted closure is finally disclosed. Those bound to the earth will always seek "the mysterious / traveling that one does outside / the cube and this takes place / in air" ("Roses" 59).

WORKS CITED

Guest, Barbara. "Roses." *Moscow Mansions.* New York: Viking, 1973. 57–59.
———. *Seeking Air.* Santa Barbara: Black Sparrow, 1978.

The Sense of Unending:
Joyce Carol Oates's *Bellefleur*
as an Experiment in Feminine
Storytelling

PERRY NODELMAN

EXPLAINING how innovation in American fiction has traditionally been understood as a manifestation of the need to escape social norms, Nina Baym says,

> There is no place for a woman author in this scheme. Her roles in the drama of creation are those allotted to her in a male melodrama: either she is to be silent, like nature, or she is the creator of conventional works, the spokesperson of society. What she might do as an innovator in her own right is not to be perceived. (77)

The anthropologist Sherry B. Ortner suggests that assumptions of this sort are universal: in all cultures, "woman is being identified with—or if you will, seems to be a symbol of—something that every culture devalues, something that every culture defines as being of a lower order of existence than itself" (72). That something is "nature"; it is opposed to culture itself, "the process of generating and sustaining systems of meaningful forms (symbols, artifacts, etc.) by means of which humanity transcends the givens of natural existence . . ." (72). Paradoxically, then, those believed to be of a lower order show their cultural inferiority by passively accepting cultural conventions, and those of a higher order show their superiority by willfully disrupting cultural conventions and engendering new ones; since women are assumed to be members of a lower order, femininity and innovation are perceived to be opposites.

Not surprisingly, critics usually identify fiction as innovative exactly because it manipulates "systems of meaningful forms." Jerome Klinkowitz says that the authors he studies in *Literary Disruptions* are "given to formal experimentation, a thematic interest in the imaginative transformation of reality, and a sometimes painful but often hilarious self-conscious artistry" (x); Robert Scholes similarly says that the authors he calls "fabulators" take "an extraordinary delight in design. . . . The structure also, by its very shapeliness, asserts the authority of the shaper" (2). In Ortner's terms, this is culture without nature, consciousness divorced from the substance it purports to order; it is pure masculinity that has decided, by implication, to make the feminine disappear.

For a woman writer, consequently, all possible choices seem equally wrong. As Baym suggests, to be silent "like nature" is to accept one's repression, and to write conventionally is to be repressed by convention. But to innovate along the usual lines is to write in explicit defiance of what has traditionally been considered to be female.

My contention is that Joyce Carol Oates's novel *Bellefleur* represents a fourth choice: a kind of writing that is neither conventional nor conventionally innovative, a novel whose innovations represent an identifiably feminine form of experimentation. I use the word "feminine" rather than "female," here and throughout this discussion, for the same reason that I use "masculine" rather than "male": to suggest that these qualities relate more significantly to cultural (and therefore changeable) assumptions about gender than they do to inherent biological factors. Indeed, Oates's "feminine" innovation suggests a means of transcending the limitations of both conventional and conventionally innovative forms of fiction that should have liberating potential for both women and men.

Oates herself has criticized the kinds of innovation I have characterized as masculine exactly because they leave out so much of perceived reality—much of it traditionally associated with femininity. She has criticized followers of Nabokov and Borges in an article in the *New York Times Book Review* for being solipsistic (June 4, 1972), and she has said that Beckett's strategy is

> to refine man out of his existence in a recognizable world. . . . If one's very existence is the phenomenal stream-of-language, if he cannot pass through the hypnotic trance of his own self-worship or the worship of invented language, he is doomed to exist within the confines of his own skull, to babble endlessly about the very process of babbling. . . . (*New Heaven* 89, 95)

Such babbling results from distance from the "world" and from a refusal to use conventional meaning-making patterns of storytelling. If the tendency to take that distance and make that refusal relates to traditional ideas of masculinity, then specifically feminine innovation could ignore or deny neither. It would be innovative even while offering both a sense that a world does exist outside the self and recognizable narratives about that world.

To assert their authority as shapers over the material they are shaping, masculine innovators "disrupt" story; we often recognize innovative writing by its fragmentations of narrative structure. But interestingly, literary experimentation involving women, either as characters in novels or as literary commentators, tends to be characterized as anything but fragmented. Feminist critics often cite the monologue that James Joyce gives Molly Bloom at the end of *Ulysses* as an example of writing unrepressed by the usual masculine assumptions about structure, and Joyce Carol Oates sees Molly's soliloquy as an attack on masculine authority: "What better way to level the pretensions of men than by having the most ordinary of Dublin voices carry us out of the novel?" (*Contraries* 185). Julia Kristeva characterizes feminism itself as a flowing stream: "by demanding recognition of an irreducible identity, without equal in the opposite sex and, as such, exploded, plural, fluid, in a certain way nonidentical, this feminism situates itself outside the linear time of identities which communicate through projection and revindication" (19–20). Speaking of her own writing, Hélène Cixous says, "I, too, overflow. . . . Time and again I, too, have felt so full of luminous torrents that I could burst" (246).

But such flowing feminine writing is not necessarily storytelling. Molly Bloom dwells on herself no less assertively or indulgently than the writers of masculine innovative fiction, and she tells even less of a connected and unified story; and Verena Andermatt suggests that the "amniotic flow" (40) of Cixous's texts is equally divorced from the conventional structure of narrative: "The tempo of their writing—indeed their lack of style—is in cadence with lacunary moments of grammatical inconsistencies, sentence-fragments, image signs, portmanteau words, litanic inscriptions and jets of letters of infinite regress" (46–47). This is pure flow divorced from narrative; it describes events without structure, just as conventional masculine innovation offers structure divorced from events. It is innovative; but in its absence of structural order it is not exactly fiction in any way we might recognize.

Yet that merely restates the paradox: for if it had the conventional structure of fiction, it could be neither innovative nor feminine—or here, female, for our usual assumptions about narrative are surprisingly bound up in our understanding of biological sexual differences; it is a critical truism that the conventional undisrupted patterns of narrative mirror maleness. When Scholes suggests that the "archetype of all fiction is the sexual act . . . the fundamental orgastic rhythm of tumescence and detumescence, of tension and resolution, of intensification to the point of climax and consummation" (26), he unconsciously echoes Beatrice Faust's description of male sexuality as "performance-oriented," emphasizing "gymnastic expertise" and with "orgasm as the desired goal" (194).

Faust also says that "female sexuality can include both intense arousal, which seeks release in orgasm, and a pleasant drift on the plateau level of arousal, which may continue indefinitely. Many women can lead satisfying and harmonious sex lives without orgasm . . ." (59). Conventional fiction mirrors the conventional male orgasmic pattern, and conventionally innovative fiction merely confirms the significance of that pattern by defiantly disrupting it in something like an act of self-centered masturbatory exhibitionism; but fiction might be both innovative and feminine if it mirrored the conventional female orgasmic pattern.[1] Such fiction would reject both the conventional orgastic pattern and the masculine innovative enterprise. Rather than disrupt the representational and sequential aspects of story by putting technique in the foreground and emphasizing the artist's "gymnastic expertise" over plot, feminine innovation would have to evoke both a recognizable and consistent reality and maintain a pleasurable flow of continuous events; but to avoid the pressure of the masculine pattern, it could not allow that flow to be dominated by the climactic end it might be seen to be moving toward.

In *Bellefleur* Oates does evoke a more-or-less recognizable world, and she does tell a story. But she evokes that world and tells that story in a way that relates to the descriptions of feminine writing I referred to earlier. In doing so, I believe, she achieves a kind of writing different from either the old conventions or conventionally innovative masculine responses to those conventions.[2]

Bellefleur is also different from much of Oates's earlier work—although not different in its thematic thrust; in fact, it is its new expression of old themes that most clearly relates it to the idea of a feminine narrative. *Bellefleur* describes how a family tries to impose its will upon the landscape of its vast estate; as commentators have pointed out, Oates has always written about people who have tried to impose themselves upon the world.[3] Suggestively similar to the innovative novelists Klinkowitz describes, Oates's characters often try to replace the world with a fiction of their own invention; a particularly obvious example is Nora, the fussy gardener in the story "Magna Mater," who "hated untidiness, borders gone wild . . . she shared with Yeats and Stevens and others of her saints a need for assertion, for staking the claims of a particularity of being in a gross universe" (189). The thrust of Oates's work is to show the danger of such self-assertion; her stories and novels characteristically describe first, how controlling people distort and manipulate themselves into a death-like rigidity or numbness, and then, how the facts of the world outside inevitably disrupt their fantasies—as in "Magna Mater," in which some drunken friends invade Nora's orderly garden and Nora asks herself, "Was the world insane, that such a horror had swept into her garden, into her life?" (209).

Bellefleur focuses on this central concern in many ways, but particularly through images of maps, walls, and names, all of which represent human attempts to define and control the world. Walls are an artificial means by which human consciousness imposes patterns of order and authority on the natural landscape; both maps and names label and define, and, like walls, represent the authority of those who provide them. Bellefleur is an estate—both a building with walls and a label on a map that claims a large chunk of the surface of the world; it represents what the first American Bellefleur, Jean-Pierre, sees as his own "lust for acquisition. . . . One stuffs oneself, it is a frenzy, the lust to lay hands on everything, to beat out others, for the others are enemies" (657). Those who inhabit the manor, many members of various branches of the Bellefleur family across the generations, are inflicted by variations of their ancestor's lust, so that the name Bellefleur comes to represent the same will to power of which the estate itself is a physical manifestation; in a chapter called "The Walled Garden," Leah Bellefleur sits symbolically within the walls of the garden inside the boundaries of the Bellefleur estate, and consults old maps as she plots to restore "The Bellefleur name: the Bellefleur empire" (188).

Later, however, the Noir Vulture swoops into this same garden and steals from it a baby Leah has commandeered as her own; Vernon Bellefleur thinks about how "the creature actually appeared in the walled garden (of all places!—of all secluded, private, *secret places*)" (379). As always in Oates, privacy is a delusion, seclusion an invitation to violation; when there are walls, things break through them.

Bellefleur is made up of variations of this story; or to be more accurate, the stories about many different Bellefleurs that make up the novel are all variations of each other. Bellefleurs either attempt to impose their will on the world and fail, or refuse their patrimony by refusing to impose their will on the world. In different generations, Jean-Pierre, his grandson Raphael, and his great-great-granddaughter Leah express the family lust for acquisition. On the other hand, there are those who resist being Bellefleurs; the poet Vernon, who believes in a world in eternal flux beyond the narrow restrictions of individual perception, tells his father, "I am not a Bellefleur" (203), and in an earlier generation, Jedediah deserts his family and civilization, seeks God and selflessness in the ever-changing wilderness, and denies not just the name Bellefleur but the validity of all names: "What a mockery, that endless stream of food and excrement, given a human name!" (546). As these passages show, Vernon and Jedediah express their defiance of the Bellefleur name by accepting and embracing a world in flux beyond the rigidifying restrictions of walls and maps and names—a world that defies attempts to define it and own it.

The endless flow of reality continually defies Bellefleur attempts to contain or control it. Emmanuel Bellefleur's project of mapping the land is never ending; "the land was always changing, streams were rerouting themselves, even the mountains were different from year to year . . ." (415). There are many actual floods of the Bellefleur estate, usually accompanied by the disappearance of Bellefleurs and the appearance of disturbing external forces. Outsiders, alien people, and even alien creatures like the Noir Vulture, break into the Bellefleur estate and disrupt its order—even its rationality, for these invasions are always the rare occasions when *Bellefleur* moves beyond realism and into fantasy. Bellefleurs find themselves sexually or otherwise involved with "natural," uncivilized people who turn into dogs, like the Doan boy, or who turn out to be bears, like Duane Doty Fox, or who may be vampires, like the Baron Ragnar Norst; the cat Mahaleel, whose arrival in a storm begins the novel, may or may not be the actual father of Leah's daughter Germaine (whose own physical expression of an un-Bellefleurish disorder is denied when her grandmother removes those parts of her body that made her a Siamese twin, and male as well as female).

This opposition between the world in flux and a family's attempts to impose authority upon it obviously relates to the masculinity of conventional ideas about self-assertion; in thematic terms, and as an ironic retelling of that typical American story about men getting rich by triumphing over a wild landscape, *Bellefleur* represents a devastating attack on conventional ideas about what it means to be civilized. But *Bellefleur* relates even more specifically to the feminist ideology of writers like Cixous and Kristeva who believe that language as we have inherited it from our male-dominated ancestors is inherently an expression of masculine authority. Throughout the novel, Oates emphasizes the power of language to replace nature with the artifice of consciousness. When Leah's son Bromwell tries to educate Goldie, a child of the wilderness, he sees it as the imposition of language upon her: "she seemed to have come from so distant a land, so remote a territory, that her very humanity was suspect. . . . It might be a challenge, a scientific challenge, Bromwell thought, to teach the child how to be human . . . how to become human, through the English language" (227).

Throughout the book, furthermore, what opposes that sort of humanity is something much like the flow supposedly characteristic of feminine speech. When young Raphael thinks of how he has survived an attack by the Doan boy by deserting his humanity and becoming fish-like, he becomes conscious of a voice that flows: "the pond's voice, the pond's subtle rhythmic murmurous voice . . ." (185). Oates often relates that inhuman voice to the world beyond the fiction-making control of human minds, as when Vernon Bellefleur says, "the poet knows that he is water poured into water," and speaks of "drowning in God—or whatever it is—I mean the poetry, the voice, the, the rhythm—And then he isn't whoever people say he is, he doesn't have a name . . ." (204). Leah's son Bromwell sums up this central opposition between flow on the one hand and names and language on the other: "wasn't life on this planet clearly a matter of a metabolic current, unstoppable, a fluid, indefinable energy flowing violently through all things from the sea worm to the stallion to Gideon Bellefleur? Why then, take Bellefleur as central in nature?" (287).

According to Ellen G. Friedman, "In Oates it is not history that lies at the heart of the human tragedy—for history is irrevocable; one simply cannot contest it—but an extreme and finally self-defeating assertion of will, self-defeating because it takes the individual even further into the recesses of his isolation, even further from an authentic relation to his world" (42–43); but in *Bellefleur*, history *is* the assertion of will; as an image of past events that channels present conceptions of reality, the Bellefleur estate represents the unidirectional and single-mindedly linear concept of time that Julia Kristeva suggests masculine consciousness has imposed upon the actual world. As such, it must be contested; Bromwell rightly concludes that "he could not escape Bellefleur without escaping history itself" (286).

But Oates does not wholeheartedly endorse those characters who try to slip past self-assertiveness and embrace the flow: she knows that one cannot negotiate the world without maps or names, even inevitably inaccurate ones, and that there is something inherently self-defeating about a consciousness like Jedediah's whose goal is its own extinction. She makes it clear that self-assertion and self-denial are equally dangerous—and equally impossible to avoid. Readings of Oates's earlier work have tended to suggest that she recommends one of two forms of conduct as alternatives to the dangers of self-assertion: either acceptance of the world as it is, or denial of the self;[4] in *Bellefleur*, however, she manages to show that *all* choices are acts of fiction-making, even those that purport to resist fiction-making—that *any* choice is doomed to be too narrow, to misrepresent, because it inevitably rejects the other possibilities. Jedediah's attempt to submerge himself in the mountains is as silly—and as logical—an act as Leah's attempt to dominate the landscape; through narrative leaps through time and place that juxtapose and counterpoint such opposite choices, *Bellefleur* reveals that they are equally ridiculous—but also, because one *must* choose, equally and gloriously human.

It is the peculiar narrative structure of *Bellefleur* that forces consciousness of this balance—a balance that Oates's earlier work misrepresents. Oates has often revealed the limitations of self-enclosed fictions in novels and stories that were themselves self-enclosed fictions with beginnings, middles, climaxes, and ends. The conventional structure of these works often seems to imply the possibility either of transcendence or of healthful adjustment to reality. As the consequences of self-enclosure lead characters toward expectably horrific climaxes in novels like *Wonderland*, readers can easily read them as admonitory parables that imply the relative desirability of adjustment or transcendence.

Some of Oates's novels before *Bellefleur* imply her concern with exactly this sort of problem. In both *Do With Me What You Will* and *The Assassins*, she includes more than one "story"; as the self-enclosed fictions of different characters intersect with each other, we come to understand how limited their perceptions are. In *The Assassins*, Hugh realizes how false his perceptions are: "The difficulty with stories, even true ones, is that they begin nowhere and end nowhere. Ultimately they encompass the entire universe and all of history. Yet—one must begin somewhere, after all! Order must be imposed upon events! *History* must be presented as story!" (101). Because *The Assassins* presents history as stories that are all limited, and does not offer a sense of an encompassing, outside world that could include all the stories, it seems particularly bleak. Alternately, although *Do With Me What You Will* works to show how Elena and Jack each break through their self-enclosed fictions and find each other, it seems merely to replace the earlier fictions with one that they both share, and one that misrepresents the world just as much as their earlier fictions did.

It is exactly the sense of a world unperceived and undistorted by anyone, a world existing outside everyone's fictions of it, a world larger than any story and containing all the stories, that *Bellefleur* successfully provides. How it does that becomes apparent in an exploration of its unusual grammar. The first sentence of *Bellefleur* contains 214 words—an outpouring expressive of the "innumerable frenzied winds" and "inarticulate longing" it describes, and also of the "flow" we might expect of woman's writing that deliberately works to contradict the shaping powers of masculine storytelling. Later sentences are equally long, often whole paragraphs. The first sentence of a chapter appropriately titled "Bloody Run" contains 736 words, including the self-descriptive "plunging with an eerie guttural music" (195); it mentions nine Bellefleurs from Jean-Pierre, the first, to one of the latest, Yolande.

One result of these long sentences is that little is left abstract or generalized throughout the book. We are told that the Noir River in flood carries not just debris, but

baby buggies, chairs, laundry that had been hung out to dry, lampshades, parts of automobiles, loose boards, doors, window frames, the corpses of chickens, cows, horses, snakes, muskrats, raccoons, and parts of these corpses; and parts of what were evidently human corpses (for the cemeteries once again flooded, and relief workers were to be astonished and sickened by the sight of badly decomposed corpses dangling from roofs, from trees, jammed against silos and corncribs and abandoned cars. . . .) (332–33)

And so on, for another 50 or so words. Other sentences tell what objects are on a table, what the furniture of a room looks like, what toys are in the nursery; and the listing of such objects inevitably evokes discussion of when they were bought, and by whom. This apparently compulsive need to fill in all the details even extends to lists of Bellefleur suicides (151–52) and "secret places" (272), and whole chapters that tell of the various cars and horses owned by the Bellefleurs, and of the variety of their "Fateful Mismatches."

Most significantly, these details are all related to each other. Despite their length, the sentences of *Bellefleur* make far too much sense to suggest anything as amorphous as the feminine language described and used by writers like Cixous. They are filled, not just with details, but with parallel constructions between dashes, with phrases and clauses in parenthesis; and this intricate grammar implies equally intricate connections among all the details—among everything that relates to the Bellefleurs, which is everything in the novel. What distinguishes *Bellefleur* as an innovative narrative, then, is not that it is a deliberately incoherent flow, but that its narrative voice so obsessively strives for coherence, for connections and explanations.

It is exactly that sort of coherence we assume to be the main quality that distinguishes a story from an incoherent description of unconnected events; paradoxically, however, it is the obsessive striving to make connections and explain details in *Bellefleur* that effectively distracts attention from its overall narrative shape, the forward movement from beginning through the middle and toward the end, of any given sentence, or of a chapter, or even of the book as a whole. Thus, the novel seems to disrupt narrative just as much as do the experimental novels by masculine writers. But far from making stories disappear, as do those other novels, *Bellefleur* does just the opposite; it tells more stories than five or six more conventional novels of its size. But it often introduces any one of those stories as an explanation for something happening in another story. At any given moment, we may be in the middle of two or three or more different stories or events in two or three different time periods, so that parts of one story interfere with the narrative sequencing of others.

For instance, the first chapter, about the arrival of Mahaleel, ends tantalizingly with the statement that "everything began on that night. And once begun, it could not be stopped" (37). But the second chapter has no apparent narrative connection to the events of the first. It tells how Raphael, merely mentioned in an aside in the first chapter and, as it turns out, of no significance in the story of Mahaleel and Leah, is attacked by the Doan boy. It is only in retrospect, after reading much further into the novel and perceiving its patterns, that one comes to understand that the story of the Doan boy's invasion of Bellefleur property interestingly parallels Mahaleel's arrival. Furthermore, and most infuriatingly, this second chapter leaves Raphael just at the moment when he seems to have drowned, at a point immediately before the story reaches its climax; it is not until the end of the next chapter that we learn, in a subclause inside another subclause of a sentence mostly about Raphael's Grand Uncle Hiram, that Raphael is not dead: instead, he is merely "so unnaturally quiet, since his near-drowning in the pond (the circumstances of which he chose *not* to explain completely to the family)" (58). Oates chooses not to explain them either; we do not hear *how* Raphael escaped drowning for another hundred pages (185).

Again and again throughout the novel, the endings of stories are missing, deferred. To use Scholes's image of orgasm, this is something like foreplay without climax, with every climax being replaced by more foreplay, a different set of exciting events that is in turn interrupted before it reaches its climax; and even when they do occur, the climaxes lose their force when they are revealed pages after the exciting events that lead up to them. Frank Kermode speaks of how "the sense of an ending" is what gives shape and meaning to all the events that precede the ending; what Oates creates in *Bellefleur* is the opposite effect: a sense of unending.

This denial of traditional storytelling does not deny the existence of the world outside the storyteller's head, and does not even deny story itself; but it *is* a denial of linear history. As the "Bellefleur Family Tree" at the front of the novel implies, Oates does tell much of the history of seven generations of the family; but she does not tell it chronologically, so that the facts of Bellefleur history are not connected by the conventional cause-and-effect relationships of narrative history. We do not move from beginning to end. We do not get complete stories in any given chapter or section. Instead, we are immersed in a sea of competing stories. The effect is of a narrator obsessively steeped, not in him or herself, but in endless details of Bellefleur history, and unable to forget any of them. It is no accident that the first chapter contains the names of no fewer than 36 members of the Bellefleur family, many of them introduced to explain facts about the house and its inhabitants that are needed to make sense of the story of the arrival of Mahaleel; but many of these Bellefleurs are introduced with identifying tags that create new mysteries, and demand that other stories be told: we hear of "Jean-Pierre, imprisoned in Powhatassie" (25) and of a drum "which Raphael Bellefleur had had covered with his own skin" (29). These imply stories we have not heard yet, and that, as it turns out, we will eventually hear.

The effect of all this is like Germaine's description of Bellefleur storytelling: "For the Bellefleurs, reminiscing, quite shamelessly jumbled 'chronological' order—indeed, to Germaine's way of thinking, they had a lofty *contempt* for it" (428). We move from Leah in the present to Jedediah in the past to Hepatica at another point in the past and then back again by grammatical rather than chronological connections; whenever one story is paralleled by, or requires information contained in, another, Oates invents a complex grammatical structure, a clause or subclause that allows her to provide it. The intricate connections of the grammar and structure of the novel imply that history is indeed real, but less significantly a linear chronology than material for endless possibilities, infinite connection and complication—numerous different stories. *Bellefleur* is much like the Tirpitz Pavilion that Leah visits—"a five-acre jumble of marvels" (265).

When Leah asks Tirpitz, "what is the theme of your pavilion?—what is the connection between all these wonderful things?" he asks her to guess the answer. Leah cannot, but Oates implies one as a drunk Noel Bellefleur thinks of "The living and the dead. Braided together. Woven together. An immense tapestry taking in centuries. . . . A tapestry. Or was it one of Matilde's ingenious quilts that looked crazy to the eye but (if you allowed her to explain, to point out the connections) made a kind of dizzying sense . . . ?" (155). *Bellefleur* is like those quilts: it is bewilderingly complicated, but makes a kind of dizzying sense, once the narrative points out the connections.

By duplicating that crazy quilt in her narrative sequencing, Oates accomplishes two things; as in her earlier work she reveals how human perception is always an act of fiction-making, and always limited—always merely one of myriad different ways of making connections; and as she had not done before *Bellefleur*, she effectively captures a sense of a world outside all the fictions—a crazy quilt that contains or evokes worlds beyond all the conflicting explanations, beyond all the stories that people make up about it.

Obviously, then, the peculiar structure of *Bellefleur* mirrors its major themes. But as well as mirroring the central ideas of the novel, its narrative structure accomplishes something equally or even more important. In deferring the endings of stories, it offers readers an unusual form of pleasure—a sense of constant mystery, endless secrets. In other words, it offers one of the main pleasures of narrative—the tension of meanings and conclusions deferred—uncontaminated by the other main pleasure—the satisfaction of a climax and an actual ending. In focusing on the continual pleasure of narrative flow as opposed to the authority of overall single-minded shaping, in deferring and downplaying climaxes and in returning again and again to the same stories and telling ever more about them, *Bellefleur* clearly echoes a sort of sexual pleasure different from the orgastic fiction Scholes describes—and similar to Faust's description of typical female sexuality.

Yet it does not entirely desert the more conventional pleasure. The structure of the novel does mirror what Kristeva calls "female time"—both "cycles, gestations, the eternal recurrence of a biological rhythm which conforms to that of nature" and "the massive presence of a monumental temporality, without cleavage or escape, which has so little to do with linear time (which passes) that the very word 'temporality' hardly fits" (16). But it does so without ever actually sacrificing the linear chronology of conventional storytelling: eventually, the stories (or at least most of them) are complete, even though the way they have been told evokes other conceptions of time than the one conception that conventional narrative rests upon. In other words, *Bellefleur* does not so much deny and dismiss linear history as add other sorts of time to it.

Bellefleur most clearly expresses linear time in that it does finally head toward a traditional climax—in the last hundred or so pages, suspense-making hints are dropped, important but thus far held-back episodes of early Bellefleur history are finally filled in (for instance, we learn that Jean-Pierre fathered not just the Bellefleur family, but its archenemies, the Varrells), and in the second to last chapter, Gideon Bellefleur drives an airplane filled with explosives into the manor, bringing to an end the house, the lives of all its inhabitants, and the novel. The climax of the novel, the event that suddenly ends all the Bellefleur stories, is itself as explosive and as conclusive as any conventional male orgasm.

The wonderful joke of a climax surfaces one last important innovation of *Bellefleur*; Oates not only reinvents the structure of narrative, she also invents an intriguing narrator. The voice that tells *Bellefleur* is as clearly and as authoritatively in control, as much a self-conscious artificer as masculine innovators are; but it also, ambiguously, enjoys sending itself up, so that even the act of producing a narrative that defies traditions is understood to be a gratuitous attempt to impose authority. When a new Bellefleur is invented for the sole purpose of making a point about Gideon 600 pages into the novel, the narrator slyly says, "little is known of Meredith Bellefleur" (619), and never mentions him again; and she slyly comments that Bromwell Bellefleur's *Hypothesis Concerning Anti-Matter*, is "eight hundred dense pages long. . . . Prefaced with an enigmatic and loosely translated remark of Heraclitus, on the nature of time: or, rather, on the nature of our conception of time" (669)—it sounds much like Oates's novel, which has just such an epigraph. In fact, the narrator constantly has characters make comments about "Bellefleur" that jokingly apply to the novel as well as the house or the family. Yolande thinks, in the middle of a chapter in which thoughts of no fewer than 20 of her relatives pass through her head, "There were so many Bellefleurs. . . . There were already enough Bellefleurs for her to contend with" (239, 242), and the narrator later tells us, "There were so many Bellefleurs, people said, but perhaps most of them had never existed. They were just stories, tales, anecdotes set in the mountains, which no one quite believed and yet could not quite disregard" (676). Jean-Pierre II asks of the "horrific" manor, "What sort of mind, driven by an unspeakable lust, had imagined it into being?" (450); and Lord Dunraven says, "there are, you know, surely you know, a dizzying profusion of plots in this house— plots, calculations, aspirations, dreams—some of them, to my way of thinking, quite mad . . ." (473).

Above all, Oates undermines her authority as narrator simply by refusing to use it. Not only does she defer explanations and solutions to mysteries, but the novel comes to its abrupt end with many mysteries left unexplained altogether. Whatever happened to Yolande after she left Bellefleur? To the boy Raphael? What exactly went on at Raoul's house? Was the old man who came to stay President Lincoln, or not? Was the old man who appeared in a flood Jeremiah, who had disappeared in an earlier flood? Gideon explodes Bellefleur before the narrator gets around to solving these and many other mysteries.

In undermining its own authority, the narrative voice allows *Bellefleur* both to have a shape and to comment on the dangers of shaping, both to use a dangerously repressive language and to change it enough to defuse its danger and its repressiveness. By reinventing the shape of narrative and the voice of the narrator, by breaking up traditional concepts and expressions of linear time in a way that implies other, more traditionally feminine ways of perceiving time but that nevertheless still expresses and allows linear time, Oates does not so much reject convention as transmute and enrich and revitalize it.

NOTES

1. Rachel Blau Duplessis connects writing and female sexuality when she suggests that Monique Wittig's writing "may also be a form of sexuality, that

multifocal female body and its orgasmic capacity, where orgasms vary startlingly and are multiple" (278).

2. In *Joyce Carol Oates: Artist in Residence*, Eileen Bender suggests that in *Bellefleur*, "Oates sets up an intriguing contrast between the chronological patriarchal saga and the cyclical rhythms of a woman's text" (112). In a sense, Bender is right; the elements of *Bellefleur* that would identify it as a woman's text do transform the novel into something like a parody of the patriarchal saga, one that parodizes by virtue of the way it contrasts with our expectations of that genre. But this means, not that *Bellefleur* itself contrasts masculine chronology with feminine rhythms, but rather that its feminine rhythms transform masculine chronology into something else, something both distinct and distinctly feminine. Bender contradictorily suggests that *Bellefleur* is both "an assemblage" of fragments and as "fluid as cinema" (118)—in terms of the definitions I offer here, that it represents at one and the same time both a fragmentary masculine form of innovation and a flowing female one. As I hope to make clear, I believe she is wrong about the former, right about the latter.

3. Joanne V. Creighton says that Oates "focuses obsessively upon the nature of the 'self' and its relationship to the 'other' " (25), G. F. Waller that "Oates's characters, especially her women, are rigidly encased in their mental ideas of the self . . ." (44), and Ellen G. Friedman that "Oates is preoccupied with the idea that the self is not a substitute for the world . . ." (4).

4. Friedman opts for acceptance: "In Oates's fiction there is no alternative to facticity, to the multifold world. . . . Her fiction documents the necessity for compromise" (20). Mary Kathryn Grant offers a more positive sort of acceptance: "There is . . . a certain resignation or acceptance of life-as-it-is in some of her early works. . . . Taken together, however, her body of novels yields a gradually developing growth toward affirmation—still to be arrived at" (7, 8). Grant believes that Oates is heading toward a "transcendent vision" (9); similarly, Creighton says, "Central to Oates's thought and to her work is a visionary conception of human experience, a belief that the ego-consciousness of our culture can be transcended personally and collectively . . ." (144); and again similarly, Waller says, "from Oates's work we sense just how crucial it is to move beyond the limitations of our isolated self-concentration. We must ultimately open ourselves to the obliteration of the ego and our fixation with its uniqueness" (23).

WORKS CITED

Andermatt, Verena. "Hélène Cixous and the Uncovery of a Feminine Language." *Women and Literature* 7 (1979): 31–48.

Baym, Nina. "Melodramas of Beset Manhood: How Theories of American Fiction Exclude Women Authors." Showalter 63–78.

Bender, Eileen. *Joyce Carol Oates: Artist in Residence*. Bloomington: Indiana UP, 1987.

Cixous, Hélène. "The Laugh of the Medusa." Marks and de Courtivron 245–64.

Creighton, Joanne V. *Joyce Carol Oates*. Boston: Hall, 1979.

DuPlessis, Rachel Blau. "For the Etruscans." Showalter 271–91.

Faust, Beatrice. *Women, Sex, and Pornography*. Harmondsworth, Gt. Brit.: Penguin, 1980.

Friedman, Ellen G. *Joyce Carol Oates*. New York: Ungar, 1980.

Grant, Mary Kathryn. *The Tragic Vision of Joyce Carol Oates*. Durham, NC: Duke UP, 1978.

Joyce, James. *Ulysses*. 1922. New York: Random, 1934.

Kermode, Frank. *The Sense of an Ending: Study in the Theory of Fiction*. New York: Oxford UP, 1967.

Klinkowitz, Jerome. *Literary Disruptions: The Making of a Post-Contemporary American Fiction*. Urbana: U of Illinois P, 1980.

Kristeva, Julia. "Woman's Time." Trans. Alice A. Jardine and Harry Blake. *Signs* 7 (1981): 13–35.

Marks, Elaine, and Isabelle de Courtivron, eds. *New French Feminisms: An Anthology*. Amherst: U of Massachusetts P, 1980.

Oates, Joyce Carol. *The Assassins: A Book of Hours*. New York: Vanguard, 1975.

———. *Bellefleur*. 1980. New York: Warner, 1981.

———. *Contraries: Essays*. New York: Oxford UP, 1981.

———. *Do With Me What You Will*. New York: Vanguard, 1973.

———. "Magna Mater." *The Goddess and Other Women*. 1974. Greenwich, CT: Fawcett, 1976.

———. *New Heaven, New Earth: The Visionary Experience in Literature*. New York: Vanguard, 1974.

———. "Whose Side Are You On?" *NYTBR*. June 4, 1972, 63.

Ortner, Sherry B. "Is Female to Male as Nature Is to Culture?" *Women, Culture, and Society*. Ed. Michelle Zimbalist Rosaldo and Louise Lamphere. Stanford, CA: Stanford UP, 1974. 67–87.

Scholes, Robert. *Fabulation and Metafiction*. Urbana: U of Illinois P, 1979.

Showalter, Elaine, ed. *The New Feminist Criticism: Essays on Women, Literature, and Theory*. New York: Pantheon, 1985.

Waller, G. F. *Dreaming America: Obsession and Transcendence in the Fiction of Joyce Carol Oates*. Baton Rouge: Louisiana UP, 1979.

LITERATURE IN TRANSLATION

Experimental Novels? Yes, But Perhaps "Otherwise": Nathalie Sarraute, Monique Wittig

GERMAINE BRÉE

Do women write "experimental" novels or not? And if they do not, is it by choice or, as has been perhaps inadvertently suggested, because of their still marginal place in literature? At the outset of this discussion we run into problems of definition and selection. The label itself looks back to the mid-1880s and to Emile Zola's blueprint for a system of relations that would enable him methodically to investigate and represent in a vast work of fiction the "real" though hidden structures and movements of contemporary French society. What Zola meant by experimental is open to doubt. In a relatively recent essay, "Emile Zola, Experimental Novelist," Michel Butor reviewed the question thoroughly, shifting the debate from a scientific to a rhetorical context, defining the specificity of the sense of the word "experimental" in relation to the act of writing.[1] The major theoretical question of the correlation between fiction and reality he thus connected to writing techniques evolved by the novelist, a basic concern of the "new novelists" that no doubt underlies the question we are considering.

Zola's conception of the novel as currently "misunderstood," in Butor's view, found little favor among his successors in an age better attuned to the Symbolic, Impressionist, or Surrealist representation of reality. That is perhaps why the French "antitraditionalist" novelists of midcentury preferred to characterize their purpose as "new," a familiar and seductive qualifier with its promise of fresh vistas and its innocuous lack of specificity.[2]

I do not propose here to redefine the aims and accomplishments of the French "new novel"; a vast bibliography disposes of that question. But in reference to my topic, I wish to point to some ambiguity in the basic terminology proposed. When discussing its premises, critics easily substitute "experimental" for "new" or "innovative," raising some troublesome questions. Are "innovative" novels necessarily "experimental"? Or, reversing the terms, are "experimental novels" ipso facto "innovative"?

Further, can there be different types of experimentation in narrative techniques, undertaken with different ends in view? An attempt to answer these questions would take me too far afield. Webster offers simplistic but nonetheless suggestive distinctions that to some extent clarify the issue. To innovate, it suggests, is to "effect a change in the established order," whereas an experiment is "a test or trial of something," "something tried to find out if it will prove effective." In the first instance then, the agent of change—the writer in the frame of our discussion—reorders a recognized form, to integrate some new facet within it, something undetected he or she has perceived. In the second instance the agent is engaged with the medium, writing; the aim is to test its potentialities and limitations, its capacity to transcend accepted codes.

One can surmise that many forms of narrative "invention" are possible, that, in a sense each writer might develop his or her own developments in form or style, excluding others. "Every time we encounter originality in a work of art, invention, no matter how gratuitous it may seem to us," Michel Butor wrote, "it obliges us little by little to remodel, from that vista, the world of which we are a part" ("Emile Zola" 20). "Originality" and "invention" define here the perceptions of the reader and correspond, for the writer, to the two poles discussed: innovation and experimentation. The dialectic of reader-writer with its intermediary phase reader-critic-writer is obvious. The "innovative" drive is more closely connected with a philosophical perception; the "experimental" with modern language theory and criticism. But it seems unlikely that outstanding novels, over the centuries, should not bear a stamp of originality, of some departure from the banal. Women novelists have not been absent from the roster of such creative writers in the past. The definition of "experimental" would have to be considerably narrowed to eliminate them, reducing the interest of the discussion. The exclusion of women novelists from the category "experimental" might then in no sense be derogatory. It could hardly be a matter of critical importance. But if we put the question in a broader frame, this exclusion seems particularly inappropriate today.

That, in France today, there are a number of women writers as active and deliberately engaged as their male contemporaries in evolving new patterns of storytelling, no one would deny; nor that their writing is highly idiosyncratic. Nathalie Sarraute, Marguerite Duras, Hélène Cixous, and Monique Wittig would rank first among them, to say nothing of Marguerite Yourcenar who can only superficially appear "midstream." With the exception of Monique Wittig, to a certain extent, they have not been neglected, far from it. But they have rarely been considered by critics for their contributions to a new "poetics" of fiction, for their willingness both to innovate and to experiment. Robbe-Grillet, Butor, and Claude

Simon have been treated as the stars of that constellation. A welcome change in that respect is Ann Jefferson's study *The Nouveau Roman and the Poetics of Fiction*, which gives Sarraute equal recognition with Butor and Robbe-Grillet in the devising and implementation of new writing strategies, requiring deliberate experimentation with the medium.[3]

I propose first to take as an example of the process of experimentation—innovation in fiction writing that has in some fashion affected the range and "poetics" of the novel—aspects of the work of Nathalie Sarraute. Her first short piece was written in 1932, some 20 odd years before the *entrée en scène* of the "new novel." Half a century later in 1983, her autobiographical text, *Enfance* (*Childhood*), was one of the best sellers of the year. In the interval she steadily published a sequence of texts, each developing further the transformations of the "models" that preceded. A brief detour will situate her more clearly in the literary panorama of the 1980s and in relation to the "experimentalist" par excellence, Robbe-Grillet.

The mid-1950s proved to be particularly interesting for the history of the "new novel." In an autobiographical text (oh scandal!) entitled *The Mirror Returns* (1954),[4] Robbe-Grillet good-naturedly demystified the programmatic declarations of his essays on fiction, the "reassuring imbecilities" they proffered, the taboo words, the linguistic theories, such as the theory of the nonreferentiality of the literary text, all of which challenged the "habitual" approach to fiction. There is, as far as I know, no such "return" among the women writers, possibly because each in her own way has been indifferent to, if not scornful of, overall theorizations as distinct from interest in specific ideas concerning the formal innovations they felt the historical conjuncture required of the novelist. The suggestion, however, could lead to another genderized distinction: women being classified as "intuitive" innovators, men as intellectually motivated experimenters. A single example would be enough to checkmate that gambit: Samuel Beckett. Sarraute's work in contrast is consistently concerned with the search for techniques adequate to the communication of a specific sense of human interaction: "experimental" describes it well.

TROPISMS AND THE QUAGMIRES OF STORYTELLING

Really, universally, relations stop nowhere, and the exquisite problem of the artist is eternally but to draw, by a geometry of his own, the circle in which they will happily appear to do so.[5] (Henry James)

When Nathalie Sarraute's name appeared among the small group of "new novelists," she was in fact already launched on what is indubitably a unique career as an "experimental" writer. In 1932 she had begun to write the first of the texts later published in a volume entitled *Tropismes* (1938) and she had then brought out two novels, *Portrait d'un inconnu* (*Portrait of a Man Unknown*) (1948), prefaced by Sartre, and *Martereau* (1953). The four Sarraute essays that came out in 1956 in *L'ère du soup-çon* (*The Age of Suspicion*) had been written between 1947 and 1956, antedating the first versions of the programmatic Robbe-Grillet essays on the "new novel": "The Use of Theory" (1955), "A Future for the Novel" (1956), "On Several Obsolete Notions" (1957). Robbe-Grillet's first novel, *Les gommes* (*The Erasers*), had come out in the same year as *Martereau* and Butor's *Passage de Milan* a year later. If I recall these facts, it is not to claim any superiority for Sarraute, merely to point to the precedency, the independence of her work.

L'ère du soupçon is a personal meditation on the writing processes that Sarraute had been trying out for some years. Much later, in the preface to the excellent translation of *Tropisms* (1963) by Maria Jolas, Sarraute warned her readers against the notion that "theorizing novelists are cool calculators who began by constructing theories, which they then decided to put into practice in their books," "lab experiments" as it were; for "no literary work can be a mere illustration of a principle however convincing." *L'ère du soupçon* describes a process: the recognition by the reader, Nathalie Sarraute, of a well-defined problem and the effort of the writer—Nathalie Sarraute—to correct it. As reader reflecting on the traditional elements of decor (description), character analysis and presentation, social commentary and plot, she briefly and approvingly sketches some examples of innovative strategy in that realm: Dostoevski, Proust, Kafka, Camus—later Ivy Compton-Burnett and Virginia Woolf. In relation to these she defines her own project, making no claim to a break with the literary tradition but rather to her role as discoverer of further regions to be explored and integrated within a continuous literary tradition of innovation in narrative creation. Her position is clear. Novels deal with the human psyche; in new ways, these novelists explore, in fiction, the psychological substrata of human activity. This as yet little known domain, when more carefully observed, dissolves that convenient entity and vehicle for moving the reader into the world of the novel via the plot, i.e., the solid character named, provided with a social status and a fixed personality. Sarraute shows the manner in which the novelists she examined brought about the "demise" of that fictive creation as she sees it. The reason for this change? In the light of the psychological knowledge of the time, the "solid" character carries no conviction.

This is the psychological domain then, which Sarraute has chosen to investigate with its consequences for the novelist. Her problem is not simple. As she sees it, the outer relations between human beings, the "stuff" of fiction, appear as the flimsiest of surface signs. These sign-gestures—tone, silence, word—emanate from the turmoil, the fluctuations, the underlying impulses of sensation and emotion that accompany human encounters and overt communications. Unconscious in great part, they are, for her, subvocal or prevocal. The technical problem of a novelist holding this view is thus defined. And it too is a difficult one: how to introduce those silent, fleeting, nonverbal moments into the narrative, which by definition rests exclusively on language; and language, the writer's tool, is a structured system that arrests and reifies and so cannot convey the fleeting aspects of human psychological life as it is really experienced.

All Nathalie Sarraute's fictions are experiments in dealing with that problem. The problem, however, has its source in a personal insight arising out of a double experience—a subjective experience and encounters with certain of its "materializations" in literary works. These in turn triggered her need to write, to explore the implications of her point of view in regard to the fiction-making process, and the writing "strategies" required. Her point of view itself is not founded on any systematized knowledge or theory: "I am absolutely unaware of the genesis or evolution of these inner movements. I wrote my first few short texts . . . *Tropisms* spontaneously, without even knowing what tropisms really were nor what they represented. My impressions guided me . . ." (*Studies* 109).

Nathalie Sarraute has spoken freely of her "research" in lectures and interviews. She designated by the metaphor "tropisms" the concealed world of psychological eddies she discerned in all human encounters. The word, first introduced in plant physiology in the mid-nineteenth century, was later also applied to animals. "Tropisms" referred technically to those movements caused in organisms by mechanical reactions to outer stimuli, chemical or physical: the sun or the temperature, for instance. She thus had to de-individualize the field under scrutiny to make visible the unconscious stratum of the psyche and free it from preconceived ethical categorization or judgment. Tropisms are common to a whole group of organisms, collective phenomena: "I gave them this name because of their spontaneous, irresistible instinctive nature, similar to that of the movements made by certain living organisms under the influence of outside stimuli such as light or heat." By analogy, in Sarraute's human world, these movements are set off by the presence of "others" or objects from the world outside. Sarraute's first attempt was to communicate, translate into words, what in her terms is wordless: "Tropisms cannot be expressed by means of the written word, but only through images capable of generating sensations. . . . To discover them requires tremendous effort, concentration, attention, preparation, work" (*Studies* 116–17). The verbal tissue of the writing is then a medium, of consequence only as it opens a way for the real adventure of the writer: communication with the reader, through words, of that which is "real" but beyond words: that is, the world of inner sensation, which the readers must be induced to recognize in themselves. The "truth" of the transcript is of the utmost importance.

Tropisms is composed of 24 short sketches, which were developed over some half dozen years. They illustrate the close connection between Sarraute's purpose and the technical experiments with narrative structures which she implements. "Tropisms," she had described as movements of attraction and repulsion, common to human organisms in contact with one another. Her sketches, consequently, narrow the field of vision, isolate apparently trivial situations and miniscule incidents of everyday city life: small groups of people, families, for instance, looking vacuously at shop windows, women gossiping in tearooms. These are anonymous, of course, described as "they"; sometimes a "she" or a "he" becomes detached, an anxious fragment of the whole; an outcast, swayed by sensations, fears, inner perturbations; separated from the reassuring collective agglomeration clad in its suffocating "miasma" of clichés.

In the first episode recalled in *Childhood*, Sarraute sets up the following scenario: a hotel in Switzerland, a governess sewing, a pair of scissors, a little girl Tachok watching, a couch upholstered in blue silk. The child seizes the scissors, announces her intent to rip the blue silk cover, and does it. What comes out from underneath is grey, messy, formless, strange. The scene is emblematic of the situations described in *Tropisms*: the ripping off of the smooth surface of the conventional attitudes, clichés, gestures. Some small shift in the mood starts the plunge into the disconcerting psychic world of some personage—a plunge not explained to the reader, but "existed." The role of the personages, as Sarraute sees it, is that of "sensitive detectors." Unsure, uneasy, they lose control over their social self, their certainties. So they reveal to the reader the frightening quagmire beneath the circumscribed reassuring patterns of the so-called real. In Sarraute's fictional world these "falls" are a source of high comedy. They lay bare the myth-making process that presides over the most quotidian relations, the "social" language that overlaps the reality with the "abominable stability of the lie," as her younger contemporary Le Clezio put it. The theme in itself could be seen as emblematic of the times.

In that frame, all the novelist's tools are called into question: point of view, character, decor, event, dialogue, relationships; the use of personal pronouns, the process of naming. The vaguely present human beings become the focus, not the activators of the microdramas developing, inwardly lived, not verbalized, not explained by some well-identified narrator, whether character or author. Sarraute, as would any good investigator, has proceeded very methodically in her successive novels, from limited situations involving closely knit family relations to more complex scenarios setting in motion coteries bound by the rhythms of habits and language codes. She evokes the attraction and repulsion that sway them, disrupting the ceremonials and word ballets under which the dangerous eddies of distrust, of suspicion, rise and fall, keeping the relations of particular individuals in perpetual mobility.

The evolution of her writing strategies, as each novel incorporates and moves beyond the last, has been thoroughly studied. It is not by chance that increasingly Sarraute raises along the way questions concerning the artist and the world of art. For it is from the psychic inner "magma" as Sarraute calls it, that the doubts arise, which destroy the immobile absolutes inscribed in a societal language out of touch with the inner hidden life of the human psyche that it seeks to stifle. The fiction writer, in fact the artist in general as Sarraute sees it, is like all human beings a myth-maker, but in a reverse process from the societal. The fiction writer unmasks the evasions, the comedies, and the truth of human life, but indirectly as it were by the narrative mode developed. In Sarraute's work the dialogue of subconversation and conversation is the means by which the unconscious struggles against the dominating social clichés are transmitted to the reader. Sarraute uses the interaction of the two languages to unmask the solid "character" and as a magnificent tool for the comical and satirical, working, as it were, of itself without the intervention of the writer. To achieve her purpose, to bring the underlying puzzled, mobile "tropisms" to life, she also experimented with time dimensions: whereas for the "outer" situations she narrows the field of vision, setting up schematically devised frames, the brief plunges into the unspoken are drawn out and balloon, extending the time- and space-frames of the incident. Paradoxically moving from outside in, from a narrow frame inward, she leads the reader to a sense of a limitless world, maintaining an aura of ambiguity without censorship, changing the expected order of presentation of the narrative. Her method is associative, not logical. But the structures adopted are not gratuitous. For according to Sarraute, their aim is to disclose certain truths. The contrast between the two spaces and their relation, the process of constant passage from one to the other, is the mimetic equivalent of a struggle inherent to human life: the social will to fix, to order and the conflicting desire to merge with the other.

The force that governs human tropisms is never named or analyzed within the fiction. It is, Sarraute says, the drive to merge with others, the desire to escape solitude. That desire is erotic in essence, but not narrowly sexual. The metaphoric language she has chosen to transcribe that upsurge is dramatized, violent, excessive; it juxtaposes with the trivial world of daily petty concerns a dangerous world of metamorphoses, aggression and destruction, a world of phantasms, of imaginary, contradictory projections. They are triggered in the mind of her personages by sudden doubt as to the apparently "real," "known," familiar distribution of roles in his or her "real" world. Here another technical problem concerning point of view arises—how to focalize, to orchestrate these inner scenarios inaccessible to all. The simplicity and indeed monotony of Sarraute's world is deceptive; it is impressive in scope and refinement.

Sarraute is well aware of the systematic codifications of the narrative mode worked out by a long line of critics and theoretical linguists. Starting from her own view of the function of the novelist in today's world, she drew from it the technical consequences and put them to work in a sequence of varied fictional situations. She took little interest in theories but consciously experimented with the narrative techniques through which the reader would perceive her world, live it, and so think it, in turn.

For the feminist critic, she proffers no genderized theory, eschews it in fact. Within the text her "sensitive detectors" can be either male or female, "he" or "she" according to their social position in an established relationship: father-daughter; father and undifferentiated children; uncle-nephew; or they can bear names: Germaine Lemaire and Alain in the relation of the revered writer and admirer. It is the tension, the relation between two emotional extremes with their undertow of questions and uncertainties that determines the tides of repulsion and attraction that give substance to the narrative, not necessarily or uniquely the sexual determination. Sarraute's originality is hers, like the space she has explored. It may seem "circumscribed" as she once admitted, but it is fully hers, and in that degree it is not only experimental, but astonishingly innovative.

Monique Wittig

> Every time we encounter originality in a work of art, invention, however gratuitous, it obliges us to remodel, from that vista, the world of which we are a part. (Michel Butor)

Virgile, non (1985), the French title of Wittig's latest "novel," presents even sophisticated readers with a conundrum. Why Virgil? Why, after Wittig has centered our attention on the poet's name, the erasing "No"? One has to move beyond the title page to realize that *Virgile, non* borrows its theme and *in part* its structure from the *Divine Comedy*, but a contemporized "Divine Comedy," situated in San Francisco, clearly designated by landmarks in its topography. Who does not know the famed Golden

Gate? The "non" then is not addressed to the poet so named, but to the figure introduced by Dante into his story, out of which a new story is emerging.

With characteristic generosity, Wittig sent me notes in answer to my query as to why she chose the Dante scenario.

> I needed a fable already familiar to everyone, one which already had a strong, total universal resonance, so that I could show the heterosexual world—in terms it could recognize—how strange that heterosexual vision seems from the lesbian point of view. I can make that vision exist universally in literary terms only by diverting one of the great classical fables.

One might entertain doubts as to "everyone's" familiarity with Dante, but not as to Wittig's very clear sense of what, as a writer, she wants to do. A self-declared lesbian writer, she is addressing a heterosexual audience to whom she proposes to present—or re-present—its sexual assumptions and practices from a dissident point of view. She does not propose to destroy their map of the "world," but merely to place it in a new perspective via the use of a "fable." The fable in question is, paradoxically, well known for its condemnation of homosexual practices.

In an unpublished study entitled "Other People's Myths," Wendy O'Flaherty[6] has raised the question of how individuals and groups live within those often unconscious myths, which seen from outside appear as "other people's lies." Those are pertinent questions in a period like ours of far-reaching change where, carried forward by technological innovations, ways of living have often moved away from ways of "thinking" one's existence. In this respect, Monique Wittig's concepts can be understood[7] in relation to the well-known intellectual configurations associated with figures such as Lévi-Strauss, Lacan, Foucault, Barthes, Derrida, and de Certeau,[8] under the impact of the often contradictory aegis of Marx, Freud, and Nietzsche. Born in 1936, Wittig, furthermore, was from the outset actively involved in the feminist movement that grew out of the 1968 student rebellion in France. In her generation there is, it seems, no other woman writer[9] who has so thoroughly and passionately sensed the significance of the contemporary currents of thought in relation to the political, social, and cultural situation of women.[10] Her point of view has been lucidly defined in articles and debates as also in her manner of living. What has been less satisfactorily explored are the experimental drives behind her work. One can maintain, and I am inclined so to do, that its originality has been obscured by the abstract grids applied to its "reading" or by shocked reactions to the thematic use of "lesbian" situations literally interpreted. Debates on "the new novel" or écriture féminine have by now acquired a rather worn "historical" cast. The questions raised by the forms Wittig classifies as "novels" have more affinity with O'Flaherty's discussion of the "storytelling" human animal, the stories spoken, written, handed down, fragmented, transformed, acted out, and reenacted. What makes Wittig's work both fascinating and disconcerting, sometimes difficult of access, is its "chamber of echoes" aspect, the layering in her text of *stories*, and stories about stories. Methods, O'Flaherty notes, are stories too.

All Wittig's fictions present rich tapestries of concrete imagery, woven throughout narratives, carried forward in a single movement—names of people, occupations, things—an uninterrupted flow, richly sensual, of colors, fragrances, flowers, movements, air, water—frescoes, I am tempted to call them, developing in sequences, but which are not an end in themselves.

"Myths," O'Flaherty notes in one of her several definitions, are "sacred narratives" that have been "accepted by tradition as embodying an important truth," serving as a "shared communal base for all educated members of a community." Essential here is the word "embodying." The "tapestry" or "fresco" aspect of Wittig's work is her manner of giving concrete "body" to invisible abstract "truths," reviving their power to reach feelings, through imagination, by their "physical" figuration. For the writer the need to experiment becomes paramount. How, working from *within* outward can she "embody" new boundaries, a new *outlook*? What stories can be developed, as one "develops" film? The communal "myth," questioned, becomes at best a "fable." As the above quotation about *Virgile, non* suggests, Wittig wishes to communicate something of importance to her audience about the way her readers construe "reality," a reality that ostracizes her group, the lesbian community.[11]

Literary strategies she adopts are carefully wrought "stories" that "embody" a movement from old narratives—whose structural constraints define relations and roles—to new alternative configurations. I shall briefly consider three of her novels that form a kind of triptych, *L'opoponax* (1964); *Les guérillères*[12] (1969); *Virgile, non* (1985).

L'opoponax can be and has been read as an example of a well-known literary genre, the *bildungsroman*, an account of a protagonist's passage from childhood to adolescence, thence to adulthood. The protagonist here is a girl, Catherine Legrand. But who is the teller of the story? Wittig, as critics have pointed out, here attributes the narrative voice to an anonymous "*on*," which in the French vernacular refers to an ungendered "we." Obviously Wittig is writing the story, but is apparently absent from the text. The last lines of the text give the reader a precious clue. In a direct reading, the story is that of an idyll: in a childhood world of girls and boys it tells of the love that grows between two girls, Catherine Legrand and Valérie Borges. The closing line of the book is: "I loved her so much that in her I still live." So far, the narrative has been developed in sequences, told in the present tense.[13] The past tense "loved" reveals the identity of narrator and story: memory.

Memory is a "utopia." What Wittig has created is a vivid "film," a flow of images, a "montage" isolating a theme: a total involvement of the children in their lives, in play, in school, in the worlds of literature, a "collective" experience within which a real new event happens: a special emotion, made of all those daily events and going beyond them. For this uncategorized feeling Catherine Legrand invents a new role, a new name "The Opoponax," a new identity as puzzling to her as the name.

The opoponax, encyclopedias tell us, is a plant with an "acrid odor," esteemed for its purifying virtues; also, differently, a kind of "perfumed myrrh." In any case, it is a pervasive presence, invisible as Catherine's strong, frustrated attraction to Valérie. Spontaneously then, Catherine has devised the mask of myth in her notes to Valérie: "I am the opoponax." A violent sequence erupts when a nearby conflagration, a schoolgirl protest, and the revelation of the threatening presence of the "opoponax" by chance coincide; Catherine is half persuaded of her magic powers as Valérie subtly recognizes and responds to her unspecified appeal. The tale then ends in a kind of coda: lights, colors, life are heightened as, in the configuration of schoolgirl friendships made visible through the ritual patterning of name, Valérie Borges and Catherine Legrand now are never separated. "*On dit*," someone says, "I loved her so much"—"*On*," the invisible presence, through whom the "recording" of an inner event, inseparable from the turbulent patterns of "reality" in which it is enclosed, can only be realized by the writer Monique Wittig; the text then is referential in the deepest sense, drawing the reader, as might a film, into the concrete re-presentation of a world modulated by a feeling that the *word* "love" by itself does not "embody." That bond between a world and a human feeling remains free of sentimentality or guilt, not of quiet, sensuous "rightness." What it presents is an unsullied image of a "true" relationship, the basis of an identity, and not a "myth."

Between *Les guérillères* and *L'opoponax* stretch the highly charged years of social unrest. They shaped Monique Wittig the political militant and advocate for women's rights, for whom they provided a stage. There is nothing militant about *L'opoponax*: it is a beautifully crafted account of a recognizable emotion. Merely, the two actors do not fit the "expected" gender roles. With *Les guérillères* the narrative drive changes.

The components of the text can hardly be overlooked, strange enough at first sight to bar the average reader from the text. Two highly visible devices break the orderly unfolding of printed words, first, the pages of juxtaposed words in block lettering, made of lists of feminine names: of goddesses, of historic characters; classical, oriental, medieval, contemporary. The opening and the closing sequences, in contrast, are made of juxtaposed segments of words that echo one another, ending with a similar notation, *Tout geste est renversement* (All action is overthrow) and *Geste renversement* (Action overthrow), indicating a circular design. The second device consists of black circles on a blank white page, which appear three times, always on the right-hand page, first as an opening to the subsequent written text, then as a kind of large punctuation mark. The written-out text between these markers develops in sequences. Once again what it suggests, formally, is a tapestry in the making, woven out of constantly changing scenes of which the reader is spectator. But of what? Who is or are the tellers of the tales? Where situated?

There is first of all an anonymous tale-bearer, who begins the story *in medias res:* "When it rains, they ["elles"] stay in the summer-house. . . ."[14] The "discourse" is modeled on the narrative style of the anthropologist, the "outsider" recording the outer patterns of life of an exotic group "elles"; but recording also what is said, sung, told by "elles," or written in the "feminaries," those guides to female sexuality, always introduced by the pervasive "they say" ("elles disent"); and further diversified by the "voices" of single, named feminine figures within the group, who are the designated "hearers." The initial "tale-bearer," the "outsider" is like a commentator running a tape carefully assembled, without explanation, a mosaic of concrete notations and a polyphony of blended but not interchangeable voices from "inside." The reader then has no option but to move with the text into the story, which is evolving on a triple level. A fourth level is a factor of imagery: the reader is drawn into a semiotic field, rich in notations, names, familiar objects, mythical allusions, which suggest the presence of a half-remembered classical world. No one has attempted as yet to disentangle, in that network, the legendary from the historical, from the invented. It bears the stamp of the author and connects with the lists of names in block letters that furnish an accompaniment to the text.

That in its overall structure, *Les guérillères* mimes classical "genres"—first the eclogue, then the epic, both familiar literary forms—has often been noted. Less so the complex thematic and semantic modulations that draw the story out of the legendary past onto the stage of contemporary history, recording women's common victory over male oppression. The "guérillères" theme appears in snatches, then gathers momentum until it triumphs in a grand finale in which Marx and Wittig join hands. The analogy with the great Shostakovich symphony celebrating the October Revolution and the defense of Leningrad can hardly be avoided, as the victorious "guérillères" join to sing the *Internationale*:[15] "The great song filled the hall, burst through doors and windows and rose to the calm sky" (144). The strange group approaches from outside as "elles" now merge into a we,[16] as the text spills over from fiction into history. The text is the "imitation" of an "action" that it mimes: "Action overthrow," an action that the symbol of the circle, the sign of the feminine, sustains until it has been erased, along with the feminaries. The reader is left to ponder the long prehistory behind the costly struggle and its "signification" as set up in the text. But the reader is not otherwise instructed. The essential, absent tale-bearer Monique Wittig has welded past, present, and projected future into a utopian literary whole of astonishing complexity and beauty rooted in a culture whose formal boundaries it transcends in a revolutionary literary "overthrow." Overthrown from within is the traditional representation of women, accomplished through pastiche and parody. Wittig has perfected a tool that serves her own deconstructive purpose, a double rhetoric of appropriation and mask, through which the "debunking" thrust of the text appears. She "appropriates" the Dante scenario; then under that mask she subverts it, reversing the meaning.

This is the tool she puts to good use in *Virgile, non*. Her selection of the referential text, we saw, was deliberate, as was the genre for the two previous novels; her intent clear, to *détourner* (i.e., subvert) the text. Further, her notes affirm her personal involvement in the writing: "The knowledge, which is not mine alone, of the hell of *Virgile, non* puts into question all philosophy and dialectic in *poetic terms*." For Wittig, Dante's text is political, but it does not, as she intends to, "stand society on its head." Rather, in Wittig's texts the figures set in motion are souls, therefore ipso facto presumably unsexed.

As she points out, the Dante story has been "pirated a hundred times," bringing readers "a shock of recognition." Her notes to me fill in the sources of allusions in the text: Djuna Barnes, Verlaine, the *New Portuguese Letters* published in France in 1972, K. Barries's *Female Slavery*, etc. A wide intertextuality.

The general structures of Dante's story are, in a manner, used. The story is told by a female character, "Wittig," who with another feminine figure Manastabal, her "guide," has undertaken a journey through hellish situations to rejoin "she" who is her "providence." Manastabal then has replaced the rejected *Virgile* of the title. The overall distribution in the Dante text is maintained: narrative; evocation of the dangerous route followed; successive descriptive scenes of grotesque group suffering; dramatic dialogue between the two voyagers, or between the voyagers and the denizens of "hell"; eventually a "happy" ending as "Wittig" and Manastabal reach "she who is my providence" in a never-never land of song, banqueting, birds, fruit, an "opera" of angels held within a prism of pure light-blue silver, ocre, orange, dazzling yellow, which recalls the last line of *L'opoponax*. But the modulations within the structure are strangely unexpected. First, the strange accouterment of the voyagers—blue jeans and shirts, a rifle slung over the shoulder—recalling the warriors of science fiction. Then, concrete notations of the landscape as the two figures advance, moving through a sandstorm. These images are compared to those of a silent "film," film being seen as a modern narrative form. The "film" is set in San Francisco, not in "another" world. There one moves in and out of hell, limbo, paradise. The sign of hell is the sandstorm; of limbo, the cafés where the travelers sit and converse while sipping tequila; and there are glimpses of paradise. There are four sequences in limbo, at different moments; five glimpses of paradise before the final arrival there of the voyagers at the end.

The story takes a strange turn as, sustained by Manastabal, "Wittig" undertakes a veritable and droll harrowing of hell. The story told is not Dante's. Hell is a "bad spot" in and out of which one can move. The figures in hell are not sinners but victims; Manastabal does not justify, as does Dante's Virgil, the tortures inflicted on them. The "fable" via the series of alternating scenes is indeed stood on its head, in the "accelerated" film of Manastabal's and Wittig's action to thrust the victims out of hell. Dante reappears in the ferocious parades of figures encountered: a wild and cruelly satiric depiction of a San Francisco parade; the processions of female figures whose physical condition luridly recalls Tillie Olsen's recapitulation of women's sad past and still extant lot: "Beaten, raped. Bought and sold. Concubinage, prostitution, white slavery. The hunt, the sexual prey . . ." (26). These are embodied, acted, performed by the text in the medieval evocations of the punishments inflicted on sinners in hell, as in Dante's successive visualizations of the analogical correspondence of sin and punishment. But in Wittig's rendering the story veers in a new direction.

When "Wittig" stepped into the role of Dante, a new perspective for the reader asserted itself within the text: a tongue-in-cheek self-parody that deflects, de-dramatizes the story. "Wittig" is a somewhat Woody Allen figure—earnest, befuddled in her role as spectator, reporter, questioner of the spectacles encountered. The dialogue with Manastabal takes new coloring: compassion, indignation, revolt. In a wild acceleration of the text, "Wittig" and Manastabal engage in a disruptive "harrowing of hell" on behalf of the generally unwilling "victims." The acquiescent Virgil of Dante is erased by the two crusaders against the dismal "reality" of pain. Chaos reigns as the "liberators" are forced to flee. It is not hard to "read" the story from signs to meaning. The victims, first, are women; the torments, physical translations of social constraints; Manastabal and "Wittig" assume the roles of liberators, and are set upon by the "victims." A double-edged satiric text surfaces, as the noble rhetoric of "women's lib" is questioned while the "myth" of lesbian asocial monstrosity is perceived as a lie. The "monstrous" lesbians, feared and vilified, rejected and ostracized by the women they see as victims, are the real proponents of a future harmonious heterosexual society. The "hellish" world depicted is, in fact, an exclusively male-dominated world where power is homosexual. But it is already an obsolete world of "shades." The stage is set for a new departure, perhaps a new narrative form. *Across the Acheron*, the title of the English translation, suggests that the hell of oppression can be left behind.

Because of Monique Wittig's brilliant visualizing techniques, I found it most rewarding to look across boundaries to another contemporary use of the *Divine Comedy*, Rauschenberg's 34 drawings for the *Inferno*, where there is no crossing the Acheron, no paradise, and the model used is simply "hell." The comparison-contrast in the structural design of the two interpretations brings out the close connection between vision and technical innovation. But this will, I hope, be the theme of another essay.[17]

NOTES

1. See Michel Butor's essay in *Repertoire IV*. This essay, like several included in *Repertoire II* and *III* (1964, 1968), is pertinent to the question discussed here.
2. Actually, the disruption of established forms of discourse had been systematically carried out with Dada and Surrealism; and in a different vein with the word games and lucid juggling with sound and syntax characteristic of Raymond Queneau and a small group of "researchers" in the creative potentialities of new patterns of words, freed from any a priori need to convey meaning (the *Ouvroir de littérature potentielle*—OU.LI.PO.—group). The "new" novelists were seeking new combinations of the basic strategies used in novel-writing.
3. In addition to Jefferson's study, see Sister Margaretta Black's dissertation on the French novel.
4. The metaphor in the title works on three levels at least. It is an obvious allusion to Stendhal's image of the novel as a mirror moving along a road, and to the rejection of the image by the dogmatic theoretician of the new novel, Ricardou. Ricardou denied the representational value of literary creation, the relation between world, word, and writer that Stendhal suggested. The "return" of the mirror is obvious in Robbe-Grillet's autobiographic project. It is also a reference to a Breton legend placed within the text as a *mise en abîme*:

the story of a mirror, lost in the shipwreck and washed up by the tide—a many-faceted symbol of the intricate patterns of memory, imagination, reflexivity, and "reality" in literary representation. A far more complex notion than Jean Ricardou's distinction between the "real" world and the "scriptural" world.

5. This quotation from James appears in Caws's *Reading Frames in Modern Fiction*. An analysis pertinent to the Sarraute enterprise is on p. 122.

6. Professor O'Flaherty holds the Mircea Eliade Chair in the History of Religion at the University of Chicago.

7. In this respect, Winifred Woodhull's dissertation on Wittig's *Les guérillères* and *Brouillon pour un dictionnaire des amantes* does a pretty thorough job. More sensitive perhaps to the actual texture of Wittig's writing and the narrative structure adopted, Hélène Wenzel's 1977 dissertation on *L'opoponax* is an excellent exegesis of that text.

8. De Certeau is less known in the United States to date. See his *La prise de parole pour une nouvelle culture* (*Speaking in Favor of a New Culture*).

9. I apologize for the use of a gender-marked designation that Wittig deplores; but how else to make my point?

10. In contrast, the position of Simone de Beauvoir has been sympathetically analyzed by Elaine Hoffman Baruch, who shows its narrow boundaries. See "The Female Body and the Male Mind."

11. "One is never happy making way for a new truth, for it always means making our way into it . . ." (Lacan, *Ecrits*). Certainly for Wittig there would be quotes to "new truth." But there is one source of truth: the truth of the body, to be deciphered and transferred into language. I owe this quotation to Nell Gifford Martin (along with most useful contributions to the brief discussion of Robert Rauschenberg's 34 drawings for the *Inferno* [1955–60], which I hope to develop in relation to Wittig's *Virgile, non* in a later study).

12. *Les guérillères*: a feminine neologism coined by Wittig from the well known nongendered noun "guerillas," kept in Le Vay's translation.

13. For an exhaustive analysis of the seven narrative sequences, see Wenzel.

14. I have used Le Vay's translation of *Les guérillères*, but in this sentence I prefer to translate "*elles*" as "they," not "the women," as Le Vay does.

15. The structural resolution is more complex, involving the merging into the text of the theme of the Funeral March.

16. See the translation by Le Vay (9, 14).

17. My grateful thanks go to Raymond Farrow and Jimmy Steintrager for their help in the presentation of this paper.

WORKS CITED

Baruch, Elaine Hoffman. "The Female Body and the Male Mind: Reconsidering Simone de Beauvoir." *Dissent* (Summer 1987): 351–58.
Black, Sister Margaretta. "Problems and Techniques of the French Novel, 1950–1970." Diss. U of Wisconsin, 1972.

Butor, Michel. "Emile Zola, Experimental Novelist." *Repertoire IV*. Paris: Gallimard, 1974.

———. *Passage de Milan*. Paris: Minuit, 1954.

Certeau, Michel de. *La prise de parole pour une nouvelle culture*. Paris: Desclée de Brower, 1968.

James, Henry. Preface to *The Princess Casamassima*. Quoted by Mary Ann Caws in *Reading Frames in Modern Fiction*. Princeton: Princeton UP, 1984.

Jefferson, Ann. *The Nouveau Roman and the Poetics of Fiction*. New York: Cambridge UP, 1980.

Lacan, Jacques. *Ecrits: A Selection*. Trans. A. Sheridan. London: Tavistock, 1977.

O'Flaherty, Wendy. "Other People's Myths." Unpubl. essay.

Olsen, Tilly. *Silences*. New York: Delacorte, 1978.

Robbe-Grillet, Alain. *Les gommes*. Paris: Minuit, 1953.

———. *The Mirror Returns*. New York: Grove, 1986.

———. *Pour un nouveau roman*. Paris: Gallimard, 1963.

Sarraute, Nathalie. *The Age of Suspicion: Essays on the Novel*. Trans. Maria Jolas. New York: Braziller, 1963.

———. *Childhood*. Trans. Barbara Wright. New York: Braziller, 1984.

———. *Martereau*. Trans. Maria Jolas. New York: Braziller, 1959.

———. *Portrait of a Man Unknown*. Trans. Maria Jolas. New York: Braziller, 1958.

———. *Tropisms*. Trans. Maria Jolas. New York: Braziller, 1967.

———. Interviewed by Liliane Atlan. *Studies in the 20th Century* 11–12 (1973): 108–23.

Wenzel, Hélène Vivienne. "*L'opoponax*: I Still Live In Her." Diss. U of California, Berkeley, 1977.

Wittig, Monique. *Les Guérillères*. Trans. David Le Vay. New York: Viking, 1971.

———. *The Opoponax*. Trans. Helen Weaver. New York: Simon, 1966.

———. *Virgile, non*. Trans. David Le Vay and Margaret Crosland as *Across the Acheron*. London: Owen, 1987.

Woodhull, Winifred. "Politics, The Feminine, and Writing: A Study of Monique Wittig's *Les guérillères* and *Brouillon pour un dictionnaire des amantes*." Diss. U of Wisconsin, 1979.

The Clandestine Fictions of
Marguerite Duras

Maria DiBattista

La femme qui écrit se déguise en . . . , en homme.
> M. Duras, *Les parleuses*

BEFORE the world can be represented, it must be felt to exist, but it is precisely this feeling that often fails Marguerite Duras. Her characters are persons displaced (by the reactive power of trauma) or banished (by the force of circumstances) to the limits of what Maurice Blanchot eerily designates as "le lieu sans lieu, le dehors" (the placeless place, the Outside) (142). In *Outside*, a collection of her journalistic pieces, Duras regards the outside world as a spectacle that claims her attention in moments of leisure or imaginative distraction, and then primarily as "cinema" (12), the unreal space of illusionistic projection. Not even Desire, the great unifier, can revoke the law of kind that prevents the mating of inner with outer reality.[1]

This general truth, which is confirmed everywhere in Duras's work, is succinctly formulated in a maxim from Duras's ambitious quest fiction, *The Sailor from Gibraltar*: "They say one person's absence can make the world a desert, but it's not so. But if the world is absent for you, no one can people it" (142). Typically, Duras evokes the world's conventional wisdom (the "*on dit*" that gives to her most personal statements the flat affect of an apothegm) only to reverse and repudiate it, thus compounding psychological with heuristic isolation. Passion can conduct the self voyeuristically outward, but it cannot displace nor cancel "the disturbing and vertiginous reality of the world" (238–39). For Duras, the world is not a desert; it is only incomplete or destitute of meaning. "Le dehors" extends to a horizon of potential significance, like the empty beach Lol Stein conjures as the image most evocative of her solitariness, a beach "empty as if God had not yet finished making it" (162) or the blank sky of Leucate in *Détruire, dit-elle* that speaks to Blanchot of the desertion of the gods (142).

I will be arguing that this visionary horizon, where meaning shimmers like a mirage, delimits the space of her writing as a specifically female domain, the domain of the clandestine. I want to consider, first, what marks this space as female, and then examine why for Duras this domain is always clandestine. Duras has maintained that men and women do not share the same relation to physical space: "A woman inhabits a place completely, her presence fills space. A man traverses, never really occupies space" (*Les parleuses* 75). This difference, Duras contends, generates the "elementary grammar of images" upon which her work is conceptually grounded. But Duras's writing does not strictly adhere to this grammar, which in any case seems to direct her cinematic rather than literary representations of the female body. Thus while her writing could be read as stories of how women attempt to realize a rich and unhurried relation to space, the most memorable of her women remain heroines *maudites* who seem to evacuate rather than inhabit the space they occupy, like the young woman of *The Square* who is amazed that "I occupy any physical place in the world at all" (9), or like Lol Stein, whose life before her "ravishment" is summarized as the story of "how a dwelling becomes empty when she moves in" (73).

Duras's retreat into self-emptying space reenacts her original desertion of the world of the Mother. This motive becomes startlingly clear in her overtly autobiographical fictions and memoirs. In these works her mother is identified with an overpopulated, even cannibalistic world that threatens to devour her and whatever creativity she may express. In Duras's novelistic recounting of her early years in Indochina, *Un barrage contre le Pacifique* (*The Sea Wall*), the mother is seen to conspire with the mad fecundity of the natural world:

> There were children as there were rains, fruits, floods. They came each year, by periodical tides, or, if you like, by crops and burgeonings. Every woman of the plain, as long as she was young enough to be desired by her husband, had her child each year. . . . This went on regularly, with the rhythm of plant-life, as if, in a deep, long inhalation, each year, the body of each woman took in and swelled with child, expelled in an exhalation a child and then, in a second inhalation, took in another. (92)

The women of the plain whose existence is regulated by this vegetal rhythm experience life as a kind of predictable natural disaster. Duras describes how rains and their fruits, women and their children are overwhelmed in a leveling flood of equivalences, but she refuses to discriminate between the anthropology and the ontology of such disastrous motherhood. The women of the plain, historically identified as the subjugated native population of Indochina in the 1920s, seem equally to be the subjects of a bleak parable of procreation.

The primordial syllable—*mère*, homonym with *mer*, the sea—summarizes for Duras the thematics of this calamitous maternity. This pun encapsulates the mother and the primal force of her madness, the madness of sowing crops and raising children where no earthly life can nor should be sustained. It is the madness of resumption itself, of the ceaseless efforts to turn back the tides of the Pacific and make the wilderness of the salt plains flower into the Promised Land pictured by colonial propaganda posters. The story of *The Sea Wall* centers on the mother's struggles to work an unworkable concession, a story that possesses, especially for the daughter caught in the spell of its unfolding, the dread fascination of a cautionary tale: "She had had so much misfortune that she had become a monster exercising a mighty spell, her children ran the risk of being forever held captive to console her in her grief, and they might never be able to leave her, but would have to go on bending to her will, go on letting themselves, in their turn, be devoured by her." Duras would elude the grasp of this demon-mother who emotionally devours her children by providing her fable with an abrupt, almost offhanded ironic moral: "There were no two ways for a girl to learn how to leave her mother" (148).

Learning how to leave mother is not a lesson easily dispatched, whether one is a young girl or a mature woman. In her study of modern literary women, Ellen Moers noted that Woolf and Colette wrote "of the power and grandeur of motherhood with an air of finality, as if what they were describing would never come again; as if there would never more be any mothers" (359). In Duras we encounter a writer haunted by the opposite anxiety. She represents the predicaments of maternity from the perspective of the daughter who fears that she will never be in the presence of anything *but* the mother. The daughter would avoid the fate of the mother, doomed to perish in battle with the very Nature whose unremitting fertility she externally (and linguistically) symbolizes: "Ever since the failure of the sea walls, there never passed a day without her planting something, no matter what, anything that would grow and give wood or fruit or leaves or nothing—anything that would simply grow" (90). In the literature of mothers and daughters, few approach and none surpass Duras's mordant account of the daughter's sullen attempts to avoid paying tribute to female creativity within this oppressive economy of abundance (an abundance that is the ironic antonym of actual prosperity). The sea wall is Duras's most abiding symbol for two different kinds of female constructions, the one maternal and symbolizing the mother's dream of hegemony over the world of natural process (the sea), the other filial, symbolizing the psychic defense the daughter-who-writes must raise to shield herself from the mother's baffled but determined will.

In *The Lover* Duras returns to her "common family history of ruin and death" to discover that hers is a history recoverable only within "the very depths of my flesh," where the deposits of both her love and her hate have been secreted. Yet it is on the threshold of this interior that silence commences, and so Duras finds herself once more dumb and immobilized before a "closed door": "I've never written, though I thought I wrote, never loved, though I thought I loved, never done anything but wait outside the closed door" (25). The closed door, symbol of her impasse, is also the threshold of her vocation as writer, a vocation to be fulfilled once this door has been opened. For Duras now understands that all previous writing, and all former loving, have merely distracted her from this primary calling: to stand in dutiful attendance on the brink of self-understanding. Indeed, one of the real triumphs of *The Lover* is Duras's description of how, with her mother now dead and laid to rest, she may "write about her so easily now, so long, so fully. She's become just something you write without difficulty, cursive writing" (29). The French *écriture courante* denotes a running hand, a writing that *flows*, presumably without impediments. Within this cursive medium, the demon-mother finally assumes a historical, and thus limited existence, and so can no longer return, like other creatures of darkness, from the dead. In cursive writing, the mother, whose adult unhappiness took the place of childish dreams, becomes a "mother either flayed by poverty or distraught and muttering in the wilderness, either searching for food or endlessly telling what's happened to her, Marie Legrand from Roubaix, telling of her innocence, her savings, her hopes" (46). Tellingly, when she remembers her mother, "it is under this particular name, her maiden name that I see her: Marie Legrand" ("Mothers" 99). Any rapprochement with the mother can only be accomplished, it would seem, by seeing through the frenzied widow who dominates the early novels and recovering, from the depths of a lost history, a portrait of the mother as a young girl.

Reacting against the mother and forswearing her destiny, Duras becomes a minimalist in staging the play of desire. Her settings are forlorn and devastated places: a barren Indochinese plain, S. Thala in *The Ravishing of Lol Stein*, or more compelling, Hiroshima. Her characters encounter each other in a village square, a park, or asylum. There they exchange stories and loves, and then part, leaving the world untransformed, everything in the place destined or assigned to it by the powers of the Outside, powers outrageously symbolized by the jackal-like cadastral agents in *The Sea Wall* and never so recklessly specified again. As Germaine Brée reminds us, Duras over the years has simplified her situations in order to isolate the moment when an "inner event seems to be taking shape" (v). The narrator of *The Sailor from Gibraltar* confirms Brée's insight in characterological terms: "One's always more or less looking for something. . . . For something to arise in the world and come towards you" (128). His own moment of "shameless" happiness, which at once expresses (through a fit of tears) and mobilizes his hysteria, comes when, gazing at Fra Angelico's "Annunication," he perceives the "angel" with "warm wings of untruth" returning his look. Duras, the memoirist spellbound before her closed door, is foretold in the narrator's transfixion as he stands poised, like an aroused and attentive Mary, on the threshold of revelation, awaiting divine instructions. So many of Duras's characters cannot change unless summoned from without (from "le dehors"). They otherwise are doomed, like the young girl of *The Square*, to criticize, but never to abandon a life in which nothing arises in spiritual greeting.

Such sacred encounters on the threshold of madness are not even conceivable for Duras except in a secluded and *inverted* world, like the one depicted in *The Sailor from Gibraltor* by Anna's atlas of the "topsy-turvy universe, a negative of the world," one that corresponds to her vision of a spiritually depopulated globe: "It also showed depths and currents. The continents were mostly as white and empty as the seas" (147). Duras takes odd comfort in these world-blankings because they allow her to survey the "ground," as yet unoccupied, of women's writing: "That's it," she asserts in an interview, "reverse everything, including analysis and criticism. . . . Reverse everything. Make women the point of departure in judging, make darkness the point of departure in judging what men call light, make obscurity the point of departure in judging what men call clarity" (Husserl-Kapit 426). Men are blinded by the dazzling but spurious lucidity of their theoretical intelligence and so have no revolutionary vision to communicate. Women should learn to see by the dim but not false light emitted by the darkness; they should trust to that obscurity that endows nothingness itself with the density of presence.[2]

Duras's own writing transpires within an inverted symbolic field in which darkness signifies the presence of an unquiet interior and white signifies the vacancy of the unreal world ruled by material logic and masculine force. Duras designates this interior, which conceals the most radical (hence transformative) of human thoughts and feelings—*clandestinité*. The underground activity of the French Resistance is the immediate historical resonance of this word. But Duras seems intent on communicating a more general idea of clandestinité, one that comprehends the categorical imperatives of women's writing: to translate this suppressed and all-too-human darkness without "clarifying" it, that is, without betraying it to the rule of reason, which is always authoritarian in Duras's psychology. These translations, which occur throughout Duras's fiction, are specifically identified as a species of clandestine writing during a series of conversations with Xavière Gauthier, published as *Les parleuses*. In their first conversation Duras remarks that women writers are often "reduced" to clandestinité and that she considers herself a "clandestine" (35). However, in the larger metaphoric (and tactical) reversals that direct Duras's thought, this banishment is also occasion for exploring "*un champ d'expérimentation*" (19)—a field of experimentation that extends beyond or beneath established forms of expression. Duras thus recuperates the clandestine as the domain (assigned or preferred?) of women's literature, the literature of an unknown and as yet unformulated language, the "silence of women."

To speak on tabooed subjects demands, besides great courage, great facility in translating such a burdened silence, and Duras has proved herself possessed of both. Yet she is not interested in becoming a kind of captive Cassandra, an inspired but unregarded prophet of a conquered female population. She remains clandestine even as she attracts public notice by communicating through an abstract ventriloquism that mimics in order to subvert the voices of vested authority. "The woman who writes," Duras once provocatively averred in the assertion that serves as my epigraph, "disguises herself as a man." The man Duras impersonates is, however, a particular kind of man, a man without affect, often without charm, indeed, to invoke the title of a novel that impressed her, a man without qualities. She assumes not just the vestige and verbal mannerisms of another sex, but impersonates the narrative figure men have often arrogated for their own questionable ends, that classical figure of psychological and grammatical detachment—the third person. The assertion that opens *Le Vice-Consul*, "Elle marche, écrit Peter Morgan," astounds because it stands in stark isolation, unattended by further sentences of contextual qualification. This fiercely univalent sentence, which is followed immediately by a new paragraph stylistically remarkable for its collation of grammatical persons, alerts us to the way a classical grammar of persons reinforces as it constructs a narrative about the relation between perceived and perceiver. The third person who observes and describes, that is who writes, is male, while the female acts and is acted upon in consequence of this male predication. *Détruire, dit-elle* is Duras's most spectacular assault on this narrative relation and the grammar that constitutes it. The destruction this text intends is registered in the syntactical shock of the title, which deploys the infinitive with a violence Blanchot admired as truly oracular (39).

Duras's experiments in sexual mimicry, then, are adroit acts of cultural sabotage. If she adopts the disguise of male authorship (as in *The Sailor from Gibraltar* or in *The Ravishing of Lol Stein*), she does so to camouflage a more serious transgression, her "making free" with tabooed erotic topics, especially in the scandalous form of adulterous passion. Duras observes: "Adultery is a . . . bugbear; however, for the conditioning of the erotic, it is irreplaceable" (*Les parleuses* 46). Duras does not appear to be interested in deciding whether this conditioning is a social or a biological fact of life, only in contending that the abolition of adultery, like the abolition of all illicit love (*amour clandestin*), while desirable, "involves somewhere the idea of loss": "I don't really like it when one says: 'All this is bad, we need to get rid of everything and regret nothing.' I regret at the same time as I cast away" (225). Duras's praise of the folly of adultery is a sign of her attachment to the topics of the clandestine. She is responding, in passages like this, to a reflex of her own writerly temperament, for she often seems drawn to the perverse excitement of a thing done in secret for its own sake. This would explain why she would regret even as she attains her liberation from clandestine existence. Duras's experimental writing is, in her own figure, *"un passage à blanc"* (45), a passage across a blanched, reclusive space where desire is either consumed or neutralized, a space that is simultaneously the realm of discovery of experiment and invention, and the domain of self-loss.

Within this experimental field, elementary distinctions of place and person are effaced to create phantasmal names worthy of Duras's de-realizing syntax. Duras's pen name is one of the most successful creations of this transformational grammar. In one of her interviews in Montreal, she responds to a remark about the importance of names in her work by revealing that her surname is Donnadieu, a name (given-unto-God) that at once reverses and puns on the terms of the God-given (Lamy 55). In fact, it is in response to a question about the writer's displacement of God in the work of creation that this biographical information is volunteered. But Duras obviously renounced any hint of such theopathic writing in forsaking her surname (with its hint of divine surrender) and assuming as pseudonym the name of a village of Lot-et-Garonne, near property her father once rented and where he died (55). Readers of Duras become accustomed to such blendings of the personal and the communal identity. Duras's exploitation of the self-substantiating property of places and place names has become a signature of her work, sometimes quite shockingly, as in the film *Hiroshima mon amour*, where Hiroshima and Nevers-en-Loire become fetishized beyond the historical suffering they designate. The film evokes the holocaust of Hiroshima from an adulterous hotel bed, a fetishization Duras admits to be a "voluntary sacrilege" (*Hiroshima* 2). The generic heroine of *Hiroshima mon amour* testifies to the reality of horrors *personally* witnessed against the generic male's repudiation of this historical impiety:[3]

Lui:—Tu n'as *rien* vu à Hiroshima. Rien.
Elle:—J'ai *tout* vu. Tout. (16)

This (male) nothing and this (female) all collapse into the intensive space of confrontation that is the film's psychological *mise-en-scène*. At film's end, the lovers' identities dissolve the place names denoting the shame of collaboration (loving a Nazi soldier) and the horror of mass death. She and he intone, as if in clandestine benediction, the visionary identifications begotten by love:

ELLE: "Hi-ro-shi-ma. C'est ton nom."
LUI: —C'est mon nom. Oui. Ton nom à toi est Nevers. Ne-vers-en-
Fran-ce. (102–03)

This erotic grammar that fuses person and place disguises but cannot eliminate the fundamental dichotomy that determines Duras's political outlook as well as her narrative strategies, the dichotomy between individual experience, provocatively figured in the autobiographical and generally erotic tenor of her work, and the traumatic historical *episode* lived by everyone, reluctantly figured in the local and global politics, the Outside, of her narratives. From this fundamental difference between the collective outer world and the inner world of the imaginary, other distinctions follow, perhaps the most morally sobering being Duras's assertion that her recently resurrected memoirs of the Liberation, *La douleur* (*The War*), are charged with "a tremendous chaos of thought and feeling . . . and beside which literary work was something of which I felt ashamed" (10). Duras claims that she could not bring herself to tamper with the original draft of these texts. She demands that in reading them we separate the *literary* from the historical as the sacred is from the profane. "Learn to read them properly: they are sacred," she intones like a high priestess—or a penitent. For *The War* is a text that assembles—but does not "construct"—a sequence of remorseful memories and guilty identifications: "Thérèse is me," she proclaims of "Ter of the Militia": "The person who tortures the informer is me. So also is the one who feels like making love to Ter, the member of the Militia. Me. I give you the torturer along with the rest of the texts" (111). The "me" so identified is strangely depersonalized, as if in ritual confession, and yet we know from her other works the intimacy subsisting between self-abasement and self-absorption.

The self-concern that inevitably conditions the sufferings of the guilt-ridden appears in a different register in Duras's mesmerizing text of self-doubling, *The Lover*. This "memoir" of her sexual initiation deliberately confounds the imagined with the remembered and confuses what was lived with what was dreamed. The resulting confusion in her text is not only intentional, but necessary, in fulfillment of its nature as "writing": "Sometimes I realize that if writing isn't, all things, all contraries confounded, a quest for vanity and void, it's nothing. That if it's not, each time, all things confounded into one through some inexpressible essence, then writing is nothing but advertisement" (8). The quest for vanity and void terminates in love-making, "when you let the body alone, to seek and find and take what it likes . . . in the force of desire" (43). What is discovered in this moment of abandonment is the vanity of the desire it consummates. For it is desire, Duras observes, "that deludes the body, that deceives" (*Les parleuses* 223). Desire can create a text of deception, but it leaves no truthful record of itself, except in the lines of the ravaged face.

The life-worn face is the initial image with which Duras presents herself in *The Lover*. She watches her own face age with the "same sort of interest I might have taken in the reading of a book," an analogy that justifies her mood of self-congratulation in remarking that her face, though "scored with deep, dry wrinkles," has not collapsed. For those scorings will help her confirm how, as a young girl, "the space existed in me for desire," how at the age of eighteen, fifteen (she is careless of strict chronology) she already was possessed of "that flagrant, exhausted face, those rings around the eyes, in advance of time and experience" (9). What the translator renders as "experience" is in French a word embracing literary as well as sexual expectations of originality, *l'experiment* (italics in original), an Anglicized locution (*experimentation* would be the normal French usage). Duras literally italicizes her riskiest translation in linking the traditional metaphor in the women's literature of self-realization— sexual discovery as self-discovery—with the *failure* to define a female "subject." For no stable relation exists between the subject who writes and the subject of her recounting. As memorist, Duras shifts restlessly and without explanation from first to third person.

The Lover seduces us by flaunting rather than disguising the literary conventionality of its autobiographical premise: associating the initiation into sexual *jouissance*, a pleasure-unto-death, with the emergence of the woman who writes. Duras remains safely within, even as she plays against the sexual orthodoxy that *only* pleasure can instruct and liberate. However, Duras's conformity to a model text promoting the sexual liberation of woman is vexed by her insistence that her life cannot be "composed" into a tendentious narrative. She is adamant on this point: "The story of my life doesn't exist. Does not exist. There's never any center to it. No path, no line" (8). She refuses to ascribe a fixed end, purpose, or structure to those human occurrences and relations that nevertheless indisputably formed the person who retells them. She writes instead of self-contained moments and their elaborately distended images. These images are then metaphorically assembled into incantatory descriptions of *situ-*

ations rather than metonymically arranged (and ideologically fashioned) into a *story* in which we can see the self unfold. To abide within the limitations of such self-contained scenes is to sacrifice certain narrative luxuries, those thrilling feats of romantic fiction in forging a series of accidental occurrences into an amorous destiny. In Duras, desire circulates, destitute of destination.

Duras will only acknowledge the reality of certain *crossings* that are fateful, like her crossing of the Mekong on an ordinary day, except this day she encountered her first lover, scion of a Chinese landowner from Fushun, wealthy and taboo. Their first meeting fails to impress on Duras's memory a distinct image, but this confounding of outlines is precisely what endows the event with "the virtue of representing, of being the creator of, an absolute" (10). This absolute is both incarnated and dispersed in a series of fragmentary memories that recall the physical appurtenances of the crossing: the dress of threadbare silk that belonged to her mother and so definitely *pertains* to her, speaks of her, who she is and where she came from; the man's hat she wears that bestows a crucial ambiguity on her self-recollection and allows her to see herself "as another would be seen, outside myself, available to all, available to all eyes, in circulation for cities, journeys, desire." She would never part from this hat because it reminds her of that moment when the "inadequacy of childhood . . . [the] inescapable imposition of nature" turned into a "provoking choice of nature, a choice of the mind" (12). The hat retains its historical value as a reminder of the futility of her provocations in the wilderness of her impoverished childhood.

These vividly ambiguous images replace and are meant to correct the "romancing" of her earlier autobiographical fictions. In assuming the burden of truthful recounting (itself, of course, an art like any other, but requiring either more candor or more guile to attain), Duras insinuates the frank intimacy of long acquaintance between the "I" who writes and the "you" who reads (and rereads) her: "So you see it wasn't in the bar at Réam, as I wrote, that I met the rich man with the black limousine, it was after we left the land by the dike, two or three years after, on the ferry, the day I'm telling you about, in that light of haze and heat" (27). Yet even told with scrupulous honesty, the past seems attended by portents of its own inevitability. Duras makes the space of recollection fateful by filling it with a series of self-projections or self-doublings, brief but psychologically "complete" portraits of women she might have turned into rather than, as it happened, she turned away from: Marie Carpenter, the American expatriate who leaves people "with the feeling of having experienced a sort of empty nightmare" (65); the collaborator Betty Fernandez who instructs her in another form of vanity—the superstition of trying to seek political solutions for personal problems; the Lady, never designated by any other name but this class word, who is "consigned to the infamy of a pleasure unto death, . . . unto the mysterious death of lovers without love" (90). These women are all more or less creatures of that nonlife that Duras locates in the realm of "publicity," life conducted in the public domain of the Outside.

Only one person escapes "the law of error"—the law of futile self-display, which holds that either desire is "in the woman who aroused it or it didn't exist" (19) and she is Hélène Lagonelle. Her name reverberates with the internal echo of *lagon*, a lagoon, secluded well for narcissistic reflection. This verbal echo is corroborated by Hélène's white body, an important social fact in a colonial country where being white is already "to have desire in you," that is, to possess the sexual prestige of the "uncolored." This body arouses Duras's talent for fantasizing. She would have gladly drowned in this pool, even as she would resist engulfment by the mad flood of maternal love: "I want to take Hélène Lagonelle with me to where every evening, my eyes shut, I have imparted to me the pleasure that makes you cry out. . . . I want it to happen in my presence, I want her to do it as I wish, I want her to give herself where I give myself. It's via Hélène Lagonelle's body, through it, that the ultimate pleasure would pass from him to me" (74). Hélène is the vehicle for Duras's sexual tenor; through her, jouissance might circulate "from him to me" and yet remain within the classical registers of *amour propre*.[4] This fantasy awaits fulfillment "On the other bank of the river. As soon as you've crossed to the other side" (75).

Of course, what Duras also finds on the other side is "this arid and terrible place" where she lives "to the exclusion of everything else"—the domain of the family. But only within this demonized space can Duras locate "the heart of my essential certainty, the certainty that later on I'll be a writer." This certainty is intermingled with her love for her younger brother. His death is the first in a series of deaths, including, much later, a stillborn child, that initiates Duras into the *douleur* of writing: "I think I can already say, I have a vague desire to die. From now on I treat that word and my life as inseparable. I think I have a vague desire to be alone, just as I realize I've never been alone any more since I left childhood behind, and the family of the hunter. I'm going to write" (103).

Her destiny as a writer is announced at the crossing between familial love and sexual love and is therefore virtually a synecdoche for the incest taboo. Incest is not an act she commits, but rather a clandestine representation she makes as she and her Chinese lover become entangled in a Faulknerian skein of cultural interdictions, the scandal of incest and miscegenation: he, the Chinese lover, making love to her "as he would his own child," a child he has illegitimately created (101); she, adoring his "member" for engendering her, haunted by the ghost of her brother, which proleptically informs her of the love she bears him, but will only recognize upon his death. Duras's *sexual* certainty that she is "the Queen of his desire" merges perilously with a fantasy of beleaguered narcissism, but that fantasy appears vindicated when after "war, marriages, children, divorces, books," her lover travels to Paris with his wife, then phones Duras to tell her "he could never stop loving her, that he'd love her until death" (117).

There is yet one final encounter in Duras's fateful crossing over to clandestine love—her traumatic contact with the local lunatic, excluded from all recognizably human society, who frightens and mocks her with a language she cannot understand, a madness she is in danger of sharing: "For me the whole town is inhabited by the beggar woman in the road. And all the beggar women of the towns, the rice fields, the tracks bordering Siam, the banks of the Mekong—for me the beggar woman who frightened me is inhabited by them. She comes from everywhere" (86). This madwoman, like the leprous beggarwoman of the *India Song* cycle or the itinerant mother with the gangrenous foot forced to abandon her child in *The Sea Wall*,[5] embodies the disfiguring power of the Outside that everywhere encroaches on Duras's essential certainty that she will be a writer. This omnipresent figure of reproach challenges the self-withdrawal that protects that certainty and on which it is grounded. She comes to symbolize for Duras the negative interpenetration of figure and world, indeed represents, at the point where internal certainty and external doubt converge, the possibility of representing the sufferings of the world, the brutalities of colonialism, the injustices of the gods who are hidden from us. And it is here, and here only, that literature stops and writing becomes sacred—here where it rejoins the world as a transgressive text insistent on its sins but pentitent for its self-absorption, its errancies of will. It is also here that the general but very real resemblance between the literature and the cinema of Marguerite Duras reveals itself. They unfold in the same definitive darkness, the amorous night of the clandestine, sequestered—but only for a time—from the Outside with its blinding lights and unanswerable realities. Ultimately Duras's art is the art of negatives that when projected assume the spectral luminousness, and all the false candor of life.

NOTES

1. Julia Kristeva speaks of a "Hiroshima of Love" in which outside and inside conjoin in an "implosion of love into death and death into love." Kristeva contemplates this catastrophe as one of the more disturbing manifestations of

Duras's postmodern "aesthetic of awkwardness." I find it difficult to endorse this rhetorical conflation of public and private, a conflation that leads Kristeva to argue that within the "psychic microcosm" of Duras's narrative subjects, "private pain absorbs political horror" (142–43). As I shall argue in the pages that follow, Duras herself is skeptical of the reality of the subject and is the last writer to offer us the descriptive plenitude—even in miniature—of a microcosm. She depicts psychic "scenes," not worlds; she is the chronicler of madness, as Kristeva says, but this madness is not so much the synecdochic event that recapitulates the insanity of modern history, but a writerly stance that places Duras not within the heart, but on the borders of reality.

2. This obscurity can be communal and political in nature. Duras, after lamenting the failures of Mai 1968, which she sees as a failure to abide a silence "equivalent to the sum of our collective respirations," reaffirmed her belief in this abandoned "communal obscurity" in which new behaviors and modes of life could have been charted (*Les parleuses* 226).

3. Duras intended the Japanese engineer to be immediately identifiable as an "international type" of advanced global capitalism. He is the moral and historical product of his times, educated in its techniques and at home in its economic and political environment, a man "who would never feel out of his element in any city of the world." The French actress Duras envisaged—and cast—possessed a "Look" at once seductive and unselfconscious (137, 139).

4. For a more elaborate and sympathetic consideration of female doubling in Duras, see Kristeva (148–51).

5. I am grateful to Suzanne Nash for this synoptic example and for her generous help with this essay.

WORKS CITED

Blanchot, Maurice. "Détruire." *Marguerite Duras*. 139–42.
Brée, Germaine. "Introduction." *Four Novels by Marguerite Duras*. New York: Grove, 1965.
Duras, Marguerite. *Détruire, dit-elle*. Paris: Minuit, 1969.
———. *Hiroshima, mon amour*. Paris: Gallimard, 1960.
———. *India Song*. Paris: Gallimard, 1973.
———. *The Lover*. Trans. Barbara Bray. New York: Pantheon, 1985.
———. *Marguerite Duras*. Paris: Albatros, 1979.
———. "Mothers." *Marguerite Duras*. 99–101.
———. *Outside: papiers d'un jour*. Paris: Michel, 1981.
———. *Les parleuses*. Paris: Minuit, 1974.
———. *The Ravishing of Lol Stein*. Trans. Richard Seaver. New York: Grove, 1966.
———. *The Sailor from Gibraltar*. Trans. Barbara Bray. New York: Pantheon, 1986.
———. *The Sea Wall*. Trans. Herma Briffault. New York: Farrar, 1985.

————. *The Square*. Trans. Sonia Pitt-Rivers and Irina Morduch. New York: Grove, 1982.

————. *Le Vice-Consul*. Paris: Gallimard, 1966.

————. *The War*. Trans. Barbara Bray. New York: Pantheon, 1986.

Husserl-Kapit, Susan. "An Interview with Marguerite Duras." *Signs* 1 (1976): 423–34.

Kristeva, Julia. "The Pain of Sorrow in the Modern World: The Works of Marguerite Duras." *PMLA* 102 (1987): 138–52.

Lamy, Suzanne and André Roy. *Marguerite Duras à Montréal*. Montreal: Spirale, 1981.

Moers, Ellen. *Literary Women*. New York: Doubleday, 1977.

NOTES ON CONTRIBUTORS

Germaine Brée is the author of *Marcel Proust and Deliverance from Time*, *The World of Marcel Proust*, *Women Writers in France*, *Twentieth Century French Literature*, *Littérature française: Du surrealisme à l'empire de la critique* among other publications.

Christine Brooke-Rose's most recent novel is *Xorandor*. She is Professor of American Literature at the University of Paris.

Marianne DeKoven is Professor of English at Rutgers University and author of *A Different Language: Gertrude Stein's Experimental Writing*.

Maria DiBattista, Professor of English and Comparative Literature at Princeton University, has written *The Fables of Anon: The Major Novels of Virginia Woolf*, as well as articles on modern narrative.

Millicent Dillon has authored *A Little Original Sin: The Life and Work of Jane Bowles* as well as two books of fiction. The editor of Bowles's letters, she is currently working on a book on Mary Cassatt and Isadora Duncan and a novel, *The Dance of the Mothers*.

Rachel Blau DuPlessis is the author of *Writing Beyond the Ending: Narrative Strategies of Twentieth-Century Women Writers* and *H.D.: The Career of That Struggle*, as well as feminist essays and poetry. She teaches at Temple University.

Kathleen Fraser is the author of seven books of poetry and the founding editor of *HOW(ever)*, a journal of experimental women's poetry. She teaches creative writing at San Francisco State College. Her most recent book is *Notes Preceding Trust*.

Ellen G. Friedman is the author of *Joyce Carol Oates* and the editor of *Joan Didion: Essays and Conversations*. She has published articles on various modern and contemporary writers and teaches English at Trenton State College.

Miriam Fuchs works in experimental literature and has published articles on such writers as Djuna Barnes, Colman Dowell, and William Gaddis. She currently teaches at the University of Hawaii.

Donna Gerstenberger is a Professor of English at the University of Washington. She is interested in modern literature and has written books on Synge, Murdoch, Richard Hugo, and modern verse drama, as well as articles on aspects of modern American and English literature.

Gillian E. Hanscombe has published fiction and poetry as well as *The Art of Life: Dorothy Richardson and the Development of Feminist Consciousness* and *Writing for Their Lives: The Modernist Women 1910–1940* (coauthored with Virginia L. M. Smyers).

Richard Martin teaches English and American literature at the University of Aachen, West Germany. He has published a book on E. M. Forster and numerous articles on contemporary British and American fiction.

Larry McCaffery has published widely on experimental writers, including *The

Metafictional Muse, Postmodern Fiction: A Bio-bibliographical Guide, and two volumes of interviews with contemporary authors—*Anything Can Happen* (with Tom LeClair) and *Alive and Writing* (with Sinda Gregory). He is Professor of American Literature at San Diego State University.

Perry Nodelman is Professor of English at the University of Winnipeg. He has published on contemporary and children's literature and is Editor of the *Children's Literature Association Quarterly.*

Marjorie Perloff, Professor of English and Comparative Literature at Stanford University, has published widely on modern and postmodern poetry and poetics. Her latest book is *The Futurist Movement: Avant-Garde, Avant Guerre, and the Language of Rupture.*

Sharon Spencer is the author of *Space, Time, and Structure in the Modern Novel* and *Collage of Dreams: The Writings of Anaïs Nin*, as well as a novel and short stories. She is Professor of English and Comparative Literature at Montclair State College.

Philip Stevick, Professor of English at Temple University, has edited *The Theory of the Novel* and *Anti-Story* and authored *Alternative Pleasures: Postrealist Fiction and the Tradition*, as well as many essays on eighteenth- and twentieth-century fiction.

Linda W. Wagner-Martin holds the Hanes Chair at the University of North Carolina at Chapel Hill. Her most recent book is a biography of Sylvia Plath. She also writes on Glasgow, Dos Passos, W. C. Williams, Levertov, Hemingway, Faulkner, and other modern writers.

Selected List of
Women Experimentalists

The following list cites mainly works by writers discussed in this volume. However, under the third generation, we have also included lesser-known contemporary experimentalists not covered herein. We list initial publication dates, as well as selected later editions or reprints. We include fiction, drama, poetry, and nonfiction.

First Generation

Dorothy Miller Richardson

Pointed Roofs. Introd. J. D. Beresford. London: Duckworth, 1915.

Backwater. London: Duckworth, 1916.

Honeycomb. London: Duckworth, 1917.

Interim. London: Duckworth, 1919.

The Tunnel. London: Duckworth, 1919.

Deadlock. London: Duckworth, 1921.

Revolving Lights. London: Duckworth, 1923.

The Trap. London: Duckworth, 1925.

Oberland. London: Duckworth, 1927.

Dawn's Left Hand. London: Duckworth, 1931.

Clear Horizon. London: Dent, 1935.

Pilgrimage including *Dimple Hill.* 4 vols. London: Dent, 1938; New York: Knopf, 1938.

Pilgrimage including *March Moonlight.* Introd. Walter Allen. 4 vols. London: Dent, 1967; New York: Knopf, 1967.

Pilgrimage. Introd. Gillian E. Hanscombe. 4 vols. London: Virago, 1979.

Gertrude Stein

Three Lives. New York: Grafton, 1909; New York: Boni, 1927; New York: Random, 1936, 1958; New York: NAL, 1985.

Tender Buttons. New York: Claire Marie, 1914; New York: Haskell, 1970.

Geography and Plays. Boston: Four Seas, 1922; New York: Something Else, 1968.

The Making of Americans. Paris: Contact, 1925; unabridged ed. New York: Something Else, 1966.

Composition as Explanation. London: Hogarth, 1926.

Useful Knowledge. New York: Payson, 1928.

Before the Flowers of Friendship Faded Friendship Faded. Paris: Plain Edition, 1931.

How to Write. Paris: Plain Edition, 1931; Barton, VT: Something Else, 1973; New York: Dover, 1975.

Lucy Church Amiably. Paris: Plain Edition, 1931; New York: Something Else, 1969.

Operas and Plays. Paris: Plain Edition, 1932; Barrytown, NY: Station Hill, 1987.

The Autobiography of Alice B. Toklas. New York: Harcourt, 1933; Harmondsworth, Gt. Brit: Penguin, 1966, 1983; New York: Modern Library, 1980.

Matisse Picasso and Gertrude Stein

with Two Shorter Pieces. Paris: Plain Edition, 1933; Barton, VT: Something Else, 1972.

Four Saints in Three Acts, an Opera to be Sung. New York: Random, 1934.

Portraits and Prayers. New York: Random, 1934.

Lectures in America. New York: Random, 1935; Boston: Beacon, 1957, 1985.

Narration. Chicago: U of Chicago P, 1935; New York: Greenwood, 1969.

The Geographical History of America. New York: Random, 1936.

Everybody's Autobiography. New York: Random, 1937, 1973.

Picasso. Trans. Alice B. Toklas. London: Batsford, 1938; Boston: Beacon, 1969; New York: Dover, 1984.

Paris France. New York: Scribner's, 1940; New York: Liveright, 1970.

What Are Masterpieces. Los Angeles: Conference, 1940; New York: Pitman, 1970.

Ida. New York: Random, 1941; New York: Cooper Square, 1971.

Wars I Have Seen. New York: Random, 1945; London: Brilliance Books, 1984.

Brewsie and Willie. New York: Random, 1946.

Selected Writings of Gertrude Stein. Ed. Carl Van Vechten. New York: Random, 1946, 1972; New York: Modern Library, 1962.

Four in America. New Haven: Yale UP, 1947; Freeport, NY: Books for Libraries, 1969.

Blood on the Dining-Room Floor. New York: Banyan, 1948; Berkeley: Creative Arts/Black Lizard, 1982.

Last Operas and Plays. Ed. Carl Van Vechten. New York: Rinehart, 1949.

Things as They Are. Pawlet, VT: Banyan, 1950.

Two: Gertrude Stein and Her Brother and Other Early Portraits. Foreword by Janet Flanner. New Haven: Yale UP, 1951; Freeport, NY: Books for Libraries, 1969.

Mrs. Reynolds and Five Earlier Novelettes. New Haven: Yale UP, 1952; Freeport, NY: Books for Libraries, 1969.

Bee Time Vine and Other Pieces 1913–1927. New Haven: Yale UP, 1953; Freeport, NY: Books for Libraries, 1969.

As Fine as Melanctha. New Haven: Yale UP, 1954; Freeport, NY: Books for Libraries, 1969.

Painted Lace and Other Pieces (1914–1937). New Haven: Yale UP, 1955.

Stanzas in Meditation and Other Poems (1929–1933). New Haven: Yale UP, 1956; Freeport, NY: Books for Libraries, 1969.

A Novel of Thank You. New Haven: Yale UP, 1958; Freeport, NY: Books for Libraries, 1969.

Alphabets and Birthdays. Freeport, NY: Books for Libraries, 1969.

Gertrude Stein on Picasso. Ed. Edward Burns. New York: Liveright, 1970.

Fernhurst, Q.E.D., and Other Early Writings. New York: Liveright, 1971, 1983; New York: Norton, 1983.

A Primer for the Gradual Understanding of Gertrude Stein. Ed. Robert Bartlett Haas. Los Angeles: Black Sparrow, 1971.

Reflection on the Atomic Bomb. Ed. Robert Bartlett Haas. Los Angeles: Black Sparrow, 1973.

How Writing is Written. Ed. Robert Bartlett Haas. Los Angeles: Black Sparrow, 1974.

VIRGINIA WOOLF

The Voyage Out. London: Duckworth, 1915; New York: Doran, 1920; New York: Harcourt, 1968.

Night and Day. London: Duckworth, 1919; New York: Doran, 1920; New York: Harcourt, 1973.

Monday or Tuesday. Richmond: Hogarth, 1921; New York: Harcourt, 1921.

Jacob's Room. Richmond: Hogarth, 1922; New York: Harcourt, 1923, 1978.

Mr. Bennet and Mrs. Brown. London: Hogarth, 1924; Folcroft, PA: Folcroft, 1977.

The Common Reader. London: Hogarth, 1925; New York: Harcourt, 1925.

Mrs. Dalloway. London: Hogarth, 1925; New York: Harcourt, 1925, 1955.

To the Lighthouse. London: Hogarth, 1927; New York: Harcourt, 1927, 1955, 1964.

Orlando: A Biography. London: Hogarth, 1928; New York: Crosby, 1928; New York: Harcourt, 1973.

A Room of One's Own. London: Hogarth, 1929; New York: Harcourt, 1929, 1957, 1963.

The Waves. London: Hogarth, 1931; New York: Harcourt, 1931, 1978.

The Common Reader: Second Series. London: Hogarth, 1932; *The Second Common Reader*. New York: Harcourt, 1932.

Flush: A Biography. London: Hogarth, 1933; New York: Harcourt, 1933, 1976.

The Years. London: Hogarth, 1937; New York: Harcourt, 1937, 1969.

Three Guineas. London: Hogarth, 1938; New York: Harcourt, 1938, 1963.

Roger Fry: A Biography. London: Hogarth, 1940; New York: Harcourt, 1940, 1976.

Between the Acts. London: Hogarth, 1941; New York: Harcourt, 1941, 1970.

The Death of the Moth and Other Essays. London: Hogarth, 1942; New York: Harcourt, 1942, 1970.

A Haunted House and Other Short Stories. London: Hogarth, 1943; New York: Harcourt, 1944, 1966.

The Moment and Other Essays. London: Hogarth, 1947; New York: Harcourt, 1948, 1974.

The Captain's Death Bed and Other Essays. London: Hogarth, 1950; New York: Harcourt, 1950, 1973.

A Writer's Diary. Ed. Leonard Woolf. London: Hogarth, 1953; New York: Harcourt, 1954, 1973.

Virginia Woolf and Lytton Strachey: Letters. Ed. Leonard Woolf and James Strachey. London: Hogarth, Chatto, 1956; New York: Harcourt, 1956.

Granite and Rainbow: Essays. London: Hogarth, 1958; New York: Harcourt, 1958, 1975.

Jacob's Room and The Waves: Two Complete Novels. New York: Harcourt, 1959.

Contemporary Writers. Ed. Jean Guiguet. London: Hogarth, 1965; New York: Harcourt, 1966.

Collected Essays. 4 vols. London: Hogarth, 1966–67; New York: Harcourt, 1967.

Mrs. Dalloway's Party: A Short Story Sequence. Ed. Stella McNichol. London: Hogarth, 1973; New York: Harcourt, 1975.

The Letters of Virginia Woolf. Vol 1: 1888–1912; Vol. 2: 1912–22; Vol. 3: 1923–28; Vol. 4: 1929–31; Vol. 5: 1932–35; Vol. 6: 1936–41. Ed. Nigel Nicolson and Joanne Trautmann. New York: Harcourt, 1975–80.

Freshwater: A Comedy. Ed. Lucio P. Ruotolo. London: Hogarth, 1976;

New York: Harcourt, 1976, 1985.
Moments of Being: Unpublished Autobiographical Writings. Ed. Jeanne Schulkind. Brighton: Sussex UP, 1976; New York: Harcourt, 1976.
Books and Portraits. Ed. Mary Lyon. London: Hogarth, 1977; New York: Harcourt, 1978.
The Diary of Virginia Woolf. Ed. Anne Olivier Bell. Vol 1: 1915–19; Vol. 2 (Bell & McNeillie): 1920–24; Vol. 3 (Bell & McNeillie): 1925–30; Vol. 4 (Bell & McNeillie): 1931–35; Vol. 5 (Bell & McNeillie): 1936–41. New York: Harcourt, 1977–84.
The Pargiters: The Novel-Essay Portion of "The Years". Ed. Mitchell A. Leaska. New York: NY Public Library, 1977; London: Hogarth, 1978.
Women and Writing. Ed. Michelle Barrett. New York: Harcourt, 1980.
The Complete Shorter Fiction of Virginia Woolf. Ed. Susan Dick. New York: Harcourt, 1985.

Second Generation

Djuna Barnes

The Book of Repulsive Women, 8 Rhythms and 5 Drawings. New York: Bruno, 1915.
A Book. New York: Boni, 1923; London: Faber, 1958.
Ladies Almanack. Paris: (McAlmon), 1928; New York: Harper, 1972.
Ryder. New York: Liveright, 1928; New York: St. Martin's, 1979.
A Night Among the Horses. New York: Liveright, 1929.
Nightwood. London: Faber, 1936. Introd. T. S. Eliot. New York: Harcourt, 1937; New York: New Directions, 1946, 1961.
The Antiphon: A Play. London: Faber, 1958.
Selected Works of Djuna Barnes: Spillway, The Antiphon, Nightwood. New York: Farrar, 1962.
Spillway. London: Faber, 1962; New York: Harper, 1972.
Creatures in an Alphabet. New York: Dial, 1982.
Smoke and Other Early Stories. Ed. Douglas Messerli. College Park, MD: Sun & Moon, 1982.
Interviews. Ed. Alyce Barry. College Park, MD: Sun & Moon, 1985.

Jane Bowles

Two Serious Ladies. New York: Knopf, 1943; New York: Dutton, 1984. In *My Sister's Hand in Mine.*
In The Summer House. New York: Random, 1954. In *My Sister's Hand in Mine.*
The Collected Works of Jane Bowles. New York: Farrar, 1966.
Plain Pleasures. London: Owen, 1966. In *My Sister's Hand in Mine.*
Feminine Wiles. Santa Barbara: Black Sparrow, 1976.
My Sister's Hand in Mine: The Collected Works of Jane Bowles. 1966. Expanded ed. Introd. Truman Capote. New York: Ecco, 1978.
Out in the World: Selected Letters of Jane Bowles: 1935–1970. Ed. Millicent Dillon. Santa Barbara: Black Sparrow, 1985.

H.D. (Hilda Doolittle)

Choruses from Iphigeneia in Aulis. Cleveland: Clerk's, 1916.
Sea Garden. Boston: Houghton, 1916.
The Tribute and Circe, Two Poems by H.D. Cleveland: Clerk's, 1917.
Hymen. New York: Holt, 1921.

Heliodora and Other Poems. Boston: Houghton, 1924.

Collected Poems. New York: Boni, 1925, 1940; New York: New Directions, 1983.

Palimpsest. Paris: Contact, 1926; Rev. ed. Carbondale: Southern Illinois UP, 1968.

Hippolytus Temporizes. Boston: Houghton, 1927; Redding Ridge, CT: Black Swan, 1985.

Hedylus. Boston: Houghton, 1928; Redding Ridge, CT: Black Swan, 1980.

Red Roses for Bronze. New York: Random, 1929; Boston: Houghton, 1931 (Extended edition).

Borderline—A Pool Film with Paul Robeson. London: Mercury, 1930.

Kora and Ka. Dijon: Imprimerie Darantière, 1934.

The Usual Star. Dijon: Imprimerie Darantière, 1934.

Nights. Dijon: Imprimerie Darantière, 1935 ("John Helforth"); New York: New Directions, 1986.

The Hedgehog. London: Brendin, 1936; New York: New Directions, 1988.

Euripides' Ion. Boston: Houghton, 1937; Redding Ridge, CT: Black Swan, 1986.

The Walls Do Not Fall. London and New York: Oxford UP, 1944. In *Trilogy.*

What Do I Love? London: Brendin, 1944.

Tribute to the Angels. London and New York: Oxford UP, 1945. In *Trilogy.*

The Flowering of the Rod. London and New York: Oxford UP, 1946. In *Trilogy.*

By Avon River. New York: Macmillan, 1949; Redding Ridge, CT: Black Swan, 1987.

Tribute to Freud. New York: Pantheon, 1956; Boston: Godine, 1974; New York: New Directions, 1984.

Selected Poems. New York: Grove, 1957; New York: New Directions, 1988.

Bid Me To Live (A Madrigal). New York: Grove, 1960; Redding Ridge, CT: Black Swan, 1983.

Helen in Egypt. New York: Grove, 1961; New York: New Directions, 1974.

Hermetic Definition. New York: New Directions, 1972.

Trilogy (The Walls Do Not Fall, Tribute to the Angels, The Flowering of the Rod). New York: New Directions, 1973.

End to Torment: A Memoir of Ezra Pound. Ed. Norman Holmes Pearson and Michael King. New York: New Directions, 1979.

HERmione. New York: New Directions, 1981.

The Gift. New York: New Directions, 1982.

Notes on Thought and Vision & The Wise Sappho. San Francisco: City Lights, 1982.

Collected Poems 1912–1944. Ed. Louis L. Martz. New York: New Directions, 1983.

Anna Kavan ("Helen Ferguson," "H. W. Edmunds")

A Charmed Circle. London: Cape, 1929.

The Dark Sisters. London: Cape, 1930.

Let Me Alone. London: Cape, 1930; New York: M. Kesend, 1974.

A Stranger Still. London: Lane, 1935.

Goose Cross. London: Lane, 1936.

Asylum Piece and Other Stories. London: Cape, 1940; New York: M. Kesend, 1980.

I am Lazarus: Short Stories. London:

Cape, 1945; London: Owen, 1978.

House of Sleep. Garden City, NY: Doubleday, 1947. Also published as *Sleep Has His House*. London: Cassell, 1948; New York: M. Kesend, 1980.

The Horse's Tale (with K. T. Bluth). London: Gaberbocchus, 1949.

Eagle's Nest. London: Owen, 1957.

A Bright Green Field and Other Stories. London: Owen, 1958.

Who Are You? Northwood, Gt. Brit.: Scorpion, 1963.

Ice. London: Owen, 1967; New York: Norton, 1985.

Julia and the Bazooka and Other Stories. London: Owen, 1970; New York: Norton, 1985.

A Scarcity of Love. London: Owen, 1971; New York: Herder, 1972.

My Soul in China: A Novella and Stories. London: Owen, 1975.

ANAÏS NIN

D. H. Lawrence: An Unprofessional Study. Paris: Black Manikin, 1932; London: Spearman, 1961; Denver: Swallow, 1964.

House of Incest. Paris: Siana, 1936; New York, Gemor, 1947; Denver: Swallow, 1958.

Winter of Artifice. Paris: Obelisk, 1939; New York: Gemor, 1942; Denver: Swallow, 1948, 1961.

Under a Glass Bell. New York: Gemor, 1944; New York: Dutton, 1948.

Ladders to Fire. New York: Dutton, 1946; London: Owen, 1963.

Realism and Reality. New York: Alicat, 1946.

Children of the Albatross. New York: Dutton, 1947; London: Owen, 1959; Chicago: Swallow, 1966.

On Writing. Hanover, NH: Oliver, 1947.

The Four-Chambered Heart. New York: Duell, 1950; London: Owen, 1959; Chicago: Swallow, 1966.

A Spy in the House of Love. New York: British Book Centre, 1954; Chicago: Swallow, 1966.

Solar Barque. Ann Arbor: Edwards, 1958.

Cities of the Interior (*Ladders to Fire*; *Children of the Albatross*; *The Four-Chambered Heart*; *A Spy in the House of Love*; *Seduction of the Minotaur*). Denver: Swallow, 1959; Introd. Sharon Spencer. Chicago: Swallow, 1974.

Seduction of the Minotaur. Denver: Swallow, 1961; London: Owen, 1961; Chicago: Swallow, 1969.

Collages. Denver: Swallow, 1964.

The Diary of Anaïs Nin. 1931–34; 1934–39; 1939–44; 1944–47; 1947–55; 1955–66; 1966–74. Ed. Gunther Stuhlmann. New York: Harcourt, 1966–80.

The Novel of the Future. New York: Macmillan, 1968; Athens, OH: Ohio UP, 1985.

A Photographic Supplement to the Diary of Anaïs Nin. New York: Harcourt, 1974.

A Woman Speaks: The Lectures, Seminars and Interviews of Anaïs Nin. Ed. Evelyn J. Hinz. Chicago: Swallow, 1975.

In Favor of the Sensitive Man and Other Essays. New York: Harcourt, 1976.

Delta of Venus: Erotica. New York: Harcourt, 1977; New York: Bantam, 1987.

Waste of Timelessness and Other Early Stories. Weston, CT: Magic Circle, 1977.

Linotte: The Early Diary of Anaïs Nin: 1914–1920. Trans. Jean L. Sherman. New York: Harcourt, 1978.

Little Birds, Erotica. New York: Harcourt, 1979.

The Early Diary of Anaïs Nin. Vol. 2: 1920–23; Vol. 3: 1923–27; Vol. 4: 1927–31. New York: Harcourt, 1982–85.

The White Blackbird and Other Writings. Santa Barbara: Capra, 1985.

Henry and June: From the Unexpurgated Diary of Anaïs Nin. New York: Harcourt, 1986.

JEAN RHYS

The Left Bank. London: Cape, 1927; New York: Harper, 1928; Freeport, NY: Books for Libraries, 1970.

Quartet (first published as *Postures*). London: Chatto, 1928; New York: Simon, 1929. Reissued as *Quartet.* London: Deutsch, 1969; New York: Harper, 1971, 1981.

After Leaving Mr. MacKenzie. London: Cape, 1930; New York: Knopf, 1931; New York: Harper, 1972.

Voyage in the Dark. London: Constable, 1934; New York: Morrow, 1935; New York: Norton, 1968, 1982.

Good Morning, Midnight. London: Constable, 1939; New York: Harper, 1939; New York: Norton, 1986.

Wide Sargasso Sea. London: Deutsch, 1966; New York: Norton, 1967, 1982.

Tigers are Better Looking. London: Deutsch, 1968; New York: Harper, 1974.

My Day. New York: Hallman, 1975.

Sleep It Off, Lady. London: Deutsch, 1976; New York: Harper, 1976.

Smile Please: An Unfinished Autobiography. London: Deutsch, 1979; New York: Harper, 1979.

The Letters of Jean Rhys. Ed. Francis Wyndham and Diana Melly. London: Deutsch, 1984; New York: Viking, 1984.

The Complete Novels. Introd. Diana Athill. New York: Norton, 1985.

The Collected Short Stories. New York: Norton, 1987.

THIRD GENERATION

KATHY ACKER

Persian Poems. New York: Papyrus, 1972.

I Don't Expect You'll Do the Same. San Francisco: Musicmusic, 1974.

The Adult Life of Toulouse Lautrec by Henri Toulouse Lautrec. New York: TVRT Press, 1975, 1978.

The Childlike Life of the Black Tarantula by the Black Tarantula. New York: TVRT Press, 1975.

Kathy Goes to Haiti. Toronto: Rumor, 1978. In *Literal Madness.*

I Dreamt I Was a Nymphomaniac!: Imagining. New York: Traveler's Digest, 1980.

New York City in 1979. New York: Top Stories, 1981.

Hello, I'm Erica Jong. New York: Contact II, 1982.

Great Expectations. New York: Grove, 1983.

Implosion. New York: Wedge, 1983.

Algeria: A Series of Invocations Because Nothing Else Works. Gt. Brit.: Aloes, 1984.

Blood and Guts in High School. New York: Grove, 1984.

My Death My Life by Pier Paolo Pasolini. London: Pan, 1984. In *Literal Madness.*

Don Quixote. New York: Grove, 1986.

Literal Madness: My Death My Life by Pier Paolo Pasolini; Kathy Goes to Haiti; Florida. New York: Grove, 1987.

Empire of the Senseless. New York: Grove, 1988.

LAURIE ANDERSON

Words in Reverse. New York: Top Stories, 1979.
United States. New York: Harper, 1984.

CHRISTINE BROOKE-ROSE

Gold. Aldington, Kent: Hand and Flower, 1955.
The Languages of Love. London: Secker, 1957.
A Grammar of Metaphor. London: Secker, 1958.
The Sycamore Tree. London: Secker, 1958; New York: Norton, 1959.
The Dear Deceit. London: Secker, 1960; New York: Doubleday, 1961.
The Middlemen: A Satire. London: Secker, 1961.
Out. London: M. Joseph, 1964.
Such. London: M. Joseph, 1966.
Between. London: M. Joseph, 1968.
Go When You See the Green Man Walking. London: M. Joseph, 1969.
A ZBC of Ezra Pound. London: Faber, 1971; Berkeley: U of California P, 1971.
Thru. London: Hamilton, 1975.
A Structural Analysis of Pound's Usura Canto. The Hague: Mouton, 1976.
A Rhetoric of the Unreal: Studies in Narrative and Structure, Especially of the Fantastic. Cambridge and New York: Cambridge UP, 1981.
Amalgamemnon. Manchester, Gt. Brit. and New York: Carcanet, 1984.
The Christine Brooke-Rose Omnibus: Four Novels: Out, Such, Between, Thru. Manchester, Gt. Brit. and New York: Carcanet, 1986.
Xorandor. Manchester, Gt. Brit. and New York: Carcanet, 1986; New York: Avon, 1988.

GABRIELLE BURTON

I'm Running Away From Home, But I'm Not Allowed to Cross the Street: A Primer of Women's Liberation. Pittsburgh: Know, 1972.
Heartbreak Hotel. New York: Scribner's, 1986; New York: Penguin, 1988.

ANGELA CARTER

Shadow Dance. London: Heinemann, 1966; As *Honeybuzzard.* New York: Simon, 1967.
Unicorn. Leeds, London: Location, 1966.
The Magic Toyshop. London: Heinemann, 1967; New York: Simon, 1968.
Several Perceptions. London: Heinemann, 1968; New York: Simon, 1969.
Heroes and Villains. London: Heinemann, 1969; New York: Simon, 1970.
Love. London: Davis, 1971.
The Infernal Desire Machines of Dr. Hoffman. London: Davis, 1972. As *The War of Dreams.* New York: Harcourt, 1974; New York: Penguin, 1986.
Fireworks: Nine Profane Pieces. London: Quartet, 1974; New York: Harper, 1981; New York: Penguin, 1987.
The Passion of New Eve. London: Gollancz, 1977; New York: Harcourt, 1977.
The Sadeian Woman and the Ideology of Pornography. London: Virago, 1979; New York: Pantheon, 1979, 1988.
The Bloody Chamber and Other Stories. London: Gollancz, 1980; New York: Harper, 1980; New York: Penguin, 1987.

Nothing Sacred: Selected Writings. London: Virago, 1982.

Nights at the Circus. London: Chatto, 1984; New York: Viking, 1985; New York: Penguin, 1986.

Black Venus. London: Chatto, 1985.

Saints and Strangers. New York: Viking, 1986; New York: Penguin, 1987.

Maxine Chernoff

The Last Aurochs. Iowa City: NOW Press, 1976.

A Vegetable Emergency. Venice, CA: Beyond Baroque, 1977.

Utopia TV Store. Chicago: Yellow Press, 1979.

New Faces of 1952. Ithaca, NY: Ithaca House, 1985.

Bop. Minneapolis: Coffee House, 1986; New York: Random, 1987.

Japan. Bolinas, CA: Avenue B, 1987.

Laura Chester

Proud and Ashamed. Santa Barbara: Christopher's, 1977.

In the Zone: New and Selected Writings. Santa Rosa, CA, 1988.

Watermark. Berkeley: The Figures, 1978.

My Pleasure. Berkeley: The Figures, 1980.

Free Rein. Providence: Burning Deck, 1988.

Susan Daitch

The Colorist. New York: Top Stories, 1986.

L.C. London: Virago, 1986; New York: Harcourt, 1987.

Lydia Davis

The Thirteenth Woman and Other Sto-

ries. New York: Living Hand, 1976.

Sketches for a Life of Wassilly. Barrytown, NY: Station Hill, 1981.

Story and Other Stories. Great Barrington, MA: The Figures, 1983.

Break It Down. New York: Farrar, 1986, 1988.

Millicent Dillon

Baby, Perpetua and Other Stories. New York: Viking, 1971.

The One in the Back is Medea. New York: Viking, 1973.

A Little Original Sin: The Life and Work of Jane Bowles. New York: Holt, 1981.

After Egypt: An Anti-Biography of Isadora Duncan and Mary Cassatt. New York: Dutton, 1989. See Jane Bowles.

Harriet Doerr

Stones for Ibarra. New York: Viking, 1984.

Margaret Mitchell Dukore

A Novel Called Heritage. New York: Scribner's, 1982; New York: Dell, 1983.

Bloom: A Novel. New York: F. Watts, 1985; New York: Dell, 1987.

Eva Figes

Equinox. London: Secker, 1966.

Winter Journey. London: Faber, 1967; New York: Hill, 1968; New York: Ballantine, 1984.

Konek Landing. London: Faber, 1969.

Patriarchal Attitudes: Women in Society. London: Faber, 1970; New York: Stein, 1970; New York: Persea, 1987.

B. London: Faber, 1972.

Days. London: Faber, 1974.

Ghosts. New York: Pantheon, 1988.

Tragedy and Social Evolution. London: Calder, 1976; New York: Riverrun, 1976.

Nelly's Version. London: Secker, 1977. New York: Pantheon, 1988.

Little Eden: A Child at War. London: Faber, 1978; New York: Persea, 1987.

Waking. London: Hamilton, 1981; New York: Pantheon, 1982.

Sex and Subterfuge: Women Novelists to 1850. London: Macmillan, 1982; New York: Persea, 1987.

Light. London: Hamilton, 1983; New York: Pantheon, 1983; New York: Ballantine, 1984.

The Seven Ages. London: Hamilton, 1986; New York: Pantheon, 1986; New York: Ballantine, 1988.

KATHLEEN FRASER

Change of Address. San Francisco: Kayak, 1966.

In Defiance (of the Rains). San Francisco: Kayak, 1969.

Little Notes to You from Lucas Street. Iowa City: Penumbra, 1972.

What I Want. New York: Harper, 1974.

Magritte Series. Berkeley: Tuumba, 1977.

New Shoes. New York: Harper, 1978.

Each Next: Narratives. Berkeley: The Figures, 1980.

Something (even human voices) in the foreground, a lake. Berkeley: Kelsey St., 1984.

Boundayr. Santa Monica: Lapis, 1988.

Notes Preceding Trust. Santa Monica: Lapis, 1987.

MADELINE GINS

Word Rain (or A Discursive Introduction to the Intimate Philosophical Investigations of G,R,E,T,A, G,A,R,B,O, It Says). New York: Grossman/Viking, 1969.

The Mechanism of Meaning (with Arakawa). Munich: Bruckmann, 1971.

Intend. Bologna: Tau/ma, 1973.

For Example (A Critique of Never) (with Arakawa). Milan: Castelli, 1974.

What the President Will Say and Do!! Barrytown, NY: Station Hill, 1984.

To Not To Die. Tampa: graphicstudio, 1986.

Essay on Multi-Dimensional Architecture. Paris: Le Soleil Noir, 1986.

JAIMY GORDON

The Fall of Poxdown. Providence: Hellcoal, 1972.

Who Knows Some of This Might Be Real. Providence: Hellcoal, 1975.

. . . The City Planner & the Mad Bomber. N.P.: Wyrd, 1976.

Love is Weal, Love is Woe. New Paltz: Treacle, 1976.

The Rose of the West: A Text for a Masque. Providence: Woodbine, 1976.

The Bend, the Lip, the Kid: Real Life Stories. New York: Sun, 1978.

Circumspections from An Equestrian Statue. Providence: Burning Deck, 1979.

Private T. Pigeon's Tale. New York: McPherson, 1979.

Shamp of the City Solo. 1974. New Paltz: Treacle, 1980.

BARBARA GUEST

Poems: The Location of Things. Garden City, NY: Doubleday, 1962.

The Blue Stairs. New York: Corinth, 1968.

Moscow Mansions. New York: Viking, 1973.

The Countess from Minneapolis. Providence: Burning Deck, 1976.

Seeking Air. Santa Barbara: Black Sparrow, 1978.

Biography. Providence: Burning Deck, 1980.

Quilts. New York: Vehicle, 1980.

Herself Defined: The Poet H.D. and Her World. Garden City, NY: Doubleday, 1984.

Musicality (with June Felter). Berkeley: Kelsey St., 1988.

BERTHA HARRIS

Catching Saradove. New York: Harcourt, 1969.

Confession of Cherubino. New York: Harcourt, 1972.

Lover. Plainfield, VT: Daughters, 1976.

The Joy of Lesbian Sex (with Emily L. Sisley). New York: Crown, 1977.

MARIANNE HAUSER

Monique. Switzerland: Ringier, 1935.

Indian Phantom Play. Austria: Zinnen, 1937.

Dark Dominion. New York: Random, 1947.

The Living Shall Praise Thee. London: Gollancz, 1957.

The Choir Invisible. New York: McDowell, 1958.

Prince Ishmael. New York: Stein, 1963.

A Lesson in Music. Austin: U of Texas P, 1964.

The Talking Room. New York: Fiction Collective, 1976, 1984.

The Memoirs of the Late Mr. Ashley: An American Comedy. Los Angeles: Sun & Moon, 1986.

LYN HEJINIAN

A Thought is the Bride of What Thinking. Willits, CA: Tuumba, 1976.

A Mask of Motion. Providence: Burning Deck, 1977.

Gesualdo. Berkeley: Tuumba, 1978.

The Guard. Berkeley: Tuumba, 1984.

Redo. Grenada, MS: Salt-Works, 1984.

My Life. 1980. Rev. and enl. ed. Los Angeles: Sun & Moon, 1987.

FANNY HOWE

Forty Whacks. Boston: Houghton, 1969.

Eggs. Boston: Houghton, 1970.

The Amerindian Coastline Poem. New York: Telephone, 1976.

Bronte Wilde. New York: Avon, 1976.

First Marriage. New York: Avon, 1977.

Holy Smoke. New York: Fiction Collective, 1979.

Poem from a Single Pallet. Berkeley: Kelsey St., 1980.

The White Slave. New York: Avon, 1980.

For Erato: The Meaning of Life. Berkeley: Tuumba, 1984.

In the Middle of Nowhere. New York: Fiction Collective, 1984.

Robeson Street. Cambridge, MA: Alicejamesbooks, 1985.

Introduction to the World. Berkeley: The Figures, 1986.

The Lives of a Spirit. Los Angeles: Sun & Moon, 1986.

JILL JOHNSTON

Marmalade Me. New York: Dutton, 1971.

Lesbian Nation: The Feminist Solution. New York: Simon, 1973.

Gullibles Travels. New York: Links, 1974.

Mother Bound: Autobiography in Search of a Father. New York: Knopf, 1983.

Paper Daughter. New York: Knopf, 1985.

GAYLE JONES

Corregidora. New York: Random, 1975; Boston: Beacon, 1986.

Eva's Man. Boston: Beacon, 1976, 1987.

White Rat. New York: Random, 1977.

Song for Anninho. Detroit: Lotus, 1981.

The Hermit-Woman. Detroit: Lotus, 1983.

Xarque and Other Poems. Detroit: Lotus, 1985.

ELAINE KRAF

I Am Clarence. New York: Doubleday, 1969.

The House of Madelaine. New York: Doubleday, 1971.

Find Him! New York: Fiction Collective, 1977.

The Princess of 72nd Street. New York: New Directions, 1979.

RHODA LERMAN

Call Me Ishtar. New York: Doubleday, 1973.

The Girl That He Marries: A Novel. New York: Holt, 1976.

Eleanor: A Novel. New York: Holt, 1979.

The Book of the Night. New York: Holt, 1984.

BERNADETTE MAYER

Moving. New York: Angel Hair, 1971.

Memory. Plainfield, VT: Atlantic, 1975.

Studying Hunger. New York/Bolinas: Adventures in Poetry/Big Sky, 1975.

Midwinter Day. Berkeley: Turtle Island, 1982.

Utopia. New York: The Figures, 1984.

DEENA METZGER

Skin: Shadows/Silence. Reno: West Coast Poetry Review, 1975.

Dark Milk. Los Angeles: Momentum, 1978.

The Axis-Mundi Poems. Los Angeles: Jazz, 1981.

The Woman Who Slept With Men To Take the War Out of Them/Tree. Los Angeles: Peace, 1981.

URSULE MOLINARO

Rimes et raisons. Monte Carlo: Regain, 1954.

Mirrors for Small Beasts. New York: Noonday, 1960.

Green Lights are Blue. New York: NAL, 1967.

Sounds of a Drunken Summer. New York: Harper, 1969.

The Zodiac Lovers. New York: Avon, 1969.

The Borrower. New York: Harper, 1970.

Encores for a Dilettante. New York: Fiction Collective, 1978.

The Autobiography of Cassandra, Princess & Prophetess of Troy. Danbury, CT: Archer, 1979.

Bastards: Footnotes to History. New York: McPherson, 1979.

Nightschool for Saints. Danbury, CT: Archer, 1981.

Analects of Self-Contempt/Sweet Cheat of Freedom. New York: Top Stories, 1983.

Positions with White Roses. New

Paltz: Treacle, 1983; London: The Women's Press, 1988.

TONI MORRISON

The Bluest Eye. New York: Holt, 1970.
Sula. New York: Knopf, 1973.
Song of Solomon. New York: Knopf, 1977.
Tar Baby. New York: Knopf, 1981.
Beloved. New York: Knopf, 1987.

JOYCE CAROL OATES

By the North Gate. New York: Vanguard, 1963.
With Shuddering Fall. New York: Vanguard, 1964.
Upon the Sweeping Flood and Other Stories. New York: Vanguard, 1966.
A Garden of Earthly Delights. New York: Vanguard, 1967.
Expensive People. New York: Vanguard, 1968.
Women in Love and Other Poems. New York: Albondocani, 1968.
Anonymous Sins and Other Poems. Baton Rouge: Louisiana State UP, 1969.
Them. New York: Vanguard, 1969.
Cupid and Psyche. New York: Albondocani, 1970.
Love and Its Derangements. Baton Rouge: Louisiana State UP, 1970.
The Wheel of Love. New York: Vanguard, 1970.
Wonderland. New York: Vanguard, 1971.
The Edge of Impossibility: Tragic Forms in Literature. New York: Vanguard, 1972.
Marriages and Infidelities. New York: Vanguard, 1972.
Wooded Forms. New York: Albondocani, 1972.
Angel Fire. Baton Rouge: Louisiana State UP, 1973.
Do With Me What You Will. New York: Vanguard, 1973.
Dreaming America and Other Poems. New York: Aloe, 1973.
The Hostile Son: The Poetry of D. H. Lawrence. Los Angeles: Black Sparrow, 1973.
A Posthumous Sketch. Los Angeles: Black Sparrow, 1973.
The Girl. Cambridge, MA: Pomegranate, 1974.
The Goddess and Other Women. New York: Vanguard, 1974; Greenwich, CT: Fawcett, 1976.
The Hungry Ghosts: Seven Allusive Comedies. Los Angeles: Black Sparrow, 1974.
New Heaven, New Earth: The Visionary Experience in Literature. New York: Vanguard, 1974.
Where Are You Going, Where Have You Been? Greenwich, CT: Fawcett, 1974.
The Assassins: A Book of Hours. New York: Vanguard, 1975.
The Fabulous Beasts. Baton Rouge: Louisiana State UP, 1975.
The Poisoned Kiss and Other Stories from the Portuguese (as Fernandez/ Oates). New York: Vanguard, 1975.
The Seduction and Other Stories. Los Angeles: Black Sparrow, 1975.
Childwold. New York: Vanguard, 1976.
Crossing the Border. New York: Vanguard, 1976.
The Triumph of the Spider Monkey. Santa Barbara: Black Sparrow, 1976.
Night-Side. New York: Vanguard, 1977.
Son of the Morning. New York: Vanguard, 1978.
Women Whose Lives Are Food, Men Whose Lives are Money. Baton Rouge: Louisiana State UP, 1978.

All the Good People I've Left Behind.
Santa Barbara: Black Sparrow,
1979.
Cybele. Santa Barbara: Black Sparrow,
1979.
The Lamb of Abyssalia. Cambridge,
MA: Pomegranate, 1979.
Queen of the Night. Northridge, CA:
Lord John, 1979.
The Step-Father. Northridge, CA:
Lord John, 1979.
Unholy Loves. New York: Vanguard,
1979.
Bellefleur. New York: Dutton, 1980;
New York: Warner, 1981.
Celestial Timepiece. Dallas: Press-
works, 1980.
*Three Plays (Ontological Proof of My
Existence, Miracle Play, The
Triumph of the Spider Monkey).*
Princeton: Ontario Review, 1980.
Angel of Light. New York: Dutton,
1981.
Contraries: Essays. New York: Oxford
UP, 1981.
Nightless Nights: Nine Poems. Con-
cord, NH: Ewert, 1981.
A Sentimental Education. New York:
Dutton, 1981.
A Bloodsmoor Romance. New York:
Dutton, 1982.
*Invisible Women: New and Selected
Poems 1970–1982.* Princeton: On-
tario Review, 1982.
*First Person Singular: Writers on Their
Craft* (edited by Oates). Princeton:
Princeton UP, 1983.
The Profane Art: Essays and Reviews.
New York: Dutton, 1983.
Last Days. New York: Dutton, 1984.
Mysteries of Winterthurn. New York:
Dutton, 1984.
Wild Saturdays and Other Stories.
London: Dent, 1984.
Solstice. New York: Dutton, 1985.
Marya: A Life. New York: Dutton,
1986.

Lives of the Twins (as Rosamond
Smith). New York: Simon, 1987.
On Boxing. New York: Doubleday,
1987.
Raven's Wing. New York: Dutton,
1987.
You Must Remember This. New York:
Dutton, 1987.
*(Woman) Writer: Occasions and Op-
portunities.* New York, Dutton,
1988.

GEORGIANA PEACHER

*Mary Stuart's Ravishment Descending
Time.* Evanston: TriQuarterly,
Northwestern UP, 1976.

JAYNE ANNE PHILLIPS

Sweethearts. Short Beech, CT: Wing-
bow/Truck Press, 1976.
Counting. New York: Vehicle, 1978.
Black Tickets. New York: Delacorte,
1979.
Hometown. Iowa City: Bookslinger,
1980.
How Mickey Made It. St. Paul, MN:
Bookslinger, 1981.
The Secret Country. Chapel Hill, NC:
Palaeon, 1982.
Machine Dreams. New York: Dutton,
1984.
Fast Lanes. New York: Dutton, 1986.

CONSTANCE PIERCE

Philippe at His Bath. New York: Fic-
tion Collective, 1983.
When Things Get Back to Normal.
New York: Fiction Collective, 1985.

CARLENE POLITE

The Flagellants. New York: Farrar,
1967; Boston: Beacon, 1988.
Sister X and the Victims of Foul Play.
New York: Farrar, 1975.

ANN QUIN

Berg. London: Calder, 1964, 1979; New York: Scribner's, 1964, 1979.
Three. London: Calder, 1966; New York: Scribner's, 1966.
Passages. London: Calder, 1969, 1979; New York: Scribner's, 1969.
Tripticks. London: Calder, 1972, 1979.

MARILYNNE ROBINSON

Housekeeping. New York: Farrar, 1980; New York: Bantam, 1987.

JOANNA RUSS

Picnic on Paradise. New York: Ace, 1968.
And Chaos Died. New York: Ace, 1970.
The Female Man. New York: Bantam, 1975; Boston: Beacon, 1987.
Kittatinny: A Tale of Magic. New York: Daughters, 1978.
The Two of Them. New York: Putnam, 1978.
On Strike Against God. New York: Out and Out, 1980.
The Adventures of Alyx. New York: Pocket, 1983.
How to Suppress Women's Writing. Austin: U of Texas P, 1983.
The Zanzibar Cat. Sauk City, WI: Arkham, 1983.
Extra(Ordinary) People. New York: St. Martin's, 1984.
Magic Mommas, Trembling Sisters, Puritans and Perverts. Trumansburg, NY: Crossing, 1985.
The Hidden Side of the Moon. New York: St. Martin's, 1987.

EVE SHELNUTT

The Love Child. Santa Barbara: Black Sparrow, 1979.

The Formal Voice. Santa Barbara: Black Sparrow, 1982.
The Musician. Santa Barbara: Black Sparrow, 1987.
Recital in a Private Home. Pittsburgh: Carnegie Mellon Press, 1988.

PENELOPE SHUTTLE

All the Usual Hours of Sleeping. London: Calder, 1969.
Wailing Monkey Embracing a Tree. London: Calder, 1973, 1980.
The Terrors of Dr. Treviles (with Peter Redgrove). London: Routledge, 1974.
The Glass Cottage: A Nautical Romance (with Peter Redgrove). London: Routledge, 1976.
Jesusa. Falmouth, Cornwall: Granite, 1976.
Rainsplitter in the Zodiac Garden. London: Calder, 1977.
The Mirror of the Giant. London: Calder, 1980.
The Orchard Upstairs. London: Oxford UP, 1980.
Prognostica. Knotting, Bedfordshire: Booth, 1980.
The Child-Stealer. London: Oxford UP, 1983.
The Lion from Rio. London: Oxford UP, 1986.

SUSAN SONTAG

The Benefactor. New York: Farrar, 1963, 1987.
Against Interpretation and Other Essays. New York: Farrar, 1964, 1986.
Death Kit. New York: Farrar, 1967, 1986.
Trip To Hanoi. New York: Farrar, 1968.
Duet for Cannibals. New York: Farrar, 1970.

Brother Carl. New York: Farrar, 1974.
Styles of Radical Will: On Photography. New York: Farrar, 1977, 1987.
I, etcetera. New York: Farrar, 1978, 1988.
Illness as Metaphor. New York: Farrar, 1978, 1988.
Under the Sign of Saturn. New York: Farrar, 1980.
A Susan Sontag Reader. New York: Random, 1983.

LYNNE TILLMAN

Living With Contradictions. New York: Top Stories, 1982.
Haunted Houses. New York: Poseidon, 1987.

MARGUERITE YOUNG

Prismatic Ground. New York: Macmillan, 1937.
Moderate Fable. New York: Reynal, 1944.
Angel in the Forest: A Fairy Tale of Two Utopias. New York: Reynal, 1945.
Miss MacIntosh, My Darling. New York: Scribner's, 1965; London: Owen, 1966; Introd. Anaïs Nin. New York: Harcourt, 1979.

PAMELA ZOLINE

The Heat Death of the Universe and Other Stories. New Paltz: McPherson, 1987.

LITERATURE IN TRANSLATION

MARGUERITE DURAS

Works translated into English

Un barrage contre le Pacifique. Paris: Gallimard, 1950; *The Sea Wall.* Trans. Herma Briffault. New York: Pellegrini, 1952; New York: Farrar, 1985.
Le marin de Gibraltar. Paris: Gallimard, 1952; *The Sailor from Gibraltar.* Trans. Barbara Bray. New York: Grove, 1966; New York: Pantheon, 1986.
Les petits chevaux de Tarquinia. Paris: Gallimard, 1953; *The Little Horses of Tarquinia.* Trans. Peter Du Berg. London: Calder, 1960; New York: Riverrun, 1980.
Des journées entières dans les arbres. Paris: Gallimard, 1954; *Whole Days in the Trees.* Trans. Anita Barrows. New York: Riverrun, 1984.
Le square. Paris: Gallimard, 1955; *The Square.* Trans. Sonia Pitt-Rivers and Irina Morduch. New York: Grove, 1959, 1982. In *Four Novels.*
Moderato cantabile. Paris: Minuit, 1958; *Moderato Cantabile.* Trans. Richard Seaver. New York: Grove, 1960. In *Four Novels.*
Dix heures et demie du soir en été. Paris: Gallimard, 1960; *Ten-Thirty on a Summer Night.* Trans. Anne Borchardt. In *Four Novels.*
Hiroshima, mon amour. Paris: Gallimard, 1960; *Hiroshima, mon amour.* Trans. Richard Seaver. New York: Grove, 1961.
Les viaducs de la Seine-et-Oise. Paris: Gallimard, 1960. In *Three Plays.*
L'après-midi de Monsieur Andesmas. Paris: Gallimard, 1962; *The Afternoon of Mr. Andesmas.* Trans. Anne Borchardt. London: Calder, 1965. In *Four Novels.*
Le ravissement de Lol V. Stein. Paris:

Gallimard, 1964; *The Ravishing of Lol Stein*. Trans. Richard Seaver. New York: Grove, 1966.

Four Novels. Introd. Germaine Brée. New York: Grove, 1965.

Théâtre I (includes *Le square*). Paris: Gallimard, 1965. *Le square* in *Three Plays.*

Le Vice-Consul. Paris: Gallimard, 1966; *The Vice-Consul.* Trans. Eileen Ellenbogen. London: Hamilton, 1968.

L'amante anglaise. Paris: Gallimard, 1967; *L'Amante Anglaise.* Trans. Barbara Bray. London: Hamilton, 1968; New York: Grove, 1968.

Three Plays: The Square, Whole Days in the Trees, The Viaducts of Seine-et-Oise. Trans. Barbara Bray and Sonia Orwell. London: Calder, 1967.

Théâtre II (including *Des journées entières dans les arbres*). Paris: Gallimard, 1968. *Des journées* in *Three Plays.*

Détruire, dit-elle. Paris: Minuit, 1969; *Destroy, She Said.* Trans. Barbara Bray. New York: Grove, 1970.

India Song. Paris: Gallimard, 1973; *India Song.* Trans. Barbara Bray. New York: Grove, 1976.

Outside: papiers d'un jour. Paris: Michel, 1981; *Outside: Selected Writings.* Trans. Arthur Goldhammer. Boston: Beacon, 1986.

La maladie de la mort. Paris: Minuit, 1982; *The Malady of Death.* Trans. Barbara Bray. New York: Pantheon, 1985.

L'amant. Paris: Minuit, 1984; *The Lover.* Trans. Barbara Bray. New York: Pantheon, 1985.

La douleur. Paris: P.O.L., 1985. *The War.* Trans. Barbara Bray. New York: Pantheon, 1986.

Les yeux bleaus, cheveux noir. Paris:

Minuit, 1987; *Blue Eyes, Black Hair.* Trans. Barbara Bray. New York: Pantheon, 1988.

NATHALIE SARRAUTE

Works translated into English

Tropismes. Paris: Denoel, 1939; rev. ed. Paris: Minuit, 1957; *Tropisms* (with *The Age of Suspicion*). London: Calder, 1963; *Tropisms* (publ. separately). Trans. Maria Jolas. New York: Braziller, 1967.

Portrait d'un inconnu. Paris: Marin, 1948; *Portrait of a Man Unknown.* Trans. Maria Jolas. New York: Braziller, 1958; London: Calder, 1959.

Martereau. Paris: Gallimard, 1953; *Martereau.* Trans. Maria Jolas. New York: Braziller, 1959; London: Calder, 1964.

L'ère du soupçon: essais sur le roman. Paris: Gallimard, 1956; *The Age of Suspicion: Essays on the Novel.* Trans. Maria Jolas. New York: Braziller, 1963; London: Calder, 1963.

Le planétarium. Paris: Gallimard, 1959; *The Planetarium.* Trans. Maria Jolas. New York: Braziller, 1960; London: Calder, 1961.

Les fruits d'or. Paris: Gallimard, 1963; *The Golden Fruits.* Trans. Maria Jolas. New York: Braziller, 1964; London: Calder, 1965.

Le silence, suivi de le mensonge. Paris: Gallimard, 1967; *Silence and the Lie.* Trans. Maria Jolas. London: Calder, 1969.

Entre la vie et la mort. Paris: Gallimard, 1968; *Between Life and Death.* Trans. Maria Jolas. New York: Braziller, 1969; London: Calder, 1970.

Vous les entendez? Paris: Gallimard, 1972; *Do You Hear Them?* Trans.

Maria Jolas. New York: Braziller, 1973; London: Calder, 1975.

Disent les imbéciles. Paris: Gallimard, 1976; *Fools Say.* New York: Braziller, 1977; London: Calder, 1977.

Théâtre. Paris: Gallimard, 1978; *Theatre: Collected Plays.* Trans. Maria Jolas and Barbara Wright. London: Calder, 1980. New York: Braziller, 1981.

L'usage de la parole. Paris: Gallimard, 1980; *The Use of Speech.* Trans. Barbara Wright. New York: Braziller, 1980.

Enfance. Paris: Gallimard, 1983; *Childhood.* Trans. Barbara Wright. New York: Braziller, 1984.

MONIQUE WITTIG

L'opoponax. Paris: Minuit, 1964; *The Opoponax.* Trans. Helen Weaver. New York: Simon, 1966.

Les guérillères. Paris: Minuit, 1969; *Les Guérillères.* Trans. David Le Vay. New York: Viking, 1971; Boston: Beacon, 1985.

Les corps lesbien. Paris: Minuit, 1973; *The Lesbian Body.* Trans. David Le Vay. New York: Morrow, 1975; Boston: Beacon, 1986.

Brouillon pour un dictionnaire des amantes. Paris: Grasset, 1976; *Lesbian Peoples: Material for a Dictionary* (with Sande Zeig). Trans. Monique Wittig and Sande Zeig. New York: Avon, 1979.

Virgile, non. Paris: Minuit, 1985; *Across the Acheron.* Trans. David Le Vay and Margaret Crosland. London: Owen, 1987.

Index

DATE DUE

GAYLORD			PRINTED IN U.S.A.